ALSO BY JACQUES PEPIN

THE OTHER HALF OF THE EGG,
CO-AUTHORED WITH HELEN MCCULLY

JACQUES PEPIN: A FRENCH CHEF
COOKS AT HOME

LA TECHNIQUE

LA METHODE

EVERYDAY COOKING WITH JACQUES PEPIN

JACQUES PEPIN'S
THE ART OF COOKING

ALFRED A. KNOPF · NEW YORK 1994

JACQUES PEPIN'S
THE ART OF COOKING

THIS IS A BORZOI BOOK PUBLISHED BY
ALFRED A. KNOPF, INC.

Most of the recipes were previously published, in
different form, in *Gourmet* magazine.

Library of Congress Cataloging-in-Publication
Data

Pepin, Jacques.
    Jacques Pepin's the art of cooking.

    Includes index.
    1. Cookery. I. Title. II. Title: Art of cooking.
TX651.P384 1987   641.5   87-4253
ISBN 0-679-74270-0 (v. 1)
    0-679-74271-9 (v. 2)

Manufactured in Japan
Published September 4, 1992
Second Printing, February 1994

To the present generation of young chefs who are creating a new standard for American cuisine. May your enthusiasm and devotion to the trade remain and endure "to the last syllable of recorded time."

ACKNOWLEDGMENTS

The process of writing a book is a long, exhilarating, and exhausting undertaking that requires a work team with complete dedication. I wish to thank the members of the team who made this book a reality. I am forever grateful to my wife, Gloria, for her faith and support; to Grandpa and Ethel, who washed all those pots; to Norma Galehouse, whose good disposition, devotion, and endurance held things together; to Susan Heller, who shared her enthusiasm and fresh ideas; to Gloria Zimmerman, for scouting the shoreline for ingredients; to Tom Hopkins, for endless days of photography; to Madeline Burrows, for smiling; to Judith Jones, for her keen eyes and discerning taste, which refined and enriched my manuscript; and to Toula Polygalaktos, Virginia Tan, and Stephanie Tevonian, whose participation is reflected on each page of the book.

CONTENTS

INTRODUCTION

The purpose of this book, the first of two volumes, is to teach you how to cook by demonstrating through the making of a dish the cooking techniques that go into a particular recipe. I have deliberately chosen a range of dishes that encompasses all the cooking procedures that a good cook needs to master, and I have played with interesting combinations of ingredients that not only taste good but make for attractive presentations.

The recipes partake of haute cuisine as well as bourgeois or everyday cooking. Many of the dishes, like the Consommé Printanier and the Saddle of Lamb with Sage-Mousse Stuffing, are elaborate and intended for special parties. Yet many of the dishes, from Farmer's-Style Soup to Gratin of Eggs Loute and Scrod Norma, are simple, fast, fairly inexpensive fare that could be served everyday.

Occasionally there are complicated procedures — from cleaning out a whole baby lamb to boning a leg of veal — that some readers may prefer to have done by their butchers, and this won't make any difference to the finished dish. You will notice that many preparations, like the Stuffed Salmon in Flaky Dough, are composed of several subrecipes (the dough, the stuffing, the lemon sauce, etc.), which can be extrapolated and used by themselves.

The dishes I have put together are not strictly of one denomination — French, American, or anything else — but rather they are based on my own personal preferences and prejudices. Like other artists and tradesmen, cooks evolve a style that reflects the times they live in. Changing lifestyles, social pressures, improvements in equipment, as well as the availability of new ingredients, are bound to change one's cooking over the years. Moreover, as one gets older, the metabolism of the body changes and the need for certain foods increases as that for others lessens. Perhaps one becomes more discriminating. I know my cooking has changed and, I hope, continues to improve.

Although my background is French, after nearly thirty years in the U.S. my cooking has certainly changed direction and, I believe, advanced as it has been influenced by the different exposures I've had in America, including the various ethnic foods, such as Chinese, Vietnamese, Mexican, and Indian, all of which I love to eat and to cook. I have always been particularly fond of Italian and Southern French food, and there are a lot of these hearty accents in my own cooking. In fact, there are really no foods that I don't like — from Spanish tapas to African couscous and Swedish smorgasbord — although I am more familiar with (and fonder of) some than others. The advantage of being in America instead of Europe is that all of these diversified cuisines are readily available, at least in large metropolitan areas, so the dedicated cook can train his palate and extend his repertoire with very little effort.

When I teach cooking, I always emphasize the functional aspects of recipes, stressing the use of fresh and healthful ingredients and explaining cooking procedures. In writing my first two books, <u>La Technique</u> and <u>La Méthode</u>, I focused on developing a cook's dexterity by emphasizing the handling of ingredients in a professional way — in other words, learning the techniques per se was the goal of these books and the recipes were incidental. Yet I realize in working with both amateurs and aspiring professionals alike that they learn more readily when they are actually doing a recipe. Perhaps there is an analogy here with the old adage that the proof of the pudding lies in the eating: a culinary technique without a finished dish as the end result is too abstract — ultimately specious. A finished dish is actually <u>a taste</u> to be defined and stored in our taste memory. And that taste can be evidenced only through a recipe which, in turn, is, of course, controlled by the mastery of the techniques involved in producing it. But the ultimate goal is the taste.

In these new recipes, I have, whenever possible, used a minimum of butter, cream, and other rich ingredients, just as I do when cooking for my family at home. However, when I felt a recipe was not successful without enrichment, I added what was needed. Some dishes are richer than others but, on the whole, the sauces are "lean" in comparison to what is served in luxurious American, French, or Italian restaurants offering the same kind of dishes that I feature here. Often I have given my sauces a little thickening by adding a dash of starch, rather than using a cream reduction or butter emulsion to thicken them. I have applied this method not only to cream and butter sauces but also to brown sauces, which end up being leaner, healthier, and just as flavorful.

I have rounded out the meat and fish dishes with accompanying vegetables, concentrating on combinations of tastes, textures, and colors, with the greater emphasis on taste. Instead of serving a series of five or six baby or diced vegetables indiscriminately with any type of meat or fish, I have chosen one or two specific vegetables, from broccoli and cauliflower to carrots and kohlrabi, as a side dish for a specific meat or fish because I felt that the combination worked well together.

Some dishes are presented whole in the bourgeois home style—as is the Veal Roast with Braised Lettuce or the Wild Mushroom-and-Herb-Stuffed Chicken — and in other instances, when more convenient, the food is presented on individual plates.

Elaborate plating and presentations of hot food are nearly impossible to do at home without affecting the taste of the food. Taking four to five minutes to arrange an individual plate works in a restaurant because the cook stands behind that single serving, prepares it, and sends it to a table before arranging another plate. But it will work for the home cook only if he or she is serving four to six people. If each plate requires five minutes to prepare, for a party of twelve it will take over one hour between the serving of the first and the last guest, and although the food may still look attractive, it will probably be cold or dry on the plate. Anything that affects the taste of the food in a negative way is wrong. The visual aspect of food, the aesthetic that complements the taste, should never be the prime factor.

Yet cold food — desserts, aspics, etc. — can and should emphasize the aesthetic of food since time spent in the preparation is not at the expense of taste. Moreover, even here, when the food has been too manipulated, too "touched," too arranged, it becomes static and loses some of its natural spontaneity and the casualness that gives a dish a certain undefinable quality and honesty.

Although I have tried in the instructions to be as practical, helpful, and to the point as possible, there is always a certain intangible aspect to the preparation and the food that is impossible to freeze on the page at times. Recipes reflect the moment and the conditions that existed when they were written down. It is difficult to explain everything from variations in temperature and humidity from day to day to the particular quirks of the equipment available or to the quality of the ingredients themselves. To account for all the possible variables in a recipe would take pages of explanation. Each time a recipe is redone, it is an adventure in itself. Things change, and such changes, although minute, in ingredients, equipment, temperature, and even the mood of the cook, will alter the result.

Recipes are only guides or helps. A thorough understanding of the principles and techniques that govern them is important to control the outcome of a dish. If, when you try a recipe, everything conspires to make your circumstances identical to mine when I wrote the recipe down, then the results will be excellent, as long as the recipe is followed. If the conditions are different, however, adjustments in the recipe are necessary to compensate for the differences.

Each individual palate is different. As you are making a recipe, adjust it to suit your own taste. After you have prepared it a few times and it is adapted to your taste, the recipe will become your own.

In creating new recipes, I have tried to look at familiar ingredients with fresh eyes and to combine them in original ways that keep the intrinsic taste of the food. The originality may come from new ways of combining ingredients as well as new techniques or new presentations.

In a restaurant, the recipes are refined further because they are done over and over. In that repetition process, new and easier ways of making the same recipe are found. Likewise at home, by making a recipe over and over you make it fit your own requirements and always find ways of making it better, faster, and more attractive.

My hope is that these recipes will inspire you enough to get you to the stove and that you will like the dishes enough to make them your own. Happy cooking!

LOWERING CALORIES

I have attempted to keep calories down throughout this book but my method is not an exact scientific one. It is based on a casual, commonsense approach. For someone interested in precise calorie counts, there are many available books with detailed, specific instructions.

Special elegant party dishes, like most of the dishes in this book, often have more calories than are found in everyday cooking. Although I have tried to keep calories as low as this type of cooking permits, many dishes are still quite rich. To lower the calories in certain of these dishes would be to destroy the intrinsic quality. So be it.

Yet, for someone interested in lowering calories, there are dishes that can be stripped of a few of their calories and at the same time preserve their good taste and elegance. Whenever possible, I have attempted to do just that and have written the "leaner version" following the original. I have done this only with recipes that would retain most of their taste, refinement, and flavor. Exact calorie counts are not given but could be calculated approximately by following the USDA Handbook No. 8.

LOW-SALT COOKING

In the last few years, the issue of salt in cooking has attracted much attention because many people are suffering from high blood pressure and have to cut down on their salt intake. Although a cook is not a doctor, a commonsense approach in cooking will help people who want to cut down on salt. The advice below is given strictly from a culinary point of view and is not intended for the person who has serious physiological problems. When the problem is severe, a doctor's recommendations and prescriptions should be followed.

When one is conditioned to eat highly salted food, it seems impossible to do without salt; food seems tasteless without it. Yet, surprisingly, with some effort and motivation one gets used to less salt and the food tastes just as good.

Yet there is no general panacea for the lack of salt, no special techniques or miracles that will make all dishes taste fantastic without salt. The aim is to compensate by choosing the right food, the proper technique, and the right spice and seasoning.

Certain types of food, such as tomatoes, carrots, mushrooms, etc., "work" without salt. You should be aware that other seemingly innocuous foods like shellfish or celery are already high in sodium. To cook without salt is a challenge that tests the cook's understanding of food and his ability to express his knowledge by compensating for its absence with other ingredients.

Some cooking techniques tend to hide the lack of salt more than others. When food – from fish to meat – is served plain, boiled or steamed, the lack of salt is very apparent unless some condiments or seasonings are added. Likewise, most liquids, like soups and stocks, taste bland without salt unless reduced to the extreme. On the other hand, food baked, roasted at a high temperature, or broiled, as well as grilled, tastes good without salt. The surface of the fish, meat, or vegetable crystallizes, forming a flavorful crust. The sugar and cooking juices caramelize and produce an intense flavor that tends to mask the absence of salt.

For foods that are bland – like a steamed fish or a boiled chicken – a mixture of sweet (maple syrup, honey) and acid (citrus juices, vinegar) along with hot pepper will do well. Most acid ingredients like vinegar, lemon juice, sour grapes (verjus), sour cream, and yogurt liven the flavor of bland foods, making the lack of salt less noticeable.

Tasty, strong-flavored salad greens, such as arugula, radicchio, or bitter chicory, enhance the flavor of other milder greens and hide the lack of salt. Mushrooms are great flavor enhancers, too, especially the dried varieties like cèpe or shiitake, which are reconstituted in water. The juice can be used as well as the mushrooms. Shiitake mushrooms are particularly meaty, strong-flavored, and satisfying, even without the use of salt.

Spices like chili powder, curry powder, allspice, ground coriander, hot pepper flakes, nutmeg, cloves, and, particularly, black pepper (ground at the last moment since its essential oils tend to evaporate quickly) are a great help.

Dried herbs like oregano, thyme, or bay leaf are quite useful, as is dry mustard. Fresh herbs, from parsley, chervil, coriander, and chives to tarragon and basil, are lifesavers. Special seasonings like grated lemon rind, horseradish, chopped garlic (kept in a little olive oil), chopped onion (washed in cold water and pressed in a towel to prevent discoloration), and chopped scallions are all very useful as replacements for salt.

Salt is a flavor enhancer, and to bring out the taste of the food without it one must learn through trial and error, adding a bit of one thing and a bit of another to heighten the flavor according to one's own palate.

Just as a painter has a series of different colors on his palette which he combines to create nuances and give complexity to a painting, the cook attempts the same with seasonings. To achieve a satisfying taste, a cook must add and taste over and over until he or she is pleased with the result. Yet, if before each addition and tasting, one has to stop to grate a lemon, search for ground pepper, chop chives, grate ginger, etc., the cooking becomes lengthy and tedious just as painting would if the artist had to open a tube of paint each time he felt he needed a little red and then close it and open another tube when he wants green and close it again before going on to another color. For the painter to express himself and for the painting to progress, the colors have to be readily available so the artist can use them in a spontaneous and almost automatic fashion. The same is true in cooking.

Therefore, fill small receptacles containing vinegar, lemon juice, freshly chopped herbs, hot pepper, dry mustard, grated horseradish, curry powder, cayenne, chopped scallions, garlic, onions, etc., so they are at the immediate disposal of the cook, enabling him or her to express his or her talent in a spontaneous manner in making any dish, from soup to meat and, like a painter giving touches and values, add a little bit of one thing, then a bit of another, until he or she is satisfied. That is the way to build a flavor without the use of salt.

Everyone has his own favorite seasonings — from a purée of garlic to grated lemon rind and fresh herbs. With some practice, the cook can create some exciting combinations, using any recipe from any book as a base for different, new taste sensations. Finally, with time and patience, the need for salt lessens and eventually becomes quite minimal.

The recipes in this book have been designed to demonstrate important cooking techniques. The techniques are noted with their step numbers at the top of the page where they appear so that you can locate them easily and refer to them again when needed.

BROWN STOCK, DEMI-GLACE AND GLACE

One of the basic ingredients of the professional chef is brown stock. To have brown stock, reduced brown stock (demi-glace or half glaze), and extract of brown stock (glace or glaze) at hand is to be able to create three-star dishes in minutes.

A stock is the liquid created by boiling bones, water, and seasonings together. If the bones are browned prior to boiling, the stock will be brown; if not, it will be a white stock. Because of the browning of the bones and meat scraps, the stock, in addition to being brown, has a nuttier, stronger flavor than the white stock — the kind of difference one would recognize between a piece of boiled and a piece of roasted meat.

To be good, a stock should cook slowly (so the fat can separate and be removed) for a long time (to get all the taste and nutrients out of the bones); it should then be strained through a very fine sieve (to remove any remaining impurities). The strained stock should be reduced until it reaches the proper flavor and consistency. Rely on your taste; sometimes the stock will have to be reduced more, sometimes less. If possible, the stock should be refrigerated overnight before using so that any remaining fat will harden on top and can be removed.

Because stock is used to create sauces that will be added to other dishes and, most of the time, will be reduced to intensify flavor, no salt is used when making it. A salty stock could overpower a sauce and cannot be reduced without becoming oversalted.

A good stock should be gelatinous, almost fat free, salt free, and fairly high in protein. Depending on the amount of elements in the bones and the amount of meat used, the yield from 10 lb. of bones will range from 3 to 6 qt. of stock. Ten to 12 hours of cooking are needed to extract enough taste from large pieces of bones.

The quantity of water used will vary according to evaporation. The kettle is usually filled with cold water at first and then replenished with water regularly, as the liquid evaporates during the cooking. The pot is never covered. Eventually, when the stock has been strained, cooled, and degreased, it can be reduced by boiling down to the proper consistency.

Brown stock is a carrier, a vehicle used to make sauce, but it is not a sauce in itself. It is used to moisten (<u>mouiller</u> in French) a stew or deglaze a pan, or it is added to other bones, such as game or lamb, to produce a different-flavored stock or sauce.

When stock is reduced by boiling, it will turn into a dark, syrupy, flavorful liquid that takes on the name of "half glaze" (demi-glace) and is concentrated enough to become a sauce. Flavored with red Bordeaux, it will become a Bordelaise sauce; with Madeira, a dark Madeira sauce; with black truffles, a Périgueux sauce, etc.

Demi-glace, high in protein and low in fat, should be almost bland (remember, no salt) so it can marry itself to and identify with the meat it accompanies without dominating it. In this manner, demi-glace can be used with beef, lamb, veal, chicken, game, etc., as well as any seasoning, from wine and brandy to truffles, so that the dish will retain its identity, personal characteristics, and individual taste.

In the making of the stock, the liquid should not come to a rolling boil; that is, the entire surface of the liquid should not tumble and turn over onto itself. As long as at least some of the surface is calm, not agitated by boiling, any fat that comes to the surface will accumulate in the still places and can be removed with a ladle. If the whole surface of the liquid tumbles down on itself in a rolling boil, the fat that comes to the top will be mixed into the stock and will eventually bind or emulsify with it. The result will be a fatty stock, cloudy because fat particles will be suspended throughout it.

When the stock has been cooked and strained, the cooked bones can be used again. The <u>remouillage</u>, or second stock from the bones, can be reduced into a meat glaze, or glace. The stockpot containing the cooked bones is filled again with cold water, brought to a boil, and simmered again for 10 to 12 hours. Strained through a fine sieve, this second liquid will be cloudier than the first because the bones are, by then, breaking into a mush. However, the gelatinous elements in the bones are extracted in that second boiling, which yields a thicker and larger quantity of glaze than could be extracted from the first boiling. It should be boiled over high heat to reduce the liquid. At this point, there will be practically no fat left in the stock and it can be reduced at a rolling boil to save time. As the liquid gets thicker and the quantity diminishes, be sure to transfer it to a smaller saucepan and reduce the heat to prevent scorching.

The resulting meat glaze has transcended the level of a sauce. It should not be used as a sauce because it is too concentrated. It should be used as a flavoring agent to strengthen a dish or a sauce. Added to a light cream sauce, it will flavor as well as thicken the sauce (see Grenadins of Veal Helen, page 276). Properly reduced, the cooled glaze can be cut into cubes and will keep in an open bag or jar almost forever in the refrigerator.

In restaurants where individual portions are cooked on order, reducing stock to create a few Tb.of sauce works particularly well and permits the cook to diversify his sauce by changing the flavoring and garnish. But be aware that the reduction can be overdone, with the resulting sauce becoming too rich and strong. A piece of beef will require a stronger, more reduced stock than a quail, which would be overpowered by too potent a sauce.

When a stock has been reduced to the proper taste and color and is still too thin, a bit of arrowroot or potato starch diluted in water will give it the proper consistency. At one time, brown stock used to be thickened with flour in what is called "espagnole sauce" (made with a brown roux, tomato paste, and brown stock), but it is rarely made nowadays. Prepared in the classic

manner of Carème or Escoffier, the sauce cooks for nearly 6 hours after the stock has been added to the roux. During that long, slow cooking, the roux breaks down and the scum and fat that come to the surface of the sauce are removed. The sauce clarifies through the long cooking and skimming until only the binding elements in the flour remain to hold the sauce together. Although this yields a clear, syrupy and flavorful sauce, nowadays it is faster, easier, and just as good to use a so-called pure starch such as arrowroot (a purified starch with only the binding elements), which thickens instantly, has no taste, and does not "dirty" the sauce. Such pure starches, which are available now but were not a hundred years ago, make it possible for us to eliminate the long cooking of the roux and sauce advocated by Carème or Escoffier.

Is it essential to have brown stock and demi-glace on hand in order to cook well? They are necessary for certain recipes, and although sophisticated classic cooking requires their use, home or country cooking does not. In our family and at friends' homes, where we have had some of our most memorable meals, brown stocks are practically never used. Natural roasting and braising give strong juices, the equivalent of a strong reduction, and often good cooks use leftover juices from chicken or pot roast the way professional cooks use demi-glace. Likewise for stock: natural roasting juices from meat or poultry can be diluted with water and used as a substitute for standard brown stock.

2 Remove from the oven and, using a large skimmer, lift out the bones and vegetables and place in a large kettle (20 to 30 qt.), preferably stainless steel or enamel. Place on top of the stove. Pour out all the fat that has accumulated in the large roasting pan and discard.

BROWN VEAL STOCK, DEMI-GLACE, GLACE

This is a general, multi-purpose, classic brown veal stock, which is used in a variety of sauces. It is reduced to make the demi-glace and even, sometimes, to make the glaze.

Yield: 5 qt. stock

10 lb. veal bones, cut into pieces of about 2–3 in. (Bones from the neck and knuckles are very gelatinous and give a syrupy, tasty stock.)
About 1½ lb. meat sinews, tendons, and scraps
1 lb. onions, peeled or unpeeled, quartered
¾ lb. carrots, washed and cut into 1-in. chunks
1 large head garlic, separated into cloves, unpeeled
1 bunch parsley or the stems from 2 bunches
½ celery heart (¾ lb.)
4–6 bay leaves
1 Tb. dried thyme
1 Tb. whole black peppercorns
1½ lb. very large ripe tomatoes (about 4 or 5) (If the tomatoes are not ripe and tasty, use about 3 c. canned Italian plum tomatoes.)

1 Place the bones and meat scraps, spread out in one layer, in 1 very large or 2 smaller roasting pans made of heavy aluminum. Place in a 400-degree oven for 1½ hours, stirring every 20 to 30 minutes. The bones should have a nice brown color but not be burned. Peel the onions if the skins are dirty or spoiled, and quarter. Wash the carrots (no peeling is necessary) and cut into 1-in. chunks. Add the carrots and onions to the bones and continue cooking, stirring a couple of times, for 45 minutes longer (approximately 2¼ hours total roasting time).

3 Add enough water to the roasting pan to cover the bottom, place back on the stove, and, using a flat-ended wooden spatula, scrape the bottom of the pan to dissolve all the solidified juices. Add these to the stockpot. Be careful not to burn the solidified juices. If they are burned, the stock will be bitter. As it cooks with the bones and is eventually reduced, it will get more bitter. If the solidified juices are burned, discard them. →

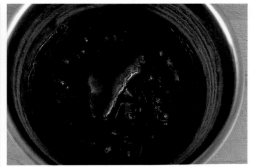

4 Fill the stockpot with water to within approximately 2 or 3 in. from the top and bring to a boil. This may take as long as 45 minutes. Boil gently for 2 hours, then skim off as much fat as you can from the top. Add the garlic, parsley or parsley stems, celery heart, bay leaves, thyme, peppercorns, and tomatoes, and bring back to a boil again. Boil very gently for 8 to 10 hours or overnight.

7 When the stock is completely cold, remove any fat that has come to the top. If necessary, place the stock back in a kettle and boil down to bring it to a 5-qt. yield. Then cool again. When it is cold, the stock should be transparent, practically fat free, salt free, and highly gelatinous.

10 To the bones, which have already been cooked for 8 to 10 hours, add enough cold water to fill up the kettle again. Bring to a boil, and again boil the bones gently for 10 to 12 hours. The stock yielded won't be as clear as the first stock since some of the bones are already breaking down into a paste. The resulting stock will be slightly cloudy but quite tasty. Strain the second boiling to make glaze. Reduce the stock on high heat in a large kettle. As the liquid is reduced, transfer to smaller and smaller pans and continue to reduce. You will notice when it is completely reduced: the mixture is almost as dark as an overcooked caramel, large bubbles appear on top, and the texture is very thick, like jam. Be careful to cook it on very low heat during the last 1½ to 2 hours of cooking so it doesn't scorch.

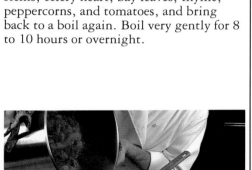

5 In the morning, strain the stock through a very fine sieve. Set aside to cool.

8 Demi-glace is only a reduced brown stock. To make it, take the original brown stock and boil it down on high heat to about 2½ qt. and cool. It should be very highly gelatinous, slightly syrupy, and have a very beautiful dark reddish-brown color.

11 Pour into a bowl, cool.

6 To help strain the stock through the fine sieve, tap the edge of the sieve gently with the palm of your hand or spatula. This moves the solids, preventing them from clogging the holes, and allows the juices to go through. If the solids are pressed with a spoon or ladle, they will be crushed and puréed and muddy the stock.

9 When cold, scoop into large chunks, which will retain their shape, wrap in plastic wrap and then aluminum foil, and freeze for later use.

12 When cold, unmold and <u>cut the hard reduced stock into cubes.</u> These can be kept in the refrigerator in an open jar (if the jar is closed, they get moldy) or in an open plastic bag. They can also be frozen; either way, they will keep almost indefinitely without spoiling.

FAST BROWN STOCK, DEMI-GLACE, GLACE (WITH POULTRY BONES)

Fast brown stock, as the name indicates, is made in less time than regular stock. The bones can also be used twice, and the second boiling, again, used to do a <u>glace de viande.</u> The recipe here is made strictly with poultry bones, and the flavor is excellent, although the color and the gelatinous texture won't be quite as rich as the stock done with the veal bones. A mixture of veal bones and poultry bones can also be used in the fast brown stock as well as in the classic version.

Yield: 2½ qt.

6 lb. poultry bones (the backs, necks, and wing tips will have skin)
2 lb. poultry gizzards
½ lb. carrots (about 4), washed and cut into 1½-in. chunks
¾ lb. onions, washed and cut into 1½-in. chunks
2 c. ripe and juicy tomatoes, diced, or canned Italian plum tomatoes
5 or 6 sprigs thyme or 2 tsp. dried thyme
3 bay leaves
2 large ribs celery
2 tsp. whole black peppercorns

1 Cut the bones into 1- to 1½-in. pieces <u>and place with the gizzards in 2 very large, shallow, heavy aluminum saucepans.</u> Place on top of the stove over high heat and cook, stirring occasionally, for 45 minutes. There is a great deal of fat in the skin of the chicken, which will be rendered during that intensive cooking. The fat is needed for the browning and will make the pieces of bone very crusty, brown, and flavorful. If chicken bones without fat are used, oil and butter should be used to brown the bones.

2 After 45 minutes of cooking on high heat, the mixture should be quite crisp. Add the carrots and onions and continue cooking for 5 minutes. Using a large skimmer, lift out the pieces of meat and vegetables and place in a large stainless-steel or enameled kettle. Cover with water and place over high heat. Discard the fat accumulated in the saucepans. Add enough water to cover the bottom of the saucepans and cook on top of the stove, stirring with a flat, wooden spatula to dissolve all the solidified, crystallized cooking juices. Add to the kettle.

Bring to a boil. Boil gently for about 30 minutes. At that point, remove as much scum and fat from the top as possible and add the tomatoes, thyme, bay leaves, celery, and peppercorns. Continue cooking for 4 to 6 hours longer. Strain the liquid through a very fine sieve. Cool.

When cold, remove all the fat, remelt the liquid, and reduce to about 2½ qt. of brown stock. It should be highly gelatinous and hold together.

To make the demi-glace, reduce the brown stock to about 1 qt. When cold, divide among small containers, or cut into chunks, wrap in plastic wrap and aluminum foil, and freeze.

To make the glace, fill the kettle containing the cooked bones with water again. Bring to a boil and reboil gently for approximately 4½ to 5 hours. Strain. Reduce, transferring the liquid to smaller and smaller saucepans as it becomes less and less. You should have approximately ½ to ¾ c. of meat glace. Cool. Unmold and cut into cubes. Refrigerate for later use.

BROWN STOCK AND LOW-CALORIE COOKING

Brown stock, demi-glace, and glace are virtually fat free (as well as salt free) when properly done and are ideal for a low-calorie diet. They give flavor and can partially replace butter and oil in some dressings and sauces.

2 To chop or slice the onion, cut it in half through the root end, which should not be removed, then lay the halves cut side down on the table. Cut vertical slices from the root end to the tip ⅛ in. apart, keeping the slices attached at the root end.

3 Holding your knife flat parallel to the table, make 2 or 3 horizontal cuts in the onion. The onion should be at the edge of the table so that the knife can be held flat. Now chop in an up and down motion into fine dice.

CREAM OF MUSSEL SOUP

The plentiful mussel is one of the least expensive and tastiest of the shellfish. The flavorful stock is excellent in soups or sauces, and the meat can be served in salads or as a garnish for soup as well as in soufflés.

Yield: 6 servings

1 medium onion
3 lb. very fresh mussels, preferably small
1 c. fruity, dry white wine
1 c. water
1 large clove garlic, crushed, with skin on
1 tsp. fresh thyme, chopped
¼ tsp. freshly ground black pepper
About 20 spinach leaves
1 Tb. potato starch dissolved in 4 Tb. water
Salt and pepper to taste
1 c. heavy cream
2 Tb. minced chives

1 **Cutting up an onion:** Use a plump, firm onion. Peel it, making sure you peel as many layers as necessary to expose the flesh completely.

4 Although mussels bought in the market are usually completely cleaned, if you pick your own you will notice that they usually come in a bunch or are held together by beards that look like dried-out grass but are a life-sustaining cord. Mussels can be kept for over a week in the refrigerator without dying or being endangered. Do not put them in a plastic bag or in water as it will kill them. Small or medium-sized mussels are tenderer and better flavored than the very large ones. They should be heavy and have a dark, shiny, blue-black shell.

6 It is not absolutely necessary to clean the shells if you don't plan to serve the mussels with the shells. If you do plan to use the shells, however, you should scrape off all the encrustations and barnacles attached to them. After scraping, place them in a large pot filled with cold water and rub them together, one against the other. Lift them up from the water, place them in clean water, and again rub them one against the other. Repeat this procedure a few more times. If the mussels were obtained from an area where there is a lot of sand or mud, place a handful of salt in the water with the mussels and let them soak for an hour or so. The salt will help them disgorge some of the sand.

8 Place the mussels in a pot, preferably stainless steel; add the wine, water, onions, garlic, thyme, and pepper, and cover. Bring to a boil, tossing or shaking the mussels to splash the boiling liquid over them. Continue to boil over high heat, stirring them once or twice, until all the shells are open. Drain in a colander, saving the juices.

5 To clean, separate the mussels, removing and discarding the dried beards that hold them together.

7 Taking a mussel in your hand, try to slide it open by making the 2 shells pivot on each other. The purpose is to find out if any of the shells are full of mud (instead of mussels), and they must be checked before cooking because one muddy mussel can ruin your dish. However, by sliding the shells, making the top shell pivot on the bottom shell, they will open and you may find that out of the entire batch there is one full of mud, which, of course, should be discarded.

9 Pour the cooking juices through a strainer lined with paper towels to remove any remaining sand, and add enough water to make 3 c. of stock. Meanwhile, remove the mussels from the shells and pull off the mantle from the top part of the mussels. This mantle tends to be tough and, since we are going to serve the mussels as a garnish for our soup, it is best to remove it. The dish will be a bit more elegant and easier to eat. You should have approximately 30 to 40 mussels. →

10 Drop the spinach leaves into boiling water and cook for about 30 seconds, long enough for them to wilt. Drain them in a colander and place in cold water to cool. Remove the cooled leaves and flatten them on the table. Cut each leaf in half to remove the center stem, which may be tough. Roll each mussel in a segment of spinach leaf, arrange them on a platter, and cover with a wet towel so they don't dry out. Place in a warm oven and heat until lukewarm before you serve with the hot soup so the little green packages will not cool off the soup.

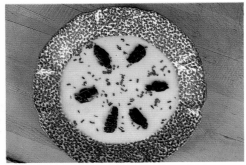

11 Return the strained stock to the sauce-pan and bring to a boil. Add the dissolved potato starch with salt and pepper, if needed, and the cream. Return to the boil and ladle the soup into 6 soup plates (approximately 6 oz. per person). The soup plates should be shallow so the garnish doesn't sink. Sprinkle with the chives and arrange the packages of mussels (5 or 6 per person) so they are visible on top of the soup. Serve immediately.

A LEANER VERSION

Replace the cream with milk and proceed according to the recipe.

1 Place the oysters with their juice in a saucepan over medium heat and cook until the temperature reaches approximately 180 degrees, stirring occasionally. This will be enough to cook the oysters; the outside of the oyster should "frill."

2 If any curd or foam rises to the surface, skim it off with a fine skimmer and discard it.

3 Place the corn flat on the table and, with a long knife, cut the kernels from the ears. Then scrape the ears with the back of the knife to remove any remaining flesh. You should have approximately 4 c. of kernels.

OYSTER AND CORN CHOWDER

This is a delightful recipe, at its best in the fall when the oysters are small and plump and the corn is very fresh. The soup base can be made ahead and, at the last moment, the oysters and corn can be added, the soup brought just to a hot temperature (180 degrees is enough to cook the oysters, and the corn should be cooked about the same). Then serve it immediately.

The cornbread is particularly nice made in tiny barquettes, or tartlet molds, to serve with the soup, although it can be made into a loaf and cut into slices.

It is preferable to poach the oysters by themselves first because at certain times of the year when the oysters are milky (at spawning time), the surrounding liquid will curdle when heated. The curdling wouldn't affect the taste of the soup but it would look curdled. If you poach the oysters beforehand, any curd will rise to the top and you can remove it with a skimmer before adding the oysters and liquid to the soup.

Yield: 8–10 servings

4 doz. oysters, shucked (see page 54), cleaned of any pieces of shell, and kept in their juices
4 c. corn kernels (about 6 ears of corn)
About 2 or 3 leeks (2 c.), sliced thin
3 Tb. butter
¾ c. chopped onions (about 1 medium onion)
About 3 or 4 cloves from 1 fresh head of garlic
3 c. milk
2 c. heavy cream
1 tsp. salt
½ tsp. freshly ground black pepper

SMALL CORNBREAD

Yield: 16 servings
½ stick butter
½ c. sliced leeks
⅓ c. flour
½ c. cornmeal
½ tsp. salt
1 tsp. sugar
1 tsp. double-acting baking powder
1 egg
3 Tb. milk

4 Most of the green from the leeks should be used. (Reserve the darker green for stock.) Cut off the root end and the tough outside of the leeks, split into fourths, and wash carefully. Slice thin. Melt the butter in a large kettle. When hot, add the onions and the leeks and sauté gently over medium heat for 3 to 4 minutes.

5 **Chop the garlic.** Be sure to use a firm head of garlic. Remove the outer skin, then hit the head of garlic with the flat of the hand to separate the cloves.

6 Cut off the root end of the cloves. Place the flat side of the knife blade on a clove, then hit it hard down and forward to crack the clove open. The crushing of the garlic will release its essential oil. Remove the skin; the meat will then come out easily.

7 Place 3 of the peeled cloves near the edge of your cutting board to make them easier to smash. Holding your knife horizontal to the board, hit the side of the blade with the palm of your hand to smash the cloves.

8 Chop the crushed garlic cloves, using an up and down motion, until they are minced fine. You should have 1 Tb. minced garlic. Add the garlic to the soup, stir for approximately 20 to 30 seconds, and add the milk and cream. Bring to a strong boil, then add the corn, oysters, salt, and pepper, and heat until the temperature reaches 170 to 180 degrees at the most.

9 **For the small cornbread:** In a skillet, melt ½ stick butter and add ½ c. sliced leeks. Sauté over medium heat for approximately 1½ minutes. Let cool. Meanwhile, in a bowl combine ⅓ c. flour, ½ c. cornmeal, ½ tsp. salt, and 1 tsp. each sugar and baking powder. Add the egg, 3 Tb. milk, and, finally, the leek mixture. Stir well and put approximately 1 Tb. in each of 16 small buttered molds. Place on a cookie sheet in a 425-degree oven for 10 to 12 minutes, until set and nicely browned.

10 Serve the soup immediately with warm small cornbread.

A LEANER VERSION

Omit the butter and replace the cream with milk in the soup. Cook the onions and leeks with ½ c. water (instead of 3 Tb. of butter) in a saucepan over high heat for a few minutes, until the water has practically evaporated and the leeks and onions are soft. Then proceed according to the recipe. Serve without the cornbread.

2 Strain the liquid through a very fine strainer. Reduce whatever liquid you have to 8 c. (2 qt.).

For finishing the lobster cream: In a bowl mix the butter and flour together with a whisk. Gather this kneaded butter—a *beurre manié*—on the whisk and add it directly to the stock, whisking so it dissolves well. Bring to a boil. (You should not have any lumps.) Add the cayenne and salt to taste (lobsters tend to be salty so be careful). Simmer 3 to 4 minutes. If there are any lumps, strain; add the cream and cognac. Heat briefly (it doesn't need to come back to a boil).

While the stock is cooking, make the dumplings from the remaining mousse used in the Lobster Sara recipe.

CREAM OF LOBSTER SOUP

Yield: 10–12 servings

Roe from 1 lobster

LOBSTER STOCK

1 Tb. butter
1 onion (4 oz.), coarsely chopped
1 leek (4 oz.), coarsely chopped
About 1½ c. liquid (reserved from lobster steaming, page 76) plus shells
2 tomatoes (about 1 lb.), coarsely chopped
1 tsp. dried thyme
2 tsp. paprika
1 c. dry white wine
3 bay leaves, crumbled
4 cloves garlic, crushed, with skin on
1 tsp. salt
16 c. water

FINISHING THE LOBSTER CREAM

⅓ stick soft butter (2 Tb. + 2 tsp.)
¼ c. flour
⅛ tsp. cayenne pepper
½ tsp. salt, if needed
1½ c. heavy cream
1 Tb. cognac

FOR THE DUMPLINGS

½ recipe of mousse in Lobster Sara (page 76)

1 **Dry roe for decoration:** Dry the roe in a 375-degree oven for 12 to 15 minutes, until dry and red. Crumble in a spice grinder or with a mortar and pestle.

To make the lobster stock: Heat the butter in a skillet and, when hot, add the onions and leeks. Sauté for 2 to 3 minutes, until they begin to brown. Add the 1½ c. liquid reserved from lobster steaming, and stir to loosen all the particles. Place in a large kettle, preferably stainless steel, and add all the lobster shells, bodies, etc., the tomatoes, thyme, paprika, white wine, bay leaves, garlic, salt, and water. Bring to a boil and cook gently for a good 3 hours.

3 Place the mousse in a pastry bag fitted with a ½-in. plain round opening. Bring a pot of water 1 to 1½ in. deep to a boil. Squeeze the mixture out of the bag, cutting it off every in. with the point of a knife, so that the little dumplings fall into the simmering water. Keep pressing the mixture out of the bag and cutting until it is all squeezed out.→

4 Cook the dumplings in 180-degree stock for about 2 to 3 minutes and remove with a slotted spoon. Place in cold water to cool, then drain. At serving time, reheat the dumplings in hot water for 1 to 2 minutes, then scoop them up with a slotted spoon and distribute them equally among the soup bowls.

5 Spoon the soup on top of the dumplings, sprinkle with the dried lobster roe, and serve immediately.

A LEANER VERSION

Make the stock according to the recipe. To the 2 qt. of stock, add ½ c. vermicelli (very thin noodles) and bring to a boil. Cook a few minutes, until the pasta is tender but still firm to the bite. Serve with a sprinkling of freshly ground black pepper on top.

FARMER'S-STYLE SOUP

This soup is called "farmer's style" in France because it is made with a piece of bacon or salted, cured pork and water. The salted pork and vegetables create a flavorful stock. For the classic soup, use the 5 vegetables listed below: leeks, carrots, celery, turnips, and potatoes. Although the soup can be made with stock, the flavor is purer and more authentic done simply with water. The soup doesn't require a long time to cook and can be made ahead, then reheated and served with croutons. Leftover soup can be puréed in a food processor, giving it another look, texture, and taste.

Yield: 6 servings

6 oz. slab bacon
2 leeks (about 8 oz.)
3 carrots (about 8 oz.)
1 rib celery
1 medium-large turnip (6 oz.)
2 large potatoes (12 oz.)
7 c. water
Salt (optional)
TO FINISH
1 clove garlic
1 Tb. finely chopped parsley
3 Tb. basil

1 Cut the bacon into ¼-in.-thick slices. Pile the slices together and cut into ¼-in.-thick strips or lardons.

2 Clean the leeks (see page 121), using most of the green. Split them open so you can wash inside and cut into ¼-in. slices. Peel the 3 carrots and cut into slices lengthwise and then into ¼-in. dice.

3 Peel the celery, turnips, and potatoes and cut into ¼-in. dice. Blanch the lardons in a Dutch oven or large, heavy pot with enough cold water to cover: bring to a boil and boil about 1 minute. Drain into a sieve and wash the lardons under cold water. Rinse the pot and place the lardons back in it. Place over high heat and fry the lardons over medium to high heat for 3 to 5 minutes, until they are well fried and have rendered most of their fat. Pour out approximately half of the fat. Add the leeks, celery, and carrots, and sauté gently over medium heat for 1 to 2 minutes. Add the water and salt, and bring to a boil. Let boil about 10 minutes, then add the turnips and potatoes. Return to the boil, cover, and boil gently for about 20 minutes. Taste for salt and add a little, if necessary, depending on the saltiness of the bacon.

4 At serving time, chop the garlic, parsley, and basil together. Add to the boiling soup and serve immediately.

A LEANER VERSION

Use 3 oz. of bacon instead of 6 oz. After the bacon fat has been rendered, as explained in step 3, pour out all of the fat (instead of half, as indicated in the recipe) and proceed according to the recipe instructions.

BLACK BEAN SOUP AUGIER

This soup is named after my father-in-law, Louis Augier, originally from Cuba. It is a good sturdy soup for winter. My version here can be made with other beans if you like, such as white or red kidney beans. Diced ham or sausage can also be added to the soup for more body, although it is quite flavorful without any meat.

Bacon cornbread is a good accompaniment; it can also be served with other soups or with a salad.

Yield: 8 servings

1 lb. black beans (sometimes called black turtle beans)
2 potatoes (¾ lb.), peeled and diced
1 tsp. salt
½ tsp. dried thyme
2 qt. water
1½ qt. chicken stock
1 c. coarsely chopped onions
2 tomatoes, diced (about 2 c.)
½ c. good olive oil
1½ Tb. red wine vinegar
¼ tsp. Tabasco
3 cloves garlic, peeled and crushed

BACON CORNBREAD

¼ lb. bacon (about 6 slices)
1 c. flour
1 c. yellow cornmeal
½ tsp. salt
1 tsp. sugar
2 tsp. double-acting baking powder
2 eggs, beaten
1 c. milk
1 ear corn (about 1 c. kernels)

GARNISHES

1 large or 2 medium onions, chopped (1½ c.)
3 hard-cooked eggs (see page 32)
Extra olive oil to serve with the soup
Extra red wine vinegar to serve with the soup →

1 Remove any stones or damaged beans and wash the beans carefully under cold water. Place in a saucepan, cover with cold water, and soak for 1 hour. (It is not necessary to soak the beans overnight; oversoaking tends to make the beans ferment and may produce indigestion or flatulence.) Lift the beans from the soaking water, place in a large pot, and add the diced potatoes, salt, and thyme. Add 2 qt. water and the chicken stock. Bring to a boil and cook, uncovered, boiling gently for about 1 hour.

2 For the bacon cornbread: While the soup is cooking, cut the slices of bacon into ¼-in. strips (lardons) and place in an ovenproof skillet. Cook over high heat for 8 to 10 minutes. When the bacon is very brown and crisp, remove and drain. Combine the flour, cornmeal, salt, sugar, and baking powder in a bowl and mix well. Add the eggs and half of the milk. Mix until smooth. Stir in the remaining milk, the corn kernels, and finally the bacon pieces.

3 Pour the mixture back into the skillet on top of the fat remaining from cooking the bacon. The fat will come up on the sides. Drag your spatula across the surface of the batter so it is streaked with some of the bacon fat.

4 Place in a 425-degree oven for 20 minutes, at which point it should be cooked, browned and fluffy. After the soup has cooked for 1 hour, add the coarsely chopped onions and diced tomatoes to the soup pot, and cook for another hour. At the end of the cooking, the mixture will have started to thicken. Be sure to scrape the bottom of the pot occasionally with a long spoon so the mixture doesn't stick.

When the soup is cooked, lift out approximately half the solids from the pot with a skimmer. Place in a food processor and process to a purée. Return the purée to the soup. (This step makes the soup thick and creamy while retaining some of the larger chunks of beans and potatoes.) If the soup is too thick, add some water to dilute according to your taste. Add the olive oil, red wine vinegar, Tabasco, and chopped garlic and stir to incorporate. Bring to a boil.

5 Prepare the garnishes: Chop the onions fine. There is a component of sulfuric acid released during chopping that tends to sting your eyes and discolor the onions. Fortunately, this component is water soluble. So place the onions in a colander or sieve and rinse thoroughly under cold water. Press the onions in a towel to remove extra liquid and place in a bowl. The onions are now mild, white, and fluffy, and will remain so, even overnight.

6 Cool and shell the eggs. An egg slicer is best for chopped eggs and ideal for egg salad. Slice the eggs across lengthwise and then lift each sliced egg and place it lengthwise on the egg slicer. Cut through, dividing the egg into neat chunks.

7 Ladle the soup into soup bowls or plates. Drizzle a little additional olive oil and a few drops of vinegar on top and add some of the chopped onions and eggs. Serve very hot with the bacon cornbread.

CONSOMME PRINTANIER

Consommé is a clarified stock. Clarification is the process whereby a coagulant – in this case egg whites – gathers in all the specks and impurities in a stock the bits of vegetable, herbs and spices, and as it cooks, forms a crust; through this crust, the stock filters and clarifies to yield a crystal-clear liquid. A good consommé is high in protein, practically fat free, and highly seasoned. Many classic recipes indicate the addition of ground beef to the clarification to strengthen the stock. But, when the stock is strong, as in this case, no extra ground beef is needed. The vegetables give a good, brisk taste and are cooked just long enough to flavor the stock.

When using a weaker stock, add 2 lb. of lean ground beef to the clarification and cook the consommé for 2 to 3 hours to render all the taste from the meat. Although this technique will yield a strong, beautiful consommé, the long cooking tends to lessen some of the fresh taste of the vegetables.

The standard white stock for the consommé can be made with beef bones or poultry bones only, as well as a mixture of both, as I do here. Game consommé is made with additions of game bones to the standard stock, and fish consommé is made with fish bones and vegetables. For the Consommé Printanier, I have chosen a garnish of tiny carrot, turnip, and zucchini rounds and miniature chicken quenelles, which give this consummate soup a springlike touch of color.

Yield: about 16 servings

WHITE STOCK

4½ lb. beef bones (some marrow bones and some neck bones with meat on them)
3½ lb. chicken or turkey bones, especially the back and neck bones
12 qt. cold water
2 large onions, peeled (about 1 lb.)
12 cloves, inserted into the 2 onions
3 leeks, white only (Keep the green for clarification.)
1 Tb. thyme leaves
1 large onion, unpeeled, cut into halves and cooked over medium heat flat side down in a sturdy steel skillet without fat for about 20 minutes, until it turns black (photograph 3)

CLARIFICATION

3 c. coarsely sliced green of leeks
2 c. coarsely sliced tops and leaves of celery, especially the leaves
1 c. parsley stems, cut into 1-in. pieces
1½ c. coarsely chopped carrots
3 sprigs fresh tarragon or 2 tsp. dried tarragon
1 tsp. dried thyme
1½ tsp. crushed black peppercorns (called *mignonnette*)
1 Tb. salt (the stock is unsalted)
6 egg whites
4 qt. white stock

CHICKEN QUENELLES

1 breast (6 oz.) chicken, cleaned of sinews and fat
¼ c. loose parsley leaves
⅔ c. heavy cream
¼ tsp. salt
⅛ tsp. freshly ground black pepper
3 c. water

VEGETABLE GARNISH

3 turnips, peeled
3 zucchini, scrubbed well
3 carrots, peeled

1 For the white stock: Notice the beef marrow bones on the far left and turkey neck bones on the right. They are gelatinous and will yield a good stock.

Place the bones and water in a large stockpot, preferably stainless steel, and bring to a boil. As it nears the boil, the gelatinous and bloody elements in the bones will come to the surface in the form of a gray foam.→

2 Skim with a fine skimmer. Boil gently, uncovered, for 1 hour. During that first hour, most of the scum and fat will come to the surface. Remove with a skimmer or ladle. It's best to remove the scum and fat during the first hour before you have seasoned the stock, as the seasonings tend to get picked up and discarded with the scum.

3 While the stock is cooking, cut the unpeeled large onion in half and cook it over medium heat in a steel or cast-iron skillet, flat side down. Cook without fat until black. Add to the stock after it has cooked 1 hour, along with the rest of the ingredients. The burnt onion will give a beautiful golden color to the consommé and is not burnt enough to impart a bitter taste to the stock. Boil gently for 5 hours, skimming the fat from the top occasionally. Strain through a fine sieve and cool overnight, reserving the bones.

4 Remove any extra fat that comes to the surface during cooling. You should have 4 qt. If your yield is greater, boil down to 4 qt. If your yield is less, add water to make 4 qt. Cool overnight, if possible, and remove any fat that solidifies on the top. The stock should be gelatinous and hold together. Cover the cooked bones again with water and boil for another 5 to 6 hours. Drain and reduce to 1 qt. of strong stock. (This extra stock is not used in our recipe and can be frozen to be used at a later date.)

5 **For the clarification:** Notice that only the green of leeks and celery and the stems of parsley are used. It is like making an infusion with tea or herbs. A fast cooking of the greens will yield a flavorful vegetable taste.

6 Mix together all the ingredients for the clarification except the stock. Heat the stock to lukewarm and stir in the clarification ingredients. Place over high heat and cook, stirring often, until the mixture comes to a strong boil.

7 You will notice that the mixture gets muddier and muddier as it comes to the boil. As soon as it comes to a strong boil, a crust, created by the albumen of the whites, forms. Reduce the heat to very low. Make a hole with a ladle in the center of the crust so the liquid can boil gently through it.

8 Remove some of the liquid through the hole with the ladle and baste the top of the crust to help it set. Repeat a few times in the first 5 minutes of cooking. The consommé should boil gently through the hole. Keep cooking it for 25 minutes and then turn off the heat. Let it sit for 15 minutes.

9 Strain the liquid through a sieve lined with paper towels or a cloth towel soaked in cold water and then wrung out. Let the consommé sit for 30 minutes. If any fat comes to the surface during this period, slide a paper towel across the top of the liquid to pick it up. Set the consommé aside until ready to use. It can be served cold as well as hot. You should have 3 qt. of consommé. Often, the clarification ingredients – i.e., what is left in the strainer, particularly if meat has been used – can be reused. Cover with water and boil gently for 2 hours. Drain. This *remouil-lage*, or rewetting, yields a clean, light stock, good for soups or for use instead of water when starting a stock from scratch.

10 **For the quenelles:** Place the breast of chicken and ¼ c. parsley in the bowl of a food processor and process for 10 seconds. Add ⅔ c. cream in a thin, steady stream and process another 15 seconds. Add ¼ tsp. salt and ⅛ tsp. pepper and process just enough to combine. Place the mixture in a pastry bag fitted with a plain tube with a ¼-in. opening. Butter a flameproof gratin dish or small roasting pan and pipe the mixture into it, forming little mounds about ¾ in. in diameter. This makes

about 40. Wet your hand and pat the tops of the dumplings to push down any "tails" and to make the tops smooth and round.

Bring 3 c. of water to a boil in a separate saucepan. Pour the boiling water on top of the small quenelles and place on the stove over low heat. Cook under the boil (about 180 degrees) for 5 to 6 minutes. Remove the quenelles with a slotted spoon and place in cold water for 10 minutes to cool. Drain and cover with plastic wrap. Set aside until serving time.

11 **To make the vegetable garnish** in the same shape as shown, a special tool – a tiny round scoop (like a miniature melon baller) about ¼ in. in diameter – is needed. Scoop tiny balls from peeled carrots and white turnips and unpeeled zucchini. Be sure to press the scoop down into the flesh of the vegetable before scooping out the balls, so the tiny balls are almost perfectly round. Cook the carrot balls in boiling water for about 5 to 6 minutes, the turnips 4 to 5 minutes, and the zucchini about 45 seconds. Drain and place the vegetable balls in cold water.

12 At serving time, reheat the vegetable balls and chicken quenelles in the consommé. For each serving ladle some consommé into a soup plate and add about 8 to 10 balls of each vegetable and 2 quenelles. Serve immediately.

A LEANER VERSION

Omit the chicken quenelles and proceed according to the recipe.

PETITE MARMITE WITH CHICKEN "BALLOONS"

A pot-au-feu is the archetype of the earthy, one-dish family meal. Meat and vegetables are cooked together with water in a large stockpot. When cooked, the meat is served with the vegetables and the broth is served on the side with bread and, sometimes, cheese. Petite marmite is the classic, more elegant version of the pot-au-feu. The rich broth is served with the vegetables and meat still in it and a garnish of croutons and grated cheese on the side.

In the petite marmite below, bones and meat are cooked first to produce a rich, lean stock and the vegetables are added along with the chicken "balloons" only ½ hour before serving. Being cooked only 30 minutes, the vegetables retain more taste, texture, and color, and produce a more flavorful soup. For presentation, the vegetables are arranged directly on top of the sliced meat in a colorful pattern. The stock is added and the vegetables are cooked without being mixed into the liquid, thus keeping their shape and arrangement.

Yield: 6 servings

STOCK

4 lb. beef bones
2 lb. chicken bones
2 lb. beef (chuck, shank, or short ribs)
4 bay leaves
1 tsp. dried thyme leaves

CHICKEN "BALLOONS"

12 chicken wings
5 oz. chicken meat (from 1 single breast or leg)
2 oz. chicken fat
¼ loosely packed c. parsley
Small dash ground nutmeg
¼ tsp. salt

VEGETABLES FOR MARMITE

3 carrots, peeled (½ lb.)
2 medium leeks, cleaned (½ lb.)
¼ white cabbage (½ lb.)
1 large white turnip, peeled (6 oz.)
5 or 6 dried shiitake mushrooms (placed in 1½ c. tepid water for ½ hour to reconstitute and drained, the liquid reserved)
1 tsp. salt

GARNISH

½ French baguette (long, narrow loaf of bread), thinly sliced
Grated Parmesan cheese in cabbage leaf

1 Cover the beef and chicken bones with cold water. Bring to a boil and cook for 2½ hours at a very gentle simmer, removing the scum as it comes to the surface. Add the beef, bay leaves, and dried thyme, and continue cooking for 2 hours longer. Strain the stock, cool overnight, and remove any fat that has solidified on top. It should yield 8 c. of stock.

Trim the cooked beef of any fat and cut into ¼-in. slices. Set aside.

To make the chicken "balloons": Cut the chicken wings above the wing tip joints on one side and above the joint at the other end, keeping only the middle segment. The object is to loosen the bones so they can be pulled out.

2 Trim off the strips of fatty skin that run along either side of the wing. It tends to be tough. (The trimmings can be frozen to use in stock or soup.)

3 Using a towel for a better grip, pull out the 2 bones; they should come out easily now that the wings have been cut at both ends.

4 Place the 5 oz. of chicken meat, fat, parsley, nutmeg, and salt in the bowl of a food processor, and process for 15 to 25 seconds, until well blended. Place the mixture in a pastry bag fitted with a ½-in. plain tip and stuff the wings until they take on a roundish, balloon shape. Don't worry if the stuffing is still visible. In a saucepan, cover with cold water, bring to a boil, and boil gently for 1 minute, drain, and rinse under cold water. Set aside until finishing the dish.

6 Place the stuffed chicken around the dish on top of the vegetables and the mushroom caps in the center. Pour the mushroom liquid on top and add the salt and 4 c. of the cooking liquid from the meat. Reserve the remaining 4 c. Bring the *petite marmite* to a boil, cover, and cook at a gentle simmer for 30 minutes.

5 **To prepare the <u>petite marmite</u>:** Arrange the meat in the bottom of an earthenware terrine or large saucepan nice enough to be brought to the table. Cut the carrots and leeks into 3- or 4-in. sticks about ½ in. thick. Pull off one cabbage leaf and reserve for use as a garnish. Cut the cabbage and turnip into wedges. Remove the stems from the shiitake mushrooms (the stems are fibrous but can be used to flavor stock) and reserve the soaking liquid. Arrange the vegetables on top of the meat in the pan.

7 Reheat the remaining stock and season with salt. Slice the baguette very thin (about ¼-in. slices). Arrange on a cookie sheet and place in a 400-degree oven for 10 to 12 minutes, until nicely browned. Arrange the grated Parmesan cheese in the center of a cabbage leaf with the croutons around on a serving plate. Present with the hot soup.

8 For an individual serving, scoop a few pieces of meat, some vegetables, a couple of chicken "balloons," and some stock into a soup plate. Serve immediately, while very hot, with extra stock, the croutons, and cheese.

23

1 Slice the onions thin by hand or in a food processor. Heat the butter and oil in a saucepan. When hot, add the onions and sauté 10 to 12 minutes on high heat, until nicely browned.

ONION SOUP GRATINEE LYONNAISE

A classic onion soup is a chicken or beef broth cooked with onions, and it can be served plain. Sometimes one slice of bread, covered with cheese, is placed on top just before serving. However, when the onion soup is combined with Swiss cheese and toasted French bread and is placed in the oven to brown, it becomes an onion soup gra-tinée or, for short, a gratinée. There are many versions of this famous soup. The standard classic version is done with chicken and beef stock; the onions, first sau-téed lightly, are combined and cooked with the stock.

In the Lyonnaise-style onion soup, the onions are cooked longer, until they reach a deep, dark mahogany color with some pieces slightly burned. Then stock or sometimes only water is added and the mixture is cooked and, eventually, pushed through a food mill. A lot of bread is used in the Lyonnaise version, usually even more than I've used in the recipe following. Sometimes it is prepared in a large soup terrine and brought to the table brown and puffy. A hole is made in the center of the crust with a ladle, and a mixture of egg yolk and port wine is poured inside the gratinée. It is then stirred together, crust and all, and the thick concoction served in hot soup plates.

A gratinée is ideal for a late supper. All of the ingredients can be ready and the soup

assembled and finished in the oven just before serving. Some cooks place the onion soup under the broiler just long enough to melt the cheese, but the recipe below is cooked in a very hot oven a longer time so that it forms a thicker and more flavorful crust than can be created under the broiler. For an onion soup not to collapse, the bowl has to be filled to the rim with stock and bread. The cheese layer on top should cover the whole surface and sides so, when it melts, it will stick to the sides of the bowl and form a crust that holds its shape without sinking into the liquid.

Yield: 6 bowls, 12 oz. each

1¼ lb. onions, peeled
1 Tb. butter
2 Tb. corn oil
1 French baguette – long, narrow loaf of bread (6–8 slices per person)
1 lb. cheese, half Emmenthaler and half Gruyère
10 c. chicken stock and/or water
1 tsp. chopped garlic (1 or 2 cloves)
¼ tsp. freshly ground black pepper
Salt to taste, depending on saltiness of the stock

2 Meanwhile, slice the bread very thin and grate the cheese. When the onions are nicely browned, add the chicken stock mixed with water or all stock or all water and the garlic. Bring to a boil and cook, uncovered, at a gentle boil for 20 minutes. Push the mixture through a food mill and add the pepper and salt.

3 Place the bread in one layer on a cookie sheet and cook in a 400-degree oven for approximately 8 to 10 minutes, until well browned on each side. Place 6 to 8 slices of the bread in each of the soup bowls and place the bowls on a cookie sheet.

4 Sprinkle about 2 Tb. of cheese on top of the bread and fill up the bowls with the soup mixture. Be sure the bowls are filled to the rim. If you need a bit more liquid, add a little water to the soup in each of the bowls.

5 Place approximately ½ c. of the combined cheeses on top of each bowl, making sure that the cheese is not only covering the bread but is touching the edge of the bowl all around so it will melt and adhere to the edge during cooking. Place the cookie sheet containing the bowls in a 425-degree oven and cook for 30 minutes.

6 When ready, the cheese, overlapping on the rim, will be attached to the bowl. If not brown enough after 30 minutes, place under the broiler for a few seconds before serving. Serve immediately, hot and puffy.

A LEANER VERSION

Reduce the amount of oil in the ingredients by half (1 Tb. instead of 2). Cook the stock and onions according to the recipe. Serve the onion soup as a clear soup, omitting steps 3 to 5, i.e., the bread, cheese, and oven baking.

COLD SORREL SOUP (GERMINY)

Germiny is the classic sorrel soup that is served in elegant French restaurants. It is usually served cold, with little pieces of fresh chervil sprinkled on top. The acidity of sorrel (high in oxalic acid) goes very well with the richness of the soup. If the soup is to be served cold, a good chicken stock should be used but not one that is so strong it becomes jelly-like when chilled.

Other more ordinary sorrel soups are made with sorrel, leeks, and potatoes, all of which are cooked with stock or water, then pushed through the food mill, and finished with cream. The germiny is made like a custard: the egg yolks are cooked into the hot broth, so one must be careful not to let the temperature rise above 180 degrees or else the eggs may become scrambled. A good cautionary measure is to reserve the cream in a cold bowl, then pour the hot soup through a fine strainer (to remove any possible scrambled particles) directly into the cold cream; this will immediately lower the temperature of the soup and prevent any further scrambling.

The soup should be fairly highly seasoned with salt and pepper when it is hot as the seasonings tend to lessen in intensity as the soup gets cold.

Yield: 8 servings

4 c. cold chicken stock
1 Tb. potato starch
4 egg yolks
¾ c. heavy cream
1 bunch sorrel (about 2 to 3 oz.), leaves cleaned of ribs
Salt to taste (depending on stock seasoning)

GARNISH

"Pluches" (whole leaves) of chervil or flat parsley

1 Mix ½ c. of the cold chicken stock with the potato starch and set aside. Mix another ½ c. of the stock with the egg yolks in a large bowl and set aside. Place the cream in a large bowl with a fine sieve on top and set aside. Bring the 3 c. of remaining chicken stock to a boil. When the stock is boiling, stir in the dissolved potato starch and bring back to a boil (ensuring that the potato starch is cooked).

2 Add the boiling stock to the cold stock–egg yolk mixture, and mix well with a whisk. Return to the soup pot and place the soup back on the stove.

3 Cook over medium heat on top of the stove, stirring with a flat wooden spatula, until the temperature reaches about 180 degrees – in about 1 to 2 minutes. Be careful not to overcook. As soon as the mixture reaches 180 degrees and thickens (the time at which the lecithin in the egg yolks thickens), pour the soup through the fine sieve directly into the cold cream. Stir to mix well.

4 Pull off any fibrous ribs from more mature sorrel leaves. Pile the leaves up, roll them into a bundle, and cut into ⅛-in. slices to shred (known as *chiffonade*). For proper slicing, note that the thumb and fingertips are tucked under and the blade of the knife is flat against the smooth side of the fingers, which act as a guide as the blade goes up and down. Put the chiffonade in a stainless-steel pan with 2 Tb. water and bring to a boil. The sorrel will melt and turn khaki color. Cook for 1 to 2 minutes.

5 Combine the sorrel with the soup. At this time, the sorrel may seem very mushy. When it is mixed into the soup, however, the strands separate again and divide through the soup, giving that wonderful, slightly acidic taste of sorrel to the soup. Taste again for seasoning.

6 Serve cold, sprinkled with pieces of chervil.

EGGS

GRATIN OF EGGS LOUTE

It is a delicate procedure to hard-cook eggs properly. So often in restaurants eggs are cooked at too high a boil, which tends to toughen the albumen and produce a rubbery white of egg. Also you'll often notice the smell of sulfur that we associate with rotten eggs and the greenish tint around the yolks; to prevent this the eggs should be started in hot tap water, brought to a boil, and simmered for 10 to 11 minutes, depending on size, then placed in ice-cold water. They should not be removed from the water until the insides of the eggs are cold. If you feel the eggs may be difficult to shell, it helps to remove them momentarily from the cold water and roll them under your hand, cracking the whole surface while they are still hot, before returning them to the cold water to finish cooling completely. In this manner, the water tends to get in between the membrane and the flesh, making the eggs easier to shell.

This Gratin of Eggs Loute has a purée of mushrooms underneath and an onion and cream sauce on top and is ideal for a light supper or lunch as well as brunch.

Yield: 6–8 servings

8 extra large eggs, hard-cooked, cooled, shelled, and sliced

MUSHROOM FILLING

1 Tb. butter
8 oz. mushrooms
½ c. thinly sliced scallions (about 3)
1 anchovy fillet, crushed (about 1 tsp.)
1/16 tsp. freshly ground black pepper

SOUBISE SAUCE

½ lb. onions, peeled and sliced thin
1 c. water
1 Tb. butter
1 Tb. flour
1 c. cold milk
½ c. heavy cream
1/16 tsp. freshly ground black pepper
½ tsp. salt
2 Tb. Swiss cheese (preferably very dry), grated →

31

1 Place the eggs in a single layer in a saucepan, cover with hot water from the tap, and bring to a boil. Lower the heat and boil gently for 11 minutes. Then pour off the hot water and add cold water and ice to cool.

Meanwhile, place 1 Tb. butter in a skillet. Wash the mushrooms carefully and chop coarse by hand or in a food processor. Add the scallions to the butter and sauté for about 2 minutes. Add the mushrooms and cook for approximately 3 to 4 minutes, until the juice of the mushrooms has been released, is boiled down, and the mushrooms are dry again.

Add the crushed anchovy and the pepper. Mix well and spread the mixture in the bottom of a 6-c. gratin dish.

Slice the eggs with an egg slicer and arrange over the filling. (Notice the light yellow color of the yolk and the absence of a green tinge around it.)

3 Sprinkle with the Swiss cheese and place under the broiler for about 3 to 4 minutes, until nicely browned. Serve immediately.

2 Place the sliced onions in a saucepan with 1 c. of water, bring to a boil, and boil for approximately 5 minutes, until the onions are almost tender and most of the water has evaporated, leaving the onions almost dry. Place in a food processor and reduce to a purée. Melt the butter in a saucepan and add the flour. Mix well with a whisk and cook for about 10 to 15 seconds. Add the cold milk. Stir with the whisk and bring the mixture to a boil, stirring often. When it boils and thickens, add the cream, the pepper and salt, and the purée of onion. Bring to the boil again and pour the sauce over the sliced eggs.

POACHED EGGS CLAMART

Poaching Eggs. The freshest and the best-quality eggs will give the best results for poaching. Eggs from free-range chickens will be high in albumen, as will very fresh eggs, and the egg white will hold its shape around the yolk and resist thinning out too much in the water during cooking. Keeping the raw eggs cold, also, will tend to contract the albumen and make the egg white hold a better shape while cooking. Vinegar is added to the water, as the acidity also tends to make the egg white retain its shape better. Salt is not necessary. It tends to break down the albumen of the white and make it more runny. Always poach one or two extra eggs in case one breaks during cooking.

Poached eggs are very useful in a kitchen. They lend themselves to a great number of combinations. They can be used cold in aspic as well as hot in various dishes, and they can be poached several hours or even a day ahead and kept in the refrigerator in clean water as is done in restaurant kitchens.

Hollandaise Sauce. Hollandaise is the mother sauce of hot emulsion sauces. First, a mixture of egg yolks is cooked with a little bit of liquid (water or lemon juice), and that combination is called a <u>sabayon.</u> Then butter is added. The butter is usually clarified, but can be added soft and unmelted instead as we are doing in this recipe. The extra moisture in the unclarified butter will make a slightly thinner sauce, but fresh butter gives the sauce a creamier taste.

For a thicker hollandaise, clarify the butter. To clarify butter, cut it into pieces into a saucepan and place in a 200-degree oven until the butter is completely melted. It will separate into two layers — a milky residue at the bottom and a transparent, oily layer on top. The oily part is the clarified butter and the milky residue can be discarded.

With the addition of a mixture of reduced vinegar, shallots, and tarragon, the hollandaise becomes a <u>*béarnaise*</u> and, in turn, the béarnaise with tomato is called a <u>*choron*</u> sauce. The addition of meat glaze makes it a <u>Valois</u> sauce, and with whipped cream folded in it becomes a <u>mousseline</u> sauce (see Salmon with Mousseline Sauce, page 125). Lemon and orange can be added also and the name changes. Hollandaise can be combined with fish sauce or other types of sauces to enrich them and help them glaze under the broiler.

It is extremely useful to know how to reconstitute a sauce that has broken down as a result of exposure to too much heat (see photographs 11 and 12). The greater the amount of egg yolk in the hollandaise, the less likely it is to break down. However, too many egg yolks can make the sauce too "yolky" in taste. Leftover hollandaise which has solidified can be kept in the refrigerator and added to béchamel or other cream sauces or soups to enrich them.

Yield: 8 servings

TO POACH THE EGGS

2 qt. water
3 Tb. distilled white vinegar
8–10 very fresh and cold eggs

FOR THE HOLLANDAISE SAUCE

4 egg yolks
3 Tb. water
2 sticks unsalted butter, softened
¼ tsp. salt
⅛ tsp. cayenne pepper

FOR THE PEAS

2 c. fresh peas (or one 10-oz. package frozen "petite" peas)
2 Tb. unsalted butter
1 Tb. water
½ tsp. salt
½ tsp. sugar

FOR THE CROUTONS

8 slices thin white bread
2 Tb. unsalted butter, softened

GARNISH

8–10 slices truffle or 8–10 slices tomato →

1 **To poach the eggs:** Combine the water and vinegar in a saucepan (preferably non-stick) and bring to a boil. Although eggs can be broken into a little dish and slid into the water, it is just as easy to crack them, one at a time, on a flat surface and then drop them directly into the saucepan of boiling water. Open the eggs with both thumbs and let them slide directly into the water, positioning your hands as close to the water as possible to avoid splashing. The eggs should be poached in simmering water, although the first one can go into boiling water, as the cold temperature of the egg will cool off the water and stop the boiling immediately. Break one egg after another, going as fast as you can so there is not too much difference in cooking time between the first and the last eggs.

2 Run a large slotted spoon across the surface of the water to make the eggs move in the water as they are poaching and prevent them from sticking to the bottom. Using a non-stick saucepan also helps resolve this problem. After the eggs have moved in the water and some of the whites hardened, they won't stick anymore. Cook the eggs from 3 to 5 minutes, depending on whether you prefer them soft or more set. As the temperature of the water rises after the addition of the cold eggs, reduce the heat. The eggs should poach at a bare simmer, as boiling water will toughen the albumen and make rubbery eggs. Lift an egg occasionally with the slotted spoon and press it lightly with your finger to determine the degree of doneness. The whites should be set, but the yolks should still be soft and runny inside.

3 As soon as the eggs are cooked to your liking, lift them out with the slotted spoon and transfer to a bowl of ice water. (This will stop the cooking of the eggs and also wash off the vinegar taste.)

4 When the eggs are cold, lift them with your hands from the water and trim off the excess shaggy edges of white with a knife. Place in a bowl of clean water and keep in the refrigerator. At serving time, the eggs can be placed in a strainer and lowered one at a time into simmering water for approximately 1 minute to make them hot, then drained on paper towels and served. If poached eggs are used in a gratin, the cold eggs can be placed directly in the gratin dish or on top of spinach or other vegetables and heated directly in the oven.

5 Notice that in the presentation of eggs one side is always nicer than the other. The underside of the egg is not as rounded and beautiful as the top. Place it so that the nicest side shows, as in the picture.

6 **For the hollandaise:** Place the yolks and water in a saucepan, preferably stainless steel or enameled cast iron. (Aluminum will discolor the sauce.) The *sabayon*, which is the first part of the hollandaise, can be made in a double boiler over lukewarm to hot water to prevent curdling or it can be prepared directly on top of the stove.

7 Start beating the mixture, making sure that you "drive" the whisk into the corners of the saucepan where the eggs will have a tendency to overcook and scramble. Cook over medium heat, alternately moving the pan off the heat while beating and then placing it back on the heat, so the mixture never gets too hot. If it comes too close to a boil, the eggs will scramble. On the other hand, if the mixture does not get hot enough during the beating, it will tend to foam too much, increase in volume, and have too light a consistency to be able to hold and absorb the butter.

8 Beat for approximately 4 minutes. The consistency of the mixture should be that of thick, soft, very smooth butter. Between the streaks of the whisk, you should be able to see the bottom of the pan.

9 Add the butter piece by piece, beating after each addition while moving the hollandaise off and on the heat to keep the temperature hot enough so the butter is absorbed and the hollandaise thickens. Season with salt and cayenne pepper. Notice that the hollandaise doesn't require much salt.

10 If the hollandaise is exposed to too much heat, it will eventually separate and break down. Notice the broken look and the butter separating from the egg yolk. First, the sauce will start getting oily at the edge when it begins to break down. As that starts to happen, you can smooth it out again by beating in 1 Tb. of hot water. However, if the sauce is completely separated, as shown in our photograph, reconstitute it as explained below.

11 Strain the mixture through a very fine strainer to separate most of the oily liquid part from the sauce.

12 Place 2 Tb. of water in a saucepan, bring to a boil, remove from the heat, and add the thick part of the broken sauce ½ tsp. at a time while beating. You will see the sauce becoming smooth again. Keep adding until you have used all of the thick part of the sauce. Then, while beating, add the liquid butter part as though you

were making the hollandaise from scratch, moving the pan on and off the heat to keep the temperature warm. If the sauce has been recooked too much or if during the process the eggs tend to scramble lightly, the mixture can be strained through a very fine strainer, a *chinois,* to alleviate the scrambled appearance.

13 **Prepare the peas:** Place 2 c. peas, 2 Tb. butter, 1 Tb. water, ½ tsp. each salt and sugar in a saucepan, bring to a boil, and cook over high heat for about 1 to 2 minutes.

For the croutons: Cut each of the 8 slices of bread with a round cutter approximately 3 in. in diameter. Butter each of the rounds on both sides with the soft butter. Arrange on a cookie sheet and place in a 400-degree oven for 10 to 12 minutes, until well browned on both sides. Set aside.

At serving time reheat your eggs in a small strainer placed in simmering water for approximately 1 minute. Place the croutons on the plates, surround them with the peas, and position a drained egg on top of each. Coat with the hollandaise sauce and decorate the top with a few peas, a slice of truffle, or thin strips of tomato.

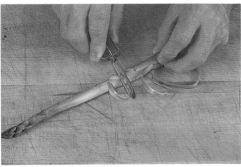

2 Peel the asparagus, starting approximately one-third of the way down the stalk; you can check with your fingernail to see if the skin is fairly fibrous there. To peel, hold the asparagus completely flat on the table, keeping your index finger and thumb on top of it, not underneath, so the asparagus lies flat and can be rolled on the table as it is peeled. Notice that the vegetable peeler is held with the thumb and fingers of the other hand flat and on top, not underneath it, so the blade is perfectly parallel to the stalk. Begin cutting near the tip end of the asparagus one-third of the way down the stalk, pushing the trimmings directly onto your fingers; there is no danger of cutting yourself. As you peel, rotate the asparagus by rolling it gently. Peel all around.

3 When all the asparagus has been peeled, break each piece at the base just above where the peeling stops, removing the trimmings and the base. The asparagus can now be tied in bundles and cooked.

MOLLET EGGS WITH STEWED ASPARAGUS

Mollet ("soft" in French) indicates eggs that have approximately the consistency of a poached egg except they are cooked in the shell like a hard-cooked egg. About 3½ to 4 minutes of cooking in simmering water is long enough, as very often the eggs are peeled and reheated at serving time. They are a bit delicate to shell and it is best done under cold water.

The stew of asparagus here is made with a combination of green and white asparagus. The white asparagus tends to be a trifle bitter and takes a bit longer to cook than the green. It is imperative to peel the asparagus, as shown in photographs 2 and 3 here, because it enables you to eat not only the tips but most of the stalk, which is covered with a fibrous inedible membrane.

Yield: 6 servings

24 asparagus spears (green, white, or a combination of both), about 4 per person
6 slices bread
1 Tb. butter
1½ Tb. corn oil
6 large eggs
FOR COOKING THE ASPARAGUS
½ c. water
¼ tsp. salt
3 Tb. butter

1 The white asparagus is on the left. The good green asparagus is in the center. (Notice that the tip is fairly tightly closed, as it should be.) On the right is an "over-the-hill" asparagus spear. The tips are opening like a flower. Fresh asparagus is firm and plump and will snap rather than bend. A soft, wrinkled specimen indicates dehydration and age.

Eliminate the butter and the oil for the croutons, trimmed as indicated in the recipe. Toast in a toaster or an oven. Reduce the amount of butter to 1 Tb. for the cooking of the asparagus. Proceed as explained in the recipe.

4 For the stewed asparagus, the stalks are lined up 6 to 8 at a time and cut on a bias into pieces about 1½ in. long. Trim the slices of bread and cut a small round (1½ in.) from the center of each with a cookie cutter. The egg will sit in the center of the hollowed-out slice of bread, which will secure it and prevent it from rolling.

Place the 1 Tb. of butter and the 1½ Tb. of oil in a skillet and, when hot, cook the 6 rings of bread for about 1½ minutes on each side, until nicely browned.

6 Arrange the asparagus on individual plates with some of its liquid. Place the crouton ring in the middle of the plate and position the egg in the hollowed-out center. Cut one of the pieces of asparagus into thin strips to decorate the top.

5 Place the eggs in hot but not boiling water (which has a tendency to make them crack), bring to a boil, and boil gently 3½ to 4 minutes, depending on the size of the eggs. Remove the eggs with a slotted spoon and transfer them to a bowl of ice water. Lift from the cold water, crack the shells, and place the eggs back in the cold water; this will make them easier to peel. While still warm, shell the eggs. Hold in ice water to stop the cooking if you are not serving immediately.

To cook the asparagus: Place the white asparagus in a saucepan in one layer. Add the water and salt. Bring to a boil, cover, and cook about 1 minute. Add the green asparagus, cover, and cook for another 1½ minutes. Add the 3 Tb. of butter in pieces, and cook the mixture over high heat until the butter mixes with the remaining water and boils together to create an emulsion. Set aside.

If the eggs are to be reheated, lower into boiling water for about 1 minute.

7 The egg is shown broken to illustrate that the consistency of the inside of the egg should be about like that of a poached egg. Serve immediately.

As an alternative serving suggestion, instead of decorating with asparagus strips, the pieces of crouton from the centers of the bread can be browned and placed on top of the eggs.

E G G S

MOLDED EGGS

The molded eggs done below in ½-c. ramekins are actually shirred eggs. They can, of course, be served directly in the ramekins, but here they are unmolded. When unmolded, the eggs look nice prepared in ramekins the sides of which have been coated either with expensive chopped truffles (truffles are at their best with eggs or potatoes) or with herbs. Other coatings might be chopped boiled ham, watercress leaves, or mushroom slices.

The eggs in the recipes following are cooked 4 minutes in the oven. (They can be cooked 1 minute less if you are going to serve them directly in the ramekins. At this stage, the eggs are too soft to be unmolded.) To be unmolded, they should be cooked from 3½ to 5 minutes, depending on personal taste. Most of the white should be set but the yolk should be runny.

With the Eggs Crécy, the chopped-truffle-coated eggs, a delicate purée of carrots thinned with the cooking juices of the carrots and enriched with cream and butter is served. The purée should be fairly liquid so it can be spread on a plate and the eggs placed in the center. For a regular purée of carrots, omit the carrot liquid so the purée is slightly thicker.

The Molded Eggs Claude are flavored with herbs, which can be changed according to availability and taste. One radish makes enough julienne for one egg. It is a delicate and slightly crunchy garnish, and the intensity of the demi-glace complements well the taste of the eggs.

In both recipes, the eggs are placed on croutons, which makes them easier to unmold and also sets them in relief above the sauce and garnish.

TWO RECIPES FOR MOLDED EGGS

MOLDED EGGS CRECY WITH TRUFFLES

Yield: 6 servings
2 Tb. butter, for the molds
6 Tb. finely chopped truffles
½ lb. carrots, peeled (about 3 carrots)
¼ tsp. salt
3 Tb. heavy cream
6 large eggs
6 slices bread
1 Tb. butter
1½ Tb. corn oil
GARNISH
1 snow pea, blanched for 20 seconds in boiling water and cut into ⅛-in. slices

MOLDED EGGS CLAUDE WITH HERBS

Yield: 6 servings
2 Tb. butter, for the molds
6 Tb. chopped herbs (a mixture of parsley, tarragon, chives, coriander, and/or chervil)
6 radishes, julienned
6 large eggs
6 slices bread
1 Tb. butter
1½ Tb. oil
1 c. demi-glace (see page 8), brought to a boil and seasoned with salt and pepper
Salt and freshly ground pepper to taste

1 **To prepare molds:** Butter generously (1 tsp. each) the half-cup molds and press into the butter the chopped truffles (in the mold on the left) or the chopped herbs (in the one on the right).

2 Cut the radishes into thin slices.

3 Stack the slices together and cut them into a fine julienne. They can be kept, if done ahead, in cold water to cover so they stay crisp.

For the purée of carrot, cut the peeled carrots into ½-in. dice. Cover with water, add a dash of salt, and bring to a boil. Cook about 7 minutes, until the carrots are just tender. Drain the carrots (reserving ⅓ c. of the liquid) and place them and the reserved liquid in the food processor. Process until finely puréed. Add ¼ tsp. salt and the cream to further liquefy the carrot mixture. Set aside until ready to serve.

5 The eggs are now just set; the centers are slightly runny and soft. They could be served in this manner or unmolded.

7 **For the Eggs Crécy with Truffles:** Place approximately 2 to 3 Tb. of the carrot purée on a warm serving plate. Position the truffled egg on the crouton in the center, and decorate the surrounding carrot purée border with blanched snow pea slices. The egg is broken to show that the consistency of the inside is about the same as that of a poached egg. Serve immediately.

6 While the eggs are cooking, cut a round a little larger than the circumference of the ramekins out of the center of each bread slice with a cookie cutter. To sauté 6 rounds, heat 1 Tb. of butter and 1½ Tb. of oil in a skillet. When hot, add the rounds and sauté approximately 1 minute on each side, until nicely browned.

For unmolded eggs, run a knife around the eggs in the ramekins to loosen at the edges. Place a round crouton on top of each and unmold the egg on top of it.

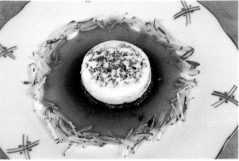

8 **For the Molded Eggs Claude with Herbs:** Arrange a border of julienned radish around individual plates. Pour approximately 2 to 3 Tb. of hot, seasoned demiglace in the middle of each plate, and place the unmolded egg on its crouton in the center. Serve immediately.

4 Sprinkle a tiny dash of salt into each of the molds and break an egg into each mold. Place the molds in an ovenproof skillet and surround with 1 in. of water. Bring to a boil on top of the stove, cover with a lid, and place in a preheated 400-degree oven for 4 minutes.

A LEANER VERSION

For the Molded Eggs Claude with Herbs: Brush the molds very lightly with melted butter – 2 tsp. should be enough for the 6 molds. Toast the croutons in a toaster or in the oven without fat. (The croutons can also be eliminated.) Proceed according to the recipe instructions.

Snow peas, when blanched and sliced thin, will form little "petals" that make a nice decoration with a dot of red in the center, either from a red pepper or a tomato.

Scrambled eggs prepared this way can be kept warm after cooking in a double boiler over 150-degree water for at least 30 minutes.

Yield: 6 servings

BREAD CASES
1 small loaf unsliced white bread
2 Tb. softened butter

MUSHROOMS
½ lb. shiitake or oyster mushrooms (about 18–20 total, 4–5 per person)
2 Tb. butter
¼ tsp. salt
1 Tb. chopped shallots
2 Tb. white wine
½ c. demi-glace (see page 8)

DECORATION
1 snow pea
1 piece of peeled red pepper or tomato flesh

SCRAMBLED EGGS
12 large eggs
½ tsp. salt
¼ tsp. freshly ground black pepper
2 Tb. butter
3 Tb. heavy cream

SCRAMBLED EGGS IN BREAD CASES WITH CANDIED OYSTER MUSHROOMS

There are two different types of scrambled eggs. The standard method of preparation is to cook the eggs long enough for firm curds to form before stirring the mixture. Then the large curds are stirred into the uncooked part of the eggs until the whole mixture consists of fairly large lumps. If this is done quickly, there should still be some soft, liquidy egg around the lumps. When served, this standard, earthier way of scrambling eggs is different but equally as good as the method shown below. Some days I crave one kind and other days the other kind.

In the recipe here, the eggs are cooked in a heavy saucepan and stirred almost continuously with a whisk in order to mix the curds, as they begin to set, into the liquid eggs. This constant stirring allows only the smallest possible curds to form, and it produces the creamiest possible mixture. To prevent the eggs from overcooking after they have reached the proper consistency and have been removed from the heat (the pan will still generate enough heat so they continue to cook), some of the uncooked eggs, which have been set aside, are stirred into the cooked eggs with cream at the end to absorb the heat of the pan, again helping to create a creamy, rich mixture.

The bread cases make an ideal receptacle for the eggs, but they should be filled only at the last moment so they don't get soggy. They are coated with a very small amount of butter and done in the oven. Although they don't get as uniformly brown as they would if they had been prepared in a skillet or deep-fried in oil, they absorb a minimum of fat and are more delicate.

Oyster, shiitake, or another type of mushroom can be used. In this recipe, the mushrooms are cooked longer than usual. In standard recipes, mushrooms are often briefly sautéed and retain a lot of moisture, which gives them a particular "bite." Cooked as shown below, the mushrooms release all their moisture and are allowed to dry and brown in the skillet; this technique makes chewier pieces and concentrates the taste to produce a rich and meaty mushroom. With the concentrated demi-glace, shallots, and white wine, the mushroom sauce makes a very substantial mixture, which balances the richness and mild taste of the eggs. The sautéed mushrooms can be used as well as a garnish for most meats and roasts.

1 Use an unsliced bread loaf that is 1 or 2 days old so it can be carved into; it should not be dry but should not be too soft either or the carving will be very difficult. Cut the bread into 6 slices, each a good 1 in. thick. Trim off the crusts all around to form a square. Then, ⅜ in. in from the edge, cut down at least ½ in. into the slice to create a border.

2 Remove the bread in the center by first slicing pieces of it out on the bias.

3 Keep cutting the inside and scraping it out to create a receptacle with an overall thickness of approximately ¼ to ⅜ in. Save the trimmings for bread crumbs. Butter the bread receptacles all around, inside and out, with soft butter (not more than about 1 tsp. of butter for each receptacle). Arrange on a cookie sheet and place in a 400-degree oven for about 7 minutes, until nicely browned all over.

4 For the mushrooms: Remove the stems from the shiitake mushrooms; although tough and fibrous, they can be used for flavor in stock. The stem of the oyster mushroom is tender enough to be used in the recipe. Wash the mushrooms if dirty. Melt the butter in a large skillet. When hot, add the mushrooms and continue to cook them over medium to high heat, until most of the moisture comes out of them and evaporates. As this occurs, the mushrooms will start sizzling in the butter again. Continue cooking for a few minutes (a total of 7 to 8 minutes), until the mushrooms are brown and almost look candied. Add the salt and the shallots, sauté for about 1 minute, and add the wine. Toss and keep cooking until most of the wine has evaporated and the mushrooms are just barely wet with the wine. Add the demi-glace, bring to a boil, and simmer 1 to 2 minutes, until it reduces and coats the mushrooms. Set aside until serving time.

5 For the decoration: Blanch a snow pea in boiling water for 20 to 30 seconds, rinse under cold water, and cut crosswise into ⅛-in. slices. The slices will open like little petals.

For the center of the "flower," peel a piece of red pepper with a vegetable peeler (or use a piece of tomato flesh) and cut little rounds with the end of a pastry-bag tip.

6 For the eggs: Break the eggs into a bowl and add the salt and pepper. Beat the eggs with a whisk to mix well. Set ⅓ to ½ c. of the raw eggs aside to be used at the end of the cooking time.

Melt the butter in a heavy saucepan. When foaming, pour in the eggs and cook over medium to low heat, stirring gently with the whisk. Be sure to get around the bottom edge of the pan with your whisk, since the eggs will have a tendency to set and harden there first. Keep cooking and whisking gently until the mixture gets very creamy.

E G G S

7 The eggs should have the smallest possible curds. Continue cooking until you can see the bottom of the pan as the whisk is drawn through the eggs.

Remove the pan from the heat; the eggs will continue cooking, especially along the edges of the pan. Add the reserved raw eggs and the cream and keep mixing; the uncooked eggs and cream will absorb the heat still generated by the pan. Then place the pan in a 150-degree water bath and keep warm until serving time, or serve immediately. →

8 At serving time, place a bread case in the center of each serving plate. Arrange 4 or 5 coated mushrooms around and fill the case with the scrambled eggs. Notice how soft and creamy the egg mixture is.

9 Decorate the tops with the snow pea "petals" and red centers and serve immediately.

OMELETS

It is both simple and difficult to make an omelet. To make a moist and tasty omelet, one needs a well-seasoned or non-stick omelet pan, considerable practice, and high heat. Fresh eggs, sweet butter, and fresh herbs are indispensable for the proper omelet.

There are two different types of omelets. To make one type, the eggs are allowed to cook undisturbed for a while until large curds are formed in the pan. Then, the mixture is spread with a fork to allow the runny eggs to set in between the curds. The procedure is repeated several times, until most of the eggs are set but they are still slightly wet in the center. The omelet is then folded in half and slid or inverted onto a plate. This technique produces large, brown, chewy curds. Therefore, the omelet has a fairly rough, knobby texture and an assertive taste.

To make a classic French omelet, the eggs are poured into foaming (but not too hot) butter and moved in a continuous motion. The fork in one hand stirs the eggs while the other hand simultaneously shakes the pan to keep the mixture moving. The object is to move the curds as they start to solidify without allowing the curds to become hardened by prolonged cooking. (Albumen will toughen when exposed to high heat for too long.) The whole mixture is stirred continuously until it sets into a mass of very fine, creamy curds. The surface of the omelet is then allowed to sit undisturbed for a few seconds, just long enough to solidify the outside and make it possible to fold. It shouldn't be left long enough for the outside to brown and become hard, as this would toughen the albumen. By stirring and shaking the liquid egg mixture as quickly as possible, you end up with an omelet that is pale yellow on top and soft and creamy in the center. The making of a single omelet shouldn't take more than 1 minute. (A similar texture is achieved in Scrambled Eggs in Bread Cases with Candied Oyster Mushrooms, preceding recipe.)

Omelets can be stuffed, made flat for a country omelet (like the Italian frittata and Spanish tortilla), or rolled, and the four recipes here exemplify the different styles.

FOUR RECIPES FOR OMELETS

FINES-HERBES OMELET: CLASSIC AND COUNTRY-STYLE

for 1 omelet
3 eggs
Dash salt and freshly ground black pepper
2 Tb. herb mixture (1 Tb. finely chopped parsley and 1 Tb. finely chopped mixture of chervil, tarragon, and chives)
1½ tsp. butter

1 **For the classic fines-herbes omelet:** For each omelet, beat the eggs with salt, pepper, and the herb mixture in a bowl with a fork until well combined; that is, when you lift up the fork, pieces of egg white should no longer separate from the yolk; the egg should be well homogenized.

For a classic French omelet, place the butter in a non-stick skillet 6 to 8 in. in diameter and melt over high heat. Swirl the butter in the pan and, when foaming, add the eggs. Holding the fork flat, stir the eggs as fast as you can while shaking the pan with your other hand. Continue without stopping to shake and stir at the same time so the eggs coagulate uniformly.

E G G S

2 Still stirring, notice that the eggs are still moist in the center and incline your pan forward so most of the eggs gather toward the far end of the pan as they set. Now stop stirring while the eggs are still moist in the center.

3 Using your fork, bring the near lip over toward the center of the omelet. Note that as the mass of eggs has moved toward the far end of the pan, they have thinned out around the edges. Only the two thin lips are flipped over, first from one end, then the other, to enclose the thick, moist center. (If the mixture were left instead to set in one even layer covering the whole bottom of the pan, it would be too spread out and would then roll up like a jelly roll; thus the center would not be moist.)

4 Press the fold into place. Note: This motion should create a roundish edge. →

5 Run your fork between the edge of the pan and the far lip of the omelet to loosen it. Using the palm of your hand, tap the handle of the pan gently to shake the omelet and make it twist and lift onto itself, so the far lip rises above the edge of the pan.

6 Fold the far lip back toward the center of the omelet, meeting the other lip. Press with the flat of the fork to make sure the omelet comes to a point at each end. While holding the serving plate in your left hand, first bang the end of the pan gently so the omelet pulls together against the edge of the pan. Then, invert the omelet onto the plate and serve immediately.

7 The omelet should be very moist, creamy, and wet in the center.

8 For the country-style fines-herbes omelet: Melt the butter in the omelet pan. Mix together the eggs, salt, pepper, herbs. When the butter is hot and the foaming has subsided, pour the egg-herb mixture into the center of the pan and cook over medium heat, allowing the eggs to set and curl at the edges. Then, with the tines of your fork, stir the eggs so the runny part fills the areas between the set curds.

9 When most of the eggs are set but still slightly liquid inside, the omelet is ready.

10 Fold the omelet in half. You will notice that the outside will have a nice brown color as opposed to the classic omelet (photographs 1 to 6), which is a pale yellow. Invert onto a plate and serve immediately.

STUFFED OMELET HUNTER-STYLE

for 1 omelet
2 tsp. butter
1 medium mushroom, diced
1 chicken liver, cut into ¼-in. dice
Salt and freshly ground black pepper
2 Tb. tomato sauce
1 tsp. chopped chives
3 eggs

1 Heat 1 tsp. of the butter and, when hot, sauté the mushroom for about 30 seconds. Add the chicken liver and dash of salt and pepper. Sauté another 30 seconds and add the tomato sauce and chives. Set aside.

2 Mix the eggs and dash of salt and pepper with your fork. Heat the remaining 1 tsp. butter in an omelet pan. When hot, add the eggs and stir, following the technique used to make a classic omelet.

3 Fold the near lip onto the omelet. Arrange most of the solids from the liver-mushroom mixture down the center of the omelet, saving the remainder for a garnish (below), pushing lightly with your fork to hold them in place.

4 Tap on the end of the handle gently, as shown in photograph 5, to bring the far lip up. Press the far lip of the omelet over the stuffing, making sure that the ends of the omelet are pointed. Bang the end of the omelet pan gently so the omelet sits at the far edge of the pan. Invert onto a serving plate. Place a little extra sauce around the omelet and a bit of the liver-mushroom mixture at each end. Serve immediately.

FLAT OMELET FARMER-STYLE

for 1 omelet

2 slices salted, unsmoked bacon, cut into ¾-in. strips
½ Idaho potato, cut into 12 unpeeled, very thin slices
2 Tb. minced chives
3 eggs
Dash freshly ground black pepper

1 Cook the bacon strips on both sides for a few minutes, until nicely browned. Add the potato slices and sauté for another 2 to 3 minutes, until the thin slices are nicely browned. Add the chives. If the bacon has rendered too much fat, pour most of it out. With a fork, beat the eggs with a dash of pepper (salt is not necessary because of the bacon).

2 Add the eggs and drag the tines of a fork between the curds to expose the runny eggs to the cooking surface.

3 When the eggs are set, still slightly creamy and liquid in the center, the omelet can be flipped over (if you feel dexterous enough), or you can slide or invert it directly onto a plate. Serve immediately.

4 The 4 omelets: From the top left, clockwise, the flat omelet farmer-style, the country-style *fines-herbes* omelet, the classic stuffed omelet hunter-style, and the classic *fines-herbes* omelet.

2 In another skillet, preferably non-stick, heat 1 tsp. of the butter. When foaming at the edge, break the 2 eggs into it and cook on low to medium heat (the edges should not brown) for about 30 seconds. Then cover the pan with a lid and continue to cook another 45 seconds to 1 minute, until all the egg white is set and the egg yolk is just shiny. Slide the eggs onto a warm plate.

SKILLET EGGS WITH BROWN BUTTER

One of the fastest and tastiest methods of cooking eggs is to drop them into a skillet and fry them. But when eggs are seared in butter that is too hot, they tend to turn crisp and curl at the edge of the white, making them tough. They should be cooked in hot, but not too hot, butter. The garnish (bread, asparagus, and mushrooms here) can be changed at will to include different kinds of diced vegetables that can be sautéed briefly for serving with the eggs.

Yield: 1 serving

GARNISHES (FOR 1 SERVING OF 2 EGGS)

About ½ slice bread
1 mushroom
1 asparagus spear
2 tsp. butter
1 tsp. corn oil
Dash salt

TO FRY THE EGGS

2 tsp. butter
2 eggs
About ¼ tsp. good red wine vinegar
Parsley leaves

1 Cut enough bread (approximately ½ slice) into ½-in. cubes to measure ¼ c. Cut the mushroom into ¼-in. dice. Peel the asparagus spear, wash, and cut into ¼-in. dice.

Place the butter and corn oil in a skillet and, when hot, sauté the bread cubes for a couple of minutes, until they are nicely browned all over. Add the asparagus and mushrooms and sauté for another 45 seconds to 1 minute, until the vegetables begin to soften and are heated through. Add a dash of salt and set aside.

3 Place the garnish on top of the eggs and add the remaining tsp. of butter to the skillet. Melt and, when it becomes a hazelnut color, pour it around the eggs and sprinkle with the red wine vinegar. Sprinkle some parsley leaves on top and serve immediately.

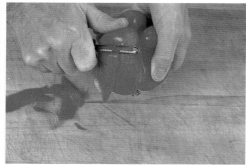

1 **For the peppers and garlic:** Peel the red pepper all around, peeling as much as you can on the top and bottom. You won't be able to get into the pleats and recesses.

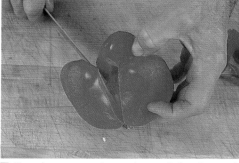

2 Cut the pepper into pieces right through the pleats where the surface was not accessible to the vegetable peeler.

3 Peel off any remaining skin with the peeler or a small, sharp paring knife. Remove the seeds and the stem and slice the peppers into thin strips.

Cut the eggplant into six ¾-in. slices. Sprinkle with salt on both sides. Heat the oil in a large skillet. When hot, add the eggplant and cook approximately 4 minutes on each side. The eggplant should be just soft and lightly browned. Cover the skillet with a lid and set aside.

Peel the garlic and slice thin. Heat the butter in a small skillet. When hot, add →

DEEP-FRIED EGGS JULIA

Although it is a classic dish, deep-fried eggs are not featured often on menus, maybe because they are a bit delicate to make. Only one egg can be fried at a time, as the egg whites splatter in the hot oil and have to be gathered together with wooden spatulas and held together until they set and start browning.

The center of a deep-fried egg should be runny and the egg requires cooking for only 1½ minutes in the hot oil. All the garnishes have to be prepared first, since, as soon as the eggs are removed from the hot oil, they should be served immediately after draining on paper towels. Instead of serving the eggs on croutons, as is done in other recipes, I have used slices of fried eggplant as a base.

The peppers are peeled with a vegetable peeler. Green, red, or yellow peppers can be peeled in this manner, providing they are plump, firm, and smooth. Another technique for peeling peppers is demonstrated in the recipe for Chicken Breasts with Chervil Mousse and Vegetable-Stuffed Peppers (page 173), where the peppers are broiled first. Broiling cooks the flesh of the pepper and imparts a particular flavor.

Yield: 6 servings

FOR THE PEPPERS AND GARLIC

1 large pepper, about 12 oz., smooth and firm
2 large cloves garlic
½ Tb. butter
⅛ tsp. salt
⅛ tsp. freshly ground black pepper

FOR THE EGGPLANT

1 medium eggplant, cut into 6 slices
¼ tsp. salt
3 Tb. corn oil
About 5 c. corn oil for frying (deep in pan)
6 eggs

GARNISH

1 small bunch fresh coriander

the red pepper, the garlic slices, salt, and pepper, and sauté for about 1 minute, just until the peppers and garlic soften a little but are still firm. Set aside.

4 Heat the 5 c. oil in a large skillet, preferably non-stick, to approximately 360 degrees. It should be at least 1½ in. deep so the eggs do not stick to the bottom of the pan as readily. Use two good wooden spatulas, dipping them into the hot oil beforehand so they are warm when ready to be used.

Break 1 egg into the oil, getting your hands as close to the oil as possible so it doesn't splatter as much when the egg hits its surface.

5 Immediately, the egg white will start bubbling and spreading. Using the 2 wooden spatulas, gather the egg white in toward the yolk.

6 Hold the egg between the spoons on one side of the saucepan in the oil to mold it into a roundish shape while it starts setting. For the yolk to be runny, the egg should cook about 1½ minutes. Fry the remaining eggs. They must be fried one at a time.

7 Remove the eggs to a paper towel to drain. Place a warm slice of eggplant in the center of each plate. Arrange some of the pepper-garlic mixture around it, and garnish the mixture with coriander leaves. Place a fried egg in the center of the eggplant. Notice that the egg cut open here has approximately the same consistency as a poached egg. Serve immediately.

- OYSTERS ON THE HALF SHELL WITH
  MIGNONNETTE SAUCE
- OYSTERS NATHALIE
- OYSTERS MADISON
- CLAMS ON THE HALF SHELL WITH COLD
  HORSERADISH SAUCE
- LINGUINE WITH CLAM SAUCE AND
  VEGETABLES
- FRIED SOFT-SHELL CLAMS AND DEEP-FRIED
  ZUCCHINI
- SOUFFLE OF MUSSELS AND BASIL BEVERLY
- HARD-SHELL CRAB LOULOU WITH
  MARINATED VEGETABLE SALAD
- SOFT-SHELL CRAB GENEVIEVE
- STUFFED SQUID POULETTE WITH KASHA
- GRILLED SQUID WITH LEMON SAUCE AND
  BROCCOLI RAPE
- OCTOPUS CATALANE
- BROILED LOBSTER BENJAMIN WITH
  CARAMELIZED CORN, POTATO FLATS, AND
  CORNBREAD
- LOBSTER SARA
- SCALLOPS NOUVELLE CUISINE
- SHRIMP "BUNNIES" CREOLE
- SHRIMP MADISON
- CRAWFISH WITH SCALLOP MOUSSE TATAN
  HELENE AND POTATO-DILL GNOCCHI
- WHELK IN HOT BROTH
- WHELK SALAD
- FROGS IN TARRAGON SAUCE
- SNAILS ROLAND
- ESCARGOT STEW WITH LINGUINE
- SEAFOOD BREAD
- FISH ROE EVELYN
- FISH FRITURE WITH FRIED CELERY LEAVES
- GOUJONNETTE OF CATFISH
- PIKE QUENELLES AND CHICKEN LIVER
  TIMBALE MERRET
- QUENELLES DORIA WITH DUXELLES SAUCE
- PATE OF FISH DUGLERE
- EEL WITH POTATO MIETTES
- EEL IN RED WINE MATELOTE
- ROAST MONKFISH IN RATATOUILLE
- MEDALLIONS OF MONKFISH STEPHANIE
- RAY MEUNIERE WITH MUSHROOMS
- POACHED RAY VALERIE WITH BROWN
  BUTTER
- BROILED BLUEFISH WITH LEMON LEEKS AND
  GARLIC WAX BEANS
- GRILLED TUNA WITH SAGE BUTTER AND SEA
  BEANS
- SALMON WITH MOUSSELINE SAUCE

(CONTINUED)

SHELLFISH & FISH

- SALMON IN SORREL SAUCE
- SALMON FILLETS IN BASIL SAUCE
- STUFFED SALMON IN FLAKY DOUGH
- GRILLED SOLE WITH HERB BUTTER
- POACHED SOLE MISTRAL
- FILLET OF SOLE ALEXANDRE DUMAS
- PAUPIETTES OF SOLE WITH LOBSTER
  MOUSSE CHRISTIANE
- SOLE COLETTE
- STEAMED SCROD NORMA
- "ANGRY" TROUT IN HOT PECAN SAUCE
  WITH HUSH PUPPIES
- FRIED WHITING COLBERT
- LONG ISLAND BOUILLABAISSE

OYSTERS

There are at least a dozen types of oysters all along the East Coast, up the Gulf of Louisiana, and along the West Coast. Although oysters are available and edible year-round, they get too milky and fatty during the spawning season and are not very good to eat at that time, especially raw on the half shell. Only medium-sized, fresh, and plump oysters are good for eating raw. The environment and the marine plants they feed on will determine the shape, size, color, and taste of the oysters. Which tastes the best, from the greenish, acidic Belon to the sweet beige Chincoteague, is purely a question of personal preference.

Like all shellfish, which spoil very quickly after dying, oysters in the shell should be alive when opened. Discard any that have opened beforehand. Your nose will determine the freshness of the oysters. A sweet, fresh seaweed and occasional iodine smell indicates a fresh oyster, while an acrid, nauseating stench indicates a spoiled one; it is unmistakable. Keep fresh unshucked oysters at about 45 degrees in a brown bag or cardboard box, with seaweed, if possible, for moisture, especially if they are to be stored for several days.

Although raw is the first choice of the real aficionado, as in Oysters on the Half Shell here, oysters can be fried, poached, broiled, or stewed. Regardless of how they are prepared, they should not be overcooked or they will toughen, especially the "frill" or "mantle," which is the lacy collar all around the body of the oyster. For large oysters, it is preferable to remove that frill before cooking, but medium or small oysters are tender enough to be consumed whole. Two more recipes follow that are ideal for the Christmas season because of the red-and-green color combination.

OYSTERS ON THE HALF SHELL WITH MIGNONNETTE SAUCE

4–6 doz. medium-sized oysters

MIGNONNETTE SAUCE

3 Tb. chopped shallots
½ c. good red wine vinegar
2 tsp. coarsely ground black pepper
2 Tb. peanut or corn oil
1 Tb. chopped fennel top, dill, or other herb
3 Tb. grated daikon or icicle radish

3–4 lemons

1 Combine all sauce ingredients and refrigerate until serving time. Prepare the oysters on the half shell following the directions on the next page. Serve about ½ tsp. Mignonnette Sauce per oyster.

BASIC PREPARATION

2 Some of the oysters available from good New York markets are, top 2 rows, from left to right, closed and open: Apalachicola, cotuit, Pacific oysters; and bottom 2 rows, from left to right, closed and open: Wellfleet, Blue Point, Belon, Chincoteague. Other well-known varieties include the Louisiana, Kent Island, Cape Cod, and the tiny, delicious Olympia, all of which can be bought locally, depending on the time of the year and the availability. →

3 Wash the oysters under cold water. Use special sturdy pointed-tip oyster knives like the ones shown in here and a thick towel or pot holder to prevent an accident.

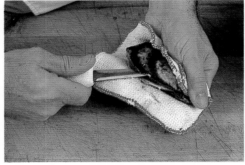

6 If the oyster shell crumbles and cannot be opened at the hinge, insert the point of the knife on the curved side of the oyster between the shells. Pry it open and sever the muscle.

8 Oysters on the half shell: The oyster should be left in the deep shell. Slide your knife under the oyster to sever the muscle and free the oyster.

4 Shucking oysters: With the oyster held firmly in the palm of your hand, pry and push the tip of the blade into the pointed end at the "hinge," between the top flat shell and the convex bottom one. You may have to exert a great amount of pressure to insert the knife between the shells at the hinge, but that is the place where you can make the cleanest opening, free of fragments of shell.

7 This technique will tend to break little pieces of shell loose inside the oyster. Be sure to remove them after the muscle is opened.

Do not wash the oysters under water as this flushes out the juices and the best taste of the oysters. Open the oysters over a bowl and retrieve the extra liquid to use in soups or sauces. At a time when a lot of oysters are opened, the extra juices can be used to rinse the oysters after opening to eliminate possible pieces of shell. Then add 1 Tb. of the juice to each oyster after the rinsing, leaving the bits of shell in the bowl.

9 Cut the lemon so it is flat at both ends. With the lemon on its side, cut halfway through with the point of a small sharp knife. Cut triangular points on a bias to give a swirl shape to the triangles.

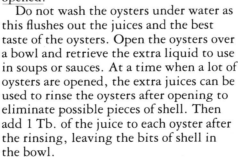

10 Arrange the oysters on a bed of shaved ice or seaweed. Serve cold with the lemon, or sprinkle with lemon juice or Mignonnette Sauce, and accompany with slices of buttered black pumpernickel bread.

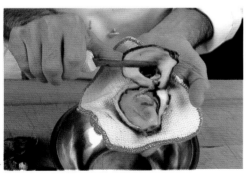

5 When you have inserted the point of the knife, press down to pop open the lid. Then move your knife back and forth, making the blade slide against the top shell inside to sever the muscle that holds both sides together. Lift up the lid.

A LEANER VERSION

Omit the oil in the Mignonnette Sauce. Proceed according to recipe instructions. Omit butter on the bread.

2 Arrange the mushrooms on 8 plates. Place a ring of red pepper in the center of each plate, and arrange 6 drained oysters within the ring. If desired, open 2 additional rings and arrange around the oysters to create a border. Add the purée of parsley to the butter sauce, coat the oysters with 2 to 3 Tb. of the green sauce, and serve. (Note: If the parsley is added to the butter sauce too early, the green will discolor.)

TWO RECIPES FOR COOKED OYSTERS

OYSTERS NATHALIE

Yield: 8 servings (6 oysters per person)
4 doz. oysters, shelled, cleaned of any
   pieces of shell, and kept in their juices
   ½ c. dry white wine
1 stick butter
Freshly ground black pepper to taste
3 Tb. water
1 or 2 large red peppers, cut into rings ⅛
   in. thick
Dash salt
2 Tb. butter (for sautéing mushrooms)
¾ lb. firm white mushrooms (approximately 16), sliced thin
3 c. loosely packed parsley leaves (preferably flat), very finely chopped or puréed
   in a spice grinder

1 Place ½ c. of the juice of the oysters with the wine in a saucepan. Bring to a boil and reduce to ½ c. Add the butter, piece by piece, mixing it well with the whisk after each addition. Season with pepper (no salt should be necessary). Set butter sauce aside.

Place 3 Tb. of water in a saucepan. Add the pepper rings and a dash of salt, and simmer gently for 1 minute at the most, just long enough to wilt and warm the peppers.

Using 2 skillets, sauté mushrooms in the remaining butter (1 Tb. per skillet) until the mushroom liquid comes out and most of it has evaporated and the mushrooms begin to sizzle again. Set aside.

Meanwhile, place the oysters in a saucepan in their remaining juices and heat on high heat to 170 degrees. The frill on the oysters should just begin to curl. Using a fine skimmer, remove any foam or curdled juices from the top.

A LEANER VERSION

Eliminate the 2 Tb. of butter for sautéing the mushrooms and ¾ of the stick of butter for the butter sauce, using only 2 Tb. of butter for the sauce. Combine 1 tsp. of potato starch with ¼ c. water and add it to the ½ c. of reduced juices in step 1. Then whisk in the 2 Tb. of butter, as explained in the recipe. To sauté the mushrooms, place 4 Tb. of water in a saucepan (preferably stainless steel) and add the mushrooms. Cook until the mushroom liquid has been released and evaporated through cooking. Proceed according to recipe.

OYSTERS MADISON

Yield: 8 servings

4 doz. oysters, shelled and kept in their
    juices (bottom shells cleaned and
    reserved)
½ c. dry white wine
5 oz. unsalted butter (1 stick and 2 Tb.)
Salt and pepper to taste
1½ lb. spinach, washed
4 Tb. peanut or corn oil
2 Tb. finely chopped garlic (about 5 or 6
    cloves)
2 Tb. finely chopped fresh ginger
1 red pepper, cut into halves, seeded, and
    cut into strips

1 Pour about half of the liquid from the
oysters into a saucepan and add the wine
to the saucepan. Bring the mixture to a
boil and reduce to about ⅓ c. Add the
butter, except 1 Tb., in pieces, whisking
constantly on low heat until all the butter
has been added. Taste and season the sauce
with salt and pepper, if needed.

Use 2 large skillets to sauté the spinach.
Place 2 Tb. of oil in each skillet and add
the garlic and ginger. Sauté for about 10
to 20 seconds, then add the spinach. (If
the spinach is wet from washing, no extra
liquid is necessary. If the spinach is dry,
add about ¼ c. water to each skillet.)
Cover and steam the spinach, mixing it to
make sure the garlic and ginger don't
burn. Cook for 2 to 3 minutes, until the
spinach is wilted and soft. Season with salt
and pepper. Set aside.

2 Add the remaining Tb. of butter to a
skillet and, when hot, add the red pepper
with a dash of salt and pepper. Sauté for
about 1 minute, just long enough to warm
the pepper and soften it slightly.

Place the shells of the oysters in the
oven to warm. Place the oysters in their
juices in a saucepan over high heat just
until they curl or "frill" at the edge. The
liquid should not boil or be heated above
about 170 degrees.

Arrange the spinach in the warm shells
and place the red pepper around the
periphery of the shells. Place 1 oyster in
the center of each shell, top with the
sauce, and serve immediately.

CLAMS

Although cherrystone clams, which are medium-sized, can be used instead of little necks (the smallest of the quahog clam), little necks are sweeter for serving on the half shell cold with their natural juices and are always welcome for a first course, apéritif or snack.

Be sure the clams are clean on the outside. If you've dug them yourself, they must be cleaned under cold running water to remove the mud from the shells and to make them disgorge sand and dirt so they are clean inside. Keep the clams in the refrigerator; they open more readily and taste better when very cold.

For spaghetti or linguine in clam sauce, my favorite clam would be cherrystone, very flavorful and tender. A good commercial pasta can be used in this dish as successfully as one made at home. It should be cooked until just slightly al dente – that is, a bit firm to the bite. This will take about 9 to 10 minutes, the same length of time it takes to make the clam sauce.

Although the clam sauce can be served as is on the spaghetti with a little Parmesan cheese, if desired, I have added seasonal vegetables to my recipe for taste, texture, and color.

CLAMS ON THE HALF SHELL WITH COLD HORSERADISH SAUCE

6 doz. little-neck clams, thoroughly cleaned

COLD HORSERADISH SAUCE

2 Tb. coarsely chopped scallions
¼ c. chopped shallots
¼ c. grated fresh horseradish
1 tsp. freshly ground black pepper
¾ c. red wine vinegar
1 Tb. olive oil
Dash salt

1 Mix together the sauce ingredients.

2 To open the clams: Holding the clam in the palm of your hand with the hinge toward you, place the blade of a small paring knife at the junction of the 2 shells. (Note: A special knife for opening clams can be used, but the paring knife works as well or better.) Press the blade with your right finger (if right-handed) so it slides between the shells. Keep cutting to sever the muscles on each side and the clam will open. →

3 Hold the shells as level as possible to avoid losing the liquor, and open them over a bowl to retrieve the juice. (The juices can be frozen or used fresh in soups, sauces, or fish stocks.) <u>Run the tip of your knife around the top shell to loosen the clam from the shell.</u>

4 <u>Run your knife underneath to loosen the clam from the lower shell</u> and to make it easier to eat.

5 The clams are presented on seaweed to keep them cool and steady, although they can be served on ice. Serve with the sauce and buttered black bread.

A LEANER VERSION

Omit the olive oil in the sauce and proceed according to the recipe.

LINGUINE WITH CLAM SAUCE AND VEGETABLES

Yield: 6–8 servings

1 tsp. salt (for the water)
1 lb. pasta (linguine or spaghetti)

FOR THE CLAM SAUCE

2 Tb. olive oil
1 Tb. butter
1 c. onions, peeled and coarsely chopped (2 medium onions)
1 tsp. oregano
¼ c. garlic (4–6 cloves), peeled and sliced
2 doz. cherrystone clams
½ c. white wine
½ tsp. freshly ground black pepper

FOR THE VEGETABLES

1 Tb. peanut oil
1 Tb. butter
8–10 asparagus spears, peeled and cut into 1-in. pieces (1 c.)
1¼ c. coarsely chopped mushrooms (4 oz.)
1½ c. ½-in.-diced zucchini (2 medium, 6 oz.)
¼ tsp. salt
⅛ tsp. freshly ground black pepper
1¼ c. ½-in.-diced, peeled, and seeded tomatoes (Retain the skin and juices for stock.)

GARNISH (OPTIONAL)

Parmesan cheese

1 Open the clams as explained in the preceding recipe, retaining the juices and placing the clams back in their own liquid. To expedite the process, sometimes it is easier to open the clams (as shown in photograph 1 of the preceding recipe) and place them in a bowl. When they have all been opened, use a teaspoon to scrape the meat out, instead of the technique explained in steps 2 and 3 of preceding recipe. Shake the clams in their own juices to release any sand or pieces of shell and lift them from the juices. Using scissors, cut the clams into halves and place in a clean bowl. To remove the sand, strain the clam liquor through paper towels directly on top of the clam pieces and set aside until cooking time. <u>A display of the vegetables, cut clams, and extra clam liquor to be used in the sauce.</u>

2 Bring about 5 to 6 qt. of water and 1 tsp. salt to the boil in a large kettle. Add the pasta.

Meanwhile, in a large skillet, heat the 2 tb. olive oil and the 1 tb. butter and, when hot, add the chopped onions and sauté for about 3 minutes. Add the oregano and the sliced garlic, and cook for about 30 seconds. Add the juice of the clams and the wine, and boil gently together for 7 to 8 minutes, uncovered. Add the clams and the pepper, bring to a boil, and simmer for about 1 minute.

4 Arrange the vegetables on top of the pasta. Serve immediately with or without grated Parmesan cheese.

3 When the pasta is cooked (about 8 to 9 minutes for dry pasta and 1 to 2 minutes for freshly made pasta), drain it in a large colander. In the kettle, heat the 1 Tb. peanut oil and 1 Tb. butter. When hot, add all the vegetables except the tomatoes. Add the salt and pepper, and sauté for about 2 minutes.

Arrange your pasta on 6 to 8 warm plates as a first course or in a large serving platter, and spoon the hot clam sauce on top. When the vegetables are cooked, add the tomatoes and toss briefly to warm.

1 Wash the clams under cold water several times, lifting them up from the water to leave behind as much sand as possible. Place in a saucepan, preferably stainless steel, and cover. Place on high heat. Within 2 to 3 minutes the clams should open and release their juices. Drain in a colander.

FRIED SOFT-SHELL CLAMS

Soft-shell clams are excellent just steamed as shown in photographs 1 and 2. They are also excellent made into chowder and are very good fried, as in this recipe. If they are fried, be sure to reserve the juices and freeze for use in other fish dishes or sauces, or season with ground pepper and drink the juice as an appetizer for dinner.

Often people cut off the siphon-like neck of the clam and discard it. This chewy part of the clam is quite good and edible, providing that the black skin on top of it is pulled off.

Yield: 6 servings

4 lb. soft-shell clams (about 6 doz.)
2 c. fresh bread crumbs (made in the food processor)
1 c. stone-ground cornmeal
¼ tsp. cayenne pepper
2 eggs
2 Tb. flour
½ tsp. salt
¼ tsp. pepper
Oil for frying (at least 3 c.)

DEEP-FRIED ZUCCHINI

4 medium zucchini, cut into ½-in. sticks, 2–3 in. long (about 50 sticks)
Oil for frying (Use same oil, strained to remove cooking particles, as was used to cook the clams.)

ANCHOVY SAUCE

½ two-oz. can anchovy fillets
3 cloves garlic
1 tsp. fennel seed
2 Tb. almonds
1 Tb. vinegar
¼ tsp. Tabasco
¼ c. olive oil

2 Remove the clams from the shells, reserving the liquid (after straining through paper towels) for another use. Be sure to pull the black skin off the long necks.

3 Combine the bread crumbs, cornmeal, and cayenne together in a shallow bowl. Mix the eggs with the flour, salt, and pepper until smooth. Dip the clams into the egg mixture and then into the bread crumb mixture, making sure they are coated well all over. Heat the oil to 375 degrees in a deep skillet or fryer. Drop the clams in, a few at a time, and cook for about 2 minutes. Drain on paper towels.

4 To prepare the zucchini: Cut the zucchini into 2- to 3-in.-long chunks. Cut the chunks into ½-in. lengthwise slices. Stack the slices together, then cut them into sticks ½ in. thick. Dip the sticks into the egg mixture, then coat with the bread crumb mixture and drop into the strained oil that has been heated to 350 to 375 degrees. Cook for about 3 to 3½ minutes. Remove to a cookie sheet lined with paper towels. Sprinkle lightly with salt.

5 To make the anchovy sauce: Purée the anchovies, garlic, fennel seed, almonds, vinegar, and Tabasco in a blender or small coffee grinder (either of which gives a better result than the food processor). When they are puréed, add the oil and blend just long enough to get the mixture smooth. If too thick, add 1 Tb. of water. Serve the fried clams and zucchini immediately with the sauce.

SOUFFLE OF MUSSELS AND BASIL BEVERLY

Although this soufflé can be made in a large soufflé dish, it is easier to serve in individual soufflé molds. The soufflés can be placed directly on plates and eaten right from the soufflé molds or can be spooned from the molds, as shown in the final photograph, and placed on individual plates with the sauce around. The basil soufflé could also be made without the mussels.

Yield: 6 individual soufflés

3 lb. very fresh mussels, preferably small
1 c. white wine
1 Tb. butter plus butter for buttering
 soufflé molds
⅓ c. finely chopped onions
⅓ c. sliced scallions
1 clove garlic
¾ c. mussel stock
½ c. heavy cream
Pepper and salt, if needed
1 Tb. potato starch dissolved in 2 Tb.
 water

BASIL SOUFFLE MIXTURE
2 Tb. butter
3 Tb. flour
1¼ c. mussel stock
Salt and pepper to taste
3 egg yolks
6 egg whites
⅓ c. plus 2 Tb. grated Parmesan cheese
1 c. fresh basil, coarsely shredded →

Making a roux-thickened sauce, 2   *Beating egg whites by hand, 3*

1 Clean the mussels according to the directions in Cream of Mussel Soup recipe (page 11). Place the clean mussels in a large stainless-steel saucepan with the white wine, cover, and bring to a boil. Boil for 2 to 3 minutes, stirring occasionally and shaking the pan until all the mussels are open. Butter 6 small soufflé dishes or soup bowls (as shown), approximately 1½ c. each. Drain the mussels in a colander and strain the juice through a strainer lined with paper towels. You should have approximately 2 c. of juice. If not, add water to make 2 c. Remove the mussels from the shells and divide among the bowls.

    Heat 1 Tb. of butter in a saucepan and, when hot, add the onions and sauté for 1½ to 2 minutes. Add the scallions, garlic, mussel stock, and the cream. Bring to a boil, add pepper and salt, if needed, depending on the saltiness of the stock. Add the dissolved potato starch, bring back to the boil, and pour equal amounts of the sauce on top of the mussels in the 6 soufflé dishes.

2 **To make the soufflé mixture:** First make a roux by melting the butter in a saucepan and, when hot, add the flour and cook for about 20 to 30 seconds. Add the mussel stock and stir well. Bring to a boil, stirring with a whisk. (The mixture will be quite thick.) Add salt and pepper to taste and the egg yolks. Stir well and bring the mixture almost to the boil again. The egg yolks will thicken the sauce further.

3 Although the egg whites can be beaten with a sturdy mixer, to beat by hand use a copper bowl and a large whisk. Beat the egg whites until stiff but not dry. Then, working very quickly so the egg whites don't get grainy, combine approximately one-quarter to one-third of the egg whites with the hot mussel sauce, mixing with the whisk. Fold in the remaining egg whites along with ⅓ c. of the Parmesan cheese and the shredded basil.

4 Spoon the soufflé mixture directly on top of the mussels and the sauce, which should still be warm, dividing it equally among the molds.

5 Sprinkle the top of the soufflés with the remaining 2 Tb. Parmesan cheese. The soufflés must be cooked immediately or the mixture will melt into the hot sauce underneath.

6 Arrange the soufflés in a large roasting pan and pour cold water from the tap around them. Place in a 400-degree oven for about 30 minutes. This is a long time to cook these small soufflés, but remember, there is cold water around them, which will heat slowly and prevent the mussels and the sauce underneath from overcooking; the soufflés will be cooking from the top. They will look puffy and lightly browned when done.

7 When the soufflés are ready, place each individual mold directly on a plate to serve. As an alternative way to serve, insert a large spoon under the soufflé mixture, lift it up, and place it in the middle of the serving plate with the mussels and sauce surrounding it. Serve immediately.

1 The difference between the male and the female crab is seen by examining the underneath side of the crab. The crab on the left with the larger skirt or apron is the female; the male, on the right, has a narrow, pointed skirt or apron. When the female is full of roe during summer (she is sometimes called "berry crab" at that time), she is most flavorful.

HARD-SHELL CRAB LOULOU WITH MARINATED VEGETABLE SALAD

Among the many different types of edible crabs, the most prized are the enormous king crabs of Alaska, the Dungeness crabs — a delicacy from the West Coast — and the stone crabs of Florida. The tiny lady crab or sand crab, which is the one that bites your feet at the beach, and the large spider crab, called <u>araignée de mer</u> in France, although edible, are not usually found in markets.

The most common specimen on the East Coast is the blue crab, which is quite inexpensive and flavorful. It becomes a greater delicacy and its price increases dramatically when it sheds its shell and becomes soft for a few days (see page 65). In its hard form, it can be sautéed in a red, spicy tomato sauce or done very simply boiled in a hot broth. It can also be sautéed with some olive oil, onion, garlic, and white wine, as in the recipe that follows.

It is a casual food that makes for convivial dining and should be enjoyed with friends, as the meat must be sucked out of the shells. Although it is excellent served with French fries or boiled potatoes, I am serving it here with a marinated vegetable salad, which is also good with many other dishes as well as for a cold buffet.

Yield: 6 servings

1 doz. hard-shell crabs
6 Tb. olive oil
2 c. onions, coarsely chopped
1 Tb. garlic, chopped (6–8 cloves)
1 c. dry white wine
½ tsp. salt
½ tsp. freshly ground black pepper
1 c. parsley, coarsely chopped

2 To kill and clean the crab, hold it with a towel so it doesn't pinch your hands with its claws; lift up the apron or skirt and twist to remove. The two large claws can also be twisted out prior to removing the apron to prevent pinching.

3 Starting at the pointed corner of the crab, lift the flap or pointed end of the shell. Remove it and retrieve any roe or liquid inside to add to the stew. Discard the upper shell. →

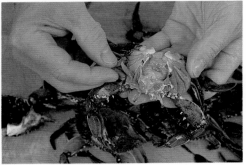

4 Notice in this she-crab all the beautiful roe and tomalley in the center. Keep this (along with any liquid), as it imparts delicious flavor to the dish.

5 Next to the roe you will notice the lungs, which are the spongy appendages on each side. Pull them off and discard, as they are not edible.

6 Crack the body in half in the center and, using a meat pounder, crack the large claw so the meat inside is more accessible when the crab is cooked.

7 Heat the oil. When hot, add the onions and sauté for 1 minute. Then, add the garlic, wine, crab (including roe and liquid), salt, and pepper. Bring to a boil, cover, and cook at a high boil for about 3 minutes. Toss the mixture well, add the parsley, and serve immediately with the marinated salad.

MARINATED VEGETABLE SALAD

Yield: 6 servings
2 c. water
½ c. white wine
⅓ c. olive oil
2 bay leaves
1 tsp. coriander seeds
1 tsp. cracked peppercorns
½ tsp. dried oregano
½ tsp. fennel seeds
1 tsp. whole allspice
¼ c. lemon juice
3 carrots (½ lb.), peeled and cut into
　sticks ½ in. thick and 1½ in. long
1 tsp. salt
½ tsp. freshly ground black pepper
¾ lb. cauliflower, cleaned and cut into
　florets
¾ lb. onions, peeled and cut into 1-in.
　dice
½ lb. mushrooms, quartered

8 Put the water, wine, oil, and spices in a saucepan, bring to a strong boil, and boil for about 8 to 10 minutes. The liquids should be reduced by almost half. Strain the liquid through a fine strainer to remove the solids. To the strained liquid add the lemon juice, carrots, salt, and pepper. Cover, bring to a boil, and cook for 3 to 4 minutes. Add the cauliflower and onions and return to the boil. Boil for 3 to 4 minutes. Finally, add the mushrooms and bring to a boil. Cover and cook again for 3 to 4 minutes longer. Let cool and serve the salad in its own juices with the crab or with other meat dishes.

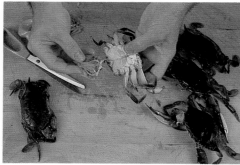

1 Lift up the skirt or apron (as shown on page 63) and twist or cut it off with scissors.

SOFT-SHELL CRAB GENEVIEVE

Once a year, the blue crabs shed their hard shells in the process of expanding and growing, and this is the time when one can enjoy one of the greatest delicacies — soft-shell crabs.

Fishermen, who gather hard-shell crabs, notice that the tip of one of the claws, then the other has turned red, which indicates that a crab will shed its shell within 48 hours. The best soft-shell crabs are those that have shed their shells only the day before; they haven't formed any hard cover yet, and the soft skin is completely edible from the leg to the top cover. Within a few days, the skin begins to harden, and crabs that have shed their shell 4 or 5 days before will have tough, leathery outsides.

In this recipe, the crabs are served on a bed of sautéed spinach, and the top is further garnished with mushrooms and asparagus. If desired, melted butter can be poured on top just before serving to enrich the dish.

Yield: 4 main-course servings or 8 first-course servings

8 soft-shell crabs (about 3–4 oz. each)

TO SAUTE THE SPINACH

2 Tb. butter
½ tsp. chopped garlic
1½ lb. spinach, trimmed and washed
¼ tsp. salt
¼ tsp. freshly ground black pepper

TO SAUTE THE CRABS

½ c. flour
½ tsp. salt
¼ tsp. freshly ground black pepper
4 Tb. butter
1 Tb. lemon juice

GARNISHES (SHIITAKE OR OTHER MUSHROOMS AND ASPARAGUS SAUTEED)

1 Tb. butter
2 c. loose fresh shiitake mushrooms (5 or 6), with tops cut into ¼-in. strips (The tough stems can be reserved to flavor stock.)
6 asparagus spears, peeled and cut into 2-in. segments and then into ¼-in. strips
Dash salt
Melted butter for enrichment (optional)

2 Cut a strip off the front part of the shell, which includes the eyes and antennae, and is tough and sometimes bitter, and discard.

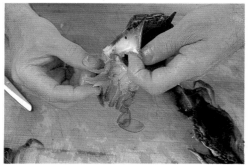

3 Lift up the top shell at both ends where it is pointed to expose the spongelike appendages on either side. Although edible in the very fresh soft-shell crab, most of the time they should be removed. Remove by pulling them off.

To prepare the spinach: Heat the butter in a large saucepan, preferably stainless steel. When hot, add the garlic and sauté for 4 to 5 seconds. Then add the spinach, which should still be wet from washing. (This will provide enough moisture for the cooking procedure.) Add the salt and pepper, cover, and cook on high heat for 3 to 4 minutes, until the spinach is thoroughly wilted and just tender. Keep warm.

SHELLFISH & FISH

4 Mix the flour, salt, and pepper together and <u>dust lightly on both sides of the crabs.</u> Slice the shiitake mushrooms and prepare the asparagus as indicated in the ingredients listing.

6 **For the garnishes:** Heat the butter. When hot, add the mushrooms and cook for about 15 to 20 seconds. Then add the asparagus and salt, and continue sautéing on high heat for about 1 minute, until the vegetables are just tender but still firm. <u>Arrange the spinach on individual plates and place 2 crabs on top for a main course.</u>

5 **To cook the crabs:** The crabs should be cooked 4 to each large skillet. (If crowded, they won't cook properly.) Divide the butter, placing 2 Tb. in each skillet. Dust the crabs all around with flour again, shaking off the excess. When the butter is hot and foamy, place the crabs, top side down, in the skillets and sauté on medium to high heat for about 1½ minutes. <u>Turn, cover the pan, and continue cooking on low to medium heat about 2 minutes longer.</u> Sprinkle the crabs with about 1½ tsp. lemon juice per skillet.

7 In the middle of the crabs, arrange the asparagus and mushrooms and, for extra richness, pour a little melted butter on top. Serve immediately.

SQUID

Squid is inexpensive (almost 90 percent of it is edible), delectable, and versatile; it can be broiled, stuffed, or sautéed, and there is almost no waste, whether you clean it yourself or buy it cleaned.

Overcooking will toughen squid. The medium-sized ones used below are very good stuffed as well as broiled. The very large ones tend to be tougher broiled and are better fried in rings or stewed.

Although the stuffed squid below is served with kasha, any other grain, from rice to couscous, will work well with the sauce of the squid. For the grilled squid, only the pen and beak (see following) are removed. In small restaurants along the Mediterranean coast, squid are even broiled whole as they come out of the water, with no cleaning whatsoever.

The bitter broccoli rape is a nice accompaniment to this earthy grilled squid.

STUFFED SQUID POULETTE WITH KASHA

Yield: 6 servings as a main course or 12 servings as a first course

About 3 lb. squid (12 medium-sized squid)

STUFFING

1 Tb. butter
½ c. finely diced or coarsely chopped carrots
1 c. coarsely chopped, loosely packed leeks
1 tsp. peeled, finely chopped garlic (2 cloves)
9 oz. coarsely chopped tentacles from the squid – see below
¼ tsp. salt
⅛ tsp. freshly ground black pepper
½ lb. shrimp, peeled
1 egg

TO COOK THE SQUID

2 Tb. butter
¾ c. diced onions
1 c. white wine
1 tsp. salt
1 tsp. freshly ground black pepper

TO FINISH THE DISH

1 Tb. butter
1 Tb. flour
½ tsp. peeled and finely chopped garlic
½ c. heavy cream
2 Tb. chopped chives

1 Wash the squid in water to clean. <u>Pull out the head and the tentacles;</u> these will come out of the body in one piece.

2 <u>Pull the pen out of the body.</u> The pen, which looks like a long piece of plastic, is the central cartilage and should be discarded.

67

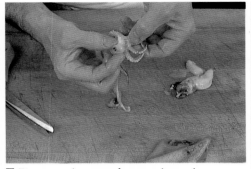

3 Remove the flap on each side of the body and pull the black skin off. Discard the skin.

4 Pull off and discard the black skin from the flaps also, and set aside.

5 Cut off the tentacles at the head and eyes.

6 Press on the round part where the tentacles come together and a knotty beak will come out of the center. Discard it. Place the tentacles in cold, salted water and rinse carefully. Lift them out of the water, leaving behind any residual sand. Cut the tentacles coarse into small pieces. (You should have about 9 oz. of tentacles.)

For the stuffing: Melt the butter in a large saucepan. When hot, add the carrots and leeks, and sauté on high heat for 1 minute. Add the garlic and the pieces of tentacles to the saucepan with the salt and pepper, and cook for about 1 minute on high heat. Remove from the heat and lift out the mixture with a slotted spoon, reserving in the saucepan any remaining juice. Let the squid mixture cool in the refrigerator.

Place the shrimp in the food processor and process briefly (about 10 seconds). Add the egg and process until the mixture is smooth. Remove and combine the shrimp paste with the cooled tentacle mixture.

7 Place the stuffing in a pastry bag without a tip. Rinse the bodies of the 12 squid, inside and out, under cold water and dry briefly with paper towels.

8 Insert the end of the pastry bag into the body of each squid and stuff the cavity. Press gently with your hand to distribute the stuffing evenly inside. Notice that the squid are stuffed only about half full because the stuffing has a tendency to expand and the squid itself will shrink considerably during cooking.

9 To cook the squid: Melt the 2 Tb. butter in the saucepan containing the juice from the stuffing preparation. When hot, add ¾ c. diced onions and place the stuffed squid on top in one layer. (It is not necessary to secure the squid's stuffing with a toothpick because they are not overstuffed.) Place the flaps from the squid around the stuffed squid and top with 1 c. white wine and 1 tsp. each salt and pepper. Cover with a buttered round of parchment paper, cut to fit the saucepan. Place on high heat and bring to a boil. Turn the heat to very low, cover the saucepan with a lid, and simmer the mixture very gently for 25 minutes.

10 Remove the cooked squid to a tray or cookie sheet. Place the round of parchment on top and keep warm by placing in a 150-degree oven or on the side of the stove. Strain the juice, pushing the solids through with a spoon to obtain most of the cooked onion, and reduce the liquid to 1½ c. In a small bowl mix 1 Tb. each butter and flour together with a whisk to make a kneaded butter. With the whisk, stir it into the reduced juice and bring the mixture to a boil, stirring constantly. Add ½ tsp. chopped garlic and ½ c. cream and return the mixture to the boil. Add 2 Tb. chives.

11 Place the squid on a platter and serve, coated with the sauce, with kasha (recipe follows).

KASHA

Yield: 8 servings
2 Tb. butter
⅓ c. chopped onions
1 c. kasha (roasted buckwheat kernels)
1 egg
2 c. chicken stock
½ tsp. salt (if chicken stock is unsalted)
⅛ tsp. freshly ground black pepper

12 Melt the butter in a saucepan and remove from the heat. Add the onions and the kasha and mix well with the butter to coat the kasha. Add the egg and mix in thoroughly with a fork. Place back on the stove and cook, stirring, over medium to high heat until the egg scrambles and mixes with the kasha and onion and the mixture becomes granulated and separated. Add the chicken stock, salt, and pepper, and bring to a boil. Reduce the heat to very low, cover tightly, and cook for 15 minutes.

Arrange the squid on a large platter with the kasha surrounding it, spoon the sauce on top of the squid, and serve immediately.

on very high heat for approximately 1½ minutes on each side. The squid will turn a beautiful pink color and the meat will firm up.

Repeat this procedure until all the squid and tentacles are cooked.

2 Mix together the oregano, olive oil, lemon juice, pepper, and salt. Arrange the squid on a large platter and spoon the sauce over it. Decorate with parsley leaves and serve immediately.

GRILLED SQUID WITH LEMON SAUCE AND BROCCOLI RAPE

Squid is excellent grilled on a conventional grill equipped with a grid or on a hamburger griddle. I use a dry cast-iron skillet in the recipe following to simulate such a griddle. The more intense the heat in the skillet, the better and faster the result.

Yield: 6 servings

3 lb. squid (12 squid)
About 2 Tb. corn or safflower oil (to cook the squid)

SAUCE

1 tsp. oregano
4 Tb. olive oil
2 Tb. lemon juice
½ tsp. freshly ground black pepper
½ tsp. salt

GARNISH

Parsley leaves

1 For the grilled squid, it is not necessary to remove the outer skin. Just pull out the head and tentacles (as explained in step 1 of the previous squid recipe) and remove with the beak and the pen (as explained in the previous squid recipe, steps 2, 5, and 6). Place the squid and tentacles in cold water to clean and lift them up from the water, placing them on paper towels to drain.

To grill the 12 pieces of squid, use 2 or 3 skillets, cooking 3 or 4 at a time in each, so the heat remains very intense and the squid are not crowded (or cook in batches). Use very sturdy (like black iron) skillets. Place the skillets on the stove over high heat for 4 to 5 minutes to allow them to get very hot. Rub the squid with the oil. Place 3 or 4 squid, flat side down, and some of the tentacles in each skillet. Cook

BROCCOLI RAPE

Broccoli rape or rabe, also called bitter broccoli, is a member of the cabbage and mustard family and is excellent served with sausages and with this grilled squid. The same recipe can be made with kale or mustard greens.

Yield: 6 servings

1 lb. broccoli rape, cleaned
¼ c. olive oil
¼ c. garlic, peeled and thinly sliced (about 5 or 6 cloves)
½ tsp. red pepper flakes
¾ tsp. salt

GARNISH

Piece of lemon rind

3 Cut off the stems of the broccoli rape up to within about 1 in. of the leaves. With a sharp knife, peel away the outer layer of the stem pieces. This will pull away easily

and the tender inside can be used in the recipe. (If the broccoli is very small, young, and tender, no peeling is necessary.)

4 Place the olive oil in a large saucepan. Add the garlic, pepper flakes, and salt, and cook on high heat for about 1 minute. Meanwhile, wash the broccoli in cold water, lifting it out of the water and shaking briefly to remove most of the water. Add it to the saucepan. (The water remaining on the broccoli is enough for the cooking process.) Cover and cook on high heat for approximately 4 to 5 minutes, until the broccoli is wilted and just tender but still a little firm.

5 Arrange the broccoli on a plate and place the freshly grilled squid on top. Decorate the center with a piece of lemon rind and serve immediately.

A LEANER VERSION

Reduce the amount of corn oil from 2 Tb. to 1 Tb. to rub on the squid. In the sauce, cut the olive oil by half. For the bitter broccoli, reduce the oil from ¼ c. to 1 Tb. and proceed according to the recipe.

OCTOPUS CATALANE

Although not commonly found in restaurants, octopus is delectable when properly cooked. When cooked either too long or too little or at too high a boil, however, it can be tough. Dipped in boiling water to stiffen for about ½ minute and served raw with its purple skin, sliced very thin, for sashimi or sushi, it will be firm but tender. Brought to a gentle boil from a cold-water start and cooked gently for 30 to 45 minutes, it will also be firm but tender. But cooked in strongly boiling water for 15 minutes it will be tough, and cooking it for hours renders it dry as well as tough.

In this recipe, the octopus is cooked and its red-purplish skin removed. As it cooks, this skin tends to become gummy and gooey, and most of it is removed after the first cooking.

Octopus coming from the market is usually dressed, and the big sac of the head has already been turned inside out and the ink sac removed. If not, it should be removed and the head just below the eyes and the beak cut off, as it is for squid (see page 67). To beat the octopus before cooking with a rolling pin or a meat pounder, as many recipes specify, doesn't seem to tenderize the meat. Still, in the Mediterranean countries, the freshly caught octopus is often pounded on racks and hung a few hours in the sun to develop a better taste.

Yield: 8 servings as a first course

1 large octopus (about 3¼ lb. dressed)
2 Tb. corn or safflower oil
1 c. ¼-in.-diced celery
¾ c. chopped onions
½ tsp. Tabasco
½ c. white wine
Salt
4 tomatoes
DRESSING

¼ c. good olive oil
1 Tb. lemon juice
1 Tb. red wine vinegar
¼ tsp. salt
GARNISH

Parsley leaves →

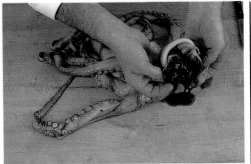

1 Turn the head of the octopus and the sac inside out if the ink sac is still there. Even though in Spain and Mexico it is used in some recipes cooked with rice (the ink used as a seasoning), here it is discarded. Wash it carefully under cold running water. Place the octopus in a pot filled with 5 to 6 qt. of cold water and bring to a boil. When it begins to boil, lower the heat to maintain a gentle boil (so it doesn't toughen the protein) and cook for 30 minutes.

2 Lift the cooked octopus out of the water and place immediately in a pan of cold water. The reddish-purplish gummy skin can now be removed. Just rub and push it off under cold water. Most of it will come off, except on the suction cups. (Note: Only a few minutes of blanching is not enough; the octopus needs longer cooking before the gelatinous skin can be slid off.)

3 Cut the meat into ½-in. pieces. You should have about 4 c. of meat and it should be firm but tender. Heat the oil in a saucepan, add the celery and onions, and

sauté for 1 minute. Add the octopus, Tabasco, wine, and salt; cover and cook over medium heat just long enough to heat the mixture through (3 to 4 minutes). Dip the tomatoes in boiling water, remove the skins, cut in halves, press the seeds out, and remove some of the ribs with a spoon (reserving the juices, ribs, and seeds for stock).

4 Arrange the warm tomato halves on a platter and spoon some of the octopus mixture into each. Mix the olive oil, lemon juice, vinegar, and salt together and sprinkle on the octopus. Garnish with parsley leaves.

5 As an alternative, cut the tomatoes into 1-in. dice and mix with the octopus along with the olive oil, lemon juice, vinegar, and salt. Serve lukewarm arranged in a salad bowl.

A LEANER VERSION

Reduce the amount of corn oil from 2 to 1 Tb. (see step 3). Reduce the olive oil in the dressing from ¼ c. to 2 Tb. Proceed according to recipe instructions.

LOBSTER

Lobster is one of the pleasures of summer in New England and, most of the time, is eaten simply steamed or boiled and served with an ear of corn and a baked potato. The fresher the lobster is from the water, the better it is. When lobster is bought from a tank, it should be bought alive, but the fact that it is alive does not guarantee it will be of high quality. Since the lobster feeds on its body meat, after a certain amount of time in the tank older lobsters will have meat on their claws and tails that has sometimes shrunk to half its original weight and has become tough and chewy.

The roe of the lobster female, a deep bottle-green substance inside the body, can be dried out in the oven and mashed into a beautiful red, granulated mixture that can be used to flavor salads and sauces or decorate the top of dishes, as it does in the Cream of Lobster Soup (page 16). The roe and the tomalley, the pale green appendage — actually the liver — inside the body, as well as the liquid from the lobster, should never be discarded, as they enhance the flavor of the stuffing in the Lobster Benjamin and the taste of the mousse in the Lobster Sara.

My version of broiled lobster is also served with potatoes and corn. The small potato flats and caramelized corn are delicate and can be served with meat as well as fish. The stuffing itself is made with the roe and cornbread (although regular bread can be used), and it should fill the cavity of the lobster and provide a protection for the meat, thus preventing it from drying out when broiled.

BROILED LOBSTER BENJAMIN

Yield: 4 servings

4 lobsters, 1¼ lb. each (including 1 c. of
  the insides and liquid)
5 Tb. butter
1 c. chopped onions
1 c. cornbread crumbs, see following recipe
½ c. chopped herbs (combination of tarragon, parsley, and chives)
¼ tsp. freshly ground black pepper
¼ tsp. salt
Olive oil and Tabasco for cooking

CARAMELIZED CORN

Yield: 4 servings
4 ears corn (1 per person)
2 Tb. corn oil
1 Tb. butter
Dash salt

POTATO FLATS

Yield: about 20
2 potatoes (12 oz.)
½ c. flour
2 eggs
½ lb. ricotta cheese
2 Tb. chopped chives
2 tsp. baking powder
¼ tsp. pepper
½ tsp. salt
2 Tb. corn oil and
1 Tb. butter per skillet

1 On the left, as indicated by the knife, is the male lobster. Notice that the first two appendages on the underside of the body under the rib cage are longer and go up between the rib. The female, on the right, has a wider body and tail, and those same two appendages are much smaller and do not extend up to the rib cage. A female is often more tender and the roe is, of course, useful for taste as well as decoration. →

2 To kill and split a lobster in half, place the point of a large, sturdy knife in the middle of the body, directly on the line that runs down the center of the shell. Push down with the knife to split the front and kill the lobster.

5 Be sure to retrieve the pale green matter (the liver or tomalley), as well as the dark green (the roe of the female) and all the liquid that comes out. This is needed for the sauce.

8 Then arrange all the lobster halves flesh side up on a cookie sheet, making certain they are approximately flat. Spoon about ⅓ c. of the stuffing onto each, filling up the cavity and covering the flesh of each lobster thinly so it doesn't dry out during cooking. Sprinkle each half lobster with approximately ½ tsp. of olive oil and a few drops of Tabasco.

Place the lobsters under a preheated broiler for 10 to 12 minutes, turning the sheet around so they cook evenly all over, including the tails and claws.

3 Turn the lobster around and, following the same cut, continue cutting down with the sturdy knife to split the lobster into 2 halves.

6 Heat the butter in a skillet. When hot, add the chopped onions and sauté for about 2 minutes, until they begin to soften, then add all the liver and roe and stir over the heat, cooking for about 1 minute. The liquid green will turn a reddish color.

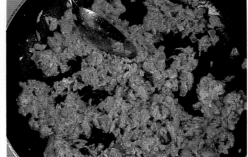

4 Be sure to remove and discard the little sac (at this point, split in half), which is the stomach, just next to the eye at the point of the head. Remove on both sides.

7 The mixture now has turned harder and is set. Remove it from the stove and combine it in a bowl with the 1 c. of cornbread crumbs, chopped herbs, pepper, and salt. Mix lightly so it doesn't get pasty.

Cover the claws of each lobster with a towel to prevent splashing and, using a meat pounder, crack them to make it easier to extract the meat after cooking.

9 For the caramelized corn: With a long knife, cut the kernels of corn off 4 ears (see Oyster and Corn Chowder, page 13) and heat 2 Tb. corn oil and 1 Tb. butter in a large skillet. When hot, add the corn and cook on high heat for 4 to 5 minutes, covering the skillet partially to prevent splattering and stirring the mixture with a spatula to release and mix in some of the brown particles from the bottom. Keep cooking until the corn gets nicely browned.

10 **For the potato flats:** Peel 2 potatoes, cut into pieces, and place in a food processor with the ½ c. flour. Process until smooth and add 2 eggs and ricotta cheese. Process until well mixed. Place the mixture in a bowl and add 2 Tb. chopped chives. Sprinkle 2 tsp. baking powder on top with ¼ tsp. pepper and ½ tsp. salt, and mix just enough to combine. Heat 2 Tb. corn oil and 1 Tb. butter in a large skillet and, when hot, add 1 good Tb. of the potato mixture per pancake, cooking 6 to 8 at one time if your skillet is large enough. Sauté approximately 2 minutes over medium to high heat on one side. Turn and cook 1 minute on the other side. These are best when served as soon as possible after cooking. They will be nicely brown with the edges darker and crunchier.

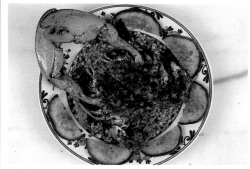

11 Arrange the caramelized corn on a large plate. Place the cooked lobster in the center and the potato flats (either whole or halved) around the outside to make a decorative pattern. Serve immediately with the extra cornbread.

A LEANER VERSION

Reduce the amount of butter from 5 to 2 Tb. for the dressing (step 6). Replace the cornbread crumbs with whole-wheat bread crumbs (step 7). Omit the olive oil sprinkled on the lobster in step 8. Proceed according to instructions. Serve without the caramelized corn and potato flats.

CORNBREAD

(regular bread can also be used in this recipe) Use what is needed for the stuffing and serve the remainder of the bread with the lobster.

1 c. yellow cornmeal
1 c. flour
2 tsp. double-acting baking powder
¼ c. grated Parmesan cheese
1 tsp. salt
1 tsp. sugar
2 eggs, beaten
¼ c. corn oil
1 c. milk
1 c. corn kernels

12 Mix in a bowl the cornmeal, flour, baking powder, cheese, salt, and sugar. Add the remaining ingredients and mix until just combined. Place in an oiled 8-in. cake pan and cook in a 425-degree oven for 20 to 25 minutes, until well done and browned. When cool, cut off and process enough cornbread to make 1 c. crumbs

LOBSTER SARA

Yield: 4 servings

4 lobsters, 1½ lb. each

MOUSSE (ENOUGH FOR THE SQUASH STUFFING AND DUMPLING SOUP GARNISH, PAGE 15)

5 oz. chicken flesh, completely cleaned
¾ c. heavy cream
2 tsp. fresh chopped tarragon
¼ tsp. salt
⅛ tsp. freshly ground black pepper
Roe and tomalley mixture
8 large squash blossoms

RED PEPPER SAUCE

2 large red peppers (6 oz. each), seeds removed, peppers cut into 1-in. squares
½ c. lobster cooking juices
½ tsp. salt
Dash cayenne pepper
4 Tb. butter

1 Place the lobsters in a steamer, 2 per deck, over 6 c. of boiling water, and steam 15 to 18 minutes. Remove the lobsters to a tray, setting aside the cooking liquid in the steamer for the sauce and the cream soup.

2 When the lobsters are cold enough, separate the tail, pressing the tail to crunch the shell. Remove the shell at the end of the tail and set it aside for decoration. See photograph 16. Reserve the other shells for soup.

3 Pull the meat off the tail and set aside. Pull the small legs off the body and set aside. Lift the top part of the shell from the body and, using a spoon, empty the entire shell. Reserve the shells for soup.

4 The red roe is in the center, the tomalley on the left, and the little sac (the stomach), which should be discarded, is held in the background. The roe from one lobster can be set aside and dried for use as a decoration in the Cream of Lobster Soup (page 15).

5 Cover the claws with a towel to prevent splattering, and crack with a meat pounder.

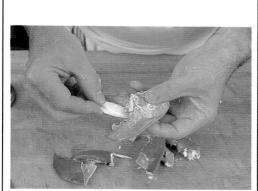

6 Separate the meat, preferably in one piece, from the shell of the claw.

7 Be sure to remove the little piece of cartilage from the center of each claw.

8 The aficionado considers the meat in the joints just above the claw the best part of the lobster. Extract this meat from the shell and set it aside. Reserve shells for soup.

9 Cut the tail crosswise into ¼-in. slices.

10 Butter a gratin dish and arrange the tail, claw, and other meat in it. Cover it with a buttered piece of waxed or parchment paper and set it aside until serving time. A good lobster will give approximately one-third to one-fourth of its original weight in meat.

Using a blender or a small spice grinder, purée the roe, tomalley, and any body liquids into a fine mixture. Chill. (You should have approximately ¾ to 1 c.)

To make the mousse: Place the 5 oz. chicken in the bowl of a food processor and process until smooth. Add the ¾ c. heavy cream in a slow stream while processing

and then add the 2 tsp. tarragon, ¼ tsp. salt, and ⅛ tsp. pepper. Combine the chicken mousse with the cold roe and tomalley mixture.

11 Place half the mousse mixture in a pastry bag fitted with a 1-in. plain tube. Open the squash flowers and remove the pistils from the inside of each blossom.

12 Squeeze the equivalent of about 2 Tb. of the mousse mixture into each blossom and close the petals around it, tucking the tips underneath.

13 Place the blossoms on a plate in a steamer and steam over boiling water for approximately 4 to 5 minutes. Set aside until ready to serve.→

SHELLFISH & FISH

77

14 **To make the pepper sauce:** Cover the pepper squares (cut from 2 large red peppers) with ½ c. lobster cooking liquid and bring to a boil. Reduce the heat and cook for about 10 minutes. By then, the peppers should be tender and the liquid evaporated. Push the peppers through a food mill to eliminate most of the skin. (You should have a good cup of liquid pepper purée.) Place the purée back in the saucepan and bring to a boil. Add ½ tsp. salt, dash of cayenne, and 4 Tb. butter, piece by piece, and mix well with a whisk until incorporated. Set aside.

16 Place a wet paper towel on top of the buttered paper covering the lobsters and warm the meat in a 250-degree oven for a few minutes until it is lukewarm. The meat should be heated slowly to keep it tender. Coat warm individual serving plates with the red pepper sauce. Arrange the lobster meat in the center, the claws on either side (to simulate the shape of a lobster), and place the reserved head and tail sections in position to complete the lobster shape. Arrange the steamed squash blossoms (cut in half lengthwise) stuffed sides down around the lobster. Serve immediately.

Note: The little potato flats made in the preceding recipe are excellent with this lobster dish as well.

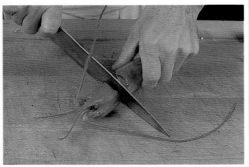

15 Cut off the front of the heads of the lobster shells, including the antennae, and the tails. Wash carefully, dry, and set aside for use later as decorations.

1 Separate the roe from the scallops and remove the tough sinewy pieces attached to the body of the scallops. Sometimes there is a tough skin on the outside of the body. If so, remove it. Wash the scallops carefully under cold water to remove any sand and cut each body into ½-in.-thick slices. Cut the roe in half lengthwise.

SCALLOPS NOUVELLE CUISINE

There are many different types of scallops, from the very tiny bay scallops (sometimes so small they get dry when cooked and should be served raw) to the slightly larger bay scallops, preferable in my opinion, and the large sea scallops. Sometimes in Maine the real St. James scallop (the coquille St. Jacques, as it is called in France) is available with the beautiful coral-colored roe on top. Not only is the roe delectable, but it makes a beautiful decoration as well.

In the recipe below, I use these Maine scallops with their roe. Each scallop tends to be quite large, weighing about 3 oz., including the roe. One scallop this size, including the roe, is enough per person. If smaller scallops are used, each person should be served the equivalent of 3 oz. with or without the roe. This dish can be served as a first course if the main course is not too rich or as a main course if the first course is rich and filling.

The tiny zucchini are served steamed and their blossoms are fried in a tempura batter. Most squash flowers can be treated in the same manner.

The scallops should not be overcooked, as they tend to toughen, but should be cooked long enough to render some of their liquid.

Yield: 6 servings

6 very large scallops (1¼ lb. total), 3 oz. each, 1 per person
    Note: If using smaller scallops, increase so that each person is served about 3 oz.
24 baby zucchini (1½ oz. each), 4 per person
⅓ c. water
Dash salt

TEMPURA BATTER

½ c. flour
1 egg yolk
⅔ c. ice-cold water
24 squash blossoms (zucchini flowers), 4 per person
2 Tb. corn or other vegetable oil
Salt

FOR COOKING SCALLOPS AND MAKING SAUCE

Roe from the scallops
Dash plus ¼ tsp. salt
½ c. dry white wine
½ tsp. potato starch dissolved in 2 tsp. water
¾ stick butter
Dash cayenne pepper

2 Trim the ends of the zucchini and wash them under cold water. Slice them thin three-quarters of the way up lengthwise from the base to create a fan. Place with the fanned pieces lying flat in a skillet, preferably stainless steel. Add ⅓ c. water to wet the bottom of the pan and a dash of salt; cover and bring to a boil for 2½ to 3 minutes. The zucchini should be tender but still a bit firm.

For the tempura batter: Mix the flour, egg yolk, and about half the water. Whisk to make the batter smooth. Then add the remainder of the water. (Be sure the water is ice cold.)

Open the flowers and check to make certain there are no insects inside. Wash under cold water and drain on paper towels. Dip the flowers into the batter and heat the cooking oil. When very hot, add the blossoms and cook on medium to high heat for about 1 minute on each side, 2 minutes totally. Drain on a wire rack. Sprinkle lightly with salt and keep warm in a 180-degree oven. →

SHELLFISH & FISH

3 **For cooking scallops and making the sauce:** In a saucepan (preferably stainless steel), combine the scallops, roe, salt, and wine, and bring the mixture to a boil, stirring occasionally. When it comes to a boil, cover with a lid, remove from the heat, and set aside so the scallops continue to cook in their own heat for 3 to 4 minutes. Strain the juice from the scallops into a measuring cup; you want ½ c. — if necessary, reduce the juice by boiling it down or add water to make ½ c. Whisk in the potato starch dissolved in water. Bring to a boil. Whisk in the butter, piece by piece, mixing with a whisk until all the butter is absorbed and the mixture has thickened. Season with a dash of cayenne.

Arrange the scallops, coated with some of the sauce, on a warm plate, distribute some zucchini and squash blossoms attractively around them, and serve immediately.

A LEANER VERSION

Reduce the amount of butter from ¾ stick to 2 Tb. and proceed according to the recipe. Omit the fried zucchini blossoms.

SHRIMP "BUNNIES" CREOLE

The shrimp here are rolled on themselves, and the shells which are left on the tails are "ears" and make the shrimp look like "bunnies." The "bunnies" can be served with the sauce used below or a different sauce, or eaten cold with a cocktail sauce.

The bit of mousse made with the trimmings of the shrimp is optional and the recipe can be done without it. The spicy tomato and hot pepper sauce, as well as the garlic spinach, makes a nice earthy complement to the shrimp.

Yield: 6 servings

24 shrimp (about 1½ lb. of 16–18-count shrimp; i.e., there are 16–18 shrimp to the lb.)
½ c. dry white wine
¼ tsp. salt
MOUSSE (OPTIONAL)
⅓ c. reserved shrimp trimmings
1 Tb. heavy cream
Dash salt and freshly ground black pepper

Red pepper rounds (cut from flesh) for "eyes"
SAUCE
1 Tb. butter
1 c. coarsely chopped onions
1 c. coarsely chopped celery
1 tsp. chopped jalapeño pepper
2 c. chopped tomatoes
1 c. water
½ tsp. salt

GARLIC SPINACH

2 Tb. olive oil
3 cloves garlic, chopped (1 Tb.)
1 lb. spinach, stems removed, washed
½ tsp. salt
¼ tsp. freshly ground black pepper

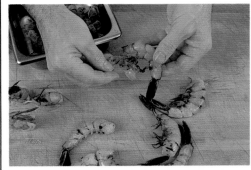

1 Shell the shrimp, leaving only the shell around the tail attached. Reserve the shells you have removed.

2 Curl each shrimp around to form the "body" of the "bunny." Cut a thin slice from the base so the "bunny" can "sit" firmly in the cooking skillet and on the plate. Reserve the trimmings for use in the mousse.

3 Curl the shrimp into a tight bunny shape. Secure with a toothpick, pushing it from the "tail" through the "head."

4 **To make the mousse:** Process the shrimp trimmings, the cream, salt, and pepper in the food processor for a few seconds, until a paste forms. Spread lightly around the "body" of each "bunny" to make it smoother. Press little cut-outs of red pepper or tomato flesh into the mousse to make "eyes."

To make the sauce: Heat the butter in a saucepan. When hot, add the reserved shells and sauté for 2 to 3 minutes. Add

the onions, celery, and jalapeño pepper, and cook a few minutes. Add the tomatoes, water, and salt, bring to a boil, and cook for 10 minutes. Push the sauce through a food mill fitted with the small screen.

5 Stand the "bunnies" up side by side in a small buttered saucepan. They should fit fairly tightly so they don't fall over. Pour the wine around the "bunnies" and sprinkle with ¼ tsp. salt. Bring to a boil, cover, and let boil 10 to 15 seconds. Leave the cover on and remove the pan to the side of the stove. Using the lid to hold the "bunnies" in the pan, pour off the cooking juices and add them to the sauce. Cook the sauce and liquid together for 8 to 10 minutes to reduce. Keep the shrimp covered in a warm place while preparing the spinach.

6 In a large saucepan, heat the olive oil. When hot, add the garlic and sauté for about 1 minute. Add the spinach, still wet from washing, and the salt and pepper. Cover and cook about 1 minute. Uncover and continue cooking for 1 to 2 minutes to get rid of most of the liquid. With a slotted spoon, lift out the spinach and arrange portions of it in the center of the individual plates. Surround with the red sauce, place 4 "bunnies" on top of the spinach "nest," pressing down to make them stand upright. Serve immediately.

SHRIMP MADISON

The tail part of the shrimp is what one usually finds at the market, sometimes frozen, sometimes fresh. It is difficult to get the whole shrimp, but the tail is the meatiest and choicest part. Frozen shrimp are quite good if defrosted slowly under refrigeration. They are used in many different ways, from the Seafood Bread (page 95) to a mousse or simply sautéed by themselves, in a variety of different styles, including the Chinese, Italian, French, and Indian.

In the version here, the shrimp are very lightly sautéed (overcooking tends to toughen the meat) and served with fresh vegetables. Shrimp are often bought so many per pound, especially in restaurants. The shrimp used below are 20–25 count, which means there are 20 to 25 shrimp per lb. The very large prawns used in restaurants are the 16–20 count, and the jumbo ones are often called "under 10," meaning there are fewer than 10 shrimp in 1 lb.

The broccoli, steamed and briefly sautéed, can complement a variety of dishes, as can the stewed tomatoes.

Yield: 6 servings

1½ lb. medium shrimp (20–25)
BROCCOLI
2 large stalks of broccoli (1¾ lb.)
2 Tb. butter
Salt to taste

COOKING THE SHRIMP
3–5 ripe tomatoes, depending on size
 (2½ c. tomato flesh)
6 Tb. butter
1 tsp. chopped garlic
½ c. white wine
1 tsp. salt
½ tsp. freshly ground black pepper
1 c. shredded basil leaves

1 Peel the shells from the shrimp: <u>Hold the tail end of the shrimp with one hand and, with the thumb and index finger of the other hand, peel off the shell from the thickest part.</u> It will come off easily. Holding the shelled part, pull gently on the flap of the tail so the shell comes off. It

will come away easily. In this recipe, the shells are not used, although they are excellent for stocks and soups and can be frozen.

2 Shrimp should be deveined if you see a strip of dark color through the flesh. This indicates that the intestinal tract is full and should be removed (for appearance rather than taste). Make an incision approximately ⅛ in. deep down the back of each shrimp to expose the intestinal tract, as shown in the picture on the right, and rinse under cool water to clean. <u>The shrimp on the left has also been cut but has nothing to be cleaned.</u>

3 To prepare the broccoli: <u>Cut the broccoli flowers from the stalks.</u> These can be cooked whole or separated into florets.

4 The stems or stalks of the broccoli are, in my opinion, the choicest part. However, they are surrounded by a thick, fibrous exterior, which should be removed. With the point of a knife and your thumb, grab the peel and pull it off in strips. If the broccoli is younger and has a thinner exterior covering, it can be peeled with a vegetable peeler. Peel until the broccoli is tender; test by piercing it with your fingernail. Cut into ¼-in. slices.

5 Cut the top of the broccoli into small florets.

6 Place the florets in the bottom layer of a two-layer steamer and the stems in the top. The sliced stems will cook faster than the florets. Bring the water in the base of your steamer to a boil. Place the broccoli layers on top, cover with the lid, and steam approximately 5 minutes for the stems and 7 to 8 minutes for the florets. The broccoli should be tender but still a bit crunchy. If serving immediately, toss with butter and a dash of salt. If you are serving later, cool the broccoli off for a few minutes under cold water to retain the green color, drain, and set aside to reheat at serving time.

7 Drop the tomatoes into boiling water (15 to 20 seconds should be long enough if the tomatoes are ripe). Remove with a slotted spoon and peel—the skin will come off easily. (If they are greenish-yellow and unripe, as they are sometimes in the winter, you may have to leave them in the water for as long as 1 minute; still, when the skin is removed, some of the flesh will come off, too.) As an alternative method, the tomatoes can be roasted on top of an open flame for a few seconds to release the skin, or the skin can be peeled off with a knife. However, to peel a large quantity, the boiling-water method is the best.

8 When the tomatoes have been peeled, cut them in halves crosswise so all the seeds and cavities are exposed. Squeeze the tomato halves to release the seeds and juice. The seeds, skin, and juice can be kept and frozen for use in stocks or sauces. Chop the tomatoes into ½- to 1-in. pieces.

9 To cook the shrimp: For 6 servings, use 2 skillets or a very large saucepan. If you use 2 skillets, melt 3 Tb. butter in each skillet. When hot, add ½ tsp. chopped garlic to each skillet and sauté for 10 seconds. Then add the tomatoes, ½ c. white wine, 1 tsp. salt, and ½ tsp. pepper, cover, and cook for approximately 1 minute. Divide the shrimp between the skillets and bring to a boil, shaking the pan occasionally, until the shrimp are just barely cooked (about 1 minute). Toss in 1 c. shredded basil and divide immediately among 6 warm plates. Reheat the broccoli and decorate the edge of the plates with the stems and florets. Serve immediately.

A LEANER VERSION

Omit the butter in the broccoli. Reheat it instead with 1 Tb. of water (just enough to create steam and prevent the broccoli from sticking to the saucepan). Reduce the amount of butter from 6 to 2 Tb. in cooking the shrimp. Proceed according to directions.

SHELLFISH & FISH

FINISHING THE CRAWFISH SAUCE

½ tsp. arrowroot dissolved in 1 Tb. water
Strained, reduced crawfish cooking juices
Dash cayenne pepper
¾ stick butter
1 head Boston lettuce

CRAWFISH WITH SCALLOP MOUSSE TATAN HELENE

The crawfish or crayfish is a sweet-water crustacean that looks like a tiny lobster; it can be found under rocks in small streams and lakes, as well as in the mud of swamps. It comes, primarily, from Louisiana and California, although several states, from Texas to Washington, are now farming them.

It is available fresh in good fish markets at certain times of the year. At crawfish festivals, whole crawfish are boiled in a spicy hot broth. To eat, one chews the body and claw, and the meat is sucked out. Usually in restaurants only the meat of the tail is served and the remainder of the body used in chowder or sauces, as in my recipe. There is so little meat in the claws that it isn't worth picking it out.

The scallop mousseline is made with a purée of scallops and whipped cream, which makes it very light and delicate. It can be served by itself, flavored with a butter and lemon sauce, or it can be used to stuff fillets of fish, as in my recipe Paupiettes of Sole (page 138), or made into a Pâté of Fish Duglère (page 108). The potato gnocchi (page 86), optional, can be served with roast or grilled meat, as well as with fish and shellfish.

Yield: 6 servings

CRAWFISH GARNISH
2 doz. crawfish
1 Tb. butter

CRAWFISH STOCK
Crawfish bodies and claws
2 Tb. butter
1 Tb. olive oil
1 c. coarsely chopped onions
½ c. coarsely chopped carrots
½ c. coarsely chopped celery
¼ tsp. thyme
¼ tsp. oregano
½ tsp. freshly ground black pepper
½ tsp. salt
2 sprigs fresh tarragon
2 Tb. cognac
1 c. white wine
1 c. chicken stock
2 c. water
2 c. fresh tomatoes, diced (2 large or 3 smaller tomatoes)

SCALLOP MOUSSELINE
½ lb. scallops
⅛ tsp. curry powder
1 c. heavy cream
⅛ tsp. white pepper
½ tsp. salt
Dash salt and freshly ground black pepper

1 Crawfish are very vivacious, and wearing a glove or using a towel may prevent getting your fingers pinched. Hold the crawfish by the tops of their bodies and break off the claws.

2 Break off the tails at the ends of the bodies. They will be sautéed separately.

3 Using a meat pounder, crush the claws so the meat is exposed to the cooking and, with a large sturdy knife, chop the bodies coarse for the sauce. Choose 6 heads that have nice antennae and reserve the ends with the antennae to use as decorations.

4 It is better to remove the intestinal tract from the tail of the crawfish, as it tends to be bitter (especially in sauce, as I am using it here). Take hold of the central flap of the tail, twist it to the left and then to the right and pull. The intestinal tract will come out attached to the flap.

7 Remove the leathery underside of the tail so the meat is exposed and can be removed easily from the remaining top part of the shell. The tails presented with the bright red part of the shell will be more attractive. Set the tails aside.

9 Strain through a fine strainer. You should have about 1¼ c. of liquid. If not, reduce by boiling rapidly or add water to obtain this amount. Set aside until ready to use.

5 Heat 1 Tb. butter in a skillet. When hot, sauté the tails for 3 to 4 minutes, until they turn red. Remove to a plate.

8 To make the stock: Heat 2 Tb. butter and 1 Tb. olive oil in a skillet. When hot, add the crushed claws and chopped bodies, and sauté for 4 to 5 minutes on high heat. Add 1 c. onions and ½ c. each carrots and celery, ¼ tsp. each thyme and oregano, ½ tsp. each pepper and salt, and cook 3 to 4 minutes longer. Add the 2 sprigs tarragon, 2 Tb. cognac, 1 c. each white wine and chicken stock, and 2 c. water, and continue to cook for 35 minutes.

Strain into a colander, pressing the shells to extract as much juice as possible. Place in a saucepan with 2 c. diced tomatoes. Bring to a boil and cook on medium heat for 10 to 12 minutes.

10 For the scallop mousseline: Butter 6 half-cup molds and refrigerate. Put ½ lb. scallops into the bowl of a food processor and process for about 10 to 15 seconds, until smooth. Add ⅛ tsp. curry powder and process again for a few seconds. With the motor running, add ¼ c. of the cream slowly and process just enough to incorporate. Place the remaining ¾ c. cream in a bowl and whip just until it holds a peak. If the cream is overwhipped, the mousseline will break down. Add the scallop mixture to the cream and combine, using a spatula or whisk. Add ⅛ tsp. pepper and ½ tsp. salt. Be sure to have the scallops, cream, and bowl cold so the texture of the mousseline is correct.

6 When cold enough to handle, shell the tails for easier serving. Because the meat inside sometimes gets mushy or doesn't have much color, keep the top part of the bright shell on the meat. With scissors, cut off the flaps on each side of the tail.

11 Place the mixture in a pastry bag without a tip. →

12 Although the molds can be filled by hand, if the mousseline is squeezed from a pastry bag with the end placed directly on the bottom of the molds, the molds will fill without any air bubbles inside. Flatten the tops of the mousselines with a spatula. Place in a saucepan and surround with lukewarm water to create a water bath.

Butter a piece of parchment paper and place it buttered side down on the mousselines. Place in a 350-degree oven for approximately 20 minutes, until cooked and firm throughout. During the cooking, the water should not go above 170 to 180 degrees or the mousselines will tend to expand and get rubbery. (They can be kept warm in hot water for 30 minutes or reheated gently in hot water for 30 minutes without affecting their quality.)

POTATO-DILL GNOCCHI (OPTIONAL)

1 lb. potatoes, unpeeled
Dash plus ½ tsp. salt
1 c. or more flour
½ c. cottage cheese
¾ c. grated Gouda or American cheese
⅓ c. finely chopped dill or basil leaves
2 eggs

TO FINISH

2 Tb. butter

13 If you decide to serve the gnocchi with the crawfish and scallop mousseline, it can be made several hours ahead and reheated as explained in step 17.

To prepare the potato-dill gnocchi: Place the unpeeled potatoes in a saucepan, cover with water, and add a dash of salt. Bring to a boil and cook about 30 minutes, until just tender but still firm. Peel the potatoes while still warm and push through a food mill directly onto a wooden board.

14 Add the salt, flour, cottage cheese, grated cheese, and dill or basil, tossing gently to mix. Break in the eggs and mix to make a dough, using a bit more flour if the dough is too sticky, which will depend on the moisture in the potatoes. Mix lightly, wrap the dough in plastic wrap, and refrigerate until cold and firm, at least 1 hour.

15 Flour the board and roll one-third of the dough into a cylinder about 1 in. thick. Cut into ½-in. slices. Repeat with the remainder of the dough.

16 Using the tines of a fork dipped in flour, flatten the gnocchi rounds, making a design at the same time.

17 Place half the gnocchi rounds in boiling water. Bring to a boil and simmer for about 5 to 6 minutes, shaking the pan occasionally to prevent them from sticking to the bottom. Remove the gnocchi to ice water and, when cold, drain and set aside until serving time. At serving time, reheat the gnocchi in hot water for 4 to 5 minutes, then drain into a bowl. Add 2 Tb. butter, a dash of salt and pepper, and toss just enough to melt the butter.

18 To finish the crawfish sauce: Add the arrowroot dissolved in water to the juice of the crawfish, add a dash of cayenne pepper, and bring to a boil. Add the ¾ stick of butter in pieces, whisking well with each addition until it is thoroughly incorporated before adding the next. When all the butter has been absorbed, bring the sauce to a boil (see Salmon with Mousseline Sauce, page 124, and hollandaise sauce, page 34).

Place the crawfish in a warm oven for a few minutes to warm. Drop 6 lettuce leaves into boiling water and leave 5 to 6 seconds, just long enough to wilt. Remove from the water, drain off excess moisture, and place on a plate. Unmold the mousselines onto a warm platter and partially wrap each with a piece of lettuce.

19 Partially coat the mousselines with the crawfish sauce and pour the rest around them. Arrange the crawfish tails around the dish, and place the reserved crawfish heads on top of the mousselines. Serve immediately with the gnocchi on the side.

WHELK

Whelk is a relative of the tiny periwinkle and the conch and, in texture and type, is similar to the land snail. It has the same lower twist or coil as a land snail, and this coil is usually removed. Whelk can be found all along the Atlantic coast and in the New York area is often known as scungilli.

Whelk meat can be quite tough and the cooking time varies. If it is cooked at a very gentle boil in plenty of water, an hour is usually long enough for medium-sized whelk to be tender. Although the meat can be ground into a paste and added to bread crumbs and other seasonings to make a good whelk fritter, most of the time it is cooked and served either in a hot broth, as I have here with my olive sauce, or it is served in a vinaigrette.

Although my recipes explain how to remove the whelk from the shell, clean, brush, and cook it, it can also be bought cleaned and even parboiled at the market, although usually not completely cooked. Even when cooked, the meat will always remain a little chewy and elastic, which is characteristic of whelk.

TWO WHELK RECIPES

WHELK IN HOT BROTH

Yield: 6 servings
1½ lb. whelk meat (prepared as instructed below), taken from 10 whelk, about 5 lb. live
1 c. sliced celery
1½ c. sliced onions
⅓ c. red wine vinegar
½ tsp. freshly ground black pepper
½ tsp. dried thyme leaves
2 bay leaves, crushed
3 scallions, cut into ½-in. pieces
1½ c. stock (water from cooking whelk)
⅛ tsp. Tabasco or ¼ tsp. hot pepper flakes or seeds
½ tsp. salt
2 Tb. butter

OLIVE SAUCE

¼ c. black olive pieces
1½ tsp. capers, drained
1½ tsp. prepared mustard, preferably hot
1½ cloves garlic, medium-sized
1½ tsp. water
¼ tsp. pepper
½ tsp. red wine vinegar
1 egg yolk
½ c. oil, half olive and half peanut or corn oil

1 Notice that the whelk has a very thick lip and some are redder inside than others. Note also that on top of the meat there is a leathery piece (called the operculum), which protects the meat.

2 Pour boiling water over the whelk and set it aside for 5 minutes. This is long enough to "set" the whelk so it can be removed from its shell.

3 Using a large kitchen fork, puncture holes directly into the foot (the hard part of the meat) and pry the meat out. It should come out in one piece.

4 Pull off the operculum on top of the meat. It may be hard to pull off; if so, cut it off.

5 Pull out the coil or twisted part at the end of the meat. This contains the liver and intestines and tends to be pasty and bitter, so discard it.

6 Split open each whelk on the rounded side to remove the long reddish-black appendage, which is part of the gut.

7 The meat is now trimmed and should be brushed to remove some of the black around the foot. Dip a strong-bristled brush in lukewarm water and scrub to remove most of the exterior black covering. The whelk is now ready to be cooked.

8 Place the meat in a large saucepan, cover with 2 qt. cold water, and add a dash of salt. Bring to a boil and simmer gently for 1 hour and 15 minutes. The whelk, when pierced with a fork, should be tender but still firm. Drain and cut into ¼-in. slices. It can be used now in the broth or in the salad recipe.

9 **For the whelk in hot broth:** Combine the prepared whelk with the 1 c. sliced celery, 1½ c. sliced onions, ⅓ c. vinegar, ½ tsp. each pepper, thyme leaves and salt, 2 bay leaves, 3 scallions, 1½ c. stock, and ⅛ tsp. Tabasco or ¼ tsp. pepper flakes, and salt. Cook very gently for 25 to 30 minutes. (You shouldn't have too much liquid remaining.) Add the butter and mix. Serve hot to lukewarm in a salad bowl with the olive sauce.

To prepare the olive sauce: Place the ¼ c. olives, 1½ tsp. each capers and mustard, 1½ cloves garlic, 1½ tsp. water, ¼ tsp. pepper, ½ tsp. vinegar, and 1 egg yolk in a food processor, and process until smooth. Add the ½ c. oil slowly with the machine on. Place in a bowl. →

SHELLFISH & FISH

WHELK SALAD

Yield: 6 servings

1½ lb. whelk (prepared in preceding
  instructions)

MUSTARD VINAIGRETTE

1 Tb. Dijon-style mustard
½ tsp. salt
¼ tsp. freshly ground black pepper
1 Tb. red wine vinegar
⅓ c. oil (olive or peanut or a mixture of
  both)
2 Tb. chopped onion
1½ tsp. chopped garlic (about 3 cloves)
1 Tb. chopped chives
1 c. ½-in.-diced tomatoes (1 or 2 tomatoes, skin removed)

DECORATION

4 large radishes, stems removed and
  halved lengthwise, with root end
  attached

1 Prepare the sauce by combining the mustard, salt, pepper, and vinegar in a bowl and add the oil, stirring constantly with a whisk until it is incorporated. Add the whelk, onion, and garlic and toss. Sprinkle with the chives and tomatoes and toss gently to mix. Arrange in a shallow bowl and decorate with the radish halves. Serve with crusty French bread and a dry white wine.

A LEANER VERSION

Whelk in Hot Broth: Omit the butter in the recipe and proceed according to the recipe instructions. Serve without the olive sauce.

Whelk Salad: Reduce the amount of oil from ⅓ c. to 2 Tb. in the mustard vinaigrette and add 4 Tb. of demi-glace (if available) or 4 Tb. of lean chicken stock to the mixture. Proceed according to the recipe.

FROGS IN TARRAGON SAUCE

Frog was a common delicacy when I was a child growing up in lower Burgundy. After a rain, my brothers and I would hunt for frogs in wet fields around ponds. We would also search for snails and wild mushrooms after summer rains.

There are many, many species of frogs but the ones preferred for cooking are the tiny pickerel, green, and brown frogs. Some of the frogs caught and used for this recipe are the larger bull frogs, mostly brown, and a smaller variety, the leopard frog, striated with yellow and green. In New York's Chinatown, one can buy fresh, live frogs even larger, weighing close to one lb. each.

Only the hind legs are eaten most of the time — which makes sense with tiny frogs. If the frogs are larger, the front legs as well as the body are meaty and yield white delicious firm flesh. Some recipes recommend boning the frogs and using the flesh in small bar-quettes or mousse. But this dish is essentially for casual eating: you can eat it with your fingers and enjoy frogs to their fullest.

Yield: 6 servings

2 lb. cleaned frogs
1 c. chopped onions
½ tsp. chopped garlic (1 or 2 cloves)
1¼ c. dry white wine
¼ tsp. freshly ground black pepper
½ tsp. salt

POTATOES

2 lb. small new white or red potatoes
Dash salt

SAUCE

1 Tb. butter
1 Tb. flour
1 c. cooking juices from frogs
1 c. heavy cream
Salt and pepper to taste
2 or 3 sprigs tarragon, chopped (enough
  for 1 Tb.)

1 The frogs can be caught with a net during the day or at night with the help of a flashlight. Hold the frog by the hind legs and hit its head on a rock to kill it. Using large scissors, cut the dead frog just under the head and front leg. Grasp the skin with one hand and pull it while holding the frog with the other hand. It will peel off easily. With scissors, cut above the feet. With a small frog, only the meaty back legs are used.

2 With a larger frog, cut the skin on the back and, using both hands, insert your finger underneath the skin and pull on each side.

3 With a firm pull, the skin will slide off easily. Cut just below the head at one end and above the feet at the other end. Remove and discard the guts.

4 Using scissors, separate the front from the back. For very large frogs, separate the legs. Wash thoroughly under cool water.

5 Place the frogs in a saucepan with the onions, garlic, wine, pepper, and salt. Bring to a boil, cover, reduce the heat, and simmer gently 6 to 7 minutes, until the meat separates partially from the bones and is just tender but still firm and slightly chewy. If the frogs are very large, increase the cooking time by 2 to 3 minutes; if they are very small (often preferred for taste), reduce the cooking time to 5 minutes.

Strain the cooking juices into a saucepan (you should have approximately 2 c.). Boil over high heat to reduce to 1 c.

For the potatoes: Wash the potatoes. Peel or, if they are very new, scrape to remove just the loose bits of skin. Clean again under water. Place in a saucepan, cover with cold water, and add a dash of salt. Bring to a boil and simmer gently just until tender, about 15 minutes. Drain the water out and set aside while you finish the sauce.

For the sauce: Using a whisk, combine the butter and flour to make a *beurre manié*. Whisk into the reduced cooking juices, mixing well, and bring to a boil. Stir in the cream and add salt and pepper to taste. Combine the frogs with the sauce and add the chopped tarragon. Bring to a boil.

6 Arrange in a serving dish with the potatoes around or on the side and a sprig of tarragon in the center. Serve immediately. If there are any leftovers, the frog meat can be picked off the bones and added to seafood dishes or used as a garnish for whole fish.

A LEANER VERSION

In the sauce, eliminate the butter, flour, and cream. Combine 2 tsp. of potato starch with 2 Tb. of water. Add to the boiling stock (see step 5) and mix well. Bring to a boil. Add 1 c. of milk and return to a boil. Proceed according to the recipe.

SHELLFISH & FISH

SNAILS

There are approximately 180 varieties of edible snails, as identified by scientists. The big white ones (<u>gros blanc</u>) available in France are known as Burgundy snails. The so-called small gray snails (<u>petit gris</u>) are the garden snails, of which there are different species. Their shells are yellowish and darker than those of the white snails.

Extremely high in protein and low in calories (if not served with butter), snails have been consumed forever, it seems. Archeologists have found fossils of snails dating back to the Quaternary period, and it is assumed they were used as a source of food very early. The Romans had a great fondness for snails; they would not only gather them from all around the Mediterranean, but would grow them.

The best snails are the so-called sleepers, picked just after their winter hibernation, and the best of these are found in vineyards. During times of hibernation, they develop an operculum, a kind of shell that closes them in. In spring, when they come out of hibernation and start their reproduction cycle (either with a mate or by themselves, since they are hermaphrodites), they are most tender, choice, and full of protein.

A snail should be left to diet or fast for 48 hours before it is eaten, so that it can clean its digestive tract and eliminate any poisonous plant or grass it may have eaten. Sometimes snails are gathered and fed bran or wheat products to fatten them and make them clean themselves, but it is not essential. It is not necessary to boil snails in salt and vinegar to make them disgorge themselves, as most recipes indicate. Since the mucus they disgorge is a protective system within themselves, the more they are sprinkled with salt and vinegar the more they disgorge themselves and the tougher the meat becomes.

The dark, twisted lower part of the shelled snail, called the cloaca, is sometimes bitter, and although some snail lovers insist that it should not be removed since it contains the liver and some of the best parts of the snail, it is not particularly attractive and most people do discard it.

After the snails have been removed from their shells and washed, they do take a while to cook. The tiny ones I used below cooked in an hour, but larger snails will require up to $2\frac{1}{2}$ to 3 hours to cook, simmering gently in a seasoned broth.

My second recipe is for a country-type dish in which the snails are cooked in their shells, the cloaca left inside, and served in a seasoned tomato sauce with pasta. The tiny sea snails — periwinkles (served in Chinese restaurants in black bean sauce) — are cooked and served the same way, in their shells.

2 Wash the snails in cold water two or three times, lifting them out of the water. Cover with cold water and bring to a boil. Boil about 1 minute and drain in a colander. Again, wash in cold water two or three times. Notice how green the water of the first cooking often is.

3 With a snail fork or needle, remove the snails from the shells.

TWO RECIPES FOR SNAILS

SNAILS ROLAND

Yield: 8 servings

COOKING OF SNAILS

2 lb. snails, about 200 of the small, dark gray garden snails (*Helix aspersa*)
1 c. white wine
1½ c. chicken stock
¼ tsp. salt
¼ tsp. freshly ground black pepper

COOKING ARTICHOKE BOTTOMS

6 medium artichokes, about 2½ lb. (½ lb. each)
2 c. water
1 Tb. lemon juice
¼ tsp. salt

FINISHING THE DISH

¾ lb. boletus mushrooms or other wild mushrooms
6 Tb. butter
1 doz. shallots (1 c.), peeled and sliced thin
1 Tb. chopped fresh thyme leaves
2 tsp. chopped garlic (5 or 6 cloves)
⅛ tsp. salt
⅛ tsp. freshly ground black pepper
½ c. chopped parsley
¼ c. chopped chives
1 Tb. Pernod

1 **To cook the snails:** These garden snails are quite small and at least 2 doz. are required per person when they are served out of the shell. Adjust the quantity if the snails are larger.

4 Remove the snails' black lower part, which looks like a coil. This dark, twisted end, the cloaca, will separate easily, although it is sometimes left on the snail by escargot lovers. Wash the snails again in cold or lukewarm water to remove any remaining mucus. Cover with the wine, chicken stock, salt, and pepper, and bring to a boil. Boil gently for 1 hour, every 10 minutes removing the scum that forms on the surface. The snails should be cooked and tender but still firm when pierced with a fork. For larger or tougher snails, increase the cooking time until the snails are tender. Cool them off in their own liquid (there should be enough liquid remaining to barely cover the snails).

5 Notice that when the snails are cold the liquid is hard like an aspic. This liquid will also be used in this recipe.

To cook the artichoke bottoms: Trim the artichokes to obtain bottoms as described on page 225. Cover with 2 c. water, 1 Tb. lemon juice, and ¼ tsp. salt, and bring to a boil. Simmer for about 12 to 15 minutes, until just tender but still a bit firm. Cool in the stock.

6 When the artichokes are cold, remove the choke from the inside of each and slice into uniform round disks with a thin slicer or knife. Cut the disks in half. They will be used as a decoration. Cut all the trimmings and other pieces into ¼-in. dice. (You should have approximately 1¼ c. of artichoke dice.)

7 When available, wild mushrooms are excellent with the snails. Several types of boletus (same family as cèpe) mushrooms are shown here. Cut ¾ lb. mushrooms into ¼- to ½-in. dice.

8 Arrange the half disks of artichoke bottoms in a flower pattern on each plate. Brush lightly with butter and warm gently in a low oven.

Heat the 6 Tb. butter in 1 very large or 2 smaller skillets. When hot, add the 1 doz. sliced shallots and cook about 30 seconds, until they start browning. Add the diced mushrooms and 1 Tb. chopped fresh thyme and sauté about 1 minute. Add the snails and 2 tsp. chopped garlic and cook on high heat, stirring, for 2 to 3 minutes. (The mixture will still be slightly wet.) Add ⅛ tsp. each salt and pepper, artichoke pieces, ½ c. chopped parsley, ¼ c. chopped chives, and 1 Tb. Pernod, and toss just long enough to heat.

9 Spoon the snail mixture into the center of the artichoke disks on the plates and serve immediately.

TWO LEANER VERSIONS

Snails Roland: In finishing the dish (step 8), reduce the amount of butter from 6 to 2 Tb. and proceed according to the recipe.

For Escargot Stew that follows: Omit the 2 Tb. of olive oil in the stew. Omit the butter in the pasta recipe and use only the 1 Tb. olive oil. Proceed according to recipe directions.

ESCARGOT STEW WITH LINGUINE

Yield: 6 servings
1 lb., about 100 garden snails
1 c. chopped onions
1 tsp. chopped garlic
¼ tsp. chopped thyme leaves
½ tsp. oregano
2 Tb. olive oil
2 Tb. vinegar
1 c. tomato juice
1 c. chicken stock
⅛ tsp. Tabasco
Salt to taste

PASTA RECIPE

1 lb. whole-wheat or regular linguine
1 Tb. olive oil
1 Tb. butter
Dash salt and freshly ground black pepper

GARNISH

Parsley leaves

1 Wash the snails under running water several minutes. Cover with water and bring to a boil. Boil 5 minutes. Again wash the snails several times in lukewarm water. Place back in a saucepan and add the onions, garlic, thyme, oregano, olive oil, vinegar, tomato juice, chicken stock, Tabasco, and salt. Bring to a boil and cook gently 45 minutes to 1 hour, until the snails are still firm but tender inside. Reduce the sauce sufficiently so it coats the snails well.

Cook the pasta in boiling, salted water for 15 to 20 minutes, until tender but still firm to the bite. Drain in a colander, reserving about ½ c. of the cooking water. Place the reserved water back in the pasta cooking pan with the olive oil, butter, and a dash of salt and pepper.

2 Toss briefly with the pasta and place on a large platter with the snails and sauce on top in the center. Sprinkle with parsley and serve immediately.

SEAFOOD BREAD

This seafood bread is a delicious and easy dish to make. It can be made with baguettes, individual oval or round rolls, as well as with a large round bread, as shown in the recipe here. It can be assembled a day ahead and kept in the refrigerator, ready for the oven.

The garlic-herb butter below can be used to flavor other dishes such as pan-fried fish, veal, or poultry, as well as sautéed vegetables. Make it in the summer when the herbs are plentiful and roll the mixture in waxed paper to make cylinders about 1½ in. in diameter. The cylinders can be frozen for a few weeks, then cut into slices and added to sautéed seafood, vegetables, or soups.

Yield: 6–8 servings
1 large round country bread (about 2 lb. and 11–12 in. in diameter)

GARLIC-HERB BUTTER

1 c. flat parsley, loosely packed (or a mixture of ½ c. parsley and ½ c. combination of basil, chives, and chervil)
3 shallots, peeled
5 medium cloves garlic
1½ sticks butter, softened

½ tsp. salt
½ tsp. pepper
1 Tb. Pernod, Ricard, or other anise liqueur
2 Tb. dry white wine

½ lb. shrimp, shelled
½ lb. scallops
½ lb. salmon
½ lb. fresh wild or domestic mushrooms
Salt and pepper
¼ c. dry white wine (to moisten the bread) →

1 Use a heavy, thick-crusted bread. The top of the bread is not used in this recipe and can be kept for another use. Only about two-thirds of the insides will be used for bread crumbs, and the remainder can be saved to use another time. Remove the top or lid of the bread: Cut down approximately ¾ in. from the sides of the loaf all around so you have a nice edge when removing the insides. Twist the soft insides left and right to loosen and pull out to create a large receptacle or shell. Place half of the insides of the bread in the food processor to make crumbs. Approximately 2½ to 3 c. of crumbs will be needed for this recipe. Set aside. Note: If the insides are very soft, cut them in pieces and dry in a hot oven or the bread will get gummy when spun in the food processor.

3 Slice the mushrooms and chop them coarse. (The mushrooms in the picture are a species of wild boletus, but any other wild or cultivated mushrooms can be used.) Sprinkle a layer of mushrooms and half the seafood on top of the buttered bread and sprinkle lightly with salt and pepper.

6 Let the bread rest 10 minutes after it comes out of the oven. Cut into large chunks with a sturdy knife and serve immediately.

2 Place the parsley, shallots, and garlic in the food processor, and process until chopped fine. Add the softened butter, salt, pepper, Pernod, and 2 Tb. white wine, and process until blended. Using a large spatula, coat the inside of the bread with some of the butter. Cut the shrimp, scallops, and salmon into 1-in. pieces.

4 Add a layer of butter, then a layer of bread crumbs and the remainder of the seafood and mushrooms.

5 Finally, spread the remaining butter on top and cover with a good layer of bread crumbs. Moisten the top of the bread crumbs with ¼ c. white wine. Place on a cookie sheet and bake in a 400-degree oven for about 1 hour. Note: If the bread is already quite dark when you buy it and you don't want it to brown much more, wrap the bottom and sides in aluminum foil before placing the bread in the oven.

FISH ROE EVELYN

Here fish roe is first lightly steamed to partially cook it, then sautéed briefly in a skillet. Although we have used a lemon sole roe, which is quite inexpensive, the roe from almost any fish can be used, the most prized being shad roe, which is much costlier.

Yield: 6 servings

GINGER SAUCE

2 tsp. grated ginger
1 tsp. minced garlic
3 Tb. soy sauce
2 tsp. rice vinegar
½ tsp. sugar

THE ROE

¾ lb. snow or sugar snap peas (about 10 per serving)
6 lemon sole roe (1½ lb. total), 4 oz. per person, which is 1 large or 2 small roe per person
½ tsp. salt
6 Tb. butter
2 c. large shallots, peeled and cut into ¼-in. slices
¼ tsp. freshly ground black pepper
2 tsp. lemon juice
½ c. loose parsley leaves, preferably flat-leaf

1 To make the sauce, mix all the ingredients.

2 To prepare sugar or snap peas: Cut off the pointed end with your fingernail and pull. You will see the string that runs all the way up the side.

3 Pull the string the length of the pea to the stem end, and break off the stem end; pull the string on the other side of the length of the pea and remove it. The strings should be removed from both sides. Set the peas aside.

4 Arrange the roe on a plate that fits in your steamer and sprinkle with ¼ tsp. of the salt. Place in the steamer on top of cold water and turn the heat to high. Cover, and when it comes to a boil and starts steaming, cook 4 minutes for large roe and approximately 3 minutes for small roe.

5 You will notice that the roe is not completely cooked (it is still partially red all around). Melt the butter in a large skillet or 2 smaller skillets to accommodate the roe in one layer. When hot, add the steamed roe, sprinkle with the shallots, pepper, and remaining ¼ tsp. salt. Cook over high heat for 1 minute, just long enough to brown the roe lightly. →

SHELLFISH & FISH

97

6 Turn the roe over onto the other side, add the peas, cover, and cook for another 2 minutes over high heat.

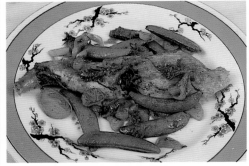

7 Remove from the heat, add the lemon juice and parsley, and cover again for 1 to 2 minutes so it cooks in its own heat. Arrange the roe on 6 individual plates with the peas, and coat each serving with about 2 tsp. of the ginger sauce. Serve immediately.

A LEANER VERSION

Reduce the amount of butter from 6 to 2 Tb. and proceed according to directions.

FISH FRITURE WITH FRIED CELERY LEAVES

A *friture* is a dish of tiny deep-fried fish. Whitebait or, as in the recipe here, the tiny fish that are found in rivers or ponds are fried to a crisp, like French fries. Small, sweet-water minnows, ablet, roach, gudgeon, and even tiny sunfish are quite delectable prepared this way. *Friture* is commonly served in small cafés along the little lakes and rivers in France, often with apéritifs before a meal.

Although some cooks fry the fish without gutting them, they tend to taste bitter that way, and the final result is well worth the extra work required to gut them.

Deep-fried celery leaves have a good, strong, slightly bitter taste. They are prepared like fried parsley (page 150) and are good to serve with different types of fried foods.

Yield: 6 servings

1 lb. small minnows or whitebait
¼ tsp. freshly ground black pepper
¼ tsp. salt
1 c. flour
4 c. loose celery leaves
Corn oil for frying (at least 1 in. deep)
Salt
GARNISH

Wedges of lemon (optional)

1 Freshly caught fish will live for a while in a pail of water. When ready to use, press and push down on the belly, starting at the head and pushing toward the tail so the guts come out. Wash the fish several times under cold water, changing the water between washings.

2 Drain on paper towels and place the tiny fish in a plastic bag with the pepper, salt, and flour. Shake so the fish are well coated with the mixture. Be sure to do this at the last moment; you cannot keep the fish floured too long, as the moisture in the fish will come out and make them gummy.

5 Arrange the fish on a platter with fried celery leaves in the center, and serve (optionally) with wedges of lemon. This is an ideal dish to serve with an apéritif.

3 Place the fish in a colander and shake to remove excess flour.

4 **To prepare the celery leaves:** Wash the leaves (if they need it) and dry very thoroughly. Heat the oil to about 400 to 425 degrees, and drop the celery leaves into the hot oil, averting your face because the oil will splatter momentarily. Stir around with a skimmer, and cook approximately 10 to 15 seconds, moving the celery in the oil. Drain on paper towels and sprinkle with salt.

Place the fish in the hot oil (about 425 degrees) and cook for 3 to 5 minutes, until crisp and brown. Lift out of the oil, place on paper towels to drain, and sprinkle with salt.

1 The skin of catfish is quite thick, just like that of eel. If the fish is to be used whole, the best procedure is to cut the skin all around the head and pull it off with pliers; it will come off easily in one piece. (Note: Be careful, as there is a long, sturdy, hard, needle-like fin on the top and on either side of the head that could puncture you. Some of these release poison and can give you pain much like that of a bee sting.) To separate the fillets, <u>cut on one side of the head, going through the thick skin with the knife.</u>

2 Turn the knife around and <u>cut through the tough rib cage, sliding your knife on top of the central bone.</u> Repeat on the other side to remove both fillets. Using a spoon, scrape the central bone to retrieve any remaining flesh, which can be added to the fish.

GOUJONNETTE OF CATFISH

Although catfish is widely used in many parts of the world as well as in the southern United States, it is only starting to be available in the Northeast. With its white, firm flesh, it lends itself to a variety of preparations, from broiling and poaching to grilling and is ideal for our goujonnette, as it holds its shape quite well and the taste is nutty and flavorful.

The goujonnette, from the French for gudgeon (a little fresh-water fish usually fried whole), can be done with any type of fish by first cutting it into little strips and then sautéing the strips briefly to make them crisp. In my recipe, the fish strips are sautéed with potato sticks and artichoke bottoms, mixed together in a delightful combination.

Yield: 6 servings

2 catfish, about 2½ lb. each, whole (gutted, skinned, and boned, the 5 lb. of fish will yield about 1½ lb. of meat)
1 lb. potatoes (3 or 4 potatoes)
4 artichokes, about 1½ lb.
1 Tb. lemon juice

FISH SEASONINGS
¼ tsp. salt
¼ tsp. pepper
⅛ tsp. cayenne pepper
1 tsp. paprika
¼ tsp. thyme leaves
½ c. flour

TO SAUTE FISH AND VEGETABLES
4 Tb. peanut oil
2 Tb. butter

TO FINISH THE DISH
1 large clove garlic, peeled and chopped fine (½ tsp.)
2 Tb. butter
¼ tsp. salt
6 to 8 leaves fresh sage (purple or green), stacked together and cut into ¼-in. strips
1 tsp. lemon juice

3 <u>Cut the rib-cage bones off</u> and remove any other bones.

4 Slide your knife under the skin to separate the meat from the skin. Clean the meat of any remaining sinew, small pieces of bone, etc.

6 When ready to cook, toss the fish pieces into a plastic bag with the salt, pepper, cayenne, paprika, thyme, and flour, and shake to coat all the pieces with the mixture, then dump into a colander and shake to remove the excess flour. Place 2 Tb. of peanut oil and 1 Tb. of butter in a very large skillet, preferably non-stick, and, when hot, add the pieces of fish in one layer. Sauté for about 5 minutes over very high heat until nicely browned all around.

8 Combine the fish with the potato-artichoke mixture. Add the garlic, 2 Tb. butter, and ¼ tsp. of salt (if needed). Toss the mixture together and place on a large platter. Sprinkle with shredded sage and lemon juice, and serve immediately.

A LEANER VERSION

To sauté the fish and vegetables (steps 6 and 7), reduce the amount of butter from 2 to 1 Tb. and the oil from 4 to 2 Tb. Omit the 2 Tb. of butter in finishing the dish and proceed according to directions.

5 Peel the potatoes and cut into 1½- to 2-in. sticks about ½ in. wide. Prepare the artichoke bottoms (see page 225). When completely clean, use a teaspoon to scrape out the choke from the inside and cut the bottoms into slices about ⅜ in. thick. Place the sliced artichokes in a bowl of water with the lemon juice until cooking time to prevent discoloration. Cut the fish into pieces about ½ in. thick and 2½ in. long.

7 Meanwhile, in another large skillet, heat the remaining 2 Tb. of oil and 1 Tb. butter and, when hot, add the potatoes. Sauté for about 5 minutes over high heat, until the potatoes start browning. Add the artichoke bottom slices and continue cooking for another 8 minutes (a total of about 13 minutes).

PIKE QUENELLES AND CHICKEN LIVER TIMBALE MERRET

A *quenelle* is a dumpling in French, and the pike quenelles, as done in the recipe here, are a specialty of the Lyon area. They are usually prepared with sweet-water fish, often pike, but sometimes with a combination of carp and pike, both firm-fleshed and high in albumen. There is less fish in Lyon quenelles than in classic quenelles made of fish, egg whites, and cream. In addition, they are heavier and denser than their classic counterparts.

Lyon quenelles are made with cream-puff dough, the flesh of the pike, and kidney fat or butter. They are sold, cooked with different sauces, in specialty stores throughout France.

It is important to poach the quenelles gently, just until they are cooked through, during the first cooking. If covered and allowed to boil, they expand, then deflate and get mushy on the second cooking. Although in this recipe the quenelles are reheated in water, they can also be reheated on top of the stove in the sauce, covered, and served just that way or reheated in the oven with the sauce in a gratin dish.

A great favorite at our table and a specialty of my cousin Merret is the combination of quenelles with a chicken-liver timbale and a fresh tomato sauce, often made with wild mushrooms — especially meadow mushrooms.

Yield: 8 servings

1 yellow pike (2½ lb. ungutted, 2 lb. gutted), about 1 lb. of meat, completely cleaned
12 oz. kidney fat of veal or young beef

PANADE (ABOUT 1 LB.)

1¼ c. milk
1¼ tsp. salt
3 Tb. butter
1¼ c. flour (6 oz.) plus additional flour for rolling out the dough
5 large eggs
½ tsp. pepper
⅛ tsp. ground or grated nutmeg

CHICKEN-LIVER TIMBALE

3 oz. chicken livers (about 3 livers), preferably the pale in color, which are milder and more flavorful
3 cloves garlic, peeled and crushed
2 tsp. butter
5 large eggs
1 tsp. potato starch
1 c. milk

¼ tsp. pepper
½ tsp. salt
1½ c. heavy cream
1 Tb. chopped parsley leaves
2 sprigs fresh thyme, chopped

TOMATO COULIS

1 Tb. butter
2 Tb. olive oil
½ c. coarsely chopped carrots
1½ c. coarsely chopped onions
4 cloves garlic, unpeeled and crushed
1 sprig each fresh thyme and oregano (¼ c. in all, loosely packed)
2 lb. ripe tomatoes, quartered
3 Tb. tomato paste (or 1 additional cut ripe tomato)
½ tsp. salt
¼ tsp. freshly ground black pepper
½ c. water
¾ lb. mushrooms, cut into 1-in. pieces

GARNISH

1 tsp. chopped chives

1 Walleye or yellow pike from the Great Lakes has good flesh for quenelles. These are not quite as tight or bluish as the more elongated pike from rivers, which are harder to obtain. Cut just under the gill, then twist your knife around, and cut alongside the central bone to lift out the fillet. Repeat on the other side.

2 If some meat is left on the bone, use a teaspoon to scrape it off and set it aside to add to the meat from the fillets.

3 Using a knife, separate the skin from the flesh at the tail. Grab the skin with one hand, and holding the knife with the other hand, cut in a jigsaw fashion, pushing forward with the knife at about a 45-degree angle. Pull on the skin at the same time to make the meat slide off it.

4 Cut off the bones from the rib cage and the strip of bones in the center of the fillet. Feel the meat with your finger and remove any additional bones. The fish should be completely boneless and yield approximately 1 lb. of meat.

5 Use the kidney fat of veal or young beef, separating the waxy fat into lumps. Remove any membrane that holds the fat together.

6 Put the fish in a food processor and process until smooth. Add the veal fat and process until the whole mixture is smooth. Be sure to process it at least 1 minute so the mixture holds tightly together. (If your food processor is small, do it in two batches.) Push the mixture through a food mill fitted with the thin screen. This will remove any filaments and fibers left in the fat. Refrigerate.

For the panade: Heat the 1¼ c. milk in a saucepan. Add ¼ tsp. of the salt and 3 Tb. butter and bring to a boil. As soon as it boils, remove it from the heat and add 1¼ c. flour all at once, stirring with a thick, heavy wooden spoon. As the ingredients combine together, the mixture will separate from the sides of the pan. Place it back on the stove over low heat and cook for about 1 minute, stirring, to dry out the mixture further. Place it on a plate, cover with plastic wrap, and press to flatten. Refrigerate to cool. (It should yield about 1 lb.)

7 When the panade is cold, place it in the bowl of a mixer. Add 5 eggs one at a time, waiting between additions for the mixture to be smooth before adding another egg. Add the remaining 1 tsp. salt, ½ tsp. pepper, ⅛ tsp. nutmeg, and the fish-fat mixture. Mix well until the mixture holds together and is smooth. Place the mixture in a bowl, cover with plastic wrap, and cool in the refrigerator for a few hours or overnight, until well set.

8 Place about one-third of the mixture on a well-floured board (be generous with the flour as the dough has a tendency to stick) and roll the dough gently with your hand, extending it to a cylinder approximately 1 to 1¼ in. thick.

9 With a knife first dipped in flour to prevent sticking, cut the cylinder on the bias into pieces of about 2 oz. each, 3 to 4 in. long and about 1¼ in. thick. Although here I am molding the mixture into an oval shape, you could also spoon it up with 2 large spoons and drop like dumplings into the hot water.

10 Roll the pieces slightly to round them at the ends by cupping your hand gently and rolling them gently back and forth on the board so the centers remain high and the ends become flatter and somewhat pointed, the segments assuming an elongated football shape. →

11 Since the dumplings are delicate, roll them gently onto the open side of a cookie sheet. Bring at least 1½ to 2 in. of water to a boil in a large saucepan. When boiling, roll the quenelles, approximately 1 doz. at a time, into the water. The temperature of the water will become lower when they are added. Let it return to about 180 degrees or just under the boil. Cook the quenelles at that temperature for approximately 12 to 15 minutes. When cooked, place the quenelles in a bowl of ice water and set aside until cold. Drain on a paper towel, cover, and refrigerate.

12 For the chicken-liver timbale: Place the 3 chicken livers, cleaned of sinews, and 3 garlic cloves in a food processor, and process until smooth. Meanwhile, heat the 2 tsp. butter in a large skillet. When hot, add the liver mixture and sauté 1 to 2 minutes, until the liver turns brownish and sets. (If left raw, the liver will sink to the bottom of the mold later.) Place it back in the food processor and process until very smooth. Add 5 eggs and 1 tsp. potato starch to the mixture and process to incorporate. Then add 1 c. milk, ¼ tsp. pepper, and ½ tsp. salt, and mix until smooth.

13 Strain the mixture through a very fine strainer into a bowl and add the 1½ c. cream, 1 Tb. chopped parsley, and 2 sprigs thyme, chopped. Pour into a 5- or 6-c. buttered mold and set the mold in a roasting pan with lukewarm water as high as possible surrounding it. Place in the center of a 375-degree oven and cook for 1 hour, or until set in the center.

14 To make the tomato coulis: Heat the 1 Tb. butter and 2 Tb. oil in a large skillet. When hot, add the ½ c. chopped carrots and 1½ c. chopped onions and sauté for 2 to 3 minutes. Add 4 cloves crushed garlic and 1 sprig each thyme and oregano and sauté for a few seconds.

15 Add 2 lb. tomatoes and 3 Tb. tomato paste. (If the tomatoes are very ripe, eliminate the paste, add 1 c. more tomatoes, then cook for 2 to 3 minutes longer.) Add ½ tsp. salt and ¼ tsp. pepper, cook over high heat 1 minute, and cover. Reduce to low heat and cook about 15 minutes. Place in a food mill with a fine screen.

Rinse the skillet with ½ c. water, pour over the coulis, and push through.

16 The tomato mixture will be grainy-looking and quite red. Bring to a boil and add ¾ lb. mushrooms. Bring back to the boil and cook, covered, 1 to 2 minutes. Set aside.

17 At serving time, bring about 2 in. of water in a saucepan to a boil and slip the quenelles into it. Cover, lower the heat, and let them poach again gently for about 10 minutes. They should be on low heat and cook just under the boil so they do not expand too much.

Unmold the chicken-liver timbale in the center of a large platter. Arrange the hot quenelles, drained and patted dry with a paper towel, around the timbale. Cover with the tomato-mushroom sauce and sprinkle with 1 tsp. chopped chives.

18 The finished dish ready for serving. Use a spoon to scoop out the liver timbale and serve one pike quenelle per person with extra sauce.

QUENELLES DORIA WITH DUXELLES SAUCE

Although quenelles usually contain fish, sometimes they are made of meat. In the recipe here, the quenelles are made with heavy cream and egg whites unlike the Lyonnaise quenelles (see Pike Quenelles, page 102), which are done with a choux paste. Lyonnaise quenelles are different in texture and more compact than the quenelles in this recipe, which are closer to a mousse in texture. In these quenelles, the albumen in the fish holds the mixture together. Therefore, one needs a fish waxy and high in albumen and as fresh as possible (frozen fish doesn't work as well). Albumen tends to contract when cold and, for that reason, all the ingredients (cream, fish, etc.) should be cold so the mixture stays firm and tight. The whiting used in this recipe has a delicate, tender, soft flesh, while the sole is more waxy and will hold the mixture better. The combination of both fish works well. Any fresh fish can be tried in combination, according to availability and one's taste.

The quenelles can be reheated and served individually, as shown in photograph 15, or served home-style in a gratin dish. The sauce is made with a purée of mushrooms, but other garnishes, like sliced mushrooms, tomatoes, herbs, etc., can be substituted.

The cucumber boats, as well as the butterfly carrots, can be used to garnish and decorate meat as well as fish or salads.

Yield: 8–10 servings

QUENELLES

2 lb. fish flesh (1 lb. lemon sole and 1 lb. whiting)
2 egg whites
3 c. heavy cream
1 tsp. salt
1 tsp. freshly ground white pepper

FISH FUMET

1 Tb. butter
1 lb. fish bones (heads, tails, etc.)
1 c. sliced onions
1 c. sliced leeks
1 c. sliced celery
2 bay leaves
½ tsp. thyme
½ tsp. freshly ground black pepper
1 c. white wine
6 c. water

CUCUMBER "CANOES"

2 cucumbers

CARROT "BUTTERFLIES"

1 large carrot

SAUCE

10 oz. mushrooms
2 c. reduced fish fumet
1 c. heavy cream
⅛ tsp. freshly ground black pepper
¾ tsp. salt
1½ tsp. arrowroot or potato starch dissolved in 1 Tb. water

1 Depending on size, you will need approximately 3 medium-sized whiting to get approximately 1 lb. of meat. Bone the whiting and remove the skin. (Don't worry if you have little pieces of skin and bone remaining in the flesh because the fish is strained through a food mill.) Keep the bones for the sauce. Place half the fish flesh (whiting and sole) in the food processor with 1 egg white. Process for 15 to 20 seconds, until the mixture is well blended. Repeat for the other batch.

2 Push the mixture through a food mill using the small screen (tiniest holes). You will notice there are sinews extracted from the fish. This straining produces a smoother, cleaner mixture. Combine the batches.

Place half the fish in the food processor. Make sure the bowl, fish, and cream are cold. With the machine on, add 1½ c. of the cream slowly in a thin stream. Mix until incorporated and add half the salt and pepper. Repeat with the remaining strained fish mixture. →

3 Combine the batches and place, covered, in the refrigerator for at least 1 hour before using.

4 **To make the quenelles:** Bring a large saucepan of water to a boil. The water should be at least 2 in. deep. Using a large serving spoon, scoop up the mixture, pressing it along the side of the bowl to smooth the top. Place a second serving spoon on the side of the mounded mixture . . .

5 and slide it underneath to lift up the quenelle and shape it further.

6 Scoop up the quenelle with the other spoon again and let it drop into the hot water. (Each quenelle will weigh approximately 2 to 2½ oz., and you should have approximately 20.) The water should not boil but remain at about 180 to 185 degrees. (If the water boils, the quenelles cook too fast and will expand, which they should not do during this first cooking.) Poach for approximately 10 minutes, turning them after 5 to 6 minutes by rolling them over.

7 When cooked, remove the quenelles with a slotted spoon and place in a bowl of ice-cold water. If they have not been molded properly with the spoons, use a knife to trim off any protrusions and make them rounded.

8 **To make the fumet:** Place the 1 Tb. butter in a large saucepan. When hot, add the 1 lb. of fish bones and sauté for 3 to 4 minutes. Add 1 c. each sliced onions, leeks, and celery, 2 bay leaves, ½ tsp. each thyme and pepper, 1 c. white wine, and 6 c. water. Mix and bring to a boil. Reduce the heat and boil gently for 35 minutes. Strain through a fine strainer. You should have approximately 2 c. of liquid.

9 **To make the cucumber "canoes":** Peel the 2 cucumbers and cut lengthwise into ½-in. slices. Cut the slices into 3 strips, removing and reserving for another use the strip with the seeded section from the center of the slices. Drop the remaining sticks in boiling water, return the water to the boil, and cook about 1 minute. Drain and transfer to cold water to cool. Then remove to paper towels to dry.

10 Cut lengthwise through the center of each stick, leaving the ends attached and creating an oblong "boat."

11 **To make the carrot "butterflies":** Cover 1 large peeled carrot with water. Bring to a boil and boil for about 10 minutes. Cool off under cold water. The carrot should be tender enough to be pierced with a knife but still firm and slightly undercooked. Cut a large chunk of carrot about 2 to 2½ in. long and carve as shown in the picture, cutting to create a design resembling the wing of a butterfly.

To create the antennae of the "butterfly," slice a very thin strip at the large rounded end of the carrot chunk, but do not cut through completely.

12 Next, using a vegetable peeler or a sharp knife, cut a very thin crosswise strip of carrot, again being careful not to cut completely through so one end is still attached to the carrot. This slice represents one wing, and the place where it is attached is the body of the "butterfly." Then cut another strip, but this time cut through the carrot to create the second wing. You can use the vegetable peeler just to start the slice and continue cutting with a knife.

13 Place the "butterfly" flat on the table and cut through the middle a bit more, until the wings just hold together at the body.

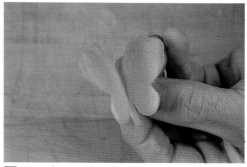

14 The "butterfly" is completely carved.

15 **To make the sauce:** Place the 10 oz. mushrooms in a food processor and process until finely chopped. Add to the 2 c. of reduced juice with the 1 c. cream, ⅛ tsp. pepper, and ¾ tsp. salt. Bring to a boil and simmer gently 4 to 5 minutes. Add 1½ tsp. arrowroot dissolved in 1 Tb. water. Bring to a boil again to thicken and set aside.

At serving time, place the cucumber "boats" in the oven for a few minutes to warm (or reheat them in water). Spread open 2 on each serving plate. Place the quenelles in gently boiling water for approximately 5 to 6 minutes to heat through. Remove with a slotted spoon and drain on paper towels. Place a quenelle in the center of each "boat." Spoon some sauce on top and around. Decorate with the "butterflies" and serve immediately.

16 As an alternative, the quenelles (2 per person for a main course) can be arranged in a gratin dish, coated with sauce, and placed in a 350-degree oven for about 30 minutes, until puffy and hot. Shake the dish every 5 to 10 minutes during the first 15 minutes of cooking to be sure the quenelles are not sticking to the bottom. Serve immediately as they come out of the oven.

SHELLFISH & FISH

1 Remove the 2 fillets from the large red snapper. Remove the bones and the skin, reserving the bone and head for soup or stock. (The bones can be frozen for a few weeks, providing the gills are removed and any blood is washed away carefully. Otherwise, the stock will be bitter.) Trim the fillets, keeping in one piece the nicest and thickest parts. You should have approximately 8 oz. of trimmings.

2 Pound the fillets lightly so they are of equal thickness throughout.

3 Butter a roasting pan or, as here, a stainless-steel platter, and place the two fillets on it. Add the trimmings to the 12 oz. of sole to make 1¼ lb. of fish flesh. Sprinkle the fillets lightly with salt and pepper.

To make the mousse: Place the 1¼ lb. of fish flesh in the food processor and process into a fine purée. The purée can be pushed through a food mill to remove any sinews and filaments (see page 105) or it

PATE OF FISH DUGLERE

A pâté of fish is often made only with a fish mousse, although sometimes fillets of fish are placed between the mousse. The pâté can be done free-form, as I do it here, or the mixture can be placed in a terrine or loaf pan and cooked in the oven either dry or in a water bath. It is served hot as well as cold, usually with a sauce.

In this recipe, I use fillets to create a base for the pâté in the shape of a fish. The mousse placed on top is formed into a fish shape and decorated with slices of carrot and scallion arranged to resemble fish scales. To make the mousse, any fish can be used, providing the flesh is high enough in albumen to assure a good mousse (see page 105). All the ingredients should be very cold. The mousse will hold better when cold because the albumen, which is the holding element in the mousse, tends to contract when cold.

The large red snapper used below is a bit drier than sole but, used in combination with sole and with the addition of cream, it works well.

Yield: 8–10 servings

FOR THE BASE OF THE "FISH"

1 four-lb. gutted red snapper
⅛ tsp. salt
⅛ tsp. freshly ground black pepper

MOUSSE

12 oz. fillets of lemon sole
½ lb. trimmings from the snapper
2 egg whites
2 c. heavy cream
¾ tsp. salt
⅛ tsp. white pepper

GARNISHES

1 carrot
2 scallions, white and light green part only, cut into thin rounds
8 oz. sliced mushrooms
¼ tsp. thyme leaves
¼ tsp. salt
1 c. dry white wine

SAUCE

1½ c. cooking liquid
½ tsp. potato starch dissolved in 1 Tb. water
1 stick butter

GARNISH

3 tomatoes, skin and seeds removed
Dash salt

can be used as is, if you desire. Add the egg whites to the purée and process until smooth. Add 1 c. of the cream, pouring it slowly and steadily on top of the fish mixture while the machine is operating. In a cold bowl beat the other c. of cream until it barely holds a peak. (See step 10 in the recipe for Crawfish with Scallop Mousse Tatan Hélène, page 85.) With a spatula, combine the partially whipped cream with the fish mixture. Add the salt and pepper.

4 Spread the mousse on top of the snapper fillets.

5 Using a piece of plastic wrap positioned on top of the mousse, shape and mold the mousse with your hand to create the form of a fish, including a tail. Remove the plastic wrap and finish the shaping with a spatula.

6 Peel a carrot and cook in water for 8 to 10 minutes, until about three-quarters cooked (it should still be firm) and cool under cold water. Using a vegetable peeler, slice strips of carrot and cut pieces to create the body details of the "mouth," "gills," etc. Cut very thin slices of scallion and embed on the surface of the mousse to simulate scales.

Arrange the mushrooms around the "fish" and sprinkle them with the thyme and salt. Pour the wine over the fish.

7 Butter half a rectangular piece of waxed paper. Fold the butter-coated half onto the unbuttered half and press together. Then open the paper and place it on top of the fish. This is a homemade lid or cover that can be pushed and molded to conform to the shape of the fish. As the fish cooks in the oven, the steam will rise from the liquid to the paper and fall back onto the fish, creating a hothouse effect and keeping the fish moist.

8 Place in a 400-degree oven for 25 to 30 minutes. It should just be cooked through. Drain any cooking liquid into a saucepan, scooping out with a slotted spoon the mushrooms that fall into the saucepan and rearranging them around the fish. Re-cover the fish and the mushrooms with waxed paper and keep warm in a low oven while making the sauce.

For the sauce: You should have approximately 1½ c. of cooking liquid. Boil to reduce to 1 c. Add ½ tsp. potato starch dissolved in 1 Tb. water to the cooking juices and bring to a boil. Add 1 stick of butter piece by piece, mixing well with the whisk, and bring the mixture to a boil. There is enough liquid to hold the butter so the mixture will not break down, even when brought to a boil. Set aside while you prepare the tomatoes.

9 Dip 3 whole tomatoes in boiling water for a few seconds. Remove the skins, cut in half, and press out the seeds (for peeling tomatoes, see page 83).

Cut the tomatoes into pieces of about 2 or 3 Tb. each. Place each, smooth side down, in a dish towel . . . →

10 and twist into a tight ball to create your own cherry tomato without skin and seeds. Place the tomato balls in a buttered dish. Sprinkle lightly with salt and place in the warm oven for a few minutes, just long enough to heat through.

11 Meanwhile, using two large metal hamburger spatulas, transfer the fish to a serving platter and add to the sauce any remaining juice that has collected around it.

Pour the sauce on top and around the fish and decorate by placing the tomatoes around the plate.

12 Cut the fish into 1-in. slices and serve hot with the sauce and tomatoes.

EEL WITH POTATO MIETTES

Eel used to be a great favorite, not only in the ancient cooking of the Romans but throughout the Middle Ages and practically up to the twentieth century. It is not, however, very commonly served in the United States. Most of the eels caught in this country are sent to Germany, Holland, and Belgium, which are the great eel-loving countries.

Eel is one of the best fish to smoke, as it is very fatty and retains the smoke well, keeping the meat very spongy, moist, and tender.

Eels are all born in the Sargasso Sea and, eventually, migrate to the different parts of the world, going up estuaries and rivers to end up in ponds, all the time getting larger and changing color. A beige color in the sea, they become dark brown in the rivers and ponds.

Very tiny eels, which are spaghetti-like and transparent, called anguilas in Spain and civelles in France, are quite common from the Basque to Spain. They are sautéed in oil with garlic and served almost like spaghetti. These so-called elvers are practically never found in U.S. markets.

If eel is smoked, it is not skinned. When sautéed or stewed, however, it must be skinned. The best eel for this purpose weighs about 1 to 1½ lb., at the most. Although the second skin underneath, a fatty layer on top of the flesh, is not always removed, in

my opinion removing it does greatly improve the taste. The first skin is pulled off and the eel is blanched. This sets the fat layer on top, which can then be scraped off or removed with a knife, and the eel is then sautéed or used in stew.

Eels can be killed when fresh by cutting off their heads. However, an easier method is to cover them with table salt; they will suffocate and die quite rapidly.

Yield: 6 servings

TO COOK THE EELS

2 eels, 1¼ lb. each
2 qt. water
Flour
3 Tb. oil
2 Tb. butter
Dash salt

TO COOK THE POTATOES

2 lb. potatoes (1¾ lb. peeled), about 6 potatoes
1 Tb. butter
1 Tb. corn oil
5 scallions, coarsely chopped (1 c.)
Dash each salt and pepper

TO FINISH

3 Tb. butter
1 tsp. chopped garlic (2 or 3 cloves)
1 Tb. red wine vinegar
½ c. shredded fresh sorrel

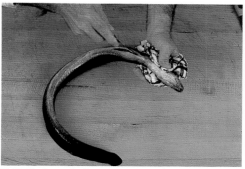

1 Kill the eels by covering with salt. They will die within a few minutes. Holding an eel with a towel, open the belly and pull the guts out. With your knife, cut the skin all around the head.

2 Tie a piece of string around the head and attach the other end to a secure object, like (as shown here) a faucet. Grab the skin at the neck with pliers and start pulling it off.

3 You could also hold the eel's head with one hand where the skin has been removed (making it less slippery) and pull the skin off with the other hand.

4 Cut off the head and, with scissors, cut off the fin on each side. Finally, cut each eel into about 5 pieces, each about 4 in. long.

5 Bring 2 qt. of water to a boil. Drop the eel pieces into the boiling water, bring it back to the boil, and boil 2 to 3 minutes. Drain the eel into a colander and rinse well under cold water until cold. When cold, peel or scrape off all the black surface, which is mostly fat, until the eel is practically clean of all that second skin and fat.

6 To cook the eels: Dry the eel pieces with a paper towel and sprinkle them with flour, coating well. Divide the oil and butter between 2 large skillets and, when hot, add the floured pieces of eel. Sprinkle lightly with salt and brown over medium to low heat for 7 to 8 minutes, turning the pieces after 3 to 4 minutes to brown evenly. Cover the skillets and set the eel aside to continue cooking and softening in its own heat for another 3 to 4 minutes.

7 For the potatoes: Peel the potatoes, cut into ¼-in. slices and then into ¼-in. dice. Wash in cold water and drain. Heat the butter and oil in a large skillet, preferably non-stick. When hot, add the well-drained potatoes. Sauté over high heat for 12 to 15 minutes, stirring occasionally, until nicely browned and cooked. Add the scallions, sprinkle with a dash of salt and pepper, and continue cooking for 2 to 3 minutes longer.

8 At serving time, arrange the potatoes and scallions on individual plates. Place 1 or 2 pieces of cooked eel on top. Melt the 3 Tb. butter in a skillet. When foaming but not too hot, add the garlic, cook for a few seconds, and then add the red wine vinegar. Heat through and spoon onto the eel. Sprinkle with the fresh sorrel (or, if not available, another type of herb). (The acidity of the sorrel tends to go well with the richness of the eel.) Serve immediately.

SHELLFISH & FISH

EEL IN RED WINE MATELOTE

This stew of eels in a red wine sauce is a specialty of Burgundy. Blanching the eel and peeling off most of the dark fat improves the taste. Sautéing the eels releases more fat from the fish, and the acidity of the red wine complements its richness. The "lion's tooth" croutons are classic and can be used with other sauced meats or stews.

Yield: 4–6 servings

2 eels, approximately 1¼ lb. each, skinned, eviscerated, and each cut into 5 pieces
1 Tb. vegetable oil
1 Tb. butter
½ c. chopped onions
½ c. chopped carrots
6 cloves garlic, chopped very fine (2 Tb.)
2 c. fruity red wine (like Beaujolais)
1 c. water
3 bay leaves
¼ tsp. thyme leaves
¼ tsp. freshly ground black pepper
¾ tsp. salt
1 Tb. butter and 1 Tb. flour (mixed together for *beurre manié*)

FOR THE "LION'S TOOTH" CROUTONS
4 or 5 slices white bread
1 Tb. butter
GLAZED PEARL ONIONS
5 oz. pearl onions (about 40), peeled
1 Tb. butter
Dash salt
½ tsp. sugar
½ c. water
GARNISH
¼ c. chopped parsley

1 Following steps 1 through 5 in the preceding recipe, blanch the pieces of eel in boiling water for 2 to 3 minutes, as indicated. Cool under cold water and peel off most of the dark fat on top of the flesh. Place the oil in a skillet and sauté the pieces of eel on high heat for 3 to 4 minutes. Drain and discard the fat.

Place the butter in a clean skillet. When hot, add the chopped onions and sauté 2 to 3 minutes. Add the carrots, garlic, red wine, water, bay leaves, thyme leaves, pepper, salt, and pieces of eel. Bring to a boil, cover, and simmer gently for 10 minutes. Remove the eel from the pan. Add the *beurre manié* with a whisk. Bring to a boil. It should thicken slightly. Place the pieces of eel back in the pan and simmer for 7 to 8 minutes longer. Set aside.

2 To make the croutons: Cut the slices of bread in half diagonally and trim the corners.

3 Round the bottom edge of each of the pointed half slices of bread to make it more attractive.

4 This technique will brown bread beautifully and requires just a minimum of butter: Coat an aluminum cookie sheet with the Tb. of butter. Rub the croutons on one side in the butter and then turn over and arrange on the sheet. Place in a 400-degree oven for 8 to 10 minutes, until brown on both sides.

5 **To cook the pearl onions:** Place the onions, butter, salt, sugar, and water in a skillet in one layer. Cook on top of the stove, covered, for 4 to 5 minutes after it comes to the boil. Uncover and continue cooking over high heat until most of the liquid has evaporated. Lower the heat to medium or low and continue cooking, tossing the onions in the remaining butter, salt, and sugar until they are glazed all around.

6 At serving time, arrange the eel on a serving platter with the sauce. Dip the tips of the croutons into the sauce to moisten and then into the chopped parsley, which will adhere to the wet tips.

7 Arrange the croutons around the eel in the red wine sauce. Sprinkle with the glazed pearl onions, and serve immediately.

SHELLFISH & FISH

MONKFISH

Monkfish (also known as belly fish, angler fish, lotte, goose fish, or frog fish) is fairly new in our markets, although it has been a favorite of European kitchens for decades. The enormous head of the fish is about three times the weight of its body, and the edible flesh is the tail consisting of two fillets alongside the central backbone. Monkfish is similar to the so-called puffer or blowfish, sometimes called "chicken of the sea," which is also quite delectable and can be found in the water off the East Coast.

The white and very firm flesh of monkfish can be broiled, stewed, or baked, or the fish roasted whole (without the head), as in my recipe following. Because it absorbs flavors well and withstands long cooking, the classic French recipe for this fish is <u>lotte à l'américaine</u>, a stew flavored with onions, garlic, tomatoes, white wine, and cognac.

ROAST MONKFISH IN RATATOUILLE

Yield: 6—8 servings

FOR THE FISH

1 3½-lb. monkfish tail (3 lb. with both
    skins and yellow fat removed)
3 cloves garlic, each cut into 3 slivers
    (9 pieces)
¼ tsp. salt
¼ tsp. pepper
2 Tb. butter

FOR THE RATATOUILLE

2 Tb. olive oil
2½ c. ½-in. slices onions
4 c. 1-in.-diced zucchini (1 lb.)
4 c. 1-in.-diced eggplant
1 large green pepper (½ lb.), seeded and
    cut into ½-in. dice (about 1 c.)
3 c. quartered plum tomatoes
1 tsp. oregano
1 Tb. finely chopped garlic (6 or 7 cloves)
1 tsp. salt
½ tsp. pepper
1 tsp. grated lemon peel
1 tsp. grated orange peel

GARNISH

Chopped parsley

1 This is the tail or edible portion of a monkfish, and this one, weighing approximately 1¾ lb., is from a fish weighing close to 6 lb., ungutted. <u>Remove the first pliable and leathery skin, which can be pulled or cut off.</u>

2 Underneath there is a second quite dark and leathery layer, which should also be removed. <u>Trim it all around, as you would trim a piece of meat, including the yellow fat (which turns dark during cooking), until you get to the white flesh.</u>

3 <u>Stud the meat with the garlic slivers</u> and sprinkle with salt and pepper.

4 Heat the butter in a large gratin dish or skillet. When hot, <u>add the fish and brown all around over medium heat for 2 minutes</u>. Place in a 400-degree oven and cook, for 20 to 25 minutes, basting after 10 minutes. Meanwhile, prepare the ratatouille.

5 **For the ratatouille:** Heat the oil in a large Dutch oven and, when hot, add the onions and sauté for 2 minutes. Add all the remaining ingredients except for the lemon and orange peels and parsley, and bring to a boil. Cover and cook for 15 minutes. Uncover and cook another 10 minutes to reduce most of the liquid. Add the lemon and orange peels and spoon the mixture around the fish. Sprinkle with parsley and serve immediately.

To serve, cut the fish into ½-in.-thick slices.

A LEANER VERSION

Reduce the amount of butter in the fish cooking (step 4) from 2 to 1 Tb. Reduce the amount of oil from 2 to 1 Tb. in the ratatouille (step 5), and proceed according to the recipe.

SHELLFISH & FISH

115

MEDALLIONS OF MONKFISH STEPHANIE

Yield: About 5 servings

1¾ lb. monkfish (1¼ lb. both skins and bones removed)
¾ c. ⅛-in.-diced carrots
½ c. ¼-in.-diced celery rib
¾ c. sliced leeks
5 or 6 sprigs fresh thyme
1 c. dry white wine
1½ c. water
½ tsp. salt
¼ tsp. pepper
⅛ oz. dried tree ear mushrooms, soaked in 1 c. warm water
4 Tb. butter

2 If there is still some skin on top of the white flesh, remove it to have the fish completely white and clean.

1 Remove both layers of skin from the fish, as explained in the previous recipe. Then cut on each side of the central bone to remove both fillets, each in one piece.

3 Cut the fish into small medallions about ¼ in. thick. Place the carrots, celery, leeks, thyme, wine, water, salt, and pep-

per in a large saucepan over medium heat. Drain the soaked tree ear mushrooms (reserving the liquid) and squeeze them, removing any stems and dirt. Cut the mushrooms into ¼-in. pieces; add to the vegetables along with the reserved juice of the mushrooms, strained through paper towels. Bring the whole mixture to a boil and boil gently for about 10 minutes, uncovered. (At this point, most of the liquid should have evaporated.)

4 Place the medallions of fish on top of the vegetables, cover, and steam the fish and vegetables. Cook about 1½ minutes on one side, turn the fish over, and cook for 1 minute on the other side (about 2½ minutes total).

5 Remove the fish and vegetables from the saucepan with a slotted spoon and arrange on individual plates. Add the butter to the remaining juices in the saucepan, mixing well to incorporate, and spoon over the fish. Serve immediately.

A LEANER VERSION

Reduce the amount of butter from 4 to 2 Tb. and follow the recipe directions.

RAY

Skate or ray (<u>raie</u> in French) is becoming more available in good fish markets. It is quite a delicate fish, but is, unfortunately, not very often utilized. Generally only the wings are used, although the central bony part of the body is good for soup. The small ray in photographs 1 and 2 is fished in North Atlantic waters, and the small wings are left whole. The wings of larger rays are cut into slices, as shown in photographs 3 and 4.

The ray is excellent poached, sautéed, or grilled. If it is to be grilled or sautéed, as in our Ray Meunière, the skin must be removed prior to cooking. The black skin, especially, tends to be quite tough and is full of needle-like prickers. When it is poached, as in the second recipe, the skin is left on and removed after cooking. Vinegar is always added to the water to eliminate the sliminess. It is often said in standard cookbooks that the ray, unlike other types of fish, tends to improve in flavor and its flesh becomes firmer after "aging" two or three days in the refrigerator. Having used it both ways, I have not seen much improvement from aging it. Therefore, I use it as fresh as possible.

RAY MEUNIERE WITH MUSHROOMS

Yield: 4 servings

2 small rays (about 1½ lb. each, whole and ungutted) or 1 large wing (about 2 lb.)
¼ tsp. salt
⅛ tsp. freshly ground black pepper
⅓ c. flour for dredging
2 Tb. butter
2 Tb. corn oil
2 c. sliced mushrooms (about 4 oz.)
Dash salt and freshly ground black pepper
TO FINISH THE DISH
2 Tb. butter
1 Tb. lemon juice
1 Tb. chopped parsley

1 The ray on the left is shown on its side with the tough, prickly black skin. On the right, it is turned over to show the underneath white side of the ray, where the mouth is and the skin is softer and smoother.

2 Cut the wings from the ray by following the bone on each side of the belly. The wings are the edible portion of the fish.

3 A large ray's wing bought at the market is approximately 1½ in. thick and weighs 2 lb. Cut the wing into 4 slabs about 5 oz. each. The pieces can now be poached or sautéed as in the recipe that follows.

6 Salt and pepper the pieces of ray and dredge with flour, shaking off any excess. Heat the butter and corn oil in a large, sturdy skillet. When hot, add the ray. Cook over medium to high heat for about 8 to 10 minutes on one side, turn, and cook approximately 6 minutes longer on the other side, a total of 14 to 16 minutes. It should be cooked through but not over-cooked. The meat should separate from the bone when pulled but still be slightly moist and pink in the center.

4 To sauté, use a sharp knife to remove the black skin, holding it with a towel if too prickly.

5 Remove the white skin underneath, using the technique shown to remove skin from fish fillets (page 102).

7 Place the cooked ray on a serving platter or, as here, on a copper dish. Add the sliced mushrooms to the drippings in the pan and cook briefly (1 minute), as they should still be firm. Season with a dash of salt and pepper, then lift the mushrooms out of the pan and scatter them on top of the ray. Heat 2 Tb. butter in a clean skillet until it is foamy and brown. Sprinkle the lemon juice on the ray, pour the hot butter on top, garnish with chopped parsley, and serve immediately.

POACHED RAY VALERIE WITH BROWN BUTTER

Yield: 4 servings

2 small rays (about 1½ lb. each, whole and ungutted) or 1 large wing (about 2 lb.)
2 qt. water
2 tsp. salt
¼ c. red wine vinegar

GARNISHES

2 slices white bread
2 or 3 radishes
1 small lemon, peeled, white pith removed
2 Tb. drained capers
2 Tb. chopped parsley
2 Tb. vegetable oil (for sautéing croutons)
1 Tb. red wine vinegar
2 Tb. butter

1 Cut the 2-lb. wing into 4 steaks, 8 oz. each. Place the water, salt, and vinegar in a large saucepan and bring to a boil. When boiling, add the ray. Return to the boil, lower the heat, and boil gently for 13 to 15 minutes. The ray should feel tender to the touch and be just cooked in the center.

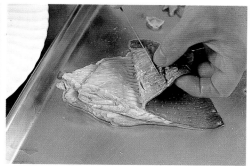

2 Drain the pieces on a tray, reserving the liquid. Lift up the skin (black and white), remove, and discard. It will slide off very easily.

3 Notice that when both skins are removed, the pieces are in two parts, separated by a tender, white cartilaginous bone in the center. Some people eat this central bone of the very small ray. For this recipe, separate the two pieces of meat and remove the central bone. The meat will slide off the bone easily. Reassemble the two pieces of meat.

4 Cut the bread and radishes into ½-in. dice. You should have ⅓ c. of diced radishes. Cut the lemon into ¼-in. dice, drain the capers, and chop the parsley. For the croutons, sauté the diced bread in the 2 Tb. of oil until nicely browned. →

5 Return the ray to the hot liquid. At serving time, drain carefully on paper towels. Place on a platter with the garnishes on top. Sprinkle with the vinegar. Heat the butter until the foaming subsides and the butter is brown. Pour over the ray and sprinkle with parsley. Serve immediately.

A LEANER VERSION

Omit the 2 Tb. of oil and brown the croutons in a 400-degree oven or make toast with the bread and cut the toasted bread into croutons. Reduce the amount of butter from 2 Tb. to 1 Tb. in step 5 and proceed according to the recipe.

BROILED BLUEFISH WITH LEMON LEEKS AND GARLIC WAX BEANS

Like tuna and other dark, fatty fish, bluefish is good only when very fresh, as it gets a strong taste when older. Since it is fatty, it is best served grilled or broiled rather than with a cream or other rich sauce.

Yield: 4 servings

TO BROIL THE BLUEFISH

1 whole bluefish, about 3 lb., ungutted (each fillet about 10 oz.)
¼ tsp. salt
⅛ tsp. pepper
1 Tb. vegetable oil

LEEKS

2 medium leeks (about 3 c. sliced)
1 c. water
¼ tsp. salt
¼ tsp. freshly ground black pepper
⅓ stick butter
1 Tb. lemon juice

WAX BEANS

½ lb. wax beans, tips removed
1 Tb. butter
½ tsp. chopped garlic (1 to 2 cloves)
Dash salt and freshly ground black pepper

1 Scale the fish in the sink to prevent the scales from splattering around. With a long, sturdy knife, cut under the fin next to the gill; then, reversing the direction of the knife blade, cut alongside the central bone and lift out the whole fillet. Turn the bluefish over and repeat to remove the other fillet. The head and bones can be reserved for soup and stock, although fatty fish don't produce as good a stock as flat or rock fish.

lemon juice, and bring the mixture to a boil. Set aside and keep warm until serving time.

2 In the center of each fillet, there is a line of bones starting below the head and extending down about 2 to 3 in. Cut on each side of the bones and lift the bones off the skin. The fillet is now completely boned out.

5 Insert your knife about 2 in. from the root end and split the leek into halves still attached at the root end. Cut parallel to the first cut so the leek is split into fourths.

8 Place the beans in boiling salted water. Return to the boil and cook, uncovered, at a strong boil for 8 to 10 minutes, until tender but still firm to the bite. Drain.

Place the fillets of bluefish skin side up on a tray under the broiler, no more than 2 in. from the heat. Broil for about 5 to 6 minutes. The skin should start to blister, brown, and crack. Do not turn the fillet over; because of the slits in the skin, it will cook through.

Arrange the leeks in the center of a platter and place the fillets on top.

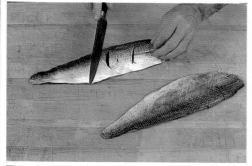

3 Make 3 or 4 slits in each fillet, cutting through the skin and approximately ½ in. deep on a slant. This will help the cooking, and the seasoning will penetrate the fish. Sprinkle with the salt, pepper, and oil, and set aside until ready to broil.

6 Run the opened leek under cold running water to remove sand that may be embedded between the leaves. At this point, the leeks can be bundled together, cooked, and served like asparagus, with a vinaigrette or hollandaise sauce (see Salmon with Mousseline Sauce, page 125). But for this recipe, after washing the leeks, proceed to the next step.

9 Melt the butter in a skillet. When hot, add the garlic, then add the beans, salt, and pepper. Sauté just enough to heat through. Arrange around the fish and serve immediately.

4 To prepare the leeks: Cut off the roots of the leeks and the first layer if fibrous or damaged. Cut off the green part of the largest leaves where tough and yellowish. As the center leaves get more tender, less of the green is removed. The pale green and more tender inside leaves are left whole. Use the trimmings (unless spoiled or damaged) for stock.

7 Cut the leeks across into ¼-in. pieces (to make approximately 3 c.). Wash carefully, drain, and place in a saucepan, preferably stainless steel, with the water. Bring to a boil and keep boiling for 5 to 6 minutes over high heat. The pieces should still be firm but tender, and only approximately ¼ c. of water should remain. If not, boil a bit longer to reduce the water to ¼ c. Add the salt, pepper, butter, and

A LEANER VERSION

Omit the oil in the broiling of the fish (step 3). On the leek preparation, reduce the amount of butter from ⅓ stick to 1 Tb. and the lemon juice from 1 Tb. to 2 tsp. In step 7, reduce the liquid in the leeks to 2 Tb. Proceed according to the recipe.

Wax beans: Reduce the amount of butter from 1 Tb. to ½ Tb. and proceed according to the recipe.

SHELLFISH & FISH

GRILLED TUNA WITH SAGE BUTTER AND SEA BEANS

Although there are different types of fresh tuna available, tuna is usually eaten from the can. In France, Spain, Portugal, and Italy, large tunas are processed according to a very strict and detailed technique. The different parts of the body, from white to darker meat, from tail meat to belly meat, are considered of different quality and used for different types of things. The Japanese use tuna a great deal in sashimi and sushi. The whiter the meat, the better the quality. When eaten raw, tuna is often soft and delicate in flavor, but somehow the taste becomes stronger when cooked. Albacore is considered the most valuable species and is the best white tuna to cook.

The tuna I am using is small, often called "bonito" or "little tunny." It is not the same quality as an albacore and the meat is quite dark. Sometimes the meat is placed in a cold brine of water and salt (about ⅓ c. salt to 2 qt. water) to leach out the blood and make the meat whiter and less accented in taste. (Notice that if the

tuna is "bled" in the brine it doesn't need any additional salt for the recipe here.) Then the tuna is boned and the skin removed. In the center of each fillet, there is a line of bones and a strip of meat (photograph 3) which is dark, strong, and bitter. It should be removed.

The tuna can be grilled briefly, as I am doing in this recipe. If it is still strong for your taste, next time place it beforehand in a mixture of 1 c. of salt to 4 c. of water 1 hour before cooking.

The small tuna depicted in the pictures following is available in New York markets during the summer and is quite inexpensive. In my small tuna, only about one-third of the total weight will be usable meat. Larger tunas yield a better percentage.

Briefly grilled, as in the recipe here, the tuna picks up a roasted taste from the hot grill, which touches the meat, but it is not completely cooked on the grill or under the broiler. It finishes cooking in its own juices without getting overcooked by the time it is served.

The sage butter is a nice complement and the sea beans, available in specialty stores or along the shore in some parts of the country, are a nice addition to the grilled fish.

Filleting tuna, 1–3

The sea beans (perce-pierre in French), called glasswort or saltwort, grow in abundance along the coast of New England. Only the young, very tender shoots should be picked. They can be eaten in salads, steamed, boiled, or sautéed. Sometimes sea beans have a central stalk that is fibrous and leathery. Still, people will eat it, pulling the meat from around the stalk. The young sprouts do not have this central stalk and are tender. They do tend to be salty, however, and I recommend soaking them in fresh water for a few hours before cooking in a large quantity of unsalted water.

Yield: 4 servings

1 tuna, about 4 to 5 lb., ungutted
¼ tsp. salt
⅛ tsp. freshly ground black pepper
1 Tb. olive oil

SEA BEANS OR GLASSWORT (PERCE-PIERRE) AND CUCUMBERS

3–4 c. sea beans (young sprouts), removed from central stalk and soaked 2 hours in cool water to remove some natural salt
3 qt. water plus 2 c.
1½ c. peeled, seeded, and diced cucumber
2 Tb. butter
Dash freshly ground black pepper

SAGE BUTTER

6 large sage leaves
⅓ stick butter (softened)
1 tsp. fresh lemon juice
⅛ tsp. salt
⅛ tsp. freshly ground black pepper

1 Cut the small, ungutted tuna on the bias under the fin by the gill in the direction of the head.

2 Turn the knife around and, holding it horizontal, cut directly on top of the central bone, separating one fillet. <u>Repeat on the other side.</u>

3 You will notice that in the center of the fillet there is a line of bones. On each side of these bones the meat is darker and tends to be bitter. <u>Remove this strip of bones and meat in the center of the fillet, as well as the skin.</u> Each fillet from the small tuna will give 2 pieces weighing about 5 to 6 oz. each.

4 In order to grill the fish properly, use a hinged metal grill and have it extremely clean and hot (see Grilled Sole with Herb Butter, page 134). To make sure that the grill is extremely hot, <u>place it on the gas stove first until red hot to give a good start to the tuna.</u>

5 Sprinkle the tuna steaks with the salt, pepper, and olive oil.

When the metal grill is red hot, <u>place the fish steaks in the center, and close the grill.</u> At this point, the grill can be placed on a hot wood charcoal grill or, as I am doing here, on a pan under the broiler, approximately 1½ to 2 in. from the heat source.

Broil the tuna 1½ minutes on one side, then turn and cook 1½ minutes on the other side. The steaks, approximately 1 in. thick, won't be quite cooked. Place them on a warm platter, cover, and set aside on top of the warm stove or in a warm oven to continue to cook in their own heat and juice. They should rest in this way for about 5 to 10 minutes before serving.

6 **For the sea beans:** Meanwhile, prepare the sea beans. <u>Notice that only the tender green shoots are used.</u> For approximately 3 to 4 c. of sea-bean sprouts, bring 3 qt. of water to a strong boil. Add the sea beans, bring the water back to the boil and let it boil, uncovered, for approximately 1 to 2 minutes. Remove the beans to ice water to cool and stop the cooking until ready to use.

7 While the steaks are resting, prepare the cucumbers. Bring 2 c. water to a boil and add the cucumbers. Return the water to the boil and immediately remove the cucumber by draining off the water. Combine the cucumber with the butter, the sea beans, and a dash of pepper, and warm on top of the stove just enough to heat through.

When the steaks have rested and been allowed to cook in their own heat for 5 to 10 minutes, you will notice some juices have been released. <u>The steaks can be served whole or cut into chunks on the bias.</u>

8 Use fresh and fragrant sage leaves. Chop the sage leaves very fine and combine with the soft butter, lemon juice, salt, and pepper.

SHELLFISH & FISH

9 At serving time, distribute the sea bean–cucumber mixture among 4 plates. Place the sliced tuna steaks with their juices in the center with approximately 2 tsp. of sage butter on top of each serving. (If you feel the meat has cooled too much, place it under a hot broiler for 1 minute before serving.) Serve immediately.

A LEANER VERSION

Reduce the amount of oil in the broiling of the tuna (step 5) from 1 Tb. to 1 tsp. In the sea beans and cucumber recipe, reduce the amount of butter from 2 Tb. to 1 Tb. (step 7). Omit the sage butter and in step 9 sprinkle the fish with the lemon juice and shredded sage. Proceed according to the recipe.

SALMON WITH MOUSSELINE SAUCE

Salmon is one of the most prized of all fish, and a whole salmon makes a rich and impressive main course for a special dinner or can be turned into a stunning presentation for a buffet centerpiece. The flesh is most delectable when it is served warm just out of the poaching broth.

The leeks in the recipe here can be cooked ahead and served cold or reheated in hot water for a few seconds so they are lukewarm. Be sure they are ready before the salmon is carved so the fish doesn't get cold.

The salmon caviar or roe is sometimes available fresh processed but usually comes pasteurized in jars of different sizes. The color of the eggs and their salted, slightly acidic taste contrasts nicely with the richness of the mousseline sauce.

The hollandaise sauce, as well as the whipped cream, can be prepared ahead but should be combined only at the last moment; otherwise the mixture will liquefy.

Yield: 14–16 servings

STOCK FOR SALMON

3 qt. water
2 tsp. salt
1½ c. diced peeled carrots
1½ c. sliced celery, preferably the leafy part
2 c. sliced green of leeks

4 bay leaves
3 sprigs thyme or 1 tsp. dried thyme leaves
2 tsp. black peppercorns or a mixture of black, green, and white
2 Tb. white wine vinegar
1 very fresh salmon, 6 lb. gutted, with the head on (about 24 in. long and 2½ in. at the thickest point)

GARNISH

Lettuce leaves and parsley

MOUSSELINE SAUCE

8 egg yolks
1 lb. unsalted butter
1 Tb. lemon juice
1 c. heavy cream, whipped firm

LEEKS AND SALMON CAVIAR

About 14–16 leeks of medium to large size (1 per person)
3 Tb. peanut or cottonseed oil
2 Tb. red wine vinegar
Salt and pepper to taste
4 oz. salmon roe caviar (about 1 good tsp. per person)

1 Place all the ingredients in a large kettle (preferably stainless steel), bring to a boil, and simmer, covered, for 15 minutes. Let cool.

2 To make a Mousseline Sauce: Make a hollandaise (see Hollandaise Sauce, page 34). The cream will be combined partially with the hollandaise when the sauce is served. To fold whipped cream ahead into warm hollandaise will cause the cream to liquefy too fast and would thin down the sauce considerably. Combining the ingredients at the last moment will give a better result.

3 Pour the stock (including solids) into the bottom of the fish poacher and place the salmon in its wire rack on top. Fill the fish poacher with additional cold water so the fish is completely submerged. If the fish poacher is not long enough (mine is 20 in. long), cut off the head of the salmon and poach it alongside the body and then position the head on the salmon properly when arranging it on the platter. (The salmon can also be served without the head.) Drape a kitchen towel on top of the fish to keep it immersed during cooking and bring the stock to about 180 to 190 degrees. (If the stock boils, the fish will have a tendency to twist and break.) Poach a 6-lb. salmon at that temperature for approximately 16 to 18 minutes, adding 5 extra minutes for each additional lb. Keep the salmon in the hot stock at least 30 minutes before serving. (If the salmon is to be served cold, let it remain in the stock as long as it takes to cool it.)

4 At serving time, lift the salmon out of the hot broth and slide it onto the serving platter. (The stock can be frozen and kept for soup or sauces.)

5 Remove the top skin and discard it.

6 Using a knife, extract the back fins (they will slide off the cooked fish when pushed) and discard.

7 Scrape the dark flesh from the top center of the fillet. (It will slide off easily.) This is mostly fat and should be discarded.

8 Arrange lettuce and parsley around the salmon. Place the head in the appropriate position and decorate the salmon with parsley. Work quickly as the salmon should be served warm.

9 To carve: Run your knife (a thin, sharp blade is best) along the middle line down to the central bone to separate the top fillet into halves. Cut across into chunks about 3 to 4 in. long, using a fork or spoon to help lift the cut portions. When the top fillet has been served, lift off the central bone gently and discard it. Cut the bottom fillet into portions, making sure to scrape off the skin and fatty tissue. Arrange on warm plates and serve immediately, garnished with the warm leeks and red caviar (recipe follows) before serving.→

SHELLFISH & FISH

10 For the Leeks and Salmon Caviar:
Trim the leeks, discarding the green leaves
(save for soup), and split them lengthwise
into fourths, leaving the root end unsplit.
Wash under cold water and tie the leeks
into bundles. Place in salted boiling
water, bring to a boil, and boil gently,
covered, for 15 to 20 minutes, until
cooked but not mushy. Drain, squeezing
out excess moisture by pressing with a
spoon, and spread out the leeks on a plate.
Season with the oil, vinegar, salt, and pepper. (The cooking liquid from the leeks
can be retained for stock, soup, or sauces.)

*Note: If the leeks are not used immediately
upon cooking, place in a pan of ice water for a
few minutes to stop the cooking, then drain and
set aside. At serving time, reheat the leeks
briefly in boiling water and season according to
the above directions.*

12 To serve, combine the hollandaise with
the whipped cream, lightly coat each
salmon piece with the sauce, and serve
immediately.

A LEANER VERSION

*Omit the mousseline sauce. To serve 14 to
16 persons, reduce 4 c. of the salmon
stock to 1 c. Add 1 tsp. of potato starch
dissolved in 1 Tb. of water to the stock
and bring to a boil. Add ½ stick (2 oz.)
butter to the stock and bring to a boil.
Serve each portion of salmon with 1 Tb.
of the sauce on top. For the leeks and
salmon caviar: Reduce the amount of oil
from 3 Tb. to 1½ Tb. and the vinegar
from 2 Tb. to 1 Tb. Proceed according to
the recipe.*

11 Split the leeks in half lengthwise and
arrange each one on a plate to create a
round receptacle for the salmon. Sprinkle
with the salmon eggs and place the salmon
in the center. At serving time, place the
warm hollandaise in a sauceboat and place
the whipped cream on top.

SALMON FILLET

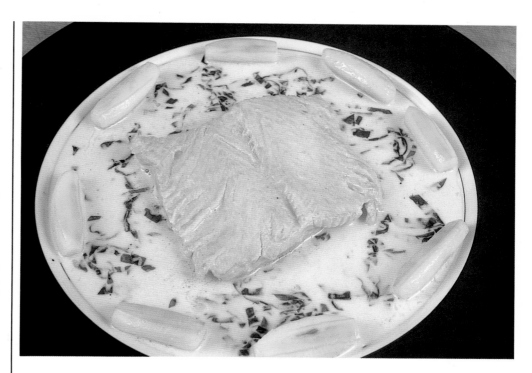

Salmon is one of the fish that restaurants use most often. It is quick to prepare and excellent tasting, providing the salmon is very fresh and completely clean, as shown in step 6 of the preceding technique.

There are many different ways to cut the fillets. In the 2 recipes here, in Sorrel Sauce and Salmon Fillets in Basil Sauce, the fillets are cut thin and about 4 in. square.

TWO SALMON FILLET RECIPES

SALMON IN SORREL SAUCE

Yield: 4 servings
1 large English-type cucumber, peeled
4 Tb. butter
Dash salt
1½ c. sorrel, loosely packed
¾ c. heavy cream
2 egg yolks
¾ tsp. salt
¼ tsp. pepper
4 salmon fillets, about ½ in. thick (4 oz. each)

2 Open the pieces to have almost square fillets 4 oz. each and ½ in. thick.

The two different salmon-cooking techniques can be used interchangeably. In one, the salmon is done under the broiler and in the other it is cooked very briefly in a skillet. If the salmon is to be prepared ahead, it can be sautéed in the skillet for approximately 20 to 30 seconds on each side, just long enough to make it barely change color. Then the skillet is removed from the direct heat, covered, and kept on top of the stove where it is warm (perhaps over the pilot light). The salmon pieces will continue cooking slowly there. Since the salmon can be prepared a bit ahead and kept warm, cooking very slowly, this method is easier when serving a dinner for 15 to 20 people. In the recipes here, the salmon is cooked and served immediately.

1 When using a whole fillet, split it in half lengthwise and cut each strip into pieces about 4 in. long and 2 in. wide. Then, <u>holding your knife flat, cut across to butterfly each piece.</u>

Making cucumber "footballs," 3–4   *Preparing sorrel, 5*

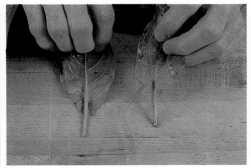

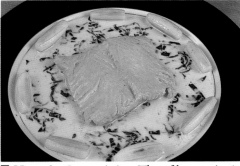

3 Cut a peeled cucumber into 1½-in. chunks. (From a long English-type cucumber, you should get about 8 pieces.) Cut each piece into quarters of equal size. Then cut out the seeds and round the corners of each piece, making it into a little oval, football shape. You should have about 8 ovals per person.

4 Cut out more of the seedy insides to smooth and shape the pieces. If using a knife is too difficult, the pieces can be smoothed with a vegetable peeler.

Bring some salted water to a boil in a saucepan and drop the cucumber pieces into it. Return to the boil and boil for 15 to 20 seconds. Then drain in a colander.

Melt 1 Tb. of the butter in a skillet and add the cucumbers. Sprinkle with a dash of salt, toss gently, and set aside.

5 Sorrel, high in oxalic acid, is particularly good with salmon, as the acidity cuts down on the richness and fattiness of the fish. The leaf, with its ends by the stems flaring outward, is easily recognizable. If the leaves are large or old, remove the tough, fibrous stems from the sorrel. Wash and pile the leaves, one on top of another, and shred into thin strips, called a julienne or chiffonnade.

Heat another Tb. of butter in a saucepan, preferably stainless steel, add the sorrel, and sauté it gently in the butter on medium heat for about 1 minute. You will notice that the sorrel will turn a khaki color. Add half the cream to the sorrel and bring to a boil.

Meanwhile, mix the remainder of the cream with the 2 egg yolks. When the sorrel sauce is boiling, add the egg yolk–cream mixture. Remove from the heat and stir. It should be hot enough for the egg yolks to thicken the mixture. Do not boil the sauce or the egg yolks will curdle. Add ½ tsp. of the salt and the pepper and set aside.

6 Heat the 2 remaining Tb. of butter in 1 very large or 2 smaller skillets (preferably non-stick). Sprinkle the 4 salmon fillets with ¼ tsp. salt and place in the gently foaming (not too hot) butter. Cook over medium to high heat for approximately 35 to 40 seconds. Using a large spatula, turn the fillets and cook another 35 to 40 seconds. Cover with a lid and set aside on the corner of the stove while you prepare the plates.

Warm up the sauce, being careful it does not boil or it will curdle. Spread the sauce on 4 large, warm plates, arrange the cucumbers (quickly rewarmed) around the edge, approximately 8 per plate, and place a salmon fillet on top of the sauce. Serve immediately.

SALMON FILLETS IN BASIL SAUCE

Yield: 4 servings
4 salmon fillets, ½ in. thick (4 oz. each), from 1-lb. salmon, completely cleaned
1 Tb. olive oil
½ tsp. salt
3 Tb. butter
3 tomatoes, peeled, seeded, and cut into ½-in. dice (2 c.), juices, seeds, and skin reserved for stock
¼ tsp. pepper
24 medium-sized basil leaves

1 Brush the fillets on both sides with the olive oil. Sprinkle with ¼ tsp. of the salt. Arrange on a cookie sheet, ready to go under the broiler. Melt the butter in a skillet and, when hot, add the tomatoes and sauté over medium to high heat for about 30 seconds, just enough to warm the tomatoes.

Meanwhile, place the fillets under the broiler about 2 in. from the heat source and cook for about 1 minute on one side. Remove the cookie sheet from the oven, turn the fillets with a large metal spatula, and place under the broiler again for another minute.

2 Arrange some of the tomato-basil mixture on 4 plates and place a fillet on top. Spoon a little of the tomato-basil mixture on top of the fish and serve immediately. Add the pepper, ¼ tsp. salt, and basil leaves to the tomatoes, place back on the stove, and again warm up for about ½ minute, just until heated through.

A LEANER VERSION

Salmon Fillets in Basil Sauce: Omit the 1 Tb. of oil in the broiling and reduce the amount of butter from 3 Tb. to 1 Tb. in step 1. Proceed according to the recipe.

STUFFED SALMON IN FLAKY DOUGH

In this recipe for salmon in flaky dough, the salmon is boned first. There are different techniques to bone salmon. In the one that follows, the fish is boned from the inside, cutting through the rib cage on each side of the central bone. Here I need approximately 2 to 2½ lb. of cleaned flesh, cut into two fillets. I used a small salmon, but one large fillet could be cut into two pieces or one chunk could be cut into several pieces and re-formed into the shape of a small salmon.

The flaky dough is not quite a standard puff paste; it has four turns instead of six and less butter than a regular puff dough. Yet it is flaky and it won't crumble when cut. It is rolled very thin and holds its shape around the salmon better than a regular puff paste.

The stuffing is made with wild mushrooms because they happened to be in season and available. Picked from a meadow, these <u>Agaricus campestris</u> are stronger and more flavorful than cultivated mushrooms. Because wild mushrooms tend to shrink and render more water, one uses more wild mushrooms than cultivated, and they are left whole.

This is a beautiful dish, ideal for an elegant party. The puff paste, the stuffing, and the boning of the fish can be done one day ahead and the whole dish assembled several hours before the party. For best results, it should be cooked at the last moment. The sauce takes only a few minutes to prepare.

Yield: 8–10 servings

1 small salmon, about 4½ lb. with head on, or a large cleaned fillet (about 2¼ lb.)

FLAKY DOUGH

2 c. flour (about 10 oz.), placed in freezer for 2 hours to cool
2 sticks butter
½ tsp. salt
½ – ⅔ c. ice-cold water (amount depending on moisture in flour)

STUFFING

½ lb. meadow mushrooms or 5 oz. cultivated mushrooms
1 Tb. butter
3 shallots, sliced (¼ c.)

4 oz. shrimp, peeled and cut into ½-in.
    dice
¼ tsp. freshly ground black pepper
¼ tsp. salt
3 Tb. chopped chives
FOR FINISHING SALMON

½ tsp. salt
⅛ tsp. freshly ground black pepper
1 egg (for wash)
FOAMY LEMON SAUCE

3 egg yolks
½ tsp. potato starch
1 c. strong chicken stock
Dash salt (amount depending on saltiness
    of stock)
Dash cayenne pepper
2 Tb. lemon juice
OPTIONAL DECORATION

Seaweed

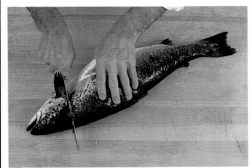

1 Cut under the fin next to the gill of the salmon on each side to remove the head.

2 From the belly side, open the salmon and cut right through the rib cage on each side of the central bone. Keep cutting until the central bone is removed.

3 Holding a knife with a sharp, thin blade almost horizontally, remove the rib cage on each of the fillets.

4 Using pliers, remove the line of bones that extends from below the head two-thirds of the way down the body. These bones go straight down into the flesh at the thickest part of the fillet, and you can feel them by rubbing the tip of a finger gently along the flesh of the salmon. If there is any meat left on the bones, scrape it off with a spoon (see page 102) and add that flesh directly onto the fillet.

5 Remove the skin from the flesh of the salmon: Pull on the skin with one hand while simultaneously pushing and cutting with a large knife held at about a 45-degree angle to the table. The blade should move in a jigsaw motion at the same time that it is pushed forward, the cutting edge scraping the skin.

6 Remove the fatty flesh (usually darker) on the surface of the fillet, using a thin, sharp knife held almost horizontally. This flesh will tend to darken more when cooked and has a stronger taste than the rest of the salmon.

7 **To make the flaky dough:** Since the flour will tend to absorb the heat generated by your hands through the manipulation of the dough, it is easier to make the dough when using cold flour directly from the freezer. Place in bowl. Cut the 2 sticks of butter into thin pieces directly into the flour. Add the salt.

8 Dump the dough out onto a floured work surface, and using a dough scraper, coarsely mix the ingredients together. Starting with a little less than ½ c., add the ice water. One-half to ⅔ c. of ice water may be used, depending on the moisture in the flour. The mixture should hold together. Try to work quickly to prevent the butter from softening and the dough from getting sticky.

9 Flour the dough. Press first with your hands, then roll the dough to extend it into a rectangle approximately 16 in. long by 10 in. wide.

10 Fold the dough like a letter into thirds. With one of the folds facing you, roll the dough again into another rectangle, approximately 18 in. long by 11 in. wide. By this time, the dough will start getting elastic and rubbery. Fold it again into thirds and wrap in plastic wrap. Refrigerate for 45 minutes to 1 hour. Then repeat the rolling and folding described above 2 more times, flouring the table lightly to prevent the dough from sticking. Notice that in photographs 9 and 10 the pieces of butter are quite visible in the dough. At the fourth turn, the pieces of butter should have practically disappeared in the dough.

11 Notice the meadow mushrooms (*Agaricus campestris*). Some are small, some larger, some opened with darker gills, some pinker. The younger the specimen, the pinker the inside; the larger and older the specimen, the darker. (Note: These flavorful mushrooms can be confused with poisonous gill mushrooms. Therefore, unless you are sure of your ability to distinguish between the poisonous and non-poisonous specimens, do not pick wild mushrooms.)

Cut off the dirty root ends from the mushrooms. They do not usually require washing. If they tend to be sandy or dirty, wash in cold water *just before using* and use immediately. (Unless used right away after washing, the mushrooms will discolor.) Leave the wild mushrooms whole unless they are very large, as they tend to shrink considerably. If using cultivated mushrooms, cut into ½-in. slices.

12 Heat the 1 Tb. butter in a skillet and, when hot, add 3 sliced shallots. Sauté about 1 minute, until the shallots soften. Then add the mushrooms and cook over medium to high heat until the mushrooms have released their juice and that juice has evaporated so the mixture starts sizzling again. Add 4 oz. shrimp, and cook for about 1 minute, just long enough for the shrimp pieces to change color. Add ¼ tsp. each pepper and salt, and 3 Tb. chives. Cool.

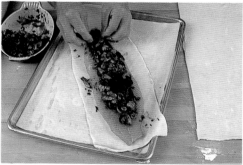

13 Line a large cookie sheet with parchment paper. During cooking, it will absorb any fat from the dough or any juice coming from the salmon. Roll the pastry into a rectangle about 16 in. wide by 16 in. long. Cut a strip 5 to 6 in. wide and place on the diagonal on top of the parchment paper on the cookie sheet. Place one of the salmon fillets on top and sprinkle it lightly with salt and pepper. Arrange the cooled mushroom-shrimp stuffing on top.

14 Place the remaining salmon fillet on top of the stuffing. Be sure that the pointed, thinner part of the fillet on one side corresponds to the larger, thicker part of the fillet on the other side, so that the shape and thickness is the same throughout, which will ensure proper cooking.

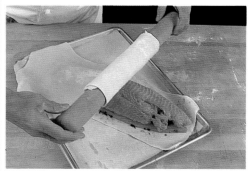

15 Roll up the remaining larger strip of dough onto your rolling pin and unroll on top of the second fillet. Brush off any flour from the surface of the dough and press it all around the edges so it conforms to the shape underneath. (Notice that the top layer of dough is larger than the bottom layer because it has to cover the top as well as the sides of the fish with enough extra dough to stick to the layer of dough underneath.)

Press the two layers of dough gently but firmly all around so they adhere well together. Place in the freezer for about 10 minutes so the dough gets firm. This will make cutting the scraps into decorations — the "fins" and "tail" — easier.

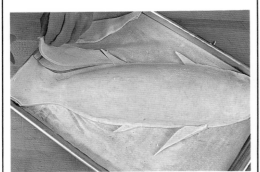

16 Remove the fish from the freezer and trim the dough all around it, designing and cutting "dorsal fins" as well as a "tail" for the "salmon" from the extra dough around the fish. Make a "gill" with a strip of trimmed dough and cut a round piece for the "eye." Decorate as you fancy.

17 Break 1 egg into a small bowl and remove about half of the white. Beat the remaining egg with a fork to make a wash. (A greater percentage of yolk will give a deeper color to the dough and the small amount of egg white will yield a shiny glaze.) Brush the "fish" with the egg wash and, using the dull side of the point of a knife, make a decorative border all around.

18 Holding the tip from a pastry bag at an angle, press it into the "fish" to imitate the scales. Place in a 375-degree oven for 45 minutes. Remove and keep, uncovered, in a warm place while making the sauce.

19 For the sauce: Place 3 egg yolks and ½ tsp. potato starch in a saucepan and mix well with a whisk. Add 1 c. chicken stock and a dash of salt and cayenne. Place over low to medium heat and whisk constantly until the mixture thickens. It will foam but should not boil. It should just reach around 180 degrees — the temperature needed to cook the starch and thicken the mixture. (This will take approximately 5 minutes.) Remove from the heat, add 2 Tb. lemon juice, and set aside. The mixture should have almost doubled in volume.

20 Use two long hamburger spatulas to transfer the "fish" to a serving platter. Decorate with seaweed around the "fish," if available.

21 Slide the "fish" onto a cutting board or platter and bring to the table. Cut into 1- to 1½-in. slices.

22 Arrange the warm slices on warm plates with the sauce around them and serve immediately.

DOVER SOLE

Authentic Dover sole, from the English Channel, has a very firm, white, and delicate flesh, which makes it particularly good to grill or poach. The grey, lemon, petrale, rex sole, or flounder available in domestic waters can be prepared in the same manner and will be perfectly adequate. However, they should be handled with extra care, especially when grilled, as their softer meat tends to break and crumble more easily than that of the firmer Dover sole. An average Dover sole weighs about 1 lb. ungutted and will yield about 6 oz. of pure flesh, which makes it an expensive delicacy.

When grilling the sole, be sure the grill is immaculately clean and extremely hot or the fish will stick to the metal. The fire is better made with wood or wood charcoal than briquettes, which are a petroleum derivative. Notice that the sole is grilled only on one side to avoid overcooking. The white skin will protect the fish during cooking, and the charcoal taste will permeate the flesh. Then the fish will finish cooking in the oven. In the poached sole recipe, take special notice of the trimming procedure, which varies from the technique used for the grilled sole.

GRILLED SOLE WITH HERB BUTTER

Yield: 4 servings as a first course

2 Dover sole, 1 lb. each, ungutted
1 tsp. peanut oil
HERB BUTTER
2 Tb. butter
1 Tb. chopped fresh herbs (a mixture of tarragon, chives, basil, dill, parsley, etc.)
1 tsp. lemon juice
Dash salt and pepper

1 Mix all the herb butter ingredients together well and keep refrigerated until serving time.

2 For the sole to be properly grilled and not stick to the metal, the grill should be extremely hot and extremely clean. This cannot be overemphasized. Cut the head off on the bias.

3 Grasp the black skin at the head and pull off. (If grey sole, flounder, etc., are used, be sure to pull the skin slowly and carefully to avoid pulling the flesh off with it.)

4 With the rounded handle of a knife, bear down on the flesh and "push" the guts out.

5 Scrape the white side with a knife or scallop or clam shell, as illustrated, to remove the scales. Wash under water thoroughly. Since the white skin is tender and holds the shape of the fish, it is generally left on, especially when the fish is to be grilled.

8 Place, unmarked side down, in a buttered dish and place in a 400-degree oven for 4 to 5 minutes to finish the cooking. Using a knife and fork, split the top fillet along the central bone and "push" both halves off the bone. They should slide easily if the sole is cooked, although it may still be slightly pink at the bones. Remove the central bone, re-form the sole to its original shape, and place on a platter.

6 With sharp scissors, cut off the fins and bones on each side of the fish. Dry thoroughly with paper towels, sprinkle with salt, and rub with peanut oil on both sides.

9 Rub each sole with 1 Tb. of herb butter and serve immediately.

A LEANER VERSION

Reduce the amount of butter from 2 Tb. to 1 Tb. in the herb butter, and proceed according to the recipe.

7 Place skin side down on the very hot grill for about 1½ minutes. Then lift the sole and place it at a 90-degree angle on the grill to form a criss-cross pattern on the white skin. Cook another 1½ minutes. The fish is marked only on the white skin side; it is not necessary to grill the sole on both sides as the charcoal taste will permeate the meat and overcooking on the grill will tend to dry the fish out.

3 Cut the folded paper as illustrated, unfold and butter. Cover the sole with the buttered paper, which will fit the contour of the fish, bring to a boil on top of the stove, and place in a 425-degree oven for 8 to 10 minutes, depending on the resting time.

4 Pour the juices and solids into a saucepan and set aside.

POACHED SOLE MISTRAL
(FOR 2 SOLE)

Yield: 4 servings as a first course
2 Dover sole, 1 lb. each, ungutted
4 Tb. butter
3 or 4 shallots, peeled and sliced (2 Tb.)
1 large red pepper (about ½ lb.), seeded, cut into 1-in. pieces, and cooked in gently boiling water for 12 minutes
½ tsp. salt
¼ tsp. freshly ground white pepper
1 sprig thyme
½ c. dry white vermouth
Salt and pepper, if needed
Blanched basil leaves (for decoration)

fins, although not used in the grilled sole, is composed of flesh as well as bones and will give taste to the cooking liquid. Therefore, it is not removed until after cooking.)

2 Butter a baking pan with 1 Tb. of butter and sprinkle with the shallots. Place the sole skin side up in the pan. Add the red pepper, salt, ground white pepper, 1 Tb. butter, thyme, and vermouth. Fold a large rectangular piece of waxed paper into fourths; center the point of the folded sides in the middle of the pan to measure the surface of the pan.

1 Clean the sole as explained in the preceding recipe up through step 4. Using sharp scissors, cut off the outside fins on each side of the sole. (The second row of

5 With a fork, push off the layer of bones on each side of the fillets. Lift the top fillet to expose the bone and remove.

Re-form the sole and transfer to a platter. Cover with the waxed paper and keep warm in a 160-degree oven while making the sauce. Push the juices and solids through a food mill fitted with the fine screen. Return the strained sauce to the cooking pot. →

SHELLFISH & FISH

135

6 Reduce the mixture by boiling to ½ c. Whisk in the last 2 Tb. of butter and add salt and pepper if needed. Sponge away any liquid that has accumulated around the sole and coat with the sauce. Decorate the top with blanched leaves of basil, as shown, or watercress or parsley, and serve immediately.

A LEANER VERSION

Omit the butter in the cooking of the sole (step 2). Do not butter the waxed paper. Reduce the amount of butter for the sauce (step 6) from 2 Tb. to 1½ Tb. and proceed according to the recipe.

FILLET OF SOLE ALEXANDRE DUMAS

Alexandre Dumas was a great gastronome who wrote a gastronomic dictionary, and the inspiration for this dish came from reading his book. This simple, flavorful, easy-to-make dish is made here with fillet of sole, but other kinds of fillets can be used. If the fillets are thick, they can be butterflied and the herbs placed in the middle. If the fillets are thin, as below, they are pounded and made into "sandwiches."

The segments of red pepper should be from peppers that will yield about 4 segments each. After the peppers are peeled and steamed, they could be served plain or stuffed with a purée of mushrooms or sautéed spinach instead of the pea purée.

The purée of peas is sweet and flavorful and has a beautiful color. To be successful, a few rules must be followed: Only tiny baby peas (which usually come only frozen) should be used. These small peas have thin skins, which liquefy better in the food processor than the thicker skins of larger peas. Second, the peas should be brought to a boil and boiled approximately 1 minute, drained, and immediately placed in the food processor. If the peas are allowed to dry out after draining, the skin shrivels, toughens, and becomes impossible to liquefy in the processor.

Yield: 6 servings

2 lb. lemon sole fillets

HERB STUFFING (ALL HERBS ARE MEASURED LOOSE, NOT PACKED)

3 scallions (½ c. minced)
1 Tb. butter
½ c. coarsely chopped chervil
⅓ c. finely minced chives
¼ c. coarsely chopped tarragon
1–2 Tb. coarsely chopped coriander
1 c. coarsely chopped parsley

COOKING THE SOLE

5 Tb. butter
¾ tsp. salt
¼ tsp. freshly ground black pepper
1 c. white wine
1 Tb. vegetable oil
1 c. fresh bread crumbs

PUREE OF PEAS

2 c. water
1 ten-oz. package frozen baby peas
1 Tb. butter
⅛ tsp. salt
¼ tsp. sugar

GARNISH

3 red peppers (6–8 oz. each), ½ per person

1 Cut down the center of a whole fillet of sole to separate it into halves. Remove the little strip of bone in the center and discard it.

2 If the fillets are large, each of the halves can again be separated into two strips. You should have about 12 pieces of approximately 2½ to 3 oz. each.

3 Wet the table, lay out the fillets, and, using a meat pounder dipped in water (to keep the flesh from tearing), pound the fillets lightly so they are of equal thickness.

4 **For the herb stuffing:** Mince the scallions. Melt 1 Tb. butter in a skillet. When hot, sauté the scallions for about 1 minute. Remove from the heat and stir in the rest of the herbs.

5 **Cooking the sole:** Butter (using 2 Tb.) a large gratin dish that can be used on top of the stove as well as in the oven. Sprinkle ¼ tsp. salt over the butter and arrange 6 fillets or pieces of fillet side by side in the dish. Place about 1 Tb. of the herb mixture on top of each fillet, sprinkle with another ¼ tsp. salt and the pepper, and cover, sandwich-style, with the other 6 fillets. Sprinkle with the remaining ¼ tsp. salt, pour wine over the fillets, and dot with 2 Tb. butter.

6 In a small skillet, heat the remaining 1 Tb. butter and the oil. When hot, add the bread crumbs and cook on medium heat, stirring almost continuously until the crumbs are dry and brown. Spoon onto the fillets and smooth the top surface. Bring the mixture to a boil on top of the stove and place in a 400-degree oven for 10 minutes.

7 Meanwhile, peel the red peppers (see Deep-Fried Eggs Julia, page 47). Divide into segments, remove the seeds, and trim each segment to make an oval receptacle. Reserve the trimmings for soup or to sauté with eggs. Place the segments in a steamer on top of boiling water. Steam for 5 minutes and set aside.

For the purée of peas: Bring 2 c. of water to a boil. Add the package of frozen peas, return to a boil, and boil for about 1 minute. Drain and immediately place in the food processor, and process for 15 to 20 seconds. Add the butter, salt, and sugar, and process for another ½ to 1 minute, until very smooth. Use to fill half the pepper segments. →

8 Serve 1 sandwich fillet whole or cut into 4 pieces per person with 1 to 2 Tb. of the natural sauce around. Place a pepper receptacle filled with the pea purée alongside and cover with another pepper segment, using it as a lid. Serve immediately.

A LEANER VERSION

Omit the butter in the herb stuffing (step 4). Combine the minced scallions with 3 Tb. water and cook for about 1 minute, until the water evaporates and the scallions are soft. Stir with the rest of the herbs. Use 2 Tb. of butter instead of 4 in cooking the sole (step 5). Omit the butter and oil in sautéing the bread crumbs (step 6); instead, spread the bread crumbs on a cookie sheet and brown in a 400-degree oven. Proceed according to the recipe. Omit the 1 Tb. of butter in the purée of peas and proceed according to the recipe.

PAUPIETTES OF SOLE WITH LOBSTER MOUSSE CHRISTIANE

The word <u>paupiette</u> refers to a piece of meat or fish that is stuffed and rolled before cooking (see Paupiettes of Veal Sara, page 279). The stuffing can be herbs, ground meat, vegetables, or a mousse. In this recipe, I use a mousse of lobster. This mousse can also be used as a garnish for soup or be served by itself.

The lobster body and shell are used to make a sauce. The roe, dried in the oven, flavors the sauce and makes a beautiful decoration. It can also enhance salads or other fish or lobster dishes. (See Cream of Lobster Soup, page 15.)

The large pieces of zucchini and carrot cut into small football shapes are very colorful and are excellent with meat as well. The "dragonfly," made from the tail, an antenna, and a leg of the lobster, is also attractive on a lobster soufflé or a lobster salad.

Yield: 6 servings

2 lb. lemon sole (1 doz. fillets)

LOBSTER MOUSSE

1 lobster, about 1½ lb., preferably female (see page 73 for identification procedure), yielding 7–8 oz. lobster meat
4 oz. shrimp, shelled and deveined (if need be)
1 Tb. herb mixture (chives, tarragon, chervil, and/or parsley)
¼ c. heavy cream
¼ tsp. salt
⅛ tsp. freshly ground black pepper

TO MAKE THE PAUPIETTES

½ tsp. salt
1 Tb. butter
5 or 6 shallots (⅓ c.)
1 c. dry white vermouth

FOR LOBSTER STOCK

1 Tb. butter
1 Tb. olive oil
1 Tb. paprika
2 tsp. chopped garlic cloves
3 c. water

SAUCE

Reduced stock
1 Tb. butter and 1 Tb. flour mixed together into a *beurre manié*
⅓ c. heavy cream

GARNISHES (CARROT AND ZUCCHINI "FOOTBALLS")

3 or 4 large carrots
2 or 3 zucchini (small to medium)
1 Tb. butter
Dash salt

1 The lemon sole fillets shown in the picture are quite large. <u>On the right fillet, there are visible lines that are fibers. This indicates that this side of the fillet was just under the skin of the sole.</u> On the left fillet, the meat is whiter and fleshier; this side was the inside of the fish touching the bones. During cooking, the fish will contract in the direction of the fiber. Therefore, the fillets should be rolled so the fibers are inside and, as they contract, the roll will tighten. The other side, fleshy and more attractive, should be on the outside.

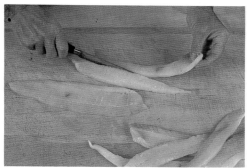

2 If the fillets are too large, <u>cut them lengthwise so the cut pieces resemble an uncut fillet</u> with a thicker end and a thinner end.

3 <u>Wet a meat pounder and the surface of the table and pound the fillets gently until</u> they are of approximately equal thickness throughout.

4 To make the lobster mousse: Kill the lobster by plunging a knife between the eyes. Place it over boiling water in a steamer and steam for approximately 1½ to 2 minutes, just enough for the flesh to firm up slightly so the meat can be <u>extracted from the shell easily.</u> Break the claw and the tail and remove the meat. The meat is still underdone, as it is gray rather than white and looks spongy.

5 If the lobster is a female, <u>remove the roe (the dark green matter),</u> place in a pan, and put into a 400-degree oven for a few minutes, until it turns red and firm. Set aside for decoration. Reserve the shells and insides of the lobster for the sauce. Reserve the end piece of the tail, 1 antenna, and 1 leg to make the "dragonfly."

For the lobster mousse: Cut the lobster meat and the shrimp into pieces and place in the bowl of the food processor with the herbs, then in the freezer for a few minutes so it is very cold. Process the mixture for a few seconds, until thoroughly mixed together. Add the cream slowly in a stream with the machine on. Add salt and pepper and process until smooth. Refrigerate again until cold.

6 Arrange the fillets of sole on the table so the side with the fibers is visible. Place the mousse in a pastry bag fitted with a plain ¼-in. tip. Sprinkle the fillets with ¼ tsp. salt and <u>pipe the cold mousse the length of the fillets,</u> reserving about 4 to 5 Tb. of the mousse for the top.

7 Spread the mousse slightly with a spatula so it is flat on the fillets, and <u>roll the fillets, starting at the thickest part, so you finish with the thinnest part of the tail.</u> →

8 With 1 Tb. butter, coat the bottom of a large saucepan. Slice the shallots coarse and sprinkle them over the bottom of the buttered pan. Using the remaining mousse and a spatula, spread some mousse on the flattest side of the rolled-up fillets so the entire top of each fillet is covered with the mousse. Place the fillets on top of the shallots, sprinkle with ¼ tsp. salt, and add the vermouth. Cut a piece of buttered parchment paper to fit (see page 135), and place it, buttered side down, on top of the fillets. Set aside.

10 Bring the paupiettes to a boil on top of the stove and place in a 400-degree oven for 10 to 12 minutes. (If the fish is to be kept warm for a while before being served, reduce the cooking time by 2 to 3 minutes.)

When the fillets are cooked, combine the juice that has accumulated in the pan with the lobster stock. Put the paper back on top of the paupiettes and keep warm in a warm oven or on top of the stove. You should have approximately 3 c. of liquid at this point. Return to the stove and reduce to approximately 1¼ c.

To make the sauce: Using a whisk, add the *beurre manié* (1 Tb. butter mixed with 1 Tb. flour) to the reduced liquid. Mix well and bring the mixture to a boil.

12 Peel 3 or 4 large carrots and cut each into about 3 chunks about 1¼ to 1½ in. long. Cut the carrot chunks in half, thirds, or quarters lengthwise, depending on how big they are, and round off the ends to make football shapes of equal size. (The trimmings can be kept for stock or soup.)

9 Meanwhile, make the stock with the lobster shells: Chop the pieces of shell coarse. Heat the butter and olive oil in a saucepan and, when hot, sauté the shells for 2 to 3 minutes with the juice in the shells and the insides. Add the paprika, garlic, and water. Bring to a boil, cover, and boil 10 minutes over high heat. Strain through a colander. The pieces of shell can also be rinsed slightly under water after straining so there is a bit more liquid added to the stock. It can always be reduced.

11 Add ⅓ c. cream, return to the boil, and strain through a very fine strainer. Set aside.

13 Prepare the zucchini in the same way: Cut 2 or 3 into chunks of about 1¼ to 1½ in. and cut each chunk in half or into 3 pieces. Shape like small footballs, reserving the trimmings for stock or soup. Bring about 2 c. water to a boil, add the zucchini, and boil for about 1½ minutes, until tender but still firm. Remove with a slotted spoon and add the carrots. Cook for about 6 to 7 minutes, until tender but firm. Set aside until serving time. You should have about 4 pieces of carrots and zucchini each per person.

14 To make the "dragonfly": Insert a wooden skewer through the first joint of the reserved lobster leg. The claw becomes the mouth of the "dragonfly." Insert the antenna inside the leg to make a long tail.

15 Push onto the skewer the 2 side appendage flaps of the lobster tail, one on each side, to duplicate the wings of the "dragonfly."

16 At serving time, arrange the paupiettes on a large platter and coat on top and around the sides with the sauce. Toss the carrots and zucchini in a skillet with 1 Tb. butter just enough to heat through. Add a dash of salt and arrange around the paupiettes. Crumble the roe and sprinkle around the platter and on top of the paupiettes, if you wish. Finally, place the "dragonfly" on top and serve immediately.

SOLE COLETTE

There are several different species of sole. For the large one required in this recipe, large lemon sole or the petrale sole of the Pacific Coast (when very large), as well as the grey sole of the East Coast, can be used. Brill, a large fish resembling a small halibut, is excellent but is rarely available in the United States. A small halibut would also be fine. All of these flat fish are related to one another, although some have firmer and moister flesh than others.

Photographs 1 through 4 demonstrate how to remove the central bone from a large flat fish so that each side, divided into 2 fillets, is held together by the head and tail. In this manner, the fish could be stuffed (as shown) and poached with the black and white skin on and the skin scraped off after cooking. The fish can be presented whole with the sauce and garnish used in this recipe.

The techniques in photographs 5 and 6 show the same recipe using only fish fillets. They are pounded and used as a wrapper on the bottom and top to enclose the stuffing, then re-formed into an elongated oval shape to approximate that of a fish. Either technique could be used for the recipe.

The stuffing is made with razor clams, but other types of clams or oysters can be used. The razor clam is very tender and meaty but tends to be quite sandy and must be washed carefully several times to ensure that all traces of sand are removed. The liquid from the clams must be strained through a paper or cloth towel to be usable.

If the sole is cooked on a large stainless-steel pan, as mine is, it could be served directly from the pan or transferred with two long hamburger spatulas to a platter, as done here, for the finished dish. The sole used is a grey sole.

Yield: 6 servings

1 grey sole, brill, or lemon sole (about 3½–4 lb., ungutted), 1¼ lb. of meat completely cleaned, or 4 fillets

RAZOR-CLAM STUFFING

1½ lb. razor clams, oysters, or soft-shell clams
5 oz. whole-wheat or other whole-grain bread (about 5 slices)
¼ c. corn or safflower oil
2 Tb. butter
1¼ c. finely chopped onions
1 leek, sliced thin (1 c.)
½ tsp. chopped garlic
2 tsp. fresh thyme leaves, coarsely chopped
4 mushrooms, cut into ¼-in. dice (1 c.)
1 egg
¼ tsp. freshly ground black pepper
½ tsp. salt

CREAM PUFF CASES (ENOUGH FOR ABOUT 8–10 SMALL CASES)

¼ c. water
2 tsp. butter
Dash salt
¼ c. flour
1 egg

"FOOTBALL" CUCUMBER GARNISH

2 cucumbers, about 1¼ lb.
1 Tb. butter
Dash salt

TO COOK THE FISH

1 c. reserved clam juice
½ c. white wine

SAUCE

1 c. of the fish cooking juices, strained
1 Tb. softened butter
2 tsp. flour
½ c. heavy cream
2 Tb. chopped chives
Salt and freshly ground black pepper to
taste

1 Using scissors, remove the outside row of bones, the ones that are visible as fins on either side of the sole. Remember that following that first row of bones – before getting into the fillet proper – there is a second layer of fins, which can be removed after cooking.

2 Run your knife (preferably a flexible, so-called fillet-of-sole knife) down the center of the sole, following the small line that separates the left from the right fillet.

Start cutting, bending the blade so it slides on top of the flat bone, and release the fillet on each side of the sole.

3 Turn the sole upside down and repeat this procedure on the other side. The meat on each side is now separated from the central bone and held just at the head and the tail of the bone. Break the bone at the neck and, using strong scissors, cut at the end of the bone on each side, next to the fin to lift the bone from the fish.

4 The bone is completely separated now. Break it at the tail and remove. The roe, if there is any, can be kept, sautéed separately, and enjoyed as a delicacy by itself. Wash the fish inside and out. The fillet on the bottom can be pushed together and the fillet on top opened to create a cavity for the filling. As indicated before, the fish could be stuffed and cooked in this manner and the skin and extra bones on the outside scraped off after cooking. In the recipe here, however, the fillets have been completely separated from the bones.

5 After separating the 4 fillets of the sole, remove the skin. Holding the end of the skin, push the flesh out, moving your knife in a jigsaw fashion, cutting the flesh at a 45-degree angle to separate it from the skin.

6 Using a little water so the meat doesn't tear apart, wet the board and the top of the sole and pound the fillets gently with a meat pounder. Be sure to work carefully as the fillets will have a tendency to tear apart. Pound all the fillets to a thickness of about ¼ in. and set aside.

Combine the crumbs, thyme, mushrooms, and onion-leek mixture; add the clams with the egg and mix well. Add the pepper and salt and mix well.

7 **To prepare the stuffing:** Wash the razor clams several times in cold water, lifting them up from the water after you finish washing so any sand remains in the bottom of the washing receptacle. If you feel they are very sandy, toss a handful of salt into cold water and let the clams soak in the salted water. It tends to help them disgorge some of the sand. Lift them out of the salted water and rinse again under fresh water. Place the clams in a saucepan, preferably stainless steel, cover, and cook over medium to high heat on top of the stove for about 5 minutes at the most, just until all the clams open.

9 Butter a large stainless-steel platter or roasting pan and place 2 fillets in the bottom. Arrange the stuffing on top, spreading it to within ½ in. of the sides, and lift up the sides of the fillet to enclose the stuffing.

11 Meanwhile, **prepare the garnish of cream puff dough:** Put ¼ c. water with 2 tsp. butter and a dash of salt in a saucepan and bring to a boil. When boiling, add ¼ c. flour all at once and mix well with a wooden spatula for about 10 to 15 seconds, until the mixture is really combined well together. Beat 1 egg in a bowl. Transfer the water-flour mixture to a clean bowl and add 1 Tb. of the egg mixture at a time, mixing to incorporate. Use the whole egg, making sure the mixture is worked until it is smooth after each addition. Butter about 9 muffin cups and place the pan in the refrigerator or freezer so the butter gets very hard. Using approximately 2 tsp. of cream puff mixture in each cup, spread with your finger to coat the bottom and sides of the mold thinly. (Don't worry if the coating is not spread evenly all over.)

8 Open up the clams completely. Save the juices and strain through paper or cloth towels to remove all the sand. You should have approximately 1 c. of juice. If not, adjust with water. Set aside. Remove the clams from the shells, and taste one to determine if they are sandy. If so, wash them carefully inside and outside one by one under lukewarm running water to remove all the sand.

Cut the bread into ½-in. cubes. Heat the oil and 1 Tb. of the butter in a skillet and, when hot, add the bread and sauté on all sides until nicely browned. Set aside to cool.

In another skillet, heat the remaining Tb. butter. When hot, add the onions and leeks and sauté 3 to 4 minutes. Add the garlic.

Place the bread in a food processor bowl and process until it is completely crumbled. You should have about 1½ c.

10 Place the 2 remaining fillets (cutting off the ends if they are too long – you can use them to patch) on top, with the whitest side showing, so the whole stuffing mixture is completely encased.

12 Place the muffin pans in a 350-degree oven for 12 to 14 minutes, until nicely cooked and browned. Let cool a few minutes and remove from the pan. Place on a cookie sheet and keep warm in a low oven →

SHELLFISH & FISH

13 Meanwhile, **prepare the cucumbers:** Peel 2 cucumbers and cut each into 3 to 4 segments about 1½ in. long. Cut each of the segments in half lengthwise and then into 3 or 4 wedges, depending on the size of the cucumber.

14 Using a sharp, thin paring knife, trim the pieces, especially on the sides containing the seeds, until the outsides are smooth and the pieces look like small, elongated footballs. Bring a qt. of water to a boil, drop the cucumbers into it, and return the water to the boil. This will take a few minutes. As soon as the water is boiling again, drain immediately into a colander. At serving time, return the cucumbers to the pan, add 1 Tb. butter and a dash of salt, and toss briefly. Serve by placing them in the warm cream-puff shells.

15 **To cook the fish:** Place 1 c. of the clam juice and the ½ c. of white wine around the fish. Butter a piece of parchment paper and tuck it so it fits all around the fish, thus preventing it from drying out in the oven. Place the stainless-steel pan on top of the stove and bring to a boil. Then place, tightly covered all around with the parchment paper, in a 375-degree oven for approximately 10 minutes. There is only a thin layer of fish around the stuffing, and it will be cooked in this length of time. The stuffing in the center, although cooked, will not be hot enough, however. Drain off the juice and strain it into a saucepan (there should be about 1 c.). Return the fish (still covered with the paper) to a low oven (about 160 to 180 degrees) to keep it warm and continue heating the stuffing while you prepare the sauce.

To prepare the sauce: Bring 1 c. of strained juice to a boil. Meanwhile, in a bowl, mix 1 Tb. softened butter and 2 tsp. flour with a whisk. Lift up the mixture on the end of the whisk and place directly into the hot juice, mixing it very quickly to prevent it from lumping. This so-called *beurre manié,* or kneaded butter, should dissolve in the juice. Bring to a boil, stirring gently with the whisk. When it boils, lower the heat and boil for about 1 minute. If lumpy, strain the sauce. Add ½ c. cream, 2 Tb. chopped chives, and salt and pepper to taste. Bring just to a boil and set aside.

Remove the fish from the oven. With 2 large spatulas, transfer it to a serving platter (or, if left on the original cooking pan, sponge out any liquid that has accumulated around the fish while it was being kept warm). Surround it with the cream-puff dough cases filled with the cucumbers. Spoon the sauce over the fish. Serve immediately.

16 This is an individual serving. The fish will cut well into 1-in. slices. Place flat with some of the sauce around it and garnish with one cucumber-filled cream-puff case. Serve immediately.

STEAMED SCROD NORMA

The steaming process, in addition to being fast, will complement the quality of a fish and keep it moist and delicate. If the fish is not super-fresh, however, it will also underline its shortcomings. Use the freshest possible fish — that is, a fish that has been out of the water no more than 24 hours.

Yield: 6 servings

6 pieces scrod fillets (1½ lb., about 4 oz. each and 1 in. thick)
1 tsp. salt
8 c. escarole (use the whitest part)
¼ c. olive oil
⅛ tsp. pepper flakes
3 cloves garlic, crushed and chopped fine (1½ tsp.)
½ c. sliced dried tomatoes, cut into strips

LEMON DRESSING

4 strips of lemon peel
1½ Tb. lemon juice
⅛ tsp. freshly ground black pepper
⅛ tsp. salt
2 Tb. olive oil

2 Tb. chopped chives

1 Sprinkle the scrod with ½ tsp. of the salt, and place on a plate in a steamer over cold water. When the water boils, steam for 5 minutes over high heat. Keep warm over the hot water until ready to serve. Meanwhile, trim the tough outside green leaves from the escarole, and cut the remainder crosswise into 1- to 1½-in. slices. You should have approximately 8 c. Place in a bowl of cold water and wash thoroughly. Lift from the water and set aside in a bowl.

2 Place the oil in a large saucepan, preferably stainless steel, add the pepper flakes, and sauté for about 1 minute. Add the garlic and cook just a few seconds until the garlic starts sizzling. Add the escarole with water still clinging to it; it will contain enough liquid so that it will begin steaming. Stir, add the remaining ½ tsp. salt, cover, bring to a boil, and cook for about 3 minutes. The escarole should be wilted but still firm. Add the strips of dried tomato and set aside for a few minutes.

Meanwhile, **make the dressing:** With a vegetable peeler, peel 4 strips of lemon peel (only the yellow part). Pile them up together and slice into very fine, short strips. Combine with lemon juice, pepper, salt, and olive oil.

Using a slotted spoon, arrange some escarole on each individual plate, place a piece of steamed fish on top, and spoon approximately 2 tsp. of the lemon dressing over the fish. Sprinkle with the chopped chives and serve immediately.

SHELLFISH & FISH

A LEANER VERSION

Reduce the amount of olive oil from ¼ c. to 1 Tb. in sautéing the escarole (step 2). Reduce the oil from 2 Tb. to 1 Tb. and the lemon juice from 1½ Tb. to 1 Tb. in the lemon dressing. Proceed according to the recipe.

Parsley

4 large mushrooms, the cap for decoration and the remainder – about ¾ c. trimmings – diced for use in the sauce (see preceding)

1 Tb. lemon juice

HUSH PUPPIES

Yield: 6 servings

1 c. flour

½ c. cornmeal

1 Tb. baking powder

¼ tsp. freshly ground black pepper

¼ tsp. salt

¼ c. chopped scallions

¼ tsp. serrano or jalapeño pepper

1 Tb. melted butter

2 eggs

½ c. milk

About 5 c. corn oil for frying

"ANGRY" TROUT IN HOT PECAN SAUCE

The commercial trout available live in markets is raised trout and, since it is very fresh, it is of good quality. Although in the wild there are other varieties such as brook and brown trout, only the rainbow is raised commercially and that is the species available in fish stores.

Trout is excellent poached, grilled, sauced, and sautéed, as in this recipe. It can be left whole or the central bone can be removed, as is done here. After boning, it can be stuffed or folded, as in my version of the "angry" trout. Folded as shown here, the trout takes up less space in the skillet and is easier to handle; also the skin on each side protects the flesh on the inside.

Even though the central bone is removed, there is still a line of small bones on each side of the fillet. These go down into the fillet perpendicular to the central bone. It is important, therefore, especially when serving this to small children, to try to remove these bones when the trout is cooked.

The sauce of pecans, hot pepper, and lemon juice is highly seasoned and anise seed gives it a distinctive flavor. The seasoning can, of course, be changed according to one's own taste.

The hush puppies served with the trout make a nice accompaniment to most sautéed or sauced meat, and the optional decoration of the three fish carved on the cap of a mush-room is fun to enhance this recipe, as well as to use in salads, aspic dishes, or poached fish. If you do these carved mushrooms, prepare them first and sprinkle them with lemon juice so they'll be ready when the fish is cooked and the trimmings will be at hand to use in the sauce.

Yield: 4 servings

4 trout (10 oz. each, ungutted, and about 8 oz. each, gutted)

¼ tsp. salt

⅓ c. flour

2 Tb. butter

2 Tb. corn oil

HOT PECAN SAUCE

½ c. pecan pieces

1 Tb. butter

½ tsp. chopped serrano or jalapeño pepper (optional)

¼ tsp. anise seed

¾ c. diced mushrooms (or trimmings from mushroom garnish; see garnish)

⅓ c. chicken stock

2 Tb. lemon juice

¼ tsp. salt

¼ tsp. freshly ground black pepper

2 Tb. butter (final addition)

1 Clip off the fins – but not the tail – with scissors and <u>cut the underside of the fish from just above the tail to the head.</u>

2 The fish can be gutted from the underside or from the gill area. To remove the gills, insert your index finger into the gill cavity, moving it from one side of the cavity to the other, and <u>remove the gills with your finger by pulling on them.</u> Most of the guts will come out attached to the gills. Wash the trout thoroughly inside and out under cold water. The trout is now ready for grilling or even poaching. For my recipe, we will bone it out.

3 <u>Cut at the tail end, below the rib cage, on each side of the central bone</u> to loosen the two fillets.

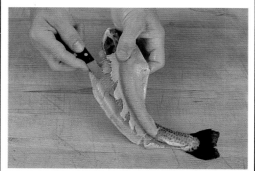

4 Place the trout on its back and, holding a small, pointed, sharp knife, cutting side up, slide the point of the blade behind the rib cage on the right side of the trout. Keep cutting behind the rib cage <u>to expose all the central bone.</u>

5 When one side is finished, <u>repeat on the other, starting at the head.</u> Slide your knife behind the rib cage until the central bone is loose and the rib cage exposed.

6 Now that the rib cage is exposed, <u>cut behind it and down,</u> to free the two fillets completely from the central bone.

7 Using your thumb and index finger, <u>pry out the bone to loosen it</u> and break it at the head as close as possible to the inside of the gill area.

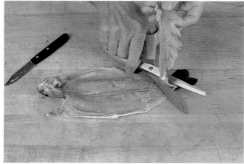

8 <u>With scissors, cut the bone at the tail</u> and cut off any extra fins and bones that are visible. The trout could now be cooked flat like a steak in just a couple of minutes.

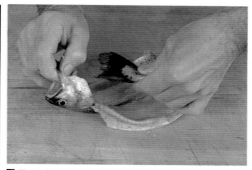

9 For this recipe, <u>fold the trout inward</u> and pull the tail through the mouth.

10 <u>The trout is ready now to be sautéed.</u> Set aside while preparing the hush puppies.

11 For the hush puppies: Combine the dry ingredients (1 c. flour, ½ c. cornmeal, 1 Tb. baking powder, ¼ tsp. each salt and pepper), ¼ c. chopped scallions, ¼ tsp. serrano or jalapeño pepper, and 1 Tb. melted butter. <u>Mix in the 2 eggs and ½ c. milk,</u> whisking to combine well. →

pepper, ¼ tsp. anise seed, and ¾ c. diced mushrooms, and sauté another minute. Add ⅓ c. chicken stock, 2 Tb. lemon juice, ¼ tsp. each salt and pepper, and heat to boiling. Set aside.

12 Heat about 5 c. oil (2 in. deep) to 350 degrees in a saucepan. (See the technique on frying for the waffle potato, page 178.) Drop approximately 1 Tb. of the hush-puppy dough at a time into the oil. The dough balls don't have to be completely round; if there are bits of dough sticking out here and there, the hush puppies will be crunchier.

17 "Draw" 3 lines to form ovals that join in the center. The design will resemble the propeller of a plane.

15 Remove the trout and place on individual serving plates. Melt 2 Tb. of butter in another skillet. When foaming and brown, combine with the pecan sauce and spoon onto the trout. Garnish with a little parsley and the optional mushroom fish decoration. Serve immediately with the hush puppies.

13 Cook 5 to 6 minutes, turning the hush puppies occasionally so they brown evenly all around. Remove to paper towels to absorb the excess oil and set aside, keeping them warm.

18 At the end of each of the blades of the propeller, "draw" the tail of a fish. This will create 3 fish intermingling together. Decorate the head of each fish and create "scales" with the point of the knife.

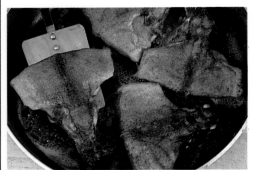

16 **To make the 3-fish mushroom decoration:** Cut the caps from 4 large mushrooms (reserving the trimmings for the pecan sauce). Cut away the top of the cap to create a "platform" or "canvas" to draw on. "Draw" with the point of a knife, cutting ⅛ in. deep, 3 equidistant lines slightly curved and joining in the center.

14 **For cooking the fish:** Sprinkle the fish with ¼ tsp. salt and dip lightly in ⅓ c. flour. Heat 2 Tb. each butter and oil in 1 very large skillet or 2 smaller ones. When hot, add the trout in one layer and cook over medium heat for 5 minutes. Turn and cook on the other side for 3 to 4 minutes. Meanwhile, **make the sauce:** In a separate pan sauté ½ c. pecans in 1 Tb. butter until golden. Add ½ tsp. chopped hot

19 With the point of a knife remove a layer of the background to set the fish design in relief. For a more complicated design, when the fish are set in relief, cut triangles into the recessed background areas between the design to create "steps." Within the triangles, cut smaller triangles, removing the pieces each time to create a series of "steps" all around the fish.

20 Trim the mushroom all around and cut off the base below the design.

21 Sprinkle some lemon juice on the finished design of the 3 fish and repeat the carving procedure on the 3 remaining mushrooms, sprinkling each with lemon juice upon completion. Use 1 per plate as a garnish for the trout or other fish dish.

FRIED WHITING COLBERT

Whiting is quite common in Europe under the name of <u>merlan</u> in France and <u>merluzzo</u> in Italy and Spain. It is an inexpensive, underestimated fish with very tender, white, and soft-textured flesh. It is ideal for a delicate mousse and quenelles. It is also good broiled as well as poached or fried. A large whiting, known as hake, is often poached and served whole, like salmon, with mayonnaise or hollandaise sauce.

In the recipe here, whitings are prepared in a classic way, dipped in beer and seasoned flour and deep-fried. They are served with a seasoned compound butter (made with butter, tarragon, lime juice, and a meat glace) and fried parsley. The Colbert compound butter, as well as the fried parsley, can be served with numerous fried fish or even sautéed meat.

Yield: 6 servings

6 whitings (½ lb. each), gutted
1 c. flour
1 tsp. freshly ground black pepper
1 tsp. paprika
1 tsp. herbs of Provence (a mixture of dried thyme, sage, oregano, and savory), crushed fine, or a mixture of oregano, thyme, and rosemary
½ tsp. salt
1 can beer
Oil for frying

COLBERT BUTTER

1 stick unsalted softened butter
2 sprigs (1 Tb.) fresh tarragon
2 tsp. lime juice
¼ tsp. freshly ground black pepper
¼ tsp. salt
1 Tb. demi-glace (see page 8), diluted and melted
2 Tb. white wine

FRIED PARSLEY

6 c. curly parsley
Corn or vegetable oil for deep frying (at least 3 c.)
Salt to taste

GARNISH

6 large mushroom caps
Lemon juice →

1 The fish are approximately ½ lb. each. Remove the gills and open the bellies. Gut the fish, making sure to <u>remove the black thin skin inside the cavities, which tends to be quite bitter</u>. Trim off the fins on the top and the bottom. The fish can be cooked this way or the central bone in the cavity can be removed. To do this, run your knife in each side of the cavity and, with your finger, pry the bone out. Break the bone at the base of the neck and the end of the cavity. The only bone left in the fish will be the bone from the end of the cavity to the tail, and it can be left in for frying.

2 After the fish are washed and dried inside and out, <u>twist each of them and insert the tail inside the mouth, pressing to make it secure</u>. It is easier to fry in this round shape. (A fish served in this way is often called whiting *en colère,* or "angry whiting," in France.)

3 <u>Hollow out the centers of 6 large mushroom caps,</u> reserving the trimmings for stocks or sauces. Brush the caps with lemon juice to prevent discoloration.

To make the Colbert butter: Combine the softened butter, tarragon, lime juice, pepper, salt, diluted meat glaze, and white wine. (This can be done in a food processor.)

4 Combine the flour, pepper, paprika, herbs of Provence, and salt. Dip the fish into the beer, coating it all over, and <u>then into the flour, covering it thickly.</u> Place in a 330- to 350-degree fryer containing at least 2 in. of oil heated to 330 to 350 degrees. The fish should be completely submerged when cooking. Cook for approximately 10 minutes, until crisp and brown.

5 Meanwhile, wash the parsley, remove the stems and dry the leaves and connecting stem pieces thoroughly. Strain the oil used for frying the whiting through paper towels to remove any cooking particles. Heat to approximately 375 to 400 degrees. <u>Drop the parsley into the oil (about 3 c. at one time), being very careful to cover your face because moisture in the parsley will cause the oil to splatter.</u> Cook, moving the parsley around with a slotted spoon or skimmer, for about 30 seconds. Drain on paper towels. Sprinkle lightly with salt. It is ready to serve.

6 Place a mushroom cap in the center of a fried fish on each serving plate and fill with the Colbert butter. Arrange some of the parsley and a few sections of lemon around the plate and serve.

LONG ISLAND BOUILLABAISSE

Bouillabaisse is a famous fish stew from the Mediterranean, made from Monte Carlo down to Perpignan. It has many different versions but is usually made with small rock fish that have too many bones to be used in other ways. Gelatinous fish like rascasse *(called scorpionfish in the U.S.) are always included, along with other rock fish of the area.*

Water is the liquid used in the stew, sometimes with the addition of white wine. Bouillabaisse is always seasoned with saffron, which is dried pistils of crocus flowers. The best saffron comes from Spain and is quite expensive because it takes over 40,000 crocuses to make a lb. of saffron.

Bouillabaisse is served as a soup or stew, or both. Sometimes the liquid of the fish, seasoned with tomato, olive oil, thyme, bay leaf, fennel, garlic, onion, etc., is served by itself with croutons. Sometimes the fish, especially when small and bony, are put through a food mill to separate the bones from the meat and liquid, and the result is served as a plain soup. Other times, shellfish, like mussels and crabs, are added and the solids are removed and served as a stew, while the broth is served at some other time.

In Marseilles and Sète, potatoes are added and a garlic sauce, called rouille *(meaning "rust" in French), is served with the bouillabaisse. This rusty-colored mayonnaise loaded with garlic contains some fish broth and is highly seasoned. My version is made with bread, potatoes, some of the fish stock, garlic, oil, and cayenne.*

Bouillabaisse is ideal for 8 to 10 people but difficult to serve for a large party. Although the fish is cooked very quickly, the bones are cooked longer to make a strong stock. In the recipe following, the bones are cooked in water and the resulting stock is strained. Then the vegetables are cut into a very tiny dice — a brunoise *— and added to the stock. The saffron, mixed with some of the stock and some grated orange rind, is added at the end (added too early, it loses some of its wonderful taste). Finally, at the last moment, the fish is poached in the strong fish and vegetable stock.*

If the dish is done in this way, it is easy for a restaurant to prepare the base ahead and, at the last moment, cook a few pieces of different fish and shellfish in the stock-vegetable mixture for each portion. The fish should be served at the peak of its taste, not overcooked, and flavored with the strong broth. The croutons and rouille *are served floating on the bouillabaisse.*

Yield: 8–10 servings

- 3 small whitings (about 1 lb.), scaled and gutted
- 2 small sea bass (about 1½ lb.), scaled and gutted
- 2 porgies (about 1½ lb.), scaled and gutted
- 3 small red snappers (about 2 lb.), scaled and gutted
- ¾ lb. medium-sized shrimp (about 25–30)
- 10 c. water
- 1 large onion (about 6 oz., to make 1 c. diced)
- 1 medium-sized leek (1 c. diced)
- 1 carrot (about 4 oz., to make 1 c. diced)
- ⅓ fennel bulb (about 4 oz., to make 1 c. diced)
- 1 rib celery (about 2 oz., to make ½ c. diced)
- 4 cloves garlic, peeled (to make about 2 Tb. sliced)
- 3 tomatoes (about 1 lb.)
- 3 or 4 large red boiling potatoes (about 2 lb.)
- 1½ lb. medium mussels (about 25), cleaned (see Cream of Mussel Soup, page 11)
- 2 Tb. olive oil
- ¼ tsp. dried crushed thyme leaves
- ½ tsp. dried crushed tarragon
- ¼ tsp. dried crushed rosemary leaves
- 1 tsp. grated orange rind
- 1 tsp. saffron crushed gently with your fingers
- 2 tsp. salt
- ½ tsp. freshly ground black pepper

ROUILLE SAUCE

- 2 slices firm-textured white bread
- 6–8 cloves garlic
- 2 slices cooked potatoes (¼ c.) from potatoes listed above
- ½ c. fish-vegetable stock from mixture above
- ½ tsp. paprika
- ⅛ tsp. cayenne pepper
- ½ tsp. salt
- 1 egg yolk
- ½ c. olive oil
- ¼ c. peanut oil

CROUTONS

- 2 Tb. corn or peanut oil
- ½ baguette (long, narrow French bread), cut into ¼-in. slices (about 40)

GARNISH

A few fennel leaves →

1 Clean the fish carefully under cool water. Be sure to remove the thin black skin inside the cavity of the whitings which tends to be bitter. Fillet the sea bass, porgies, and red snappers and shell the shrimp, reserving the bones. Cut the whitings across into pieces of about 2 in., leaving the bones in. (There is just a central bone in the whiting, and if it is removed the fish will tend to turn into a purée when cooked.) There should be approximately 2½ lb. of fish, cut into pieces, and ½ lb. of shrimp, cleaned.

2 Cut each of the fillets into 2 pieces and assemble the vegetables for the bouillabaisse.

Place the bones and shrimp shells in a saucepan with 9 c. of the water. (There will be approximately 4¼ lb. of bones and shells.) Be sure there is no blood or gills in with the bones, or the stock will be bitter. Bring the bones and water to a boil and boil gently, uncovered, for 20 minutes.

3 Cut the onion, leek, carrot, fennel, and celery into ¼-in. (or smaller) dice. Slice the garlic. Peel the tomatoes and seed (see Shrimp Madison, page 83), reserving skin, seeds, and liquid for a stock another time. Cut the tomatoes in ½-in. dice. Wash the potatoes, cover with water, bring to a boil, and cook until tender, 30 to 35 minutes, depending on size. Drain and set aside.

4 Place the cleaned mussels in a saucepan with the remaining c. of water. Cover and bring just to the boil. Remove the mussels as soon as they open. Separate the mussel shells, reserving the juice in a bowl and keeping only the shell halves containing the mussels. Let the juice rest for a while, then pour off the liquid on top carefully, leaving any sandy sediment in the bottom of the bowl. Add this liquid to the fish stock.

5 Heat the 2 Tb. olive oil in a large skillet or sauté pan and, when hot, add the garlic, onion, and leek. Sauté 2 to 3 minutes, add the celery, carrot, fennel, and crushed herbs, and cook over low heat for 2 to 3 minutes. Strain the fish stock through a fine strainer. You should have approximately 8 c. Add the stock to the vegetables. Bring to a boil again and cook 10 minutes.

6 Mix the grated orange rind and the crushed saffron with ¼ c. of the fish stock.

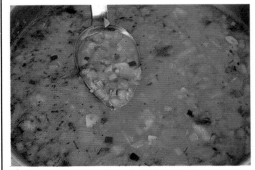

7 Add the tomatoes and the saffron–orange rind mixture to the stock and bring to a boil. Add the salt and pepper and set aside.

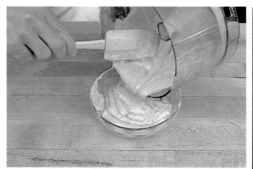

8 **For the rouille:** Place the 2 slices bread and 6 to 8 garlic cloves in a food processor and process until finely chopped. Cut 2 slices (about ¼ c.) from the cooked potatoes, add to the bread crumbs and garlic, and process until smooth. Add ½ c. of the fish stock with vegetables in it. Process until smooth. Add ½ tsp. each paprika and salt, ⅛ tsp. cayenne, and 1 egg yolk and process to combine. Finally, with the motor going, add ½ c. olive oil and ¼ c. peanut oil and process again until smooth. Remove to a bowl and keep at room temperature until serving time.

10 Just a little before serving time, bring the vegetable-broth mixture to a boil and add the fish. Return the mixture to the boil and boil gently 1½ to 2 minutes at the most. When the fish start to curl, it will be ready. Add the shrimp, return to a light boil, remove from the heat, and set aside. A single boil will be enough to cook shrimp that size.

13 Spread some of the *rouille* on about half the croutons and top with a few fennel leaves for decoration. Serve the bouillabaisse with extra croutons and *rouille*. For a hotter dish, sprinkle the *rouille* with an extra little dash of cayenne.

A LEANER VERSION

Use 1 Tb. of oil instead of 2 Tb. in the cooking of the vegetables and stock (step 5). Proceed according to the recipe.

In the rouille *sauce: Eliminate the egg yolk and peanut oil and reduce the amount of olive oil from ½ c. to 2 Tb. Proceed according to the recipe. (The sauce will be flavorful but not as smooth as in the original recipe.) For the croutons, omit the oil and brown the bread in the oven. Proceed according to the recipe instructions.*

11 The fish, now curling, is cooked. Slice some of the potatoes and place them in a saucepan with the mussels. Add 1 or 2 ladles of stock. Heat gently and keep warm on the side until serving time.

9 **For the croutons:** Spread the 2 Tb. corn or peanut oil on a cookie sheet and arrange the baguette slices (about 40) on top. Press the slices so they absorb a little of the oil and turn them over. (This technique uses a minimum amount of oil and produces a crisp and flavorful – but not too rich – crouton.) Place in a 400-degree oven and cook for about 10 minutes. The croutons should be browned on both sides.

12 To serve, place 1 or 2 slices of the warmed potatoes in the bottom of each plate with 2 or 3 mussels around them. Stir the stew gently so as not to break the pieces of fish. Place a few pieces of the fish (different varieties) and some of the vegetables in each plate, and spoon some juice over everything.

SHELLFISH & FISH

153

POULTRY

EVISCERATING A CHICKEN OR OTHER POULTRY

Although chicken, duck, pheasant, etc., are usually purchased cleaned, plucked, and eviscerated, the dedicated cook needs to know the proper technique for eviscerating poultry.

1 The technique used to eviscerate a chicken is the same as that for eviscerating a pheasant, duck, grouse, or even smaller birds, such as quail or squab.

The feet, which are very gelatinous, are good used in stock. Sometimes they are left on the chicken to create a decoration and give a certain elegance to a dish. In the recipes here, one of the chickens is roasted with the feet left on and one with them removed. If you leave them on or if you use the feet in a stock, the thick scaly skin that covers the feet should be peeled off, which is easily done if the feet are passed over the flame of a gas range. Roast the feet all around until the skin starts to blister; then, using a towel to prevent burning your hand, rub the skin off. It will come off easily.

2 Trim each side of the feet, keeping only the center claw with the tip cut off. →

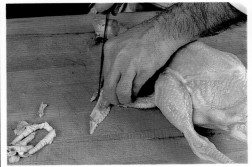

3 For aesthetic reasons, trim the ends of the wing tips and the small protrusion, or nubbin, on the side of each wing tip.

4 Fold the wings as illustrated to hold them in place. To clean out the chicken: Place the chicken on its belly and press the skin of the neck underneath to make it taut on top. Slit the neck skin the length of the neck with a sharp knife.

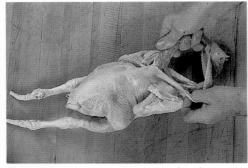

5 Separate the neck from the skin by pulling with both hands.

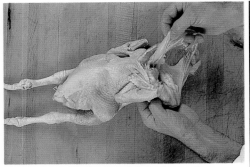

6 Separate the layer of skin from the trachea and crop (which is the first stomach) attached to it.

7 Placing the chicken on its back, pull the crop and skin up. Push your finger in along the backbone. On each side of it, run your finger up and down along the rib cage on each side and all around. The object here is to loosen the lungs in the area close to the neck opening.

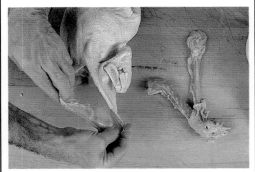

8 Cut the neck and sac at the opening. Notice how the skin of the neck is nice and clean inside and large enough so that it can be folded back onto the chicken back to cover the whole opening.

9 With the chicken on its back, cut near the tail to enlarge the opening, cutting away the little round pieces of meat on the tail.

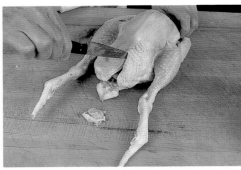

10 Then, using a knife, slit the skin in the center from the tail to the point of the breast, or sternum, to enlarge the opening.

11 Slip your finger inside and remove the 2 large pieces of fat, one on each side of the opening. Loosen completely and pull the entire insides out.

12 If the insides have been properly loosened, they will come out in one piece. To identify these parts, <u>starting at the bottom are the lungs, then the heart and the liver, and, finally, the gizzard, or the second stomach, with the fat around it.</u> Separate these organs to clean.

13 <u>Notice that on top of the liver there is a green bag. This is the gall bladder, and the green liquid bile inside is extremely bitter. Cut off the sac without breaking it.</u> If any of the liquid spills on top of the liver, cut away the areas that have been touched by the bile as they will be very bitter. If store-bought livers are green in spots, it means that bile has spilled there, so be sure to remove contaminated areas.

14 Remove the fat around the gizzard and <u>slit it on the fleshier side to open it.</u>

15 Open it and <u>remove the little sac inside full of gravel. Discard it.</u>

16 The chicken, completely eviscerated. In front, from left to right, the neck, the heart, the liver, the gizzard, and the fat. When you buy a chicken at the supermarket, you will find a package in the cavity with the liver, heart, and gizzard all cleaned.

POULTRY & GAME

GRATIN OF GRITS

5½ c. light chicken stock
1 tsp. salt
¼ tsp. pepper
1 c. grits
½ c. heavy cream
2 Tb. Parmesan cheese

SALAD

6 c. Boston lettuce
CHICKEN FAT DRESSING
1 small clove garlic, crushed and chopped
  fine (¼ tsp.)
¼ tsp. salt
¼ tsp. pepper
2 tsp. red wine vinegar
1 Tb. olive oil
2 Tb. rendered chicken fat (reserved from
  cooked chickens)
2 Tb. chicken gravy

GARNISH
Sprigs of parsley or watercress (optional)

❶ The chicken can, of course, be roasted according to the instructions here without the stuffing. However, the stuffing between the flesh and the skin of the chicken will keep the flesh moist and flavor it.

To make the stuffing: Cover the dried mushrooms with 1½ c. of lukewarm water and set aside for at least 1 hour. Remove and press the mushrooms between your palms to extract most of the water, reserving it for use in the sauce. If the pieces of mushroom are large, slice them into smaller pieces. Heat the oil and butter in a large skillet and, when hot, add the fresh mushrooms and sauté for 3 to 4 minutes, until most of the juice is released. Add the dried mushrooms, salt, pepper, garlic, and parsley, stir well to mix, and set aside to cool.

WILD MUSHROOM-AND-HERB-STUFFED CHICKEN

Stuffing a chicken usually means only one thing: filling the bird's cavities with a flavorful mixture. Here I have chosen a mixture of dried wild and fresh mushrooms and stuffed it not into the cavities but into the spaces created by separating the skin from the flesh. Stuffing chickens this way allows the flavors of the stuffing to permeate the meat better than when the stuffing is in the cavities, separated from the meat by bone. It also ensures meat that is not only flavorful but moist, for the stuffing provides an extra layer of insulation from the drying effects of the oven's heat.

Basting also enhances moisture retention, but in this recipe I baste the chickens only at the end of the cooking time, when they're turned breast side up. Up till that point, they are on their sides so their juices run into, rather than away from, the breast meat, and this — plus the oil and butter in the stuffing — makes the chickens essentially self-basting. The result is a tender, moist roast chicken that is excellent in combination with our gratin of grits and Boston lettuce salad with chicken fat vinaigrette.

Trussing serves a number of purposes: It keeps the stuffing in place, promotes even browning, and guarantees an attractive presentation. It also makes the chickens more compact when fitting several into a roasting pan is necessary. The trussing method preferred depends as much on whether the cook wants the neck and tail cavities closed during cooking as on purely aesthetic considerations for serving.

Yield: 8 servings

2 chickens, 2¾ to 3 lb. each
WILD MUSHROOM STUFFING
2 oz. sliced dried mushrooms, preferably
  cèpe (*Boletus edulis*)
1½ c. lukewarm water
8 oz. fresh mushrooms, sliced
1 Tb. olive oil
1 Tb. butter
¼ tsp. salt
¼ tsp. pepper
1 tsp. garlic, chopped
¼ c. chopped parsley
CHICKEN GRAVY
2 Tb. fat from cooking chicken
The liquid from the mushrooms
1 tsp. arrowroot mixed with 1 Tb. cognac
  and 1 Tb. water
Salt and pepper to taste

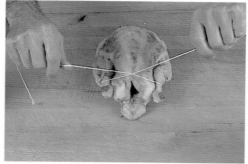

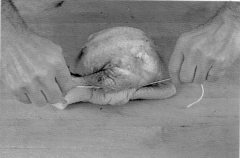

2 Lift the skin of the neck and cut on each side of the wishbone. With your thumb and index finger, pry the wishbone out (see page 171, step 3). Insert your finger between the skin and the flesh at the neck opening of the chicken and push your hand inside to loosen the skin, not only around the breast but also around the legs. Do not loosen the back skin too much, just the top surface and the sides. Repeat with the second chicken.

4 There are different ways to truss the chicken. The trussing will hold the stuffing inside and will also give a nice, plump shape to the breast, so it cooks evenly and looks better on the serving platter.

    Trussing Method 1, without trussing needle: Be sure to use a fairly thick cotton kitchen twine so it doesn't cut your fingers or the meat of the chicken. Slide the string under the tail of the chicken and around the tips of the drumsticks. Then cross the string above the chicken.

7 Tie a knot, making several loops instead of just one. The object is to make a knot that holds without someone's finger securing it. Secure further with a second knot. In this trussing technique, notice that the string does not go across the top of the breast of the chicken (which would mark the top and make it less attractive); it should just pass around the tips of the legs and extend along the sides and behind the neck and the wings.

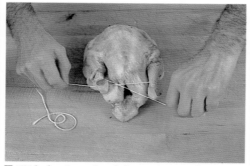

3 **To stuff the chickens:** Place a chicken standing on its tail in a bowl to secure it in the right position. Stuff by inserting the mushroom mixture between the skin and the flesh, pushing it evenly throughout the chicken, including the sides of the legs. Divide the mixture between the 2 chickens.

5 Slide both ends of the string under the tips of the drumsticks to create a figure 8.

8 **Trussing Method 2, with a trussing needle:** In the following 4 pictures, the trussing technique actually creates a design like an X with a closed bottom and top. Thread a long, thin trussing needle with string, and starting at the soft spot on the lower part of the thigh near the carcass, push your needle through, coming out on the other side in the middle of the leg, between the thigh and the drumstick. Pull through. →

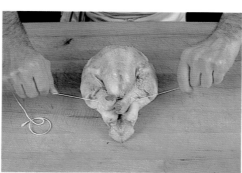

6 Pull the string together, which will tighten and close up the tail opening. Be sure the legs are pushed back snugly against the chicken and the breast is up. Bring the 2 pieces of string around the sides of the chicken until they join at the neck or next to the wing and tighten the string. It should secure the hanging skin of the neck and anchor behind the wing so it doesn't slide off.

POULTRY & GAME

161

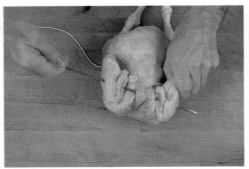

9 Place the chicken breast side down. With the trussing needle and twine, <u>go through the wing, the skin of the neck, and the opposite wing</u>. Pull through.

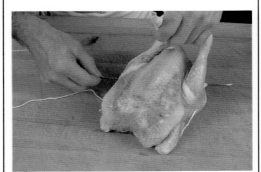

10 Turn the chicken over again onto its back and push the needle <u>from the center of the leg to the lower part of the thigh on the opposite side</u>, a reverse of what was done in photograph 8.

11 Be sure that the legs are pressed back against the breast of the chicken, <u>then come across above the leg with the needle and thread</u>. Secure with the same kind of knot used in step 7.

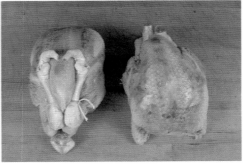

12 <u>Notice that the chicken on the left, with its legs folded, was trussed using the trussing needle, while the chicken on the right was trussed without it.</u>

13 Use a heavy aluminum or copper roasting pan for the best heat transfer and the best juice. If you think that the chicken may stick to your pan, <u>place 2 small pieces of buttered parchment paper in the bottom of the pan and place the chickens, on their sides, in the pan.</u> The paper will prevent sticking and the chickens will brown through it. Roasting the chickens on their sides brings their juices down into their breasts, and the only area exposed is the back, which does not have to be basted. As a result, the breast will stay moist.

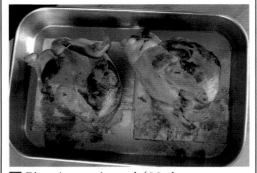

14 Place in a preheated 400-degree oven for 1 hour to 1 hour and 10 minutes, depending on the chickens' size, <u>turning them onto the other side after approxi-</u>

mately 30 minutes. At the end of the total cooking period, place the chickens on their backs and cook for another 10 minutes in the oven, basting at the beginning and the end of that 10-minute period.

15 Remove the roast chickens from the oven. <u>Notice that the chickens are placed on their sides or breast side down so the juices continue to flow into the breasts.</u> After a few minutes, remove the trussing string and keep the chickens warm on top of the stove or in a 140- to 150-degree oven. Do not cover them with aluminum foil or they will start steaming and taste reheated before long.

16 **To make the gravy:** Before discarding the pieces of parchment paper, be sure to scrape off and recover any solidified juices that may be clinging to them. If there is a lot of fat in the drippings, scoop it out, leaving only about 2 Tb. of fat to give taste to the gravy. Set the extra fat aside to use in the salad. Add the soaking liquid of the dry mushrooms to the roasting pan, place the pan on top of the stove, and stir with a flat spatula to loosen all the coagulated juices. <u>Strain the liquid into a small saucepan.</u> You should have about 1¾ c. of juice. Add 1 tsp. arrowroot mixed with 1 Tb. cognac and 1 Tb. water mixture to the sauce, stir, and bring it to a boil so it thickens. Season with salt and pepper and set aside.

17 **For the gratin of grits:** While the chicken is roasting, bring the 5½ c. of chicken stock, 1 tsp. salt, and ¼ tsp. pepper to a boil in a large saucepan and, when boiling, add 1 c. grits slowly while stirring. Cook 35 to 40 minutes over low heat, stirring occasionally so they don't stick. After 40 minutes of cooking, the mixture should be fairly thick but not pasty. This much can be done ahead.

Butter a 6-c. gratin dish and pour the grits mixture into it. At this point, the dish can be completed or set aside to be finished at serving time. If set aside for 15 to 30 minutes, the top will harden. When ready to complete cooking, pour the ½ c. cream on top of the surface, sprinkle with 2 Tb. Parmesan cheese, and place the gratin in the middle of the oven under the broiler (but not too close) for 10 minutes to brown the surface. Remember that if the gratin is kept too long before it is put into the oven, it will tend to harden too much and will have to be softened with a little milk.

18 **To make the salad:** Meanwhile, clean 6 c. of Boston lettuce by first removing the outer leaves that are very green or damaged. Then cut away the tops of the larger remaining leaves, which may be too bitter or strong tasting. Cut on each side of the center rib of each of these larger leaves and discard the ribs with the tops. Remember this is only necessary with the larger, tougher leaves. As you get closer to the center of the head, the leaves get tenderer. For the next layer of leaves, remove and discard the tops of the leaves and cut them in half through the center of the rib, which is already more tender. If the leaves are too big, you can break them into smaller pieces. Then wash the greens in a lot of cold water, being sure to lift them up from the water and not squeeze or press them in any way, as they bruise easily. Dry in a salad dryer.

Toss the lettuce with the dressing at the last moment before serving, as it is a tender salad and will wilt quickly because of the acid in the vinegar. It should be served cool but not cold, and the leaves should be well drained of water so there is no extra liquid to dilute the dressing. Combine ¼ tsp. each crushed garlic, salt, and pepper, 2 tsp. red wine vinegar, 1 Tb. olive oil, and 2 Tb. of the fat from the cooked chicken (but not the chicken gravy). Toss the salad in the dressing, place in a salad bowl, and sprinkle the chicken gravy on top. Serve immediately.

19 At serving time, place the roasted chickens on a large platter with some of the sauce on top and around them. Decorate the cavity opening with parsley or watercress, if desired, and serve immediately with the gratin of grits and the salad.

A LEANER VERSION

Omit the oil and butter in the stuffing. Place ¼ c. water with the mushrooms in a skillet to start cooking and proceed according to the recipe. Stuff, truss, and roast the chicken according to the recipe. In step 16, scoop out and discard all the fat or as much as you can retrieve from the drippings. Finish the sauce according to the recipe. Omit the gratin of grits. Salad: Omit the 2 Tb. chicken fat and the 1 Tb. olive oil and replace with 3 Tb. of the chicken gravy, a total of 5 Tb. for the salad. Proceed according to the recipe.

POULTRY & GAME

ALTERNATIVE METHOD FOR SERVING CHICKEN

As an alternative to carving the chicken in the dining room, you can also carve it in the kitchen and re-form it on a platter for serving in the dining room.

1 With the cooked chicken on its side, insert a fork into the center of the leg. Cut with the point of a sharp knife around the skin and lift up the leg. It will break at the hip joint. Hold the chicken on the table with the flat side of the knife and pull the leg up. It will separate. Repeat on the other side to remove the other leg. Then, with the chicken still on its side . . .

2 . . . cut at the shoulder joint and down along the breast. Insert your knife into the shoulder at the thickest part of the breast and pull up. The wing should come off with a part of the breast on it. Repeat on the other side.

3 The only part left on the carcass is the center of the breast, the sternum. Cut by the wishbone and push the breast off; it should separate from the sternum bone.

4 Place the carcass of the chicken on a platter and replace the center breast on top of the bone.

5 Place the 2 wings and breast pieces on each side, holding them with your fingers.

6 Then wedge in place the 2 legs, which will hold the pieces together.

7 Place some of the sauce around the re-formed chicken and garnish with parsley and watercress. Serve immediately.

BALLOTINE OF CHICKEN LUCETTE

The three <u>ballotines</u> depicted here are stuffed with vegetables. In addition to being quite colorful, they are inexpensive and very tasty. Try one of our variations below or invent your own filling.

This technique for the boning out of the chicken is used also when making a standard <u>galantine</u>, which is a cold pâté with the forcemeat wrapped in the skin and the meat of the chicken. Although the chicken could be roasted directly, steaming it first for a few minutes adds moisture, firms up the meat, and makes it easier to handle for the roasting.

The red pepper purée is the softest of the three mixtures and, therefore, the hardest to handle. But, with a little care, the chicken can be held securely in a small piece of aluminum foil.

A good accompaniment for this dish is the Swiss Chard au Gratin on page 169, which can be prepared while the chicken is roasting.

Yield: 12 servings (3 chickens)

3 chickens, 3 lb. each
¾ tsp. salt
⅜ tsp. freshly ground black pepper

RED PEPPER FILLING

1 large red pepper (about ¾ lb.)
1 tsp. potato starch dissolved in 1 Tb. cold water
Dash salt and freshly ground black pepper
1 Tb. chopped chives

SPINACH AND CHEESE FILLING

1 Tb. butter
1 tsp. chopped garlic (about 2 or 3 cloves)
½ lb. spinach, stems removed, cleaned
¼ tsp. salt
1 c. Fontina cheese, grated

MUSHROOM AND ONION FILLING

1 oz. dried shiitake mushrooms (about 12 pieces), soaked in 2 c. warm water
4 oz. cultivated mushrooms
1 Tb. butter
2 c. sliced onions
¼ tsp. salt
Dash freshly ground black pepper

BROWN GARLIC SAUCE

36–40 cloves garlic, peeled (3 per person)
2 tsp. soy sauce
Juice of the chicken
2 tsp. potato starch dissolved in 1 Tb. water
Salt and freshly ground black pepper to taste

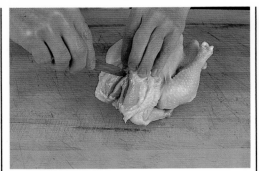

1 Cut the chicken wings, leaving only the first joint at the shoulder. Keep the trimmings for stock. Lift up the skin by the neck and slide a small, sharp paring knife on each side of the wishbone, which forms a pointed triangle. Using your thumb and forefinger, push the bone out, prying at the point where the bone is held in the sternum, or breastbone.

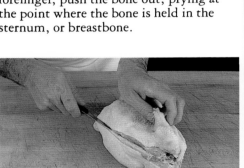

2 Place the chicken on its side and make an incision through the skin of the back from the neck to the tail.

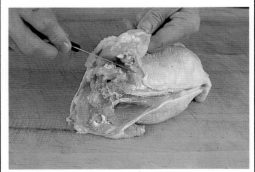

3 With the chicken on its side, lift up the skin at the shoulder joint. Move the wing and you will notice that there is a joint there. Place your knife where the joint is and cut, wiggling the knife so it cuts through the joint. Repeat on the other side at the shoulder.

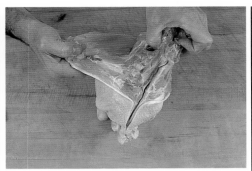

4 Holding the chicken carcass securely through the bone of the shoulder, with the thumb and forefinger of one hand, take hold of the wing at the joint with the other hand and pull. It will come off the bone on the whole side of the carcass in the back. Repeat on the other side.

5 The meat is still attached to the bone at the breastbone. Place two fingers on each side of the bone and pull down. The chicken is now completely free from the top and is holding only at the joint of the leg.

6 With the chicken on its side, cut off the little oyster of meat next to the joint of the hip.

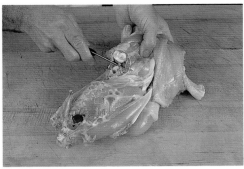

7 Open up the leg and crack at the joint of the hip, then cut through the joint to sever the large sinew. Now pull the leg free from the carcass.

8 Repeat on the other side and, finally, pull the whole carcass free of the meat.

9 The only things left attached to the carcass are the fillets on each side of the breastbone. Slide your thumb or finger underneath and pull them off.

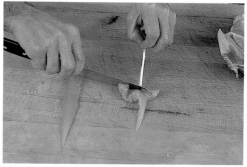

10 Holding one of the fillets flat on the table, with a knife scrape the meat free from the sinew that runs through the fillet, pushing the meat off so the sinew comes out in one place. Repeat with the other fillet.

11 To remove the leg bone, cut around the tip of the thigh bone so it can be held. Holding the blade of the knife perpendicular to the bone, start scraping the meat down off the bone until you get down to the joint. Cut around the joint with the knife and, again, scrape the bone of the drumstick down to the tip of the leg.

12 Break the bone at the end from the inside so the outside skin is not torn and the knuckle at the end of the drumstick is left intact. (This end knuckle will be trimmed off after cooking because the meat would shrink if cut before cooking.) To remove the wing bone, cut around the joint where it is held and pull the bone off.

Then prepare the 3 different fillings.

For the red pepper filling: Clean 1 large pepper and cut it into 1-in. pieces. Cover with cold water, bring to a boil, and boil for about 5 minutes. Drain well and, while still warm, place in the bowl of a food processor. Purée as fine as you can and then put through a food mill fitted with a fine screen or push through a strainer to remove the little pieces of skin from the pepper. Place the purée in a saucepan on the stove and cook it for about 7 to 8 minutes, stirring, until it thickens. It should be the consistency of tomato paste and you should have approximately ½ to ¾ c. Add 1 tsp. potato starch dissolved in 1 Tb. water and bring to a boil, stirring. Add the salt and pepper and mix well. Set aside to cool. When cool, stir in the chives.

For the spinach and cheese filling: Place the 1 Tb. butter in a skillet and heat until it turns a brown color. Add the 1 tsp. chopped garlic, stir about 5 seconds, and add ½ lb. of spinach, just wet from being washed so there is enough moisture to create steam. Sauté for about 2 to 3 minutes, add ¼ tsp. salt, and set aside to cool.

For the mushroom and onion filling: When the 1 oz. dried mushrooms have softened in the 2 c. water, drain them (reserving the liquid) and cut away and discard the part of the root where there may be dirt. Chop the mushrooms in the food processor along with the cultivated mushrooms. Melt the 1 Tb. butter in a large skillet and, when hot, add the 2 c. sliced onions. Sauté for about 5 minutes over medium to high heat, until the onions are nicely browned. Add the mushrooms, ¼ tsp. salt, and a dash of pepper and sauté for 2 minutes longer, until the water released from the mushrooms evaporates and the mixture sizzles again and is dry. Let cool.

13 Spread the 3 chickens out on the table, sprinkle each with ¼ tsp. of the salt and ⅛ tsp. of the pepper, and spread each chicken with a different stuffing. After the spinach mixture has been spread on the chicken, top it with the c. of cheese. Place each chicken's fillets on top of the stuffing. Start folding the chickens, bringing back the skin to try to re-form each one into its natural shape.

14 Place a piece of aluminum foil over the seam on the back of the chicken stuffed with the soft red pepper filling. Then, turn the chicken breast side up so the aluminum foil is underneath, helping to hold the shape.

15 To truss the chickens: Cross the legs of one of the chickens and attach together with kitchen twine.

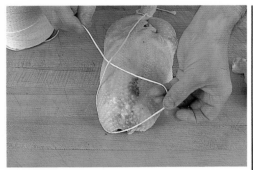

16 Tie the chicken with a double knot at the drum end. <u>Make a loop at the opposite end</u>, then slide it underneath to within ½ in. of the drum end and pull to tighten the loop (called the half-hitch).

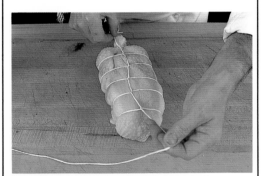

17 Repeat the loops down the whole <u>length of the chicken.</u>

18 When the chicken is secure on top, roll it gently until it is back side up, and secure it on the back also, <u>finishing by tying the twine at the crossing of the legs where the tying began</u>. Notice that the skin on the back is overlapping to hold the stuffing inside. Repeat with the other chickens. Place each chicken on a plate (not necessary if there is aluminum foil underneath) and place in a steamer basket. If you have a three-layer steamer, you can put 1 chicken in each of the layers. Bring 4 c. of water to a boil in the steamer. When boiling, place the chickens over the boiling water, cover, and steam for about 10 minutes.

Remove the chickens, reserving the liquid left (about 1½ c.) for the sauce. Place the chickens in a roasting pan, making little holes in the aluminum foil surrounding the one with the red pepper filling so the juices that are released will flow into the pan. Place in a 425-degree oven for 30 minutes. Baste with the pan juices every 10 minutes.

19 <u>Remove the chickens from the roasting pan</u> (a lot of juice will have accumulated in the pan) and discard the string and aluminum foil, since the chickens are set by now. Keep the chickens warm in a 150-degree oven or in a warm place on top of the stove. Strain the juice into a saucepan, adding the juice reserved from the steaming process, and let it rest a few minutes until the fat comes to the surface. Skim off as much fat as possible. Add the reserved mushroom-soaking water to the juice also. (You should have approximately 2 c. of liquid – if you have more, reduce to 2 c.; if you have less, add enough water to make 2 c.)

For the sauce: Cover the 36 to 40 cloves of garlic with cold water. Bring to a boil and simmer gently for 5 minutes. Drain. Add the blanched garlic and 2 tsp. soy sauce to the juice of the chicken, bring to a boil, and boil gently for 10 minutes. Add 2 tsp. potato starch dissolved in 1 Tb. water to the sauce to thicken it. Season with salt and pepper to taste.

20 Arrange the *ballotines* on a serving platter. Cut a slice about ¾ in. thick from the end of each and arrange in the front. Spoon the garlic cloves and sauce around them, coat with the sauce, and serve immediately with the Swiss Chard au Gratin (next recipe).

A LEANER VERSION

Spinach filling: Omit the cheese and reduce the amount of butter from 1 Tb. to ½ Tb. Proceed according to the recipe.

Mushroom and onion filling: Reduce the 1 Tb. butter to ½ Tb. and proceed according to the recipe. Steam and roast the chicken as indicated in the recipe. Be sure to remove most of the fat from the cooking juices (step 19). In step 20, cut the <u>ballotines</u> into slices and remove the skin before serving.

SWISS CHARD AU GRATIN

Although the whole Swiss chard can be used, green and white together, the white is usually served cut into pieces in a gratin or around a roast with the juice while the green by itself is used in soups or made into a purée, as with spinach.

In my recipe below, I make a purée of the green and I prepare the white ribs in a cream sauce and combine the two, although either recipe could be served by itself.

Yield: 6 servings
2¼ lb. Swiss chard (1¼ lb. ribs, 1 lb. greens)
1 Tb. lemon juice
TO PREPARE THE GREENS
2 Tb. butter
¼ tsp. salt
⅛ tsp. freshly ground black pepper
TO PREPARE THE WHITE RIBS
1 Tb. butter
1 Tb. flour
¾ c. cold milk
½ c. heavy cream
½ tsp. salt
⅛ tsp. freshly ground black pepper
½ c. plus 2 Tb. grated white Vermont-type Cheddar cheese or Swiss cheese

1 Separate the ribs from the leaves: If the chard leaves are small, cut the ribs where the greens begin. If they are large, cut in a triangular way to remove more of the rib from the green.

2 When all the green and white have been separated, cut the ribs lengthwise into equal pieces about ½ to ¾ in. wide.

3 There is a layer of skin on both sides of the rib that should be removed, especially in older specimens. First, with a sharp knife cut three-quarters of the way through the ribs crosswise at 2-in. intervals. Then break into pieces at each cut and pull the rib from the uncut layer of skin underneath. The skin will separate from one side. Remove the skin from the other side by using a knife to separate it from the rib along one edge and then pulling it off the rib. As you clean the ribs, place them in a qt. of water with 1 Tb. of lemon juice to prevent them from discoloring. They should be about 2 in. long by ½ in. wide.

To prepare the greens: When all the pieces have been cleaned and separated (you should have about 1¼ lb. of ribs and 1 lb. of greens), place ½ in. of water in a stainless-steel pan and bring it to a boil. Add the greens, return to the boil, and cook for 4 to 5 minutes. Then drain, cool under cold water, and press with your hands to extract some of the water. Place in a food processor and reduce to a purée (you should have 1½ c.). Heat the 2 Tb. of butter for the greens and, when the butter begins to turn brown, add the purée of green chard, salt, and pepper, and mix

enough so the purée gets hot. Arrange in the bottom of a 6-c. gratin dish.

To prepare the ribs: Place the ribs in their lemon water on the heat and bring to a boil. Boil for about 5 minutes, until just tender. Drain.

4 Melt the butter in a saucepan, add the flour, mix well with a whisk, and cook for about 10 to 20 seconds. Add the cold milk. Bring the mixture to a boil, stirring with the whisk until it thickens. When it boils, add the cream, salt, pepper, and ½ c. of the cheese. Mix well and bring to a boil. Combine with the Swiss chard ribs.

Pour the mixture on top of the green purée, sprinkle with the remaining cheese, and place under the broiler for about 5 minutes, until nicely browned all over.

POULTRY & GAME

CHICKEN BREASTS WITH CHERVIL MOUSSE AND VEGETABLE-STUFFED PEPPERS

Stuffed chicken breasts make an elegant and flavorful dish for a special party. The mousse used to stuff the breasts is made with the meat from the legs. If all the leg meat of the 3 chickens is used (approximately 1½ lb.) as done below, there will be some mousse left over. The extra mousse can be formed into dumplings and served as a garnish for soups or as a filling for patty shells. It can also be cooked in small ramekin dishes or soufflé or baba molds and served hot or cold. If you prefer to make only the exact amount needed for the recipe here, cut the ingredients by a third (1 lb. leg meat instead of 1½ lb.).

The mousse can be flavored with other types of herbs, mushrooms, or different spices. The stuffed breast can be served with the pan drippings only rather than the cognac sauce served here. The appearance of the dish is enhanced by little rounds of red pepper used as a decoration.

The poblano peppers used in the vegetable-stuffed pepper recipe are sometimes mild and

sometimes quite hot. Using them or not is a matter of personal taste, and if you prefer a mild pepper, use the elongated sweet green peppers, sometimes called Italian peppers, instead. The vegetable stuffing is delicate and lean, ideal to serve with a dish as rich as these stuffed chicken breasts.

The chickens can be boned ahead, stuffed, and sautéed at the last minute. The stuffed peppers can also be prepared ahead and cooked at the last minute. Two-and-one-half-lb. chickens yield fairly large portions and breasts of larger chickens will be too copious for one person.

Yield: 6 servings

3 chickens, 2½ lb. each

FOR THE MOUSSE

1½ lb. chicken leg meat
⅓ c. chopped ice
1 c. chervil, loose
1 c. heavy cream
1 tsp. salt
¼ tsp. freshly ground black pepper

CHICKEN STOCK

4 lb. chicken bones
5 qt. cold water
1 large or 2 small leeks (If you have green of leek, use it and reserve the white for another use.)

1 large onion, cut into eighths
2 carrots, cut into large pieces
2 ribs celery or 2 c. of the leafy ends of celery (see Braised Celery, page 303)
3 bay leaves
½ tsp. dried thyme leaves
½ tsp. whole peppercorns

FOR THE VEGETABLE-STUFFED PEPPERS

8 green and red poblano peppers (about 3 oz. each)

STUFFING

1 Tb. butter
1 Tb. corn oil
1 c. ¼-in.-diced onions
1 c. ¼-in.-diced carrots
1 c. water
2 c. cauliflower florets (cut into ½- to 1-in. pieces)
1 c. ½-in.-diced zucchini
½ tsp. finely chopped garlic
¼ tsp. freshly ground black pepper
¼ tsp. salt
2 Tb. olive oil

FOR SAUTÉING THE CHICKEN BREASTS

¼ tsp. salt
2 Tb. butter

COGNAC SAUCE

1 c. strong chicken stock
½ c. dry white wine
1 c. heavy cream
1 tsp. potato starch dissolved in 1 Tb. water
1 Tb. cognac
¼ tsp. freshly ground black pepper
¼ tsp. salt

GARNISH

1 red pepper, peeled with a vegetable peeler (see Deep-Fried Eggs Julia, page 47), cut into at least 12 small rounds

1 Cut off each wing close to the shoulder joint, leaving only a tiny piece of bone on the body for looks. The wings can be used in stew or stock. (See step 16.)

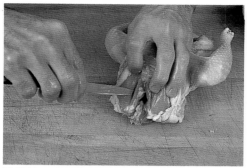

2 Slide a knife along each side of the wishbone. Insert your thumb and finger to loosen the wishbone and pry out.

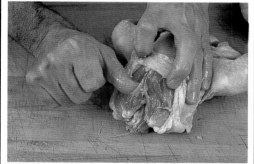

3 Slide your thumb behind the wishbone and pull it out.

4 Cut along the breastbone on each side, slicing the skin of the neck in half. The object here is to divide the chicken in half and keep the longest possible pieces of skin. Place the chicken on its side and cut the skin alongside the backbone.

5 Lift up the skin at the shoulder joint and place your knife on the joint where the wing is attached to the body. (You can find out where the joint socket is by moving the little piece of wing tip that remains.) Cut right through the joint of the shoulder.

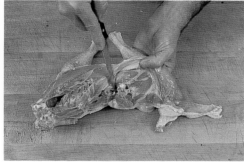

6 Grab the joint of the shoulder and the wing stump and pull, holding the carcass flat on the table with one hand and pulling with the other until the meat comes off the bone as far as the thigh joint. Remove the little oyster of meat near the back and break the leg-thigh at the joint, which will open. Cut through the joint (there is a large sinew there) and pull this half of the chicken completely loose.

7 Separate the leg from the breast, being sure to cut the skin so that more of the skin stays on the breast than the leg. Repeat with the other side of the chicken. The only pieces of meat left now are the little fillets still attached to the breast. Slide your finger behind the fillets and pull them off the carcass on both sides. Remove the sinew from the fillets (see Ballotine of Chicken Lucette, step 10, page 167).

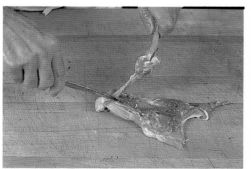

8 Lift up the skin of the breast all around, using the point of the knife if necessary, so the skin is completely loosened except where it is attached at the wing stub. If there is a lot of fat on the inside of the skin, scrape most of it off with the flat edge of the knife blade.

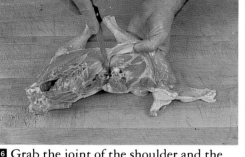

9 Pull the skin off the leg and cut to loosen first the bone of the thigh and then the drumstick bone. Remove both bones in one piece.

10 Holding the little tendons in the drumstick with a towel so they won't slide, scrape with a knife to remove as much meat from the tendons as possible. Each breast with the fillet will weigh approximately 6 oz., and the meat of each leg will weigh about 4 oz., making 20 oz. of meat from the whole chicken, with the rest of the weight being in bones (4 lb. of bones, necks, gizzards from the 3 chickens).

11 **For the mousse:** Place the 1½ lb. of chicken leg meat and the ⅓ c. ice in a large food processor with the 1 c. chervil. Process for about 10 seconds, clean the bowl all around with a rubber spatula, pushing the scrapings back into the mixture in the bottom of the bowl. Process 10 seconds more, clean the sides of the bowl again, and process another 10 seconds.

12 Add the 1 c. cream in a slow stream along with 1 tsp. salt and ¼ tsp. pepper while the machine is running, and process briefly to mix. Transfer to a bowl. Notice the texture is smooth and slightly spongy. Refrigerate until ready to use.

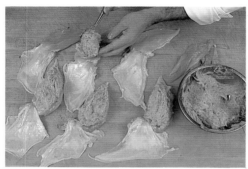

13 Place the chicken breasts skin side up on the work surface, pull back the skin, and spoon about ½ c. of the mousse on top of each breast. Arrange one of the pieces of fillet meat on one side of each of the breasts, pressing it into the mousse.

14 Bring the skin back on top of the mousse so it encases the whole surface.

15 Hold a stuffed breast skin side down in the palm of one hand and try to bring the edges of the skin around to the underside of the breasts. The skin will not wrap all around. Repeat with each breast. Refrigerate, skin side down, covered, until serving time.

16 **Make the chicken stock:** Place the 4 lb. of chicken bones in a stockpot and cover with 5 qt. of cold water; bring to a boil over high heat. During the first half hour of cooking most of the scum will come to the surface. Skim it off with a skimmer and discard it. As no more scum rises, some of the fat will come to the surface; scoop it off with a ladle as it appears and discard it. After the first half hour of cooking, add 1 large or 2 small leeks, 1 large onion, 2 cut-up carrots, 2 ribs celery, 3 bay leaves, ½ tsp. each thyme leaves and peppercorns, and continue cooking, uncovered, at a very gentle boil for 2½ hours. Drain through a large strainer into another pot. You will have 2 qt. of strong chicken stock. Let cool and skim any additional fat from the surface.

17 **For the peppers:** Arrange 8 peppers on a broiler pan and place them under a hot broiler, no more than 1 in. from the heat source, turning until the peppers blister all around, from 13 to 15 minutes. Immediately place the peppers in plastic bags. Close the bag and set aside for 10 minutes. Steaming in their own heat in the plastic bag will help the peppers release their skin.

18 Remove the peppers from the bag and peel off the skin; it will come off fairly easily. Tear the peppers open carefully, scoop out the seeds, and scrape off the membranes on the inside. Try, if possible, to leave the stem of the pepper in place as it looks more attractive this way for serving.

19 **For the stuffing:** Heat 1 Tb. each butter and corn oil in a skillet. When hot, add 1 c. each diced onions and carrots. Sauté approximately 1 minute and add 1 c. of water. Cover, bring to a boil, and cook 3 minutes. Add 2 c. cauliflower and 1 c. zucchini, cover, and continue cooking for another 3 minutes, until most of the water has evaporated. Remove the lid, add ½ tsp. chopped garlic, ¼ tsp. each pepper and salt, and continue cooking until most of the water has evaporated and the mixture is sizzling. Cool to lukewarm.

Stuff each of the peppers with approximately 2 to 3 Tb. of the stuffing, exercising as much care as possible, but don't worry if the peppers split a little. Fold the peppers back on top of the stuffing to reconstruct them and place in a gratin dish or casserole. Sprinkle with 2 Tb. olive oil, cover with a piece of parchment paper, and place in a 400-degree for 15 minutes.

20 Meanwhile, **sauté the chicken breasts:** Sprinkle the chicken with ¼ tsp. salt and heat 1 Tb. butter each in 2 skillets, preferably non-stick. When hot, add the chicken skin side down and sauté for about 4 minutes over high high. Cover, reduce the heat, and cook gently for 10 minutes. Note that the chicken is cooked only skin side down so the meat doesn't toughen. Remove the cover from the chicken and continue cooking until the juices are reduced and the chicken is sizzling again in the fat. The chicken should be nicely browned. Remove to a platter.

21 Remove the peppers from the oven, brush them with the oil from the cooking dish, arrange in a serving dish, and set aside until the chicken is ready to serve.

22 In the pan in which the chicken was cooked there will be a lot of fat in the drippings because of the skin. Boil down the drippings until the juice of the chicken crystallizes on the bottom of the skillet and creates a solidified glaze and the fat breaks down and is clear on top. Let it sit for 1 to 2 minutes and then pour off and discard most of the fat. Add ⅓ c. of water to the remaining juice, bring it to a boil, and strain through a sieve. Reduce again until you have about 3 Tb. of concentrated juice (see glace de viande, page 7). →

POULTRY & GAME

A LEANER VERSION

Stuffed peppers: Reduce the amount of corn oil from 1 Tb. to ½ Tb. and the olive oil from 2 Tb. to 1 Tb. Omit the butter and proceed according to the recipe.

23 For the sauce: Bring the 1 c. chicken stock and ½ c. white wine to a boil and reduce to 1 c. Add 1 c. cream, bring to the boil again, and add 1 tsp. potato starch dissolved in 1 Tb. water. Add 1 Tb. cognac and ¼ tsp. each pepper and salt and strain through a fine sieve.

For the pepper garnish: With a vegetable peeler, remove the skin from as much of the pepper as possible. Cut the pepper into pieces and remove the seeds. Using the ½-in. tip of a pastry bag tube, cut out circles, splitting them in half crosswise if too thick.

24 Arrange the chicken breasts on a serving platter, pour the sauce over them, and sprinkle glace of chicken (the concentrated juice left in the pan) on each.

25 Garnish with the red pepper rounds for color and serve with the stuffed peppers.

CHICKEN JEAN-CLAUDE WITH WAFFLE POTATOES

Yield: 6 servings

3 chickens, 2½ to 3 lb. each

ALMOND STUFFING

1 Tb. butter

3 scallions, chopped (about 1 c.)

1 3-oz. piece country-style ham or prosciutto, coarsely chopped (½ c.)

4 oz. chanterelle or cultivated mushrooms, cut into ¼-in. dice (1½ c.)

⅓ c. slivered almonds, roasted in a 400-degree oven until light brown, about 6 to 8 minutes

4 oz. mozzarella cheese (preferably raw buffalo-milk mozzarella), chopped or coarsely grated

⅛ tsp. freshly ground black pepper

FOR THE CHICKEN BREASTS

6 chicken breasts

½ tsp. salt

2 Tb. butter

¼ c. chopped shallots

FOR THE SAUCE

Drippings from the chicken breasts and legs

½ tsp. potato starch dissolved in 1 Tb. water

Salt and freshly ground pepper to taste

GARNISH

1 bunch watercress

FOR THE WAFFLE POTATOES

3 large Idaho potatoes, peeled (about 1½ lb.)

5 c. corn or cottonseed oil (1 in. deep in skillet)

Dash salt

The dark meat of chicken — the drumsticks and thighs — always takes longer to cook than the breasts. Moreover, when the skin is left on, the cooking time has to be increased further. In this recipe, the chickens are each separated into 4 pieces — the 2 legs and the 2 breast halves. The breasts are boned and skinned so they require only a minimum of cooking. The skin is left on the boned legs, which are stuffed and cooked like small *ballotines*. The breasts and legs are cooked in different ways and each is a distinctly different recipe that can be made on its own. But here the two recipes are combined and served with waffle potatoes.

The waffle potatoes are cut on a special piece of equipment called a *mandoline*, which has a corrugated blade that cuts the potatoes into waffle-like slices. During the cooking process, the oil goes through the little holes created and makes a dry, crunchy potato. If the waffle potatoes are served with the chicken recipes here, they can be made first, as they keep well, like potato chips.

Corn and cottonseed oils withstand high temperatures, do not give a taste to the food, and are ideal for frying potatoes as well as other fried foods. The oil should be cleaned and strained after each use. After many uses, the oil eventually breaks down, gets foamlike, and does not produce a crisp, dry product any longer. It should then be discarded. In professional kitchens, the fresh oil is used for delicate things such as apple fritters and then goes on to be used for frying potatoes or other vegetables. Next, it may be used for croquettes or breaded foods and, finally, as the last use, for fish, such as the Fish Friture (page 98) or the Fried Whiting Colbert (page 149). The sequence cannot be reversed; it has to start with delicate things, like fruit, that cannot be fried in an oil in which fish has been cooked.

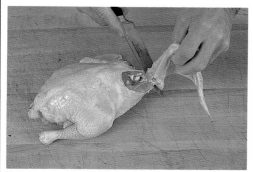

1 Remove the wings of the chickens at the joint of the shoulder, cutting and prying your knife into the joint. The wings are not used here, but save them to sauté with rice, make into stew, or use in chicken soup or stock. →

2 To remove the chicken legs, place the chicken on its side and lift the leg. The weight of the chicken will help with the boning out. <u>With the point of a sharp knife, cut the skin all around the leg.</u> The leg, which is attached to the body only by the skin, will separate by itself but still be attached at the joint of the thigh. Cut off the oyster (the roundish piece of meat on the back of the carcass).

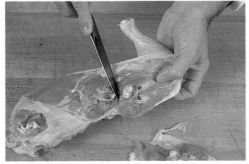

3 Hold the leg at the thigh bone and crack it open to expose the joint. <u>Cut right through the joint of the femur and pelvis, through the large sinew,</u> and pull the leg off; it will come off in one piece. Chop off the tip of the drumstick.

4 Remove the wishbone from the breast (see page 171) and pull the skin off the breast. With the chicken on its back, cut alongside the breastbone on each side to separate both breast halves. Place the chicken on its side and cut at the joint of the shoulder; <u>grasp the end of the breast while holding the carcass firmly on the table and pull</u>; the breast will come off in one piece. Repeat on the other side with the other leg and breast. The only thing left on the carcass now will be the 2 fillets; slide your finger behind the fillets and lift them out. Remove the little sinew from the fillets (see page 167) and place them back inside the breasts where they belong.

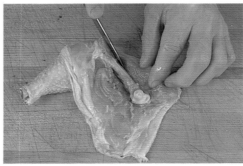

5 To bone the leg, <u>cut on each side of the thigh bone</u> and slide your knife underneath, separating the thigh bone from the meat.

6 <u>Hold the thigh bone and cut all around the joint at the knee to loosen.</u>

7 <u>Scrape down the drumstick bone and pull it off.</u> The leg is now boned. Loosen the meat from the skin of the thigh area. The meat can be pulled more toward the center with the layer of skin all around and used as a wrapper.

8 **Make the stuffing for the legs:** Melt the 1 Tb. butter in a skillet. When hot, add the 3 chopped scallions and ½ c. chopped ham or prosciutto, and sauté about 1 minute, until the scallions are wilted. Add the 1½ c. mushrooms and sauté for a minute longer. Remove from the heat and add the ⅓ c. roasted almonds, 4 oz. chopped mozzarella cheese, and ⅛ tsp. pepper. Taste for seasoning. The addition of salt depends on the saltiness of the prosciutto. Stir and mash the mixture with a fork to mix. Divide the stuffing among the 6 legs, <u>pushing some of it inside the drumsticks with your fingers</u>.

9 Fold in the sides of the thigh meat to enclose the stuffing and reconstruct the leg into its original shape. Overlap the skin slightly, if possible, to hold in the stuffing.

10 Place each leg in a piece of aluminum foil about 9 in. long and 12 in. wide. Wrap tightly to enclose, pinching the ends of the foil to seal the packages.

11 Arrange the packages in a roasting pan and place in a preheated 400-degree oven for approximately 30 minutes. Let cool about 10 minutes, until they can be handled. Open the packages carefully while the mixture is still warm so the foil doesn't stick to the skin of the chicken. Unwrap and reserve the accumulated juices.

12 Arrange the little *ballotines* in a roasting pan with their juices and place about 4 to 5 in. from the heat source under a broiler for about 5 to 10 minutes so they brown nicely on top. During this time, cook the breasts of chicken.

13 **For the chicken breasts:** Sprinkle the chicken breasts with ½ tsp. salt and melt 2 Tb. butter in a large skillet. When hot, add the 6 chicken breasts, flesh side up, and sauté over medium to high heat for about 2 minutes on one side.

14 Turn the breasts and sauté about 2 minutes on the other side; they won't be quite cooked but, at that point, sprinkle the ¼ c. chopped shallots on top, cover the pan with a lid, and set aside on the corner of the stove so the meat continues to cook in its own heat for about 5 minutes while the legs are browning under the broiler.

To make the sauce: Combine the drippings from the breasts and the legs in a saucepan, bring to a boil, and add ½ tsp. potato starch dissolved in 1 Tb. water. Bring back to the boil and add salt and pepper, if needed.

15 **For the waffle potatoes:** If a mandoline is not available, the potatoes can be sliced thin into potato chips in a food processor or by hand and fried and served as potato chips.

Peel 3 large potatoes and wash under cold water. The mandoline blade should be open about ⅛ in. beyond the thickness of the ridges so that the slices, when cut, don't divide into strips but hold together. Holding a potato in the palm of your hand, slide it in one direction over the blade. Notice that the fingers are pointing to the left side of the picture.

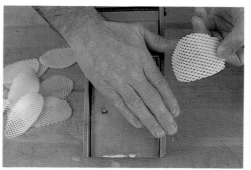

16 Bring the potato up and pivot your hand 45 degrees so the ridges of the potato are now perpendicular to the blade and your fingers are pointing in the opposite direction. Slice the potato at this angle across the blade. Keep cutting, alternating left to right after each slice, to create the desired design. The potatoes should be criss-crossing on each slice. →

17 Wash the potatoes in cold water after slicing and dry well (in a salad dryer, if available). If the potatoes are not well dried, they will splatter excessively in the oil. Pour 1 in. of oil into a skillet and heat to 400 to 425 degrees. Add about half the potatoes (about 25 to 30 slices) to the oil and cook, stirring occasionally with a skimmer, until nicely browned, approximately 3 minutes. Remove to a cookie sheet covered with paper towels. Add a dash of salt. Just like potato chips, these potatoes are served at room temperature or just lukewarm.

18 For each portion, arrange a half breast of chicken with a stuffed leg on a plate and spoon about 1½ to 2 Tb. of the natural gravy around them. Garnish with a little bunch of watercress in the center. Serve with the waffle potatoes.

1 rib celery, cut into 1-in. pieces
3 cloves garlic, crushed, with skin on
2 Tb. tomato paste
1 bay leaf
1 tsp. thyme leaves

HONEY SAUCE

¼ c. sugar
¼ c. red wine vinegar
Reduced duck stock
1 Tb. honey
¼ tsp. salt
⅛ tsp. freshly ground black pepper
½ tsp. potato starch dissolved in 1 Tb.
  water, if needed

SWEET POTATOES IN HONEY

3 lb. sweet potatoes (2 large or 3 small)
2 Tb. butter
¼ tsp. salt
⅛ tsp. freshly ground black pepper
3 Tb. honey

GLAZED SHALLOTS

35 shallots (¾ to 1 lb.), peeled (4 per
  person)
1 Tb. butter
1 Tb. sugar
¼ tsp. salt
1½ c. water

BRAISED DUCK WITH GLAZED SHALLOTS AND HONEY SWEET POTATOES

In this recipe, the duck can be cooked several days ahead and re-sautéed at the last moment. By being cooked in its own fat, which doesn't get absorbed into the meat, the duck meat doesn't dry out or get stringy. The result is a very moist, tender, delicately flavorful duck.

If the pieces of duck are salted and allowed to cure in the salt for a couple of days prior to cooking and then cooked in duck fat in a low oven for a couple of hours, the result is <u>confit</u>, or preserved duck. The pieces are then stored in their own fat in a cold cellar and used throughout the winter in famous dishes, such as cassoulet, the bean dish from the southwest of France.

In my recipe, the rich reduced stock is defatted and flavored with an acidic sweet mixture made of vinegar and sugar. Large Long Island–type ducks are ideal for this preparation. The fat remaining after the duck has been sautéed can be used for other recipes, like the Leek and Mushroom Pie (page 247), or for sautéing potatoes or other vegetables.

The technique used to glaze shallots here can be used as well for glazing pearl onions or pieces of white turnips or carrots. The sweet potato makes a nice accompaniment and, like the shallots, can be served with most roasted meat or poultry. The cracklings are ideal sprinkled on a salad. Preferably, they should be eaten the same day they are made, since their nutty taste disappears after one day and the cracklings eventually taste rancid.

Yield: 8 servings

2 ducks, 4 to 5 lb. each

FOR THE DUCK

½ tsp. salt
¼ tsp. freshly ground black pepper

FOR THE CRACKLINGS

¼ tsp. salt
¼ tsp. freshly ground black pepper
2 c. water (for deglazing)

STOCK

Bones from the duck carcasses plus necks
  and gizzards
2 Tb. butter (if bones are devoid of fat or
  skin)
1 c. coarsely chopped onions
1 c. coarsely chopped carrots
Reserved drippings from browning duck
  and cooking cracklings

1 Cut each duck into 4 pieces, keeping the skin of the neck for cracklings and the bones for stock. Remove the wing tips (the first joint), which will be used for the stock. Keep the second joint, which will be braised with the duck. Lift up the skin of the neck and cut from one shoulder joint to the other along the wishbone – which is like a half circle – and slide your thumb underneath and pry to remove it. (It is always good to remove the wishbone, even when roasting a whole duck, since that facilitates the carving.) →

2 Place the duck on its side, grab a leg, and lift it until the duck is almost lifted off the table. In this manner, the weight of the duck is used and helps in separating the leg from the carcass. With the tip of your knife, cut the skin around the leg, which will separate from the body. Keep cutting the skin all around until you touch the backbone.

3 Place the leg so the thigh bone is parallel to the backbone and lift up to crack it open at the joint. Cut right through the sinews of the joint of the leg, and keep pulling and cutting to separate the leg entirely from the body. Repeat with the other leg.

4 To separate the breast halves, place the duck on its back and, with a sharp knife, cut along the breastbone on each side to separate the 2 halves. Notice that the flesh is not very thick at the breastbone.

5 Place the duck on its side, hold the wing bone, and move it with one finger. Place your finger under the skin on the shoulder joint. As you move the wing bone, you will feel the movement. Cut with your knife through the joint, wiggling the blade to make it slide into the joint. Repeat on the other side, through the joint of the other breast.

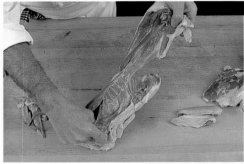

6 Grab the wing at the joint with one hand and, holding the carcass through the bones with the other hand, pull the breast off in one piece. Repeat on the other side with the other half.

7 The only things to be removed now are the 2 small fillets on the sternum, or breastbone. Slide your finger underneath and pull each fillet out.

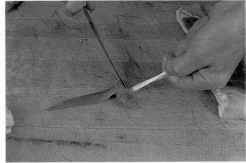

8 Inside each fillet, there is a long sinew. Holding the sinew at the end, scrape the meat from the sinew with the knife.

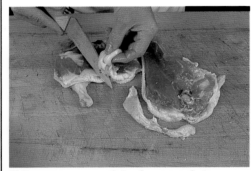

9 Remove some of the fat around the meat of the breast and leg and cut off the tips of the drumsticks for use in the stock. Repeat with other duck.

10 The cut duck: In the back on the left are the bones cut into 1½- to 2-in. pieces; the extra fat from the inside and the skin, cut into 1-in. pieces for use as cracklings; and the 2 pieces from the wings. Underneath are the 2 breast halves with the fillets next to them and, below, the 2 legs.

11 Place the 8 pieces of duck, skin side down (reserving the fillets), in 1 very large or 2 smaller sturdy aluminum or non-stick saucepans. Sprinkle with the salt and pepper, and brown on high heat for 17 minutes (only on the skin side). The skin should have shrunk considerably during this time and be quite crisp, and a great deal of fat will have accumulated in the pan. Place the duck pieces in a large casserole with the fat.

13 Strain the crackling through a fine strainer directly on top of the pieces of duck in the casserole. The duck should be almost covered with the fat. The cracklings can be used in salads or sprinkled lightly with salt and pepper and passed around as apéritif food.

Deglaze the pan used for the cracklings and the saucepan used for browning the duck with 1 c. of water for each and reserve the liquid for the stock. Heat the oven to 325 degrees, cover the duck, and place in the oven for 45 minutes.

15 **To make the stock:** Place the bones with the necks and gizzards in one layer in a large saucepan. If there is no extra fat or skin, use 2 Tb. butter to brown the bones. Brown over high heat for about 5 minutes, then lower the heat to medium and continue browning for another 20 minutes. The bones should be nicely browned all around. Add 1 c. each chopped onions and carrots and continue browning for another 5 minutes to get good crystallization of the bones, carrots, and onions.

Remove the bones and vegetables with a slotted spoon, place in a stockpot, discarding any fat accumulated in the pan. Add 3 c. of water to the drippings to dissolve all the solidified juices, and add the mixture to the stockpot along with the 2 c. reserved drippings from the the pans used for cracklings and browning the duck. Add the rib of celery, 3 garlic cloves, 2 Tb. tomato paste, 1 bay leaf, 1 tsp. thyme, and 16 additional c. of water (4 qt.). Place over high heat, bring to a boil, skim the top of any fat, and boil gently for 3 to 3½ hours.

12 Meanwhile, place all the extra fat in a saucepan and heat on top of the stove to make cracklings. When hot, add the pieces of skin and fry, stirring occasionally, over medium to high heat for 25 to 30 minutes, until the pieces are really crisp and most of the fat is rendered.

14 When the duck is cooked, remove it from the oven. Add the 4 small fillets to the casserole, cover, and let it rest for 30 minutes. Lift out the pieces and place them in a large container. Pour the clear fat on top of the duck, cool, cover, and refrigerate. (Notice that in the bottom of the pan where the duck was cooked there is a layer of juice that came out of the meat during cooking, so all is not fat. Skim off only the fat and reserve the juice for the stock.)

16 **For the sauce:** Strain the mixture through a very fine sieve into a saucepan. (You should have about 4 c.) Let the mixture rest for 10 to 15 minutes so any remaining fat can come to the top. Remove as much fat as possible and then bring the remaining stock to a boil and reduce over high heat to about 1½ c. of strong stock.

In another saucepan, mix ¼ c. each sugar and vinegar and heat until it caramelizes. Then add the reduced stock,

1 Tb. honey, ¼ tsp. salt, and ⅛ tsp. pepper. At this point, the sauce may have enough viscosity. If you feel it should be a bit thicker (as is the case here), add ½ tsp. potato starch dissolved in 1 Tb. water. Set aside.

17 Remove the duck from the refrigerator. It will be embedded in solid fat if the duck has been cooked ahead.

For the sweet potatoes in honey: Wash 3 lb. of potatoes thoroughly under water and cut into 1½-in.-thick slices. Cover with cold water, bring to a boil, and boil for 5 to 6 minutes. Set aside.

18 **For the glazed shallots:** Place the 35 peeled shallots in a single layer in a large skillet with 1 Tb. butter, 1 Tb. sugar, ¼ tsp. salt, and 1½ c. water. Bring to a boil and cook gently, covered, for about 5 minutes. Then remove the lid and continue to cook until most of the liquid evaporates and the shallots remain with butter, sugar, and salt. This will create a caramel, and the shallots will be glazed in the mixture. When the juices begin to caramelize, roll the shallots in the juices to glaze them all around. The shallots should hold their shape, but be cooked and tender to the bite.

19 Melt the 2 Tb. butter for the sweet potatoes in 1 large or 2 smaller skillets. Add the slices of sweet potatoes in one layer. Sprinkle with ¼ tsp. salt and ⅛ tsp. pepper and brown for 2 to 3 minutes on each side. Add 3 Tb. honey to the pan, cover, reduce the heat to very low, and continue cooking for 4 to 5 minutes. Set aside, covered, until ready to serve.

For the duck: Divide the pieces of duck, skin side down, between 2 skillets. Cook over high heat for about 1 minute, then reduce the heat, cover the skillet, and continue cooking for 12 to 15 minutes. (The object here is to warm up the duck and recrust the skin on the outside, melting as much fat out of it as possible.) The meat should be moist and the skin very crisp.

20 Cut the sweet potato slices in half and arrange alternately with the glazed shallots around a large platter. Place the pieces of duck in the center and coat with the sauce. Serve immediately.

CASSOULET PIERRE LARRE

The <u>cassoulet</u> is a famous stew of white beans from the southwest of France. It takes its name from the pot in which it used to be cooked. There is considerable polemics in southwest France as to whether the true <u>cassoulet</u> comes from the town of Carcassonne, Toulouse, or Castelnaudary, each of which claims the authorship of the dish. Furthermore, between those larger towns, each village and, for that matter, each chef or home cook does his own version of the cassoulet.

In general, the beans are flavored with large sausages and the dish will contain poultry (goose or duck), one meat (pork, mutton, or lamb), and pork rind. Sometimes all of these ingredients are included. The pork rind gives some gelatinous texture in addition to flavoring the dish. The cassoulet is better made ahead and will keep a few days in the refrigerator.

In the recipe here, I am combining roast pork and roast duck with the beans, but only at the last moment to retain a crisper exterior to the meat. In the classic preparation, all the cooked meat is combined with the beans in a large Dutch oven or casserole, topped with bread crumbs, and baked in the oven until crisp. Either version is good and the choice comes down to a matter of personal preference.

Any of several types of sausages available at the market can be used, or one can be made according to the directions here. The small white beans are sold under the name of white beans, pea beans, and navy beans. The dried beans are usually from the previous year's crop and do not need long presoaking. In fact, overnight soaking makes the beans ferment (as indicated by gas bubbles on top of the water) and they will be harder to digest and more likely to cause flatulence. This is the ideal one-dish dinner and, followed by a salad and a fruit dessert, it makes an excellent meal.

Yield: 8–10 servings

PUMPKIN SEED SAUSAGE

1½ lb. coarsely ground pork (from the shoulder or butt) that is approximately 25 to 30 percent fat
1 Tb. salt
¼ tsp. saltpeter (optional)
¾ tsp. freshly ground black pepper
2 Tb. shelled green pumpkin seeds
2 Tb. red wine

BEAN STEW

2 lb. small dried white beans
1 small smoked pork butt, fully cooked, about 1½ lb. (1¼ lb. trimmed)
3 onions (about ¾ lb.)
¾ lb. pork rind
2 large carrots, peeled (about ½ lb.)
2 ribs celery, peeled (about ¼ lb.)
3 qt. plus 1 c. water
1 Tb. salt

BOUQUET GARNI (TIED IN A PIECE OF CHEESE-CLOTH)

3 bay leaves
12 whole cloves
1 tsp. dried thyme

DUCK AND PORK ROASTS

1 pork shoulder blade roast (approximately 4 lb.), with some of the shoulder blade bone still in
4 cloves garlic, each cut into 2 or 3 slivers
1 duck (approximately 4½ lb.)
½ tsp. salt
¼ tsp. freshly ground black pepper
1 c. water

BREAD TOPPING

2 c. bread crumbs (from approximately 4 slices bread)
¼ c. fat from the duck and pork roasts
¼ c. chopped parsley

1 If the sausage is to be made fresh, combine the ingredients 48 hours ahead so the sausage has time to cure. Mix together the ground pork, salt, saltpeter (for a pink color), pepper, pumpkin seeds, and wine. →

Studding a roast with garlic, 5

2 Place the mixture on a piece of plastic wrap and roll it into a sausage approximately 9 in. long by 2 in. thick. Let cure at least 48 hours under refrigeration.

3 Spread the beans out in a large roasting pan. Sort through them, putting aside any that are dark, spoiled, or split in half and any stones. Discard the damaged beans and stones, place the remainder in a colander, and rinse under cold water.

4 Place the beans in a large saucepan or stockpot. The pork butt or shoulder is bought precooked but is recooked with the beans. It usually comes covered with net and wrapped in plastic. Remove the plastic and the net and cut off the thick skin around the meat. Place with the beans and add the onions, pork rind, carrots, celery, water, salt, and the bouquet garni. Bring to a boil, cover, and simmer at a gentle boil for about 1 hour and 15 minutes.

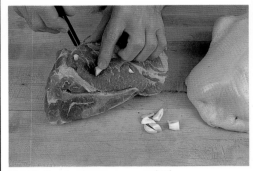

5 While the beans are cooking, prepare your roast: Pierce the pork roast here and there about ½ in. deep with the point of a sharp knife. Push the garlic slivers (pointed end first) into the slits in the meat.

6 Place the duck in a large roasting pan with the pork roast. Sprinkle ¼ tsp. of the salt and ¼ tsp. pepper on the pork roast and ¼ tsp. salt inside and outside the duck. Roast both meats in a preheated 400-degree oven for 1 hour.

After 1 hour, pour the fat off the pork roast and the duck. There will be approximately 1½ c. Turn the roast over, place both meats back in the oven, decrease the heat to 375 degrees, and cook for another hour.

7 Meanwhile, after cooking 1 hour and 15 minutes, the beans should be tender. There will still be quite a lot of liquid in the pan. Remove the solids (vegetables, pork rind, and pork butt) and discard the bag of seasonings. Place the beans back in the pot with the liquid.

8 Chop the cooked onions, carrots, and celery coarse and cut the pork rind into pieces of about ¼ to ½ in. Cut the pork butt into 1-in. pieces and place all the vegetables and meat back in the pot with the beans.

9 Unroll the sausage and place it in the bean pot, pushing it down into the liquid. Place back on the stove, bring to a boil, and simmer gently, partially covered, for about 25 minutes. Set aside.

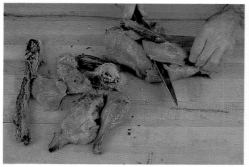

fat from the duck and pork roast on top. Place in a preheated 375-degree oven for approximately 45 minutes to 1 hour, until nicely browned.

10 Meanwhile, remove the pork roast and the duck from the oven. Pour as much fat out of the roasting pan as possible. Add 1 c. of water to the pan, cook 2 to 3 minutes on top of the stove, stirring, to dissolve all the solidified juices, and strain. You should have approximately ¾ to 1 c. of juice. Set aside.

Cut the duck into 8 pieces (the 2 legs and 2 sides of the breast each cut into 2 pieces).

12 Remove the sausage from the cassoulet and cut into ¾-in. slices. When ready to serve, place a 6-oz. ladle of the bean mixture on a warm plate with a piece of the duck, a piece of the sausage, and a piece of the roast pork. The bean mixture should still be slightly wet. Sprinkle with a spoonful of the bread crumbs.

15 Serve the cassoulet immediately, directly from the pot.

11 Cut the roast of pork into ½-in. slices. Place the meat and duck back in the roasting pan to keep warm in the turned-off but still warm oven. Heat approximately ¼ c. of the fat from the duck and pork roast in a skillet. When hot, add the 2 c. bread crumbs and cook over medium to high heat for 3 to 4 minutes, stirring, until nicely browned. Add the ¼ c. parsley, mix, and remove to a plate.

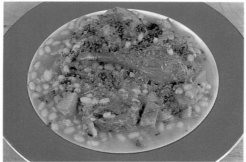

13 Spoon about 1 Tb. of the reserved juices over the cassoulet and serve immediately. Although this is not the conventional way to serve the cassoulet, it is easy to serve this way because you can distribute the meats evenly among the plates, and the meat tends to be crisper than when it is reheated with the beans.

14 For a more conventional cassoulet, arrange the pieces of roasted pork, duck, and the sausage in a Dutch casserole and layer with the cooked beans. Cover the top with a mixture of unbrowned bread crumbs and parsley and drizzle ¼ c. of the

SQUAB DANNY K.

Squab, which is young domesticated pigeon 3 to 5 weeks old, is a good transition (for those squeamish about gaminess) between domesticated poultry and real game, such as pheasant and woodcock. It is dark meat but doesn't have a gamy taste. Squab is pigeon that hasn't yet flown and has been fed to make it tender. An older pigeon, after it flies, will be tough and should be braised. The toughness will be recognized at the breastbone, the end of which will still be cartilaginous and soft in squab, but hard as wood in the pigeon. This hardness indicates an older, tougher animal.

Squab liver doesn't have a gall bladder — that little green sac filled with bile. Therefore, it doesn't need cleaning like the liver of other poultry.

Boning out the squab makes it easier to eat, and the bones are used to make the sauce. The squabs can be boned out a day or two ahead and the stock prepared completely ahead. The same technique used here for boning out the squab can be used for chicken, Cornish hen, or smaller birds, such as partridge or woodcock.

Dipping the boned squabs in boiling water tightens the skin and makes them plump again. Although reduced in size, the whole bird is now a compact piece of meat. Roast squab should be served slightly pink, as shown in the photograph.

The sauce is accented with red wine and garnished with gizzard, heart, liver, and lung as well as mushrooms, which make a nice, flavorful accompaniment to the bird. The lime peas in tomato saucers can be used to garnish other birds or meat as well as fish. The tomatoes should not be cooked, just warmed, so there is a taste of raw tomato. The peas, well accented with lime, should be cooked at the last moment. Tiny, tender baby peas, which usually come frozen, are the best choice, unless one has access to freshly picked peas.

The squabs are placed directly on top of a wire rack in the oven and roasted at a high temperature, with a pan placed underneath to catch the fat that drains out of the birds as they cook. This way, the squabs brown all around. The addition of honey mixed with water, the same technique as used for Peking duck, sweetens the skin and gives it a beautiful dark brown caramel color.

Yield: 6 servings

FOR ROASTING

6 squabs, 1 lb. each
1 tsp. honey mixed with ¼ c. water
½ tsp. salt

STOCK

Squab bones
½ c. coarsely chopped carrots
½ c. coarsely chopped onions
5 c. water
1 c. red wine
Tomato seeds and skin trimmings (see
    below)

GIBLET SAUCE

1 Tb. butter
⅓ c. chopped onions
Reserved gizzards, hearts, livers, and
    lungs, cut as indicated here
2–4 mushrooms cut into ¼-in. dice
    (½ c.)
1 tsp. potato starch dissolved in 1 Tb. red
    wine
Reduced stock
½ tsp. salt
¼ tsp. freshly ground black pepper
Defatted, strained juice from cooking the
    squabs

GARNISHES

Bunch watercress
1 tsp. garlic chives or regular chives,
    chopped

LIME PEAS IN TOMATO SAUCERS

3 tomatoes (about 1¼ lb.), peeled (see
    page 83)
2 Tb. butter
1 package (10 oz.) frozen baby peas,
    defrosted, or 10 oz. garden-fresh small
    peas
¼ tsp. salt
⅛ tsp. freshly ground black pepper
¼ tsp. sugar
1 tsp. finely grated lime rind

1 Fresh squabs weigh approximately 1 lb. each. They should be eviscerated. (Refer to page 157 for eviscerating chicken.) Notice that in the photograph the squab has been eviscerated. The head and neck, wings, and squab body are, left to right, in the foreground and the fat, heart, lungs, and liver are, left to right, in the background. The gizzard is being opened while the guts, which have to be discarded, are on the right of my hand.

2 After cutting through the fleshy part of the gizzard, as shown in photograph 1, the sharp knife should go through the skin so the gizzard can be opened and the inside pulled out in one solid lump. Inside is a sac containing digested food. Remove this sac carefully to avoid breaking it, and discard.

3 Cut the meat from the gizzard: Placing the gizzard flat on the table, cut off the lump of flesh on both ends by cutting down, sliding your knife along the skin and lifting up the two little lumps. Finally, remove the piece of flesh from the center. You should have 1 larger and 2 smaller pieces of gizzard.

4 The gizzard in the back has been opened (as shown in photographs 1 and 2) and the sac removed. The gizzard in the front has the pieces of meat taken from it. The skin from the gizzard can be added to the stock. Cut the gizzards and hearts into slivers and the liver into ½-in. pieces.

5 Boning out the squab: Lift the skin at the neck of the squab and run your knife along each side of the wishbone. Push your thumb and index finger along the bone on each side to pry it out. Pull it out. →

POULTRY & GAME

187

6 Cut at the joint of the shoulder on each side of the wishbone. (See technique for boning out chicken in Ballotine of Chicken Lucette, page 166.) Push with your index finger and the side of your thumb inside through the opening made by the knife. The object is to loosen the meat all around the central carcass.

7 The most delicate part of the operation is to separate the skin from the back of the bird, as it adheres very tightly there and will tend to tear. Using the tip of your index finger, push between the skin and the back carcass to loosen the skin. Go slowly to avoid tearing the skin.

8 After the meat has been separated from the back and around the shoulder, lift out the breast meat, prying to separate it from the top of the breastbone without tearing the skin. The fillets are still attached to the central carcass.

9 When it is loose from the carcass, turn the flesh inside out (like taking off socks), pulling the meat down, separating it from the carcass. The fillets are still attached to the central carcass.

10 Keep pulling down until all the breast meat is separated and most of the carcass – up to the joint of the hip on each side – is visible. Notice that the fillets are still attached to the carcass.

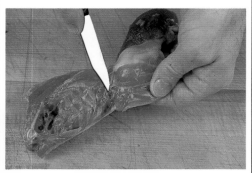

11 Holding the squab by the thigh bone, cut right through the hip joint and pull so the leg separates from the carcass. Repeat on the other side.

12 To remove the bones of the leg: With the squab still inside out, scrape the meat from the thigh bones with a knife and cut all around the knee joint. Keep scraping to loosen the meat from the drumstick bone.

13 Break the bone at the foot. Leave the knuckle in to hold the skin in place and prevent it from shrinking. Pull off the wing bones on either side.

14 Run your thumb along the carcass on each side of the breastbone and remove both fillets, pulling them off on both sides.

15 Turn the squab right side out. It is now completely boned out except for the knuckles. In the front is the whole carcass, in the middle, from left to right, are the 2 fillets, the bones of both legs, and pieces of bones from the wing joints. In the back is the boned squab.

16 On the plate, starting at the top left and continuing counter-clockwise, are the pieces of gizzard cut into slivers and, below, the hearts, cut into slivers, then the livers, cut into ½-in. pieces, and, finally, the lung at the top right. Melt the fat from the inside of the squabs in a large roasting pan. Add the carcass bones, coarsely chopped. Place over medium to high heat and brown for about 15 minutes, until nicely browned all around.

17 **For the stock:** Add ½ c. each chopped carrots and onions to the bones, cook 5 minutes, then add 5 c. water, 1 c. wine, tomato trimmings, and skin. (Look at photographs 20 and 21 on cleaning the tomatoes to obtain the skins, seeds, and trimmings for the stock.) Bring to a boil and cook 30 minutes. Strain, pressing the solids to extract the juices, and discard the solids. Let the liquid rest about 5 minutes and remove as much fat as possible. You should have approximately 2 c. of stock remaining. Reduce by boiling down to 1½ c.

    For the sauce: Heat the 1 Tb. butter in a skillet. When hot, sauté ⅓ c. onions for about 1½ minutes, and then add the gizzards and hearts and sauté about 1 minute longer. Add 2 to 4 diced mushrooms, sauté about 1 minute, and, finally, add the livers and lungs, and sauté for another minute over very high heat. Meanwhile, dissolve 1 tsp. potato starch in 1 Tb. wine and add it to the reduced stock. Combine the giblet mixture with the reduced stock and add ½ tsp. salt and ¼ tsp. pepper. Set aside.

18 Secure the skin of the neck of the squab with a toothpick so it wraps around the opening of the neck and submerge each bird in boiling water for about 5 to 10 seconds. You will notice that the skin will get tight and the squab, although smaller, will take on its original shape. Brush the squab with the honey-water mixture on all sides.

19 At cooking time, preheat the oven to 450 degrees. Sprinkle the squabs with ½ tsp. of salt and place them on a rack in the center of the oven with a large roasting pan on the rack beneath to catch the fat. Roast for about 15 minutes. The squabs should be nicely browned all around.

    Remove the squabs to a plate and keep warm. Pour out as much of the fat as possible and strain the remaining juice on top of the sauce and combine with it.

20 **For the lime peas in tomato saucers:** Drop 3 tomatoes into boiling water briefly (see page 83), remove, and peel. Place the tomatoes stem side down on the table, and cut each of them on either side of the center to create 2 saucers. The center, which will now look like a wedge, as well as the skin and seeds, is used in the stock, as indicated in step 17.

21 Using a spoon, scoop out the insides of the tomato saucers to create small receptacles of tomato flesh. Again, add the seeds to the stock. Place the tomatoes on a tray or cookie sheet in a warm oven just long enough to take the chill off. The tomatoes should be served raw.

22 Heat 2 Tb. of butter in a saucepan and, when hot, add the 10 oz. peas, ¼ tsp. salt, ⅛ tsp. pepper, and ¼ tsp. sugar. Cook about 2 minutes to heat the peas. Add 1 tsp. grated lime rind and toss to mix for 15 to 20 seconds.

Arrange the roast squabs on a large platter with the tomato saucers in between. Fill the saucers with peas, coat with some of the sauce, and place watercress in the center. Pass the rest of the sauce at the table. Serve immediately.

23 The squabs can also be arranged on individual plates and partially sliced. Notice that the squab is solid with meat and slightly pink. Pour the sauce around, garnish with the tomato saucers filled with peas, and sprinkle with 1 tsp. chopped garlic chives or regular chives. Serve immediately.

A LEANER VERSION

Lime peas in tomato saucers: Reduce the amount of butter from 2 Tb. to 1 Tb. and proceed according to the recipe.

QUAIL CYNTHIA WITH WILD RICE

Raised quail are readily available in specialty markets throughout the country. Unfortunately, they are hard to obtain fresh, and the frozen birds do not have the quality of the fresh ones. Yet they can be flavorful if defrosted very slowly under refrigeration so they do not lose too much moisture. If you are lucky enough to obtain wild quail, you'll find they have more and better flavor than raised ones.

Unlike woodcock or pheasant, quail does not age well and should be eaten fresh. There is an expression in France that quail is best eaten "at the point of the gun barrel," meaning, of course, that it should be eaten when just killed.

In the recipes here, the quail are boned, and the bones used to make a flavorful stock and sauce. The little birds are sautéed briefly skin side down so the skin is cooked and brown while the flesh on the other side remains moist, slightly pink, and tender. The boned quail can also be stuffed, reformed into their original shapes, and cooked in the oven or served cold in pâtés or aspic.

The wild rice flavored with mushrooms, pignolia nuts, and chicken livers (which should be replaced with the quail heart and liver, if available) is a flavorful accompaniment. This rice can be served with other types of game or poultry as well as meat.

The corn makes a crunchy and buttery enhancement to the quail, besides adding beautiful color. The corn kernels are not blanched but just sautéed briefly so the starch is not even set and the kernels remain very juicy and sweet, with a crunchy texture.

Yield: 6 servings

12 quail, 4 oz. each, unboned
2 Tb. good olive oil
½ tsp. powdered thyme

STOCK

Bones from the quail
2 Tb. butter
1 c. chopped carrots
1 c. chopped onions
1 c. diced tomatoes
½ c. chopped celery
½ tsp. cracked black pepper
6 c. water
Reserved mushroom liquid and stems from wild rice recipe (page 191)

SAUCE

2 c. stock
1 Tb. cider vinegar
1 tsp. potato starch dissolved in 1 Tb. water
⅛ tsp. freshly ground black pepper
½ tsp. salt

WILD RICE WITH PIGNOLIA NUTS AND MUSHROOMS

2 oz. dried Black Forest or other dried
   mushrooms (¾ c., chopped, after soaking), with liquid and stems reserved for
   stock
4 c. water
1 c. wild rice
2 Tb. butter
⅓ c. pignolia nuts
1½ c. chopped onions
½ c. raisins
½ c. diced celery
3 or 4 chicken livers, cut into ½-in. dice
   (¾ c.)
¾ tsp. salt
½ tsp. pepper

TO SAUTE THE QUAIL

2 Tb. butter (1 in each of 2 skillets)
Salt and freshly ground black pepper
CORN KERNEL GARNISH
2 Tb. butter
3 c. corn kernels (about 4 ears)
¼ tsp. salt
GARNISHES
Nasturtium blossoms and leaves (optional)
Chopped garlic chives

1 Cut the skin along the back of the quail. Sever the joint of the shoulder on either side of the neck. See the boning out of chicken (Ballotine of Chicken Lucette, page 166), and squab (Squab Danny K., preceding recipe). A knife is needed to cut the back skin and shoulder joints, but the rest of the boning can be done with the fingers.

2 Holding the wing bone, pull out the wing on each side of the neck to separate the carcass from the meat. Although still held at the breastbone, most of the quail meat should be separated from the carcass.

3 Pull the breast to separate it from the sternum. Notice that the little fillets are still attached to the bone. They will be removed later.

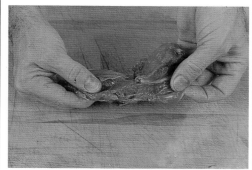

4 Break the leg bone at the hip joint and pull it off. As you break and pull, the leg will separate from the back carcass. Pull the carcass off. The only 2 pieces left on the carcass now are the fillets; slide your finger between the meat and the bone and remove the fillets. Set aside. The quail is now opened flat, with the bones of the legs and wings still in place.

5 Using your finger, stand the thigh bone up so the joint is on the table, and grasping the bone as you would a pencil, push your fingers down the length of the bone, scraping the meat off as you go down. The thigh bone is now clean.

6 Continue pushing and separating the meat from the knee joint. Now push down the drumstick bone to separate the meat. Break the bone off at the joint of the foot.

7 For the stock: Trim the wings and remove the little piece of bone in each. The quail is completely boned out with the fillet separated (in front) and the bones (on the side), ready for the sauce. Rub the boned quail with olive oil and powdered thyme and refrigerate, covered, until cooking time.

   Chop the bones coarse. Heat the butter in a skillet. When hot, add the bones and cook over medium heat for 10 to 15 minutes, until brown. Add the carrots, onions, tomatoes, celery, pepper, and water, and cook gently for a total of 45 minutes after the mixture comes to a boil.

Meanwhile, soak the mushrooms in 1½ c. of lukewarm water. After 20 to 25 minutes the mushrooms will be soaked through. Drain and add the liquid and the tough stems of the mushrooms to the stock for the remaining 20 minutes or so of cooking. Chop the caps coarse and set aside.

To make the sauce: When the stock is cooked, drain, straining through a fine strainer. You should have about 2 c. Boil down to reduce to 1¼ c. Add the vinegar and dissolved potato starch, bring to a boil, add pepper and salt, and set aside.

8 **For the wild rice:** Bring the 4 c. water to a boil and pour it over the 1 c. rice in a saucepan. Cover and let soak for 45 minutes. Drain. Return the rice to the saucepan with 4 c. cold water, bring to a boil, and boil gently for 30 minutes. Drain.

Meanwhile, add 1 Tb. of the butter to a skillet. When hot, add the ⅓ c. nuts with 1½ c. chopped onions and cook together for 3 to 4 minutes, until lightly browned. Add ½ c. raisins, ½ c. diced celery, and ¾ c. chopped mushroom caps and continue cooking for 2 to 3 minutes longer.

9 Melt the remaining Tb. of butter in a skillet. When hot, add the pieces of liver and sauté over the highest possible heat for about 20 to 30 seconds. Combine the mushroom mixture, rice, and ¾ c. diced liver together, add ¾ tsp. salt and ½ tsp. pepper, and set aside, covered, in a warm oven.

10 **To sauté the quail:** Heat 1 Tb. butter in each of 2 skillets. Sprinkle the quail lightly with salt and a dash of pepper and, when the butter is hot, cook the quail, except for the fillets, skin side down over high heat for about 2 to 2¼ minutes. Remove from the heat, turn the quail over, add the fillets, cover, and leave off the heat while you prepare the corn. Note that the quail have been cooked only about 2 minutes over high heat, which is enough to cook the skin. The heat generated in the covered pan will be just enough to cook the meat.

For the corn kernel garnish: Heat 2 Tb. butter. When hot, add 3 c. corn kernels and ¼ tsp. salt. Sauté for 3 to 4 seconds, cover, and cook for about 3 minutes over medium to high heat.

11 Meanwhile, arrange the wild rice on a platter and place the quail on top, skin side up. Place the sauce in the skillet used for cooking the quail. Bring to a boil and spoon over the quail.

12 Arrange the corn around the quail. Decorate with nasturtium flowers and leaves in the center and sprinkle with chopped garlic chives. Serve immediately.

ROAST WOODCOCK POPAUL WITH SOUFFLEED POTATOES

The native American woodcock is from the same family as the snipe, similar but not quite the same as the *bécasse* of Europe, which is larger and slightly different in color. Woodcock is considered by many gastronomes to be the finest of the game birds. Because it feeds on insects and empties itself as it starts to fly, the woodcock is ordinarily cooked with its insides left in the body. They are removed afterward and used (except for the large gizzard) to make a *farce* or stuffing, which is placed in a bread receptacle with the roasted bird on top. In our recipe, the insides are removed before the bird is cooked and sautéed separately to make the *farce*. The woodcocks in our recipe are small and are cooked briefly so the breast meat remains moist and pink.

A woodcock's taste will improve if it is aged before cooking — certain birds take to aging better than others and the woodcock is one of them. Leaving it for 3 or 4 days in the refrigerator, ungutted with its feathers on, will improve its flavor. However, over-aging gives it a strong taste and makes it indigestible.

The Savoy cabbage, as well as the bread receptacles and the *farce* mixture, makes a nice accompaniment. The souffléed potatoes can be served with most grilled or sautéed meat, from beef and veal to poultry. Souffléed potatoes are made from regular sliced potatoes as well as from crinkled potato slices. The crinkled slices, cut on the mandoline, take longer to cook. The first cooking of the potatoes may be done hours ahead, as is usually done in restaurants, and the final cooking just before serving.

Yield: 4 servings

4 ungutted woodcocks, 6 to 8 oz. each
1½ Tb. butter
Salt and freshly ground black pepper

CABBAGE GARNISH

½ head Savoy cabbage (about 10 oz.), 6 c. sliced
2 Tb. butter
1 Tb. oil
½ c. coarsely chopped prosciutto ham
½ c. coarsely chopped onion
¼ tsp. caraway seeds
2–3 cloves garlic, chopped (1 tsp.)
1 c. water

BREAD RECEPTACLES

½ loaf unsliced firm-textured white bread
4 tsp. butter

POMMES SOUFFLEES

3 large Idaho potatoes, peeled
About 3 qt. oil (preferably cottonseed or corn oil), divided between 2 frying pans
Salt to taste

FARCE GARNISH

1 Tb. butter
1½ Tb. chopped shallots
3 mushrooms, coarsely chopped (½ c.)
Reserved woodcock entrails, chopped
1 small clove garlic, chopped
⅛ tsp. salt
⅛ tsp. freshly ground black pepper
1 tsp. cognac
2 tsp. drippings from cooking the woodcocks

SAUCE

1 Tb. cognac
½ c. demi-glace (see page 7)
Salt and freshly ground black pepper to taste

1 After the woodcocks have been aged a few days in the refrigerator, pluck them, being very careful not to damage the skin. It is a tedious and delicate job, but they develop a better flavor if aged with the feathers on. When the feathers have been removed, the woodcocks can be singed on top of a gas flame to burn off the very fine feathers, and the little pieces embedded in the skin can be removed with the point of a knife. →

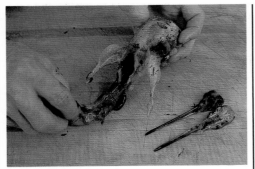

2 Cut the heads off at the neck and cut the necks off the bodies. The necks can be placed next to the woodcocks during roasting to lend flavor. Keep the heads for decoration, plucking them carefully or removing the skin. They can be split in half, as shown in the picture, to enhance the final presentation and guarantee, in a sense, the authenticity of the birds. (See technique for eviscerating chicken, page 157.) Pull out the insides and remove the gizzard and discard it. The rest of the insides including the intestines will be used to make a *farce.* Chop coarse and set aside.

4 Heat the butter and oil in a saucepan. When hot, add the prosciutto and onion and cook for 1 to 2 minutes. Add the caraway seeds, garlic, water, and cabbage. Cover and cook gently for 20 minutes. By then the water should have almost evaporated and the cabbage should be just moist. If the cooking is too fast and the water evaporates too soon, the cabbage will start browning. To prevent this, add a little water. On the other hand, if there is still too much moisture when the lid is removed, cook a few minutes, uncovered, to evaporate the excess.

6 To make the pommes soufflées: Peel the potatoes and trim at both ends so that when cut all the slices will be of equal size. All the trimmings can be reserved (in cold water) for soups, mashed potatoes, etc.

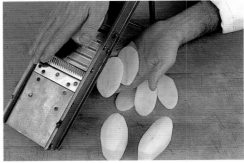

3 For the cabbage: Cut the cabbage into ½-in. slices (you should have about 6 c.).

5 To make the receptacles: Cut the bread into 1- to 1¼-in.-thick slices. Remove the crust from around the outside and carve out the center to make receptacles (see Scrambled Eggs in Bread Cases with Candied Oyster Mushrooms, page 41). With the point of a knife or a spatula, butter the bread cases very lightly all over, using 1 tsp. of butter per case. Place on a tray or cookie sheet and into a preheated 400-degree oven and cook for 10 to 12 minutes, until nicely browned all around. Set aside.

7 Cut by hand or on the straight side of a mandoline approximately ⅛ to 3/16 in. thick at the most. Place the slices in cold water as they are cut to prevent discoloration.

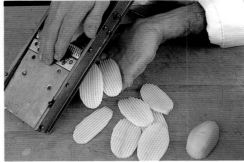

8 The slices can also be cut on the crinkle edge of the blade, as used for waffle potatoes (see Chicken Jean-Claude with Waffle Potatoes, page 177). Cut straight down, making sure that the thickness of the potato between the crinkles is still at least ⅛ in., making the whole slice about ⅜ in. thick. Wash the potatoes in cold water and dry on paper towels. The plain sliced potatoes will take approximately 4 to 5 minutes to cook in the first frying, and the crinkled slices, being thicker, about 6 to 7 minutes. Heat oil (at least 1½ in. deep) in 2 deep skillets. The oil in 1 skillet should be approximately 300 degrees, and in the other, 350 to 375 degrees.

9 Place about 15 to 20 of the crinkled slices in the skillet with the 300-degree oil and shake the pan, being careful not to splatter yourself. After you get the proper rhythm established, it is not difficult. Keep shaking for about 6 to 7 minutes, until "blisters" appear on some of the slices. In that first cooking, the potato slices should not brown; the object of the shaking while cooking is to allow a soft skin to form on the surface of each slice, which then will hold the moisture inside. If the slices brown too quickly, remove the skillet from the heat, still shaking, and return it to the heat when the oil has cooled a little, cooking until blisters begin to form.

10 Remove about 4 or 5 slices at a time with a skimmer or slotted spoon and dip immediately into the 350- to 375-degree oil. The slices should puff immediately. Notice that 3 potato slices (across the center) have puffed nicely while 2 slices have not. As soon as the slices puff, lift them from the hot oil and place on a cookie sheet lined with paper towels. They will deflate almost immediately since they are not cooked enough to hold their shape. However, having once inflated, they will reinflate when browned at serving time.

11 Keep transferring a few potato slices at a time from the 300-degree oil to the 350–375-degree oil. You will know which ones will successfully inflate as they do so almost immediately. Place those on a cookie sheet lined with paper towels and set the others aside. The inflated potatoes will deflate. Cover with a towel or plastic wrap, and place in a cool place until ready to finish at serving time. The slices that do not inflate can be used as regular fried potatoes or eaten on the spot.

12 Just before serving, refry the potatoes. Place the slices in 350–375-degree oil and cook, stirring and turning with a skimmer, long enough so they retain their puffy shape and brown evenly all around. Remove to a cookie sheet lined with paper towels.

13 Sprinkle lightly with salt. On the right are the potatoes with the crinkled edges and on the left, being held, are the potato slices with the straight edges.

14 To make the potatoes more attractive, it is conventional to serve them in a napkin folded into an artichoke design. Other potatoes, vegetables, as well as cookies or candies, can be served in the same decoratively folded napkin. Place a piece of aluminum foil in the center of a square napkin so it covers the center of the napkin. Bring the 4 corners of the napkin up so they join in the center.

15 Bring the 4 "new" corners you've created to the center and turn the napkin over. Again, fold the 4 corners toward the center. →

16 Holding the corners so they don't unwrap, place the napkin around the base of an upside-down glass and press all around so the napkin molds to the shape of the glass. Start pulling the pointed edges of the napkin out, as though you were pulling on the leaves of a real artichoke. Keep pulling until the last layer of "leaves" (where the aluminum foil is) starts showing.

17 Turn the napkin over. It is now ready to be filled with souffléed potatoes or something else. Place on another napkin or directly on a plate.

18 **To make the farce garnish:** Melt the 1 Tb. butter in a skillet. When hot, add 1½ Tb. chopped shallots and sauté 1 minute. Add ½ c. chopped mushrooms, cook another 1 to 2 minutes, and add the chopped entrails. Cook about 1 minute

until the entrails change color and become firm. Add 1 chopped garlic clove, ⅛ tsp. each salt and pepper, and 1 tsp. cognac. Set aside and keep warm.

19 **To cook the woodcocks:** Preheat the oven to 450 degrees. Melt 1½ Tb. butter in a skillet. Sprinkle the woodcocks lightly with salt and pepper. When the butter has melted, add the woodcocks, placed on their sides, and cook for 1 minute in this position over high heat. Turn and cook on the other side for another minute. Place the necks and heads around the birds and place in the oven for 5 minutes. The woodcocks are cooked sufficiently when, after a breast is punctured with a needle, the juice emitted is pink, indicating that the meat of the woodcocks is pink at the breast.

20 Mix about 2 tsp. of the drippings from cooking the woodcocks into the farce garnish. Place the cabbage on a platter with the bread receptacles in the center. Fill the receptacles with the farce. Meanwhile, to make the sauce, add the 1 Tb. cognac, ½ c. demi-glace, and salt and pepper to taste to the skillet used to cook the woodcocks. Bring to a boil.

21 Arrange the woodcocks on top of the farce and place the heads, with beaks crossed, for decoration on top. Spoon a little sauce over the woodcocks and serve immediately.

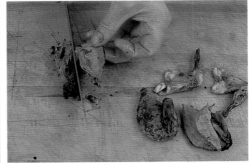

22 It is easier to eat woodcocks that have been partially boned out, and you can serve them individually that way: separate the 2 legs by pulling them off the bodies. Cut off the wings at the shoulders and pull off the breast on each side. You now have the 2 breast pieces and 2 legs. By twisting out, remove the bones of the thighs on the 2 legs and cut the top of the breastbone and separate the meat from the carcass.

23 On individual plates, arrange the breast bones in the center of the bread receptacles with the breast meat and the partially boned-out legs on each side. Spoon sauce on top and serve immediately with the pommes soufflés.

RABBIT BLANQUETTE

A rabbit stew in cream sauce is ideal for a large party; it doesn't need much more than an hour of cooking time if the rabbit is young (about 3 months old). If the rabbit is larger and older, increase the cooking time until the meat feels tender, just a bit firm when pierced with the point of a fork.

The rabbit stew, or blanquette, and the dumplings can be done several days ahead, but do not add the mushrooms, pearl onions, or cream until the last moment when reheating to ensure a fresher, better taste. In case your rabbit has the skin still on and is not eviscerated, steps 1 through 4 of this recipe will show you how to prepare it for cooking. Otherwise, pick up at step 5.

The corn fritters should be made at the last minute to achieve the best result. They tend to get soft and lose their crispness if they sit too long. If made ahead, however, they can always be placed on a cookie sheet and warmed in a hot oven or under a hot broiler to crisp them a little before serving.

Yield: 8–10 servings

2 2¾-lb. young rabbits
½ stick butter
2 c. coarsely chopped onions
¼ c. flour
1 Tb. chopped garlic (about 3 or 4 cloves)
8–10 sprigs fresh thyme or 1½ tsp. dried thyme
1 sprig fresh oregano or ½ tsp. dried oregano
4 c. water
2 c. chicken stock
½ tsp. pepper
2 tsp. salt

FOR THE DUMPLINGS

2 rabbits' livers, hearts, and kidneys (about 6 oz. total)
¾ lb. pork, at least ⅓ fat, from the shoulder, cut into ½-in. dice
1 large clove garlic, chopped
½ c. chopped parsley
¼ tsp. pepper
½ tsp. salt
1 lb. tiny white pearl onions (60–70), peeled
1 lb. oyster mushrooms, chanterelles, or cultivated mushrooms
1½ c. heavy cream

CORN FRITTERS

Yield: About 2 doz.
1¼ c. flour (about 6–7 oz.)
2 tsp. double-acting baking powder
1 egg
¼ tsp. salt
1 c. ice-cold water
2 c. corn kernels (cut from about 2 or 3 ears)
About ½ c. corn or cottonseed oil

1 To skin the rabbits, make an incision in the center of the back skin with a sharp knife. Insert 2 fingers of each of your hands in under the skin and pull to separate the skin into 2 pieces.

2 Keep pulling on the skin so it slides off the flesh.

3 Pull the skin down the back legs and sever at the foot.

197

4 Pull the skin on the side of the head and pull the 2 front legs through and sever at the foot. Cut at the neck. Remove the livers, kidneys, and hearts (weighing about 6 oz. in all) and set aside for the dumplings.

5 Cut each of the rabbits into 7 or 8 pieces, depending on size. You should have 2 back legs, the 2 front legs with some of the rib part, and the back in 3 pieces. Sprinkle with salt and pepper.

6 Melt the butter in 1 very large saucepan or 2 skillets and, when hot, place the pieces of rabbit in one layer in one or both skillets. Brown for 10 minutes over medium to high heat, turning the rabbit pieces so they are nicely browned all around. Add the chopped onions and cook briefly, for 2 to 3 minutes. Sprinkle with the flour and stir to mix well. Finally, stir in the garlic, thyme, oregano, water, stock, pepper, and salt. Mix well and bring to a boil, stirring to ensure that the mixture doesn't stick to the bottom of the pan. Then lower the heat, cover partially (leaving an opening just large enough to allow some of the steam to escape), and cook over very low to medium heat for 1 hour, boiling very gently.

7 While the rabbit is cooking, **prepare the liver dumplings.** Place the livers, hearts, and kidneys in the food processor and process until smooth. Add the ¼ lb. pork and chopped garlic clove, and keep processing until the mixture is smooth again, for about 1 minute. Add the ½ c. parsley, ¼ tsp. pepper, and ½ tsp. salt, and process again, just enough to mix. Remove and place in a bowl.

Place 1½ in. of water in a large, flat saucepan and bring to a boil. Lower the heat to stop the boiling and, using a large spoon, drop the equivalent of 2 Tb. (about 1½ oz.) of the liver mixture into the hot water. You should have approximately 1 doz. liver dumplings. The water should not boil. Keep cooking the dumplings in the water (heated to approximately 170 degrees) for 10 minutes. Remove with a slotted spoon and set aside.

8 When the rabbit is cooked, remove with a slotted spoon and place in a large clean saucepan.

9 Strain all the sauce from the rabbit through a fine sieve directly onto the pieces of rabbit. In a separate pot, cover 1 lb. of pearl onions with cold water, heat on top of the stove, and boil gently for 5 minutes. Drain. Clean the 1 lb. of mushrooms.

10 Add the dumplings, the pearl onions, the mushrooms, and 1½ c. cream to the rabbit. Place back on the stove and bring to a very light boil and simmer gently, covered, for 10 to 12 minutes. Serve with corn fritters.

11 **For the corn fritters:** Place the 1¼ c. flour, 2 tsp. baking powder, 1 egg, ¼ tsp. salt, and 1 c. water in the food processor and combine just until smooth. Add 2 c. corn kernels and process for 5 to 6 seconds, just enough to break the kernels partially. Remove to a bowl.

Heat up 2 large saucepans and add ¼ c. oil* to each pan. When the oil is very hot, drop full tablespoons of the fritter batter (about 7 per skillet) into each skillet. The mixture will spread a little.

12 Cook over high about 2 minutes at the most on each side. Lift out and set on a tray and continue making the rest of the fritters until all the batter is used up. You should have about 2 doz.

13 Serve the corn fritters immediately with the Rabbit Blanquette.

A LEANER VERSION

Omit the corn fritters and the dumplings; the rabbits' livers, hearts, and kidneys can be added to the rabbits (step 10). Omit the cream in the recipe, reduce the amount of flour from ¼ c. to 2 Tb. and the water from 4 c. to 3 c. Proceed according to the recipe.

VENISON STEAK WITH BLACK CURRANT SAUCE AND CHESTNUT PUREE OR BRAISED CHESTNUTS

The distinctive tastes of venison and chestnuts make them a particularly complementary autumn pairing. Numerous varieties of chestnuts exist, but in France the cultivated species, containing a single large nut, is called a _marron_, as opposed to the wild _châtaigne_, smaller, less sweet, but also more delicate and less cloying than a _marron_.

Chestnuts lend themselves to a multitude of uses. A classic confection, _marrons glacés_, or sweet, glazed whole chestnuts, are imported from France and sold in boxes like chocolates or in syrup at specialty-foods shops; these chestnuts have been cooked slowly in a sugar syrup until they absorb it and become tender. (My recipe for braised chestnuts is also based on the slow absorption of the cooking liquid, but a savory one.) Dehydrated peeled chestnuts from Italy are available in many specialty-foods shops, too, as are cans of chestnut purée, with or without the addition of sugar and vanilla (be sure to read the labels care-

fully). Whether chestnut purée is purchased or homemade, it can be used on the sweet side in such desserts as the famed Mont Blanc, a cone-shaped mound of the purée topped with drifts of whipped cream, in imitation of its mountain namesake, or a Turinois, combining chocolate, chestnut purée, butter, and rum. On the savory side the purée can be a base for soufflées; whole chestnuts can be steamed, boiled, roasted (New York street vendors sell them this way in winter), or braised; and chestnut pieces may be used in soups, stuffings, or pâtés.

Peeling chestnuts means removing both the outside and inside skins, or the shell and membrane, respectively. (If you have seen chestnut flour — used for cakes or pancakes or as a thickener in soups — you will recall specks of red, which are, in fact, particles of the membrane that were not refined out.) Peeling chestnuts should be done while the chestnuts (already slit) are still quite hot. Although chestnuts may be peeled after being either boiled, deep-fried, or — as here — roasted, the incision is always essential to keep the nut from exploding. Buy heavy, shiny, large chestnuts, if possible, and look for warning signals: pinholes indicate the likely presence of worms, and breaks in the skin are a sign that the nut may be old and dry inside.

The tenderest venison steaks come from the properly aged rack or loin of a deer no more than a year old. The cut is expensive, but a 4- to 5-oz. steak should be enough for one person when it is served with the proper accompaniments and garnishes.

The venison available in specialty shops is raised in large parks and is comparable in quality and taste to its wild counterpart. Extremely lean, the deep-red meat should be cooked rare or medium rare. Overcooking (unless you are using lesser cuts for a stew, for example) will result in dry, chewy meat. The steaks in my recipe gain some extra tenderness by being marinated. They should be fork-tender when served.

I offer here two versions of venison with black currant sauce. Although the ingredients of both dishes are basically the same, the mix-and-match of the cranberry relish, braised and puréed chestnuts, and zucchini boats is different, creating two distinct presentations.

Yield: 8 servings

CHESTNUT PUREE

2 lb. chestnuts, peeled as explained here
3 c. chicken stock (unsalted)
1 rib celery, cleaned
1 tsp. salt, or more
3 Tb. butter
½ c. heavy cream
Pepper and sugar to taste

ZUCCHINI BOATS

1 medium-sized zucchini, cleaned
Butter

BRAISED CHESTNUTS

2 lb. chestnuts, peeled as explained here
3 c. brown stock, unsalted (see page 7)
½ tsp. salt
3 Tb. butter

FOR THE VENISON STEAKS

1 whole or double loin, bone in, about 5 lb. (This will yield 2 single loins, 1½ lb. each, and 2 lb. of bones.) Make a stock with the bones or freeze for future use. Since the bones are not needed in this recipe, the loins could be bought boned.
4 Tb. butter

MARINADE (for about 10 steaks)

3 Tb. peanut oil
1 Tb. lemon rind
2 Tb. lemon juice
½ tsp. thyme leaves

BLACK CURRANT SAUCE

½ c. good red wine vinegar
1 c. fruity red wine
4 Tb. black currant jam or preserves
2 c. demi-glace (strong reduced brown stock) (see page 7)
4 Tb. butter (at room temperature) to finish the sauce
Salt and pepper to taste

GARNISH

Parsley leaves

CRANBERRY RELISH

1 12-oz. package fresh cranberries
1 hot jalapeño pepper, seeded and chopped fine (2 Tb.)
2 tsp. julienne (fine strips) from the skin of 1 orange
½ tsp. freshly ground black pepper
½ c. honey
⅓ c. white distilled vinegar
¼ tsp. ground allspice
1 tsp. mustard seeds
½ tsp. salt

1 Combine all the ingredients for the cranberry relish in a saucepan (preferably stainless steel), cover, and bring to a boil. Boil gently, covered, for 10 to 12 minutes. Cover and refrigerate. Serve with game, pâté, or roasted poultry. It is better done one day ahead, as it develops taste after a few hours.

2 To peel the chestnuts: Using the point of a sharp, pointed paring knife, score each chestnut on both sides. Ideally, the chestnut should be cut practically all around. Do not cut deeper than ¼ in. through the chestnut. Only the two layers of skin should be cut. Notice the knife is held so that only the tip of the blade is protruding from the hand, thus giving you more strength and control as you make the cut. A sharp knife is needed.

3 Place no more than 25 scored chestnuts in a roasting pan or on a cookie sheet and place in a preheated 400-degree oven for about 20 to 25 minutes. The chestnuts are much easier to peel when hot, and it is better to make several small batches and peel them before they cool than attempt to roast them all in one batch. Remove and peel off both layers of skin while the chestnuts are still hot. Use a towel to hold the chestnuts and a knife to cut the recalcitrant skin and pry them out. Repeat with the second lb.

4 For chestnut purée: Note: It is not essential that all the reddish inside skin be removed from the chestnuts for puréeing because they will be strained through a food mill.

Place the chestnuts, chicken stock, celery, and 1 tsp. salt in a saucepan. Bring to a boil and cook, partially covered, for about 45 minutes. You should have about 1 to 1½ c. of cooking liquid, at the most, remaining. Push the chestnuts as well as the liquid through the food mill. Add the butter and cream, mix well, and add salt, pepper, and even a dash of sugar to taste. Keep warm in a covered double boiler. Serve in the small zucchini boats.

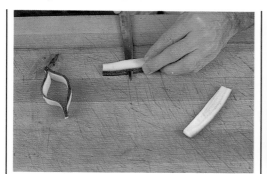

5 **Zucchini boats:** An elegant way of presenting a purée of chestnuts or other puréed vegetables, these receptacles are easy to make. Cut a piece of zucchini about 3½ to 4 in. long and slice into ¼-in. slices. Cut each slice into halves lengthwise, each about ¾ in. wide. Place in a saucepan, cover with water, and boil for about 1½ minutes. Rinse under cold water and drain. Place flat on the table and, using a small knife, cut through the slices along the whole length except at both ends. Stand the slices up and "open" to create a receptacle for the purée. Brush with butter and warm for a few minutes in the oven at serving time.

7 **For the venison steaks:** Trim the loins of any sinews and cut each loin into 5 steaks, about 4 oz. each.

8 Flatten the steaks with a meat pounder to about ½ in. thick. Roll the steaks in the marinade and cover with plastic wrap. Let macerate, refrigerated, for at least 2 hours, turning the steaks occasionally.

At serving time, place 2 Tb. butter in each of 2 skillets. Salt and pepper the steaks on both sides and place them in the hot butter, 4 steaks per skillet. Cook on high heat for 4 to 5 minutes, about 2½ minutes on each side. Remove to a platter and keep warm while making the sauce.

9 **For the black currant sauce:** Deglaze both skillets with the ½ c. vinegar and 1 c. red wine. Stir well to mix all the solidified juices and combine all the juices in 1 skillet. Reduce to about ⅔ c., then add 4 Tb. black currant jam and 2 c. reduced stock. Boil on high heat for 1 to 2 minutes to reduce and concentrate the sauce. Add the 4 Tb. butter, tablespoon by tablespoon, and the juices emitted from the reserved steaks. Do not boil the sauce. Strain through a fine strainer. Serve the steaks and sauce on very hot plates with cranberry relish and chestnut purée in zucchini boats.

6 **For braised chestnuts:** Place the 2 lb. peeled chestnuts in a saucepan so they are in one layer and add 3 c. stock and ½ tsp. salt. Cover, bring to a boil, and boil gently for 20 minutes. Add 3 Tb. butter. Partially uncover (halfway) the chestnuts, and keep boiling gently until most of the liquid is evaporated and the liquid remaining forms a glaze thick enough to coat the chestnuts. Serve as a vegetable or mix in a stuffing.

10 For a variation, serve each steak with braised chestnuts and cranberry relish in a zucchini boat.

A LEANER VERSION

Omit the chestnut purée and/or braised chestnuts. In the cranberry relish: Reduce the amount of honey from ½ c. to ¼ c. and proceed according to the recipe instructions. Reduce the amount of peanut oil from 3 Tb. to 1 Tb. in the marinade. Omit the 4 Tb. of butter in the black currant sauce. Sauté the steak, lightly coated with the oil from the marinade, in a non-stick pan, and proceed according to the recipe.

BEEF

- CHATEAUBRIAND WITH CORN PUREE IN
  CREPE BARQUETTES AND MUSHROOM
  TIMBALES WITH TRUFFLE SAUCE
- FILLET TAIL SAUTE MADELINE WITH
  KOHLRABI
- SHELL ROAST NAPA WITH TOMATO COULIS
  AND ONION CUSTARD
- FIVE-PEPPER STEAK WITH RATATOUILLE
  RAVIOLI
- RIB ROAST CLAIRE WITH YORKSHIRE
  PUDDING AND MUSTARD AND
  HORSERADISH SAUCE
- GRILLED "BUTCHER STEAKS" (SKIRT, FLANK,
  TENDERLOIN) WITH BEEF-CORIANDER
  CREPINETTES, PORK-SPINACH
  CREPINETTES, AND POTATO-CHEESE-
  STUFFED ONIONS; ARTICHOKE BOTTOMS
  OR HEARTS, FLORENTINE ARTICHOKE
  BOTTOMS MORNAY
- CONNECTICUT POT ROAST

PORK AND HAM

- PORK STEAKS WITH PORT AND PRUNES
  WITH APPLE AND ONION STEW
- HAM GEORGIA

LAMB

- SADDLE OF LAMB WITH SAGE-MOUSSE
  STUFFING
- RACK OF LAMB PROVENCALE WITH
  ARTICHOKE BOTTOMS HELEN
- BREAST OF LAMB LYONNAISE
- LOIN OF LAMB IN SAGE-MOUSSE STUFFING
  WITH EGGPLANT AND STEWED TOMATOES
- LAMB CHOPS IN AMBUSH, FAVA BEANS
  NEYRON, LEEK AND MUSHROOM PIE
- EPIGRAMS OF LAMB WITH STEWED BEANS
- GRILLED LEG OF LAMB ROBERT WITH PUREE
  OF SPINACH WITH CROUTONS AND EGGS
- ROAST BABY LAMB WITH SHALLOT SAUCE
  WITH GARLIC-BREAD ARTICHOKES AND
  VEGETABLE TEMPURA

VEAL

- GRILLED VEAL CHOPS WITH SHALLOTS AND
  BEANS
- VEAL CHOPS MENAGERE EN PAPILLOTE
- BONING OUT A LEG OF VEAL
- COCOTTE VEAL SHANKS ANNIE
- ESCALOPES OF VEAL COLETTE WITH
  POTATOES PARISIENNE AND
  RED SWISS CHARD
- FRICADELLES OF VEAL RENEE WITH
  BRAISED ENDIVE

(CONTINUED)

- GRENADINS OF VEAL HELEN WITH SLICED
  ARTICHOKE BOTTOMS
- VEAL VIENNA
- PAUPIETTES OF VEAL SARA WITH SAUTEED
  EGGPLANT
- VEAL ROAST WITH BRAISED LETTUCE
- VEAL CURRY WITH PEAR CHUTNEY AND
  BROWN RICE
- ROGNONNADE OF VEAL WITH WHEAT
  SQUARES AND PATTYPAN SQUASH
- GRILLED SHOULDER OF VEAL WITH HERB
  BUTTER WITH POTATO AND CORN
  PACKAGES

INNARDS

- BRAISED BEEF TONGUE WITH LENTILS
- POACHED CALVES' BRAINS
- CALVES' BRAINS FINANCIERE
- CALVES' BRAINS WITH BROWN BUTTER
- CALVES' LIVER SLIVERS WITH GRAPE AND
  CURRANT SAUCE AND FETTUCCINE OR
  RAVIOLI
- GRILLED DUCK LIVERS WITH HALF-DRIED
  TOMATOES
- GRILLED LAMB KIDNEYS WITH STUFFED
  MUSHROOMS
- LAMB KIDNEYS IN MUSTARD SAUCE WITH
  BRAISED CELERY
- STUFFED VEAL KIDNEYS BICHON WITH
  POTATO AND TRUFFLE CAKE
- VEAL KIDNEYS SAUTE MARRAINE
- BREADED SWEETBREADS WITH TARRAGON
  SAUCE WITH GRATIN OF BUTTERNUT
  hot2SQUASH
- BRAISED SWEETBREADS IN MIREPOIX WITH
  CREAM CHEESE BARQUETTES
- BLACK SAUSAGE BICHON WITH PUREE OF
  TURNIPS AND POTATOES AND APPLE-
  BREAD CHARLOTTES
- CHITTERLING SAUSAGES WITH SPICY RICE
  AND APPLE RINGS
- MUSTARD PIGS' FEET WITH GATEAU OF
  POTATOES WITH NIPPY SAUCE
- BRAISED TRIPE TITINE WITH STEAMED
  POTATOES
- PISTACHIO SAUSAGE IN BRIOCHE WITH
  MUSHROOM SAUCE

BEEF

FILLET OF BEEF

The fillet is the tenderest muscle of the beef. Located next to the kidney inside the belly, it is protected by the ribs and is covered with a thick layer of white, rich fat – suet – which can be melted for deep-frying.

Often the fillet is cooked whole, completely cleaned of fat, sinews, and tendons, and sometimes, as shown in photographs 6 and 7, it is divided into steaks that take on different names – from châteaubriand (see recipe next page) to tournedos and filet mignon. These are usually grilled or sautéed. The "chain" is a long strip attached lengthwise to the side of the fillet. It is made of sinews, fat, and meat and should be removed and cleaned, as shown in photographs 2 and 3.

The fillet lends itself well to a sauce (see the Madeira-truffle sauce, page 209). When completely trimmed, it can end up tasting pasty if not properly cooked. The timbale of mushrooms served with it is rich and flavorful, and the mushrooms in the timbale are enhanced by the expensive mushrooms called truffles in the sauce.

The small barquettes of crêpes filled with corn purée are delicate, sweet, and attractive. Notice that the fresh corn kernels are first blended in the food processor and then pushed through a food mill to remove any skin that was not pulverized in the processing. The resulting mixture is fairly liquid but thickens as it comes to a boil during the short cooking.

When bought from a butcher, the whole fillet usually is packed "Cryovax," that is, placed in a plastic bag with the air sucked out and replaced by nitrogen (an inert gas). Sealed in this manner, the beef keeps in the refrigerator for over a week, but, once the bag is opened, the fillet should be cleaned, divided into its separate steaks, and used right away or frozen.

The fillet used here came partially cleaned of the large layer of fat and weighed about 7¼ lb. With the fat, it would weigh about 9 to 9½ lb.

CHATEAUBRIAND WITH CORN PUREE IN CREPE BARQUETTES AND MUSHROOM TIMBALES WITH TRUFFLE SAUCE

Yield: 6–8 servings

2 châteaubriand steaks, 1¼ lb. each, cut from 1 whole fillet (partially cleaned, 7¼ lb.; completely trimmed, about 4½ lb.)
½ tsp. salt
½ tsp. freshly ground black pepper
3 Tb. butter

MADEIRA-TRUFFLE SAUCE

3 Tb. truffle peelings, finely chopped
2 Tb. cognac
½ c. Madeira or cognac
1 c. demi-glace (page 7)
½ tsp. potato starch dissolved in 1 Tb. water

MUSHROOM TIMBALES

3 Tb. butter
⅓ c. chopped shallots
2 small cloves garlic, peeled and sliced
12 oz. mushrooms, washed and coarsely chopped
1 tsp. salt
½ tsp. freshly ground black pepper
4 eggs
1 c. heavy cream

CROUTONS (10)

2 Tb. softened butter
10 slices firm-textured bread

CREPE BARQUETTES

½ c. flour
1 egg
¼ c. water
1 Tb. chopped parsley
⅓ c. milk
1½ tsp. oil
Dash salt
Oil for deep-frying

CORN PUREE FILLING

4 c. corn kernels (from 4 or 5 ears)
1½ Tb. butter
½ tsp. salt

GARNISH

Red pepper rounds (see photograph 16)

PREPARING THE WHOLE FILLET

1 Here is the whole fillet Cryovax, as it comes from the butcher or slaughterhouse.

2 Separate the long strip called the "chain," pulling it from the fillet proper. Cut it off.

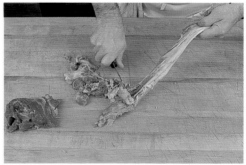

3 The chain is full of sinews and it would be difficult to remove them one by one, but, because the meat is very tender, it can simply be scraped from the sinews. Holding the chain at one end, scrape the meat from the chain with a knife or a spoon. The meat can be transformed into delicious steak tartare, hamburger, or chopped steak, and the sinews used in stock.

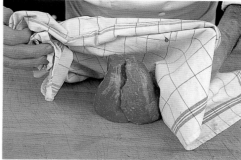

4 Remove the small layer of fat from the top of the fillet. Remove the layer of thick sinew under the layer of fat and reserve it for stock. The fillet is now completely cleaned on top. Turn it over and trim the underside, if necessary. Discard the fat and reserve the sinews and tendons for stock.

6 The fillet is usually divided into pieces. Here the large tip of the fillet, which is slightly pointed, is cut into one large steak called a châteaubriand (see below), weighing from about 1¼ to 1½ lb. This piece of meat will serve at least 3 people. Next, the whole center of the fillet, which is the same thickness, is cut into "hearts of fillets," or tournedos, about 7 to 8 oz. each.

In the recipe that follows, I use two châteaubriands. The second one could be cut from the same fillet (although that is not shown in the photograph). To do this, cut from the center of the fillet a second piece of approximately the same size as the first piece.

8 For the châteaubriand, stand the large piece of fillet pointed side up and place a towel around it.

5 In my recipe, I am not cooking the whole fillet. However, if you want to do this, fold the thin tail in on itself. To do so, tuck the tail under and then secure the thin end of it with a string before cooking. Tied this way, the fillet, though shortened slightly, is the same thickness throughout and will cook evenly.

7 From left to right is: the head of the fillet, the châteaubriand; seven tournedos; 2 smaller fillets (filets mignons), about 3 oz. each; and, finally, the tail of the fillet, cut into strips 2 to 3 in. long by ½-in. thick (see next recipe, Fillet Tail Sauté Madeline, page 210, for cutting of strips).

9 Gather the towel around to hold the fillet and, using a meat pounder, pound the meat so it flattens and takes on a roundish form as you hold it in shape with the towel. Repeat steps 8 and 9 for the second châteaubriand.

10 The châteaubriand is now ready to be cooked. It is an oval shape about 7 in. long by 5 in. wide and approximately 1¼ in. thick. Set aside in the refrigerator until ready to cook. →

11 **For the mushroom timbales:** Butter 6 or 8 small molds well with 1 Tb. of butter. Melt the remaining 2 Tb. butter in a large skillet and add ⅓ c. chopped shallots. Sauté for 1 minute. Add 2 sliced garlic cloves and sauté 10 seconds longer. Add 12 oz. mushrooms, cover, and cook on medium heat for 5 minutes. Uncover and keep cooking until all the moisture has evaporated and the mixture is sizzling. Place in a food processor and process until very smooth (about 2 to 3 minutes). Mix in 1 tsp. salt, ½ tsp. pepper, 4 eggs, and 1 c. cream. <u>Pour into the molds, which are placed in a larger pan.</u> Fill the pan with lukewarm water as high around the molds as possible, and bake in a preheated 325-degree oven for about 35 to 45 minutes, or until set. Keep warm in water until serving time. Note: The water should not boil or the mixture will expand and create air bubbles, making it less smooth.

12 **For the croutons:** Butter a roasting pan with 2 Tb. of softened butter. With an oval cookie cutter, cut the croutons out of 10 slices of bread. <u>Press the croutons into the butter, turn them over,</u> and place in a 400-degree oven for approximately 10 minutes, until nicely browned all around. If the croutons brown faster on the bottom, turn them over during cooking so they brown evenly on all sides.

13 **For the crêpe barquettes:** Combine the ½ c. flour, 1 egg, and ¼ c. water. Mix with a whisk until smooth, and add 1 Tb. parsley, ⅓ c. milk, 1½ tsp. oil, and dash of salt. To make the crêpes, butter lightly a 7-in. non-stick pan and place over medium to high heat. When hot, pour 2 to 3 Tb. of the crêpe batter into one side of the pan and quickly swirl and shake the pan to spread the batter as quickly as possible over the whole surface. Cook about 1 minute, turn, and cook about 8 to 10 seconds on the other side. Remove to a platter. Continue making the crêpes (they can be made ahead), stacking them on top of one another and covering with plastic wrap so they don't dry out. Note: After the initial buttering of the pan, no further buttering is necessary.

When ready to make the barquettes, cut each crêpe in half. Press each half crêpe into the bottom of a small mold with a scalloped or plain edge. Place another mold on top, press the crêpe into place, and <u>trim off the excess crêpe that extends above the mold.</u>

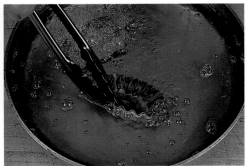

14 Place the crêpes (still held like the filling of a sandwich between the 2 molds) into 350-degree oil (preferably corn or cottonseed oil) and cook for about 1¼ to 1½ minutes. <u>If the molds tend to separate, hold them together under the oil with tongs.</u>

15 Separate the molds from the crêpes, which should be crisp and brown all around. If they require a bit more browning on the bottom, place the unmolded crêpes back in the oil for a few seconds.

16 **For the corn purée:** Place the 4 c. corn kernels in a food processor and process until puréed. <u>Push through a food mill to remove any coarse bits of skin.</u> The mixture, at this point, will be quite loose. Just before serving, place the purée in a saucepan with the 1½ Tb. butter and ½ tsp. salt, and bring to a boil. As it boils, it will thicken. Stir well with a whisk and set aside.

For the pepper round garnish: Using a vegetable peeler, remove the skin from a section of red pepper and, with a pastry bag tip, cut little rounds from strips of the flesh. Set aside for decorating the corn purée.

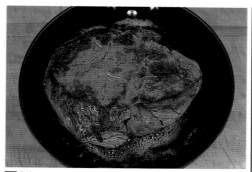

☑ To sauté the châteaubriands:
Sprinkle both of the pieces of fillet with ½
tsp. each salt and pepper. Each should be
cooked in a separate skillet, as shown in
the photograph (or one very large skillet)
so they are not crowded. Heat half of the
butter (1½ Tb.) in each skillet. When
hot, add the châteaubriands and cook over
medium to high heat for about 6 minutes
on one side, turn, and cook approximately
6 minutes on the other side for rare or
medium-rare. Set the châteaubriands on a
plate and place in a 130- to 150-degree
oven to rest for at least 15 to 20 minutes
while making the sauce.

☑ For the Madeira-truffle sauce: If you
have whole truffles instead of peelings
(which can be bought in cans), peel off the
skin and chop it fine. The rough peel of
the truffles is used in the sauce, and the
remaining whole truffles can be stored,
covered with Madeira or cognac, and
refrigerated. They will keep practically
indefinitely and can be used in other dishes
such as pâtés or galantines. Combine the 3
Tb. chopped truffle with 4 Tb. cognac.

Pour ¼ c. Madeira and ½ c. demi-
glace in each of the 2 skillets used to cook
the châteaubriands. Bring to a boil and
scrape to loosen all the drippings from the
cooking. Strain the mixture through a fine

strainer into a saucepan. Add ½ tsp.
potato starch dissolved in 1 Tb. water to
the mixture, stirring, and bring to the
boil again. Then, at the last minute, add
the truffles and cognac. The flavor of the
truffles, distinctively acquired through the
nose, tends to disappear if added too far
ahead.

☑ At serving time, unmold the timbales
of mushrooms and arrange on the croutons. Fill the barquettes with the corn
purée and dot with little rounds of pepper.

☑ Here is one châteaubriand, with ½-in.
bias-cut slices, served with corn-filled barquettes and mushroom timbales arranged
at each end. Coat the meat and the timbales lightly with the sauce and serve
immediately.

☑ For an individual presentation, place
two ½-in. slices of châteaubriand on a
plate with sauce around them and a bit
on top. Arrange a mushroom timbale,
lightly coated with the sauce, and a corn
barquette beside the fillet, and serve
immediately.

2 Cut the kohlrabi into ⅛-in.-thick slices. You should have 5 to 6 c., about 8 to 10 pieces per person. In each of 2 skillets, heat 1½ Tb. vegetable oil and 1½ tsp. butter. When hot, sauté half the kohlrabi slices in each skillet over medium heat for about 15 to 20 minutes, tossing occasionally to brown somewhat uniformly. They should be tender but still firm. Add the garlic, parsley, and salt to the kohlrabi, stirring briefly to heat the mixture through, and place in a pan in a warm oven while sautéing the fillet tails. (The same skillets used for cooking the kohlrabi can be used for cooking the fillet tails.)

FILLET TAIL SAUTE MADELINE

The tail of the beef fillet, completely cleaned of all sinews and fat, can be sautéed in a number of different ways. In the recipe here, it is seasoned simply with salt, pepper, paprika, and cayenne, sautéed briefly in butter, and served with kohlrabi. Sautéed potatoes could be done in the same manner as the kohlrabi and used instead. However, although the kohlrabi slices take longer to cook than potatoes, they are different and are quite delicious. This is a fast country dish and the kohlrabi should be started first, as it takes longer to cook than the fillet.

Yield: 6 servings

KOHLRABI

2½ lb. kohlrabi, 2¼ lb. peeled, trimmed, and sliced
3 Tb. vegetable oil
1 Tb. butter
1 tsp. chopped garlic
2 Tb. chopped parsley
¼ tsp. salt

SEASONING MIXTURE

1 tsp. salt
½ tsp. freshly ground black pepper
1 tsp. paprika
Dash cayenne

FILLET TAIL SAUTE

3 Tb. butter
1½ lb. beef fillet tails (about 4 oz. per person), cut into strips ½ in. thick and 1¼ to 1½ in. long

GARNISH

Chopped parsley

1 Peel the kohlrabi, removing the thick, fibrous skin. The flesh should be firm and white and should not smell strong.

3 Combine the ingredients for the seasoning mixture. Heat 1½ Tb. butter in each of 2 skillets. Sprinkle the pieces of fillet with the seasoning mixture. When the butter is hot, add the fillet and sauté over very high heat for 2 to 3 minutes, tossing occasionally so the meat browns all around but does not overcook.

4 Arrange the kohlrabi in a circle on each individual plate.

5 Place the sautéed fillet in the center of the kohlrabi with any natural juices that have collected in the pan. Add a sprinkle of parsley and serve immediately.

SHELL ROAST NAPA

The shell of beef extends from the last rib of the rib roast to the back leg. The whole piece, used for porterhouse steaks (also called T-bone steaks), includes the T-bone in the center with the strip on one side and the tenderloin or fillet on the other side. After the fillet and bone have been removed, the remaining piece of meat is often called a strip or shell. That shell can be cut into steaks (see Five Pepper Steak with Ravioli, page 214), which take on different names according to which part of the country you live in.

In the butchering technique here, I explain how to clean up the whole shell and divide it into steaks and, in the recipe, how to prepare a shell roast with a rich Cabernet Sauvignon sauce. The concentrated winy sauce is balanced by the mild custard of onion, which can be served with or without the coulis of fresh tomato on top. The tomato coulis is lightly cooked, mild, and doesn't conflict with the wine sauce. This custard of onion with the coulis of tomato is excellent as a first course for a family dinner and goes well with poultry and other meats.

Yield: 6–8 servings

THE SHELL OR STRIP, BONE IN

1 19-lb. shell or strip

SHELL ROAST

1 3-lb. shell, completely trimmed, with "chain" attached
½ tsp. salt
½ tsp. freshly ground black pepper
2 Tb. butter

NAPA SAUCE

1 Tb. butter
½ c. sliced shallots
½ tsp. peppercorns, cracked
3 cloves garlic, peeled and sliced
½ tsp. dried thyme leaves
2 bay leaves, crushed
3 anchovy fillets in oil
2 c. red Cabernet Sauvignon wine
1½ c. demi-glace (see page 7)
½ tsp. potato starch dissolved in 1 Tb. water (if needed to thicken sauce)
Salt and freshly ground black pepper, if needed

GARNISH

Parsley

TOMATO COULIS

4 tomatoes (1½ lb.)
1 Tb. tomato paste (if the tomatoes are not especially red and ripe)
½ c. water
½ tsp. salt
½ tsp. sugar

Boning out a shell roast of beef, cutting steaks, 2–8

ONION CUSTARD

Yield: 10–12 servings
1½ lb. onions, sliced
3 Tb. butter
2 cloves garlic, chopped coarse (½ tsp.)
1 c. water
1 c. heavy cream
1 tsp. salt
½ tsp. freshly ground black pepper
6 eggs

CROUTONS

2 Tb. softened butter
10 large round croutons, cut from 10
   slices of firm-textured bread

3 Following the contour of the bone, separate the bones from the meat. Trim away most of the fat underneath and on top of the meat. (There are approximately 5½ lb. of fat and about 2½ lb. of bones on this piece of meat.)

6 Now the top of the strip can be cleaned of the large gelatinous sinews, which are excellent in white as well as brown stock. Remove by pulling on a strip of sinew with one hand while cutting and sliding the knife against the sinew with the other hand to get it off with as little meat attached as possible.

1 The whole strip or shell, bone in (approximately 19 lb.), with fillet removed. Start removing the pieces of fat.

4 At one end of the strip, there is a triangular piece of meat lodged on top of the strip and separated from it by a large sinew. Although this triangular piece is often left in place and the steaks cut directly through it, it is preferable to remove it because the connecting sinew is tough. Following the contour of the sinew, cut off the triangle of meat.

7 When the whole shell is trimmed (there is still a little bit of the front flap and chain attached to it), most of the fat and sinews have been removed. Cut off about a 3-lb. piece of the shell for the Shell Roast Napa.

2 Slide your knife between the bone and the meat and, standing the roast on the end of the chine bone (backbone), continue cutting alongside the chine bone to separate it from the meat.

5 The triangular piece of meat is being removed and can be used as a steak. (It weighs approximately 8 oz., more or less, depending on the size of the shell.)

8 Cut the rest of the shell into ¾- to 1-in.-thick steaks of approximately 10 oz. each. Depending on the size of the shell, it will yield approximately a dozen steaks in addition to the 3-lb. roast, bones and sinews (which can be used for stock), and fat. The steaks can be wrapped in plastic wrap and then in aluminum foil and frozen individually for later use. If the steaks are frozen, be sure to defrost them slowly, still wrapped, under refrigeration.

9 **For the onion custard:** Sauté the 1½ lb. sliced onions in 2 Tb. of sizzling butter for approximately 10 minutes in a large saucepan. Add 2 chopped garlic cloves, mix well, and add 1 c. of water. Cover and cook over medium to low heat for about 5 minutes. Uncover and cook over high heat until most of the moisture has evaporated (about 3 minutes). Then place the onions in the food processor and process until very smooth. Add 1 c. cream, 1 tsp. salt, ½ tsp. pepper, and 6 eggs to the mixture in the processor and process until smooth. Butter ¾-c. baba molds with the remaining Tb. butter, fill with the onion mixture, and place the molds in a roasting pan. Surround the molds with tepid water (water should come two-thirds of the way up the molds). Place in a preheated 325-degree oven for 35 to 45 minutes, until well set. The water should not get too hot or the timbales will expand and lose some of their smoothness. Let sit in the warm water until ready to serve.

For the croutons: Prepare 10 round croutons, following the instructions on page 208.

10 **To roast the meat:** Sprinkle the roast with ½ tsp. each salt and pepper. Heat 2 Tb. butter in a large, heavy skillet. When hot, add the roast and brown on all sides over medium to high heat for 5 to 6 minutes. Place in a 425-degree oven for 20 to 25 minutes if the roast is fairly thick, like the one shown here. If it's thinner, reduce the cooking time by a few minutes.

11 Let the meat rest in a warm place (130- to 150-degree oven or on top of a warm stove) for at least 30 minutes before serving.

Meanwhile, **make the tomato coulis:** Place the 1½ lb. of tomatoes, 1 Tb. tomato paste (if needed), and ½ c. water in a saucepan. Bring to a boil, cover, and cook 10 minutes. Push the tomatoes through a food mill fitted with the fine screen, add ½ tsp. each salt and sugar, and set aside.

12 **For the sauce:** Heat the 1 Tb. butter in a saucepan. When hot, add ½ c. sliced shallots and ½ tsp. peppercorns, and sauté for 1½ to 2 minutes. Add the 3 sliced garlic cloves, ½ tsp. thyme, 2 bay leaves, and 3 anchovies, crush together, and cook 1 to 1½ minutes longer. Add 2 c. wine, bring to a boil, and cook approximately 15 minutes, until reduced to about ¾ c.

From the skillet where the shell was cooked, pour out all but 1 Tb. of the rendered fat. To the skillet add the wine reduction and 1½ c. demi-glace. Boil together over medium heat for approximately 5 minutes and strain through a fine strainer, pressing on the solids to extract the juices. Then reduce the sauce to 1½ c. Add ½ tsp. potato starch dissolved in 1 Tb. water, if needed, to thicken the sauce lightly, and salt and pepper to taste, if needed.

13 Cut the roast into ¼- to ⅜-in.-thick slices after it has rested.

14 For an individual serving, place some very warm sauce on a hot plate and arrange 2 slices of the shell roast on top of the sauce. Dribble a little additional sauce on top. Serve immediately with an onion custard unmolded on a crouton and topped with a Tb. of tomato coulis.

Yield: 6 servings

RATATOUILLE RAVIOLI

1 Tb. olive oil
1 Tb. peanut oil
1 large, coarsely chopped onion (about 6 oz.) (1¼ c.)
¾ lb. unpeeled eggplant (2 small), coarsely chopped
½ lb. green pepper, seeded and coarsely chopped (1¼ c.)
¾ lb. zucchini (2), coarsely chopped
¾ lb. tomatoes, seeded and coarsely chopped (2 c.)
3 cloves garlic, crushed and chopped (1 tsp.)
1 tsp. salt
Dash cayenne pepper

RAVIOLI PARSLEY DOUGH

2 c. flour
¼ tsp. salt
½ c. loose parsley
2 egg yolks
⅓ c. water
1 Tb. olive oil

PEPPER STEAKS

¼ c. mixture of black, white, green, Jamaican, and Szechuan peppercorns
6 shell steaks (each 10 oz. and ¾ to 1 in. thick)
2 Tb. butter
½ tsp. salt
4 Tb. chopped shallots
4 Tb. cognac
1 c. demi-glace (see page 7)
Dash salt, if needed
2 Tb. butter (to finish the sauce)

FIVE-PEPPER STEAK WITH RATATOUILLE RAVIOLI

The pepper steaks here are approximately ¾ to 1 in. thick and weigh about 10 oz. each. Steaks weighing 6 to 7 oz. could be used instead if the garnish were more copious and the menu larger. It is conventional to use cracked black peppercorns, called mignon-nettes, for pepper steak. These are used in different types of sauces for flavor. In the recipe here, however, I use five different types of dried peppercorns: black, white (which is the same as the black with the shell removed), green (also the same berries but unripe, with a lot of flavor and less hot-ness), Jamaican (also called allspice), and, finally, Szechuan (which is the flavorful, mild bud of a flower and is used in Chinese cooking).

In this recipe, the sauce is finished with shallots, cognac, and demi-glace. Some-times, as a variation, the sauce is deglazed with red wine instead of cognac and finished with the demi-glace, while, at other times, the steak is finished with heavy cream.

The ratatouille ravioli is spicy and fla-vorful. Although the dough for the ravioli is rolled with a pasta machine here, it can be rolled by hand (see Squash-Stuffed Ravioli, page 297). The ratatouille should be made ahead to be used cold. The vege-tables must be chopped fine enough so they can be pushed through a pastry bag fitted with a ½-in. plain tube. The ratatouille should be well cooked and most of its mois-ture removed so the filling is not too liquid.

Four to 5 ravioli per person will be enough for a garnish with the pepper steak. However, if served as a course in itself, the quantity should be doubled. The yield given here — about 60 to 64 ravioli — is enough for about 6 to 8 people as a main course and will serve twice that many as a garnish. To serve the ravioli by itself, poach for about 4 minutes in boiling water, drain, sprinkle with melted butter, a dash of salt and pep-per, and serve immediately with freshly grated Parmesan cheese. The uncooked ravioli can also be frozen for a few days and then cooked (directly from the freezer) by being dropped into boiling water for about 5 minutes.

1 To make the ratatouille mixture:
Heat the olive and peanut oils in a large saucepan. When hot, add the onion and sauté 2 minutes. Add the eggplant and green pepper and cook for 5 minutes over medium heat, stirring occasionally, until browning begins. Then add the zucchini, tomatoes, garlic, and salt. Mix well, cover, and cook over very low heat for about 20 minutes. Remove the cover and cook over medium heat, stirring occasionally, until most of the liquid has evaporated, 12 to 15 minutes. Add a dash of cayenne, remove to a bowl, and cool.

To make the ravioli dough: Process the flour, salt, and parsley in a processor for about 30 seconds. Add the egg yolks, water, and oil, and process again until the mixture begins to pull away from the sides of the bowl and form into a ball. Press together, wrap in plastic wrap, and refrigerate for at least 1 hour. When ready to roll, divide the dough into 4 segments. Run each segment through the pasta machine on the large setting.

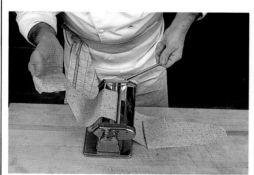

2 Push the dough back through the machine several times, changing the setting, until you reach the level (usually #7) where the dough becomes extremely thin (less than 1/16 in. thick). Each quarter of the dough will give you a rectangle about 24 in. long by 5 in. wide. Cut each rectangle in half crosswise, giving you 2 rectangles, each 12 in. long by 5 in. wide. Place one of these rectangles on a piece of waxed paper and brush it with water.

3 Fill a pastry bag fitted with a 1/2-in. plain tube with the cold ratatouille mixture. Pipe neat mounds (about 1/2 Tb. each) of the ratatouille mixture approximately 1 in. apart in 2 rows the length of the pastry.

4 Place the other rectangular piece of dough on top, pressing with your fingers in between the stuffing so the top layer of dough sticks to the wet surface of the bottom layer.

5 Using an inverted shot glass or the dull side of a cookie cutter about the size of the mounds, press around each mound to compact the stuffing into uniform rounds.

6 Using a larger cutter, cut the ravioli into neat rounds. Repeat with the remaining dough and filling until they are used up. The trimmings can be rerolled for immediate use or cut into pieces and used as a garnish in soup.

7 Lift up and remove the trimmings of the dough from the waxed paper. Since the ravioli are all arranged on the waxed paper, it is easier to place them with the paper on a tray in the freezer or refrigerator if you are not going to use them right away, or if you are, cook them immediately by sliding them into boiling water to cook gently 4 to 5 minutes.

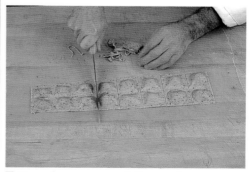

8 To make square ravioli, use the same technique as in steps 3 and 4, pressing with your fingers in between the dough-covered mounds. Then cut between the mounds, making square ravioli.

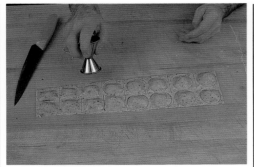

9 To improve the appearance of square ravioli, <u>press around the mounds with a cookie cutter or inverted shot glass</u> so the stuffing is marked and defined neatly inside the squares. When ready to serve, slide into boiling water and cook gently for 4 to 5 minutes. The green ravioli dough will get paler during the cooking. Lift from the water and serve immediately brushed with butter or, as in the recipe below, with some of the steak sauce.

10 <u>Roll the corner of a heavy saucepan over the peppercorns.</u> Gather them together and roll the bottom of the pan over them again to crush further.

11 Spread the ¼ c. cracked-pepper mixture on the table and place the steaks on top. Turn the steaks, <u>patting them gently to coat them with pepper on all sides.</u>

12 Use 2 skillets to sauté the steaks. Place 1 Tb. of butter in each skillet. When hot, add 3 steaks to each skillet, sprinkle them lightly with ½ tsp. salt, and sauté over high heat for approximately 2½ minutes. <u>Turn and sauté 1½ minutes on the other side.</u>

13 <u>Remove the steaks to a platter.</u> Keep warm in a 130- to 150-degree oven while finishing the sauce. Add the 4 Tb. chopped shallots to the skillets and sauté for about 30 seconds. Then add the 4 Tb. cognac, flame (to burn off the alcohol), and add 1 c. demi-glace. Combine the mixtures in one of the skillets, bring to a boil, season lightly with salt, if needed (remember that the demi-glace is not seasoned and may need salt), and strain through a fine strainer. Finally, whisk the additional 2 Tb. of butter into the sauce, mixing until well incorporated.

14 Place the steaks on very warm plates with the ravioli (about 4 per person) around them. Spoon the sauce (about 2 to 3 Tb. per serving) over the steak and the ravioli. Serve immediately.

A LEANER VERSION

In sautéing the steaks (step 12), reduce the amount of butter from 2 Tb. to 2 tsp. (1 tsp. per skillet). Omit the 2 Tb. butter to finish the sauce (step 13). Proceed according to the recipe, preferably using a non-stick pan. Reduce the 1 Tb. of olive oil and 1 Tb. of peanut oil in the ratatouille to 2 tsp. of olive oil. Proceed according to the recipe. In step 14, heat up the ratatouille and serve (instead of the ravioli) with the steaks.

RIB ROAST CLAIRE WITH YORKSHIRE PUDDING

A rib roast is usually comprised of 7 ribs and extends from the first rib, called the small end (the part closest to the fillet or New York strip), to the neck at the end of the shoulder, called the large end, which touches the shoulder and is less desirable because it has layers of fat between the meat.

The rib-eye steaks, shown in photograph 4, can be broiled, sautéed, or prepared like the châteaubriands (page 209). In this recipe the rib roast is cleaned almost completely of fat and the top covered with a very peppery, spicy mixture, which turns dark when roasted but flavors the meat.

For my version of Yorkshire pudding, some trimmings of the meat attached to the bones are added to the batter along with some reserved fat from the roast beef. To serve by itself or with poultry, the same pudding can be made, substituting 4 Tb. of oil for the fat and eliminating the pieces of meat.

The mustard and horseradish sauce can be made well ahead as it will keep for several weeks in the refrigerator. It gives a spicy accent to the meat and can also be served with most pâtés or cold cuts.

Yield: 8–10 servings

CLEANING A WHOLE RIB ROAST

1 21–25-lb. 7-rib standing rib roast

RIB ROAST CLAIRE

1 7½-lb. rib roast

SEASONING MIXTURE

2 Tb. crushed dried oregano
1 Tb. crushed dried thyme leaves
1 Tb. paprika
2 tsp. freshly ground black pepper
1/16 tsp. cayenne pepper
½ tsp. salt

YORKSHIRE PUDDING

½ c. reserved beef fat
1 c. meat trimmings
2 c. sliced leeks
1 c. flour
5 eggs
2 c. milk
1 tsp. salt
½ tsp. freshly ground black pepper
½ c. chopped parsley

MUSTARD AND HORSERADISH SAUCE

¼ c. freshly grated horseradish
3 Tb. old-fashioned coarse-ground mustard
2 Tb. honey
½ tsp. freshly ground black pepper
Dash salt

GARNISH

Red pepper segments, peeled, for use as receptacles for the sauce

1 The whole rib is covered with a thick layer of fat, which should be removed first. Pull and cut between the fat and the meat so the fat layer will lift up in one piece. If there is a thin strip of meat attached to the fat, cut it off, chop, and reserve for a good steak tartare, hamburger, or chopped steak.

2 Cut along the chine bone, removing the bone along with the fat and sinew. The only bones left on the rib roast are the ribs. Removing the chine bone makes it much easier to carve in between the ribs at the table. Our roast yields approximately 4½ lb. of trimmings, mostly fat. Remove whatever meat is usable from the trimmings and reserve for hamburger. The chine bone weighs approximately 1 lb.; reserve it. →

MEAT

217

3 Separate the meat into 2 pieces by cutting between the fourth and fifth ribs, counting from the smaller end. Reserve the piece with the small end for the rib roast.

4 Trim the other piece of meat and cut into steaks approximately 10 to 11 oz. each. You should have about 7 or 8 steaks.
   Trim most of the fat from the piece of rib roast. Trimmed, it will weigh approximately 7½ lb. There are about 7 lb. of fat in the trimmings of the roast and the steaks. Discard this fat. Wrap the steaks in plastic wrap and aluminum foil and refrigerate or freeze. If frozen, defrost slowly under refrigeration when ready to use.

5 Mix together the seasoning ingredients. Pat the seasoning mixture onto the top and sides of the rib roast. Place the roast in a large roasting pan. Surround with the chine bone and some sinews. Place in a preheated 425-degree oven for 30 minutes. Baste with the fat that has accumulated in the pan during roasting, reduce

the heat to 375 degrees, and cook for 1 hour longer. At that point, the inside temperature of the roast won't be much more than 75 degrees. Turn off the oven and let the roast sit in its pan in the oven for at least 45 minutes to 1 hour to rest and continue to cook in its own heat.

6 The roast is now cooked. Baste with the fat, remove to a plate, and keep warm in the oven.

7 Reserve approximately ½ c. of fat for the Yorkshire pudding. Discard the remainder. Pick about 1 c. of meat off the bones and add to the reserved fat. The pieces of meat will be almost like cracklings. Place a c. of water in the roasting pan with the chine bone and bring to a boil on top of the stove. Set the roast beef on top and place back in the still warm shut-off oven to continue resting and cooking in its own heat. If the oven is needed to cook the pudding, keep the meat on the back of the stove while cooking the pudding and then place it back in the oven when available to warm up slightly before serving.

8 For the Yorkshire pudding: In a large, preferably non-stick, ovenproof skillet (about 10 in. in diameter and 2 in. deep), heat the ½ c. reserved fat and 1 c. trimmings of meat from the bones (see preceding step). When hot, add 2 c. sliced leeks and sauté gently for 2 to 3 minutes over medium heat. Meanwhile, mix 1 c. flour and 5 eggs until smooth and add 2 c. milk, 1 tsp. salt, ½ tsp. pepper, and ½ c. chopped parsley.

9 Add the flour-egg-milk mixture to the sautéed leeks and place in a 400-degree oven for 30 minutes. Reduce the heat to 350 degrees and cook an additional 10 minutes.

10 Remove from the oven. The pudding has risen up the sides of the pan and fat has accumulated in the middle. Scoop out and discard the fat or baste the pudding with it.

11 Place a flat lid on top of the pudding and <u>invert it.</u>

12 Place a plate on top of the inverted pudding and <u>turn upright, so the pudding is right side up and ready to serve.</u>

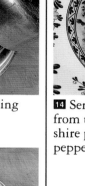

13 Make the mustard and horseradish sauce: Combine the ¼ c. grated horseradish, 3 Tb. mustard, 2 Tb. honey, ½ tsp. pepper, and a dash of salt. Make receptacles for the sauce out of segments of red pepper. <u>Cut the meat into ¼- to ½-in. slices</u> and place one slice per person on warm plates.

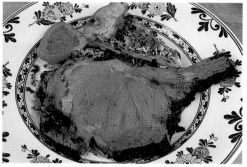

14 Serve the meat with some of the juice from the pan (1 Tb. per serving), Yorkshire pudding, and mustard sauce in red pepper receptacles.

GRILLED "BUTCHER STEAK"

When grilling steak on an open grill, beef rib steak, shell steak, strip steak, Porterhouse steak, or T-bone steak — all expensive cuts — are usually used, although the steaks on the following pages are as flavorful, leaner when properly trimmed, and much less expensive than the cuts I've just mentioned. The following steaks, juicy and tender when properly prepared, are the favorites of butchers and are, consequently, called "butcher steaks." The skirt steak, hanging tenderloin, flank steak, and oyster steak are all butcher steaks and they are shown here except for the smallest of the four, the oyster steak (l'araignée in French). Like the "oyster" in the chicken (Chicken Breasts with Chervil Mousse, page 171), it is found nested in the hollow part of the pelvic bone next to the joint of the hip.

As indicated in the veal chop and fish grilling (Grilled Veal Chops, page 264, and Grilled Sole with Herb Butter, page 134), the grill should be very clean and very hot. I use wood or wood charcoal (a partially burned wood) rather than briquettes. The wood lends a better flavor to the steak than the briquettes, which are a petroleum derivative.

There are two spicy seasonings. Mixture 1 is spicier than mixture 2, but they both can be used interchangeably on the hanging tenderloin as well as the flank or skirt steak. The skirt steak, called hampe or manteau in French, is often cut into individual 4- or 5-oz. steaks, pan-fried, and served with the shallot mixture used with the hanging tenderloin. The skirt steak is the inner diaphragm muscle and hangs inside the cavity of the beef carcass in the rib-cage area. It has fibers that run across the steak, widthwise, as opposed to the flank steak, in which the meat fiber goes lengthwise. The skirt steak shrinks and tightens somewhat during cooking and gets thicker and quite moist.

The flank steak (bavette in French) is an inside muscle, part of the side of the animal. Flat and oval with elongated fibers, it is also called "London broil" or "plank steak." Although it is excellent broiled or grilled, it is also good butterflied, stuffed, and braised. Because of the fibers in the meat, it is important to slice the flank steak crosswise in thin slices against the grain. Otherwise it will be chewy and stick between your teeth. There are two flank steaks (bavette d'aloyau and bavette de flanchet in French). The first one is very narrow, thicker, and is not found in markets in the U.S., although sometimes it is sold as skirt steak. The second (bavette de flanchet) is larger, thinner, and is what we know as a regular flank steak.

The hanging tenderloin (onglet in French) is a narrow, fairly thick (about 2-in.) piece of meat. It hangs inside the cavity of the animal between the two tenderloins, attached to the backbone. Unfortunately, it is not often found in open markets but it can be ordered special from a butcher. The oyster steak, l'araignée (the spider) in French, is so called because there is a central line or muscle that runs the length of the meat and the fiber extends from this line in a pattern resembling a spider web. Each steak weighs about 8 to 10 oz. They are not used in the recipe here.

The skirt, flank, and hanging fillet are ideal for grilling. Although the cook would usually choose only one of the three steaks shown here, I have cooked one of each to show the differences in the texture distinctive to each. I am serving them with crépinettes and stuffed onions. The word crépinette is French for caul fat. Caul fat, also called "omentum" or "mesentery," looks like a lacy membrane. It holds the organs of the pig inside the abdominal cavity. It is a strong, transparent membrane with little lines of fat in it, which give it a lacy appearance. It is used to wrap whole pâtés or individual sausages or crépinettes as done here. It flavors and bastes the meat from the outside and holds the ingredients together. The sausages can also be done without the caul fat if it is not available, although they may not be as flavorful or attractive.

There are two types of crépinettes here, one made with beef and flavored with roasted and crushed coriander seeds, and another made with pork meat flavored with garlic, spinach, and onion and bound together with chicken livers. Both kinds of crépinettes could be served by themselves cold like a pâté or hot with mashed potatoes as a country dish.

The stuffed onions are flavorful and moist because of the stuffing made with the onion trimmings, cooked potatoes, and cream cheese. They make a nice accompaniment to most roasts or sautéed meats. Although their preparation is explained and pictured at the end of the recipe, if you decide to prepare the stuffed onions with the grilled beef, prepare and stuff them ahead — even the day before — and finish them in the oven at serving time.

As an alternative, artichoke bottoms or hearts would make an attractive and delicious accompaniment, either simply braised or stuffed as in *Florentine Artichoke Bottoms Mornay.* The recipes start on page 224, and you should do the initial preparation ahead of time.

It is imperative that the meat be left to rest after grilling. It is on the grill just long enough to sear the surface and give it a charred flavor. Resting in a warm oven (130 to 150 degrees) allows the meat, which has contracted during cooking, to relax and finish cooking in its own heat. As the meat relaxes, the juices flow back through it, ensuring that the whole piece will be uniformly pink from the first slice to the last.

PORK-SPINACH CREPINETTES

Yield: About 8 crépinettes
5–6 oz. spinach
1 Tb. butter
½ c. chopped onions
2 cloves garlic, chopped very fine
2 chicken livers
1¼ lb. ground pork
¾ tsp. salt
¼ tsp. freshly ground black pepper
1 or 2 pieces of caul fat (about ½ lb.)

POTATO-CHEESE–STUFFED ONIONS

Yield: 6 servings
6 medium onions (2¼ lb.)
STUFFING
2 c. onion trimmings (from onions listed above)
2 Tb. butter
1 Tb. vegetable oil
1 large potato (7 to 8 oz.), cooked with skin on and drained
½ tsp. salt
¼ tsp. freshly ground black pepper
4 oz. cream cheese
2 Tb. chopped chives
1 Tb. grated Parmesan cheese

FOUR RECIPES FOR GRILLED BUTCHER STEAKS WITH CREPINETTES

GRILLED SPICY HOT SKIRT STEAK

Yield: 4–5 servings
1 skirt steak (2 lb. untrimmed, 1¼ lb. trimmed)
1 tsp. vegetable oil
¼ tsp. salt
SPICY SEASONING NO. 1
In a spice grinder, place together and grind into a powder:
1 tsp. mustard seed
½ tsp. cardamom powder
1 tsp. paprika
⅛ tsp. cayenne pepper
½ tsp. fennel seed

GRILLED FLANK STEAK

Yield: 4–5 servings
1 flank steak (2½ lb. untrimmed, 1¾ lb. trimmed)
1 tsp. vegetable oil
¼ tsp. salt
SPICY SEASONING NO. 2
In a spice grinder, place together and grind into a powder:
½ tsp. powdered cumin
½ tsp. thyme leaves
1 tsp. black peppercorns
¼ tsp. powdered cloves
½ tsp. coriander seeds

GRILLED HANGING TENDERLOIN

Yield: 4–5 servings
1 hanging tenderloin (3 lb. untrimmed, 1½ lb. trimmed)
1 tsp. vegetable oil
¼ tsp. salt
¼ tsp. freshly ground black pepper
SHALLOT GARNISH
1 Tb. butter
10 shallots, peeled and sliced (1 c.)
Dash salt and freshly ground black pepper
3 Tb. coarsely chopped parsley
2 Tb. dry white wine

BEEF-CORIANDER CREPINETTES

Yield: About 8 crépinettes
2 tsp. coriander seeds
1½ lb. ground beef (hamburger meat, not too lean)
1 tsp. salt
¼ tsp. freshly ground black pepper
1 Tb. sherry
2 scallions, coarsely chopped (¼ c.)
1 slice bread for bread crumbs (about ⅓ c.)
1 or 2 pieces of caul fat (about ½ lb.)

PREPARING THE STEAKS

1 For the skirt steak: Pull off the layer of skin on both sides. You will notice that the skin on both sides is not removed lengthwise but rather from side to side, following the fiber of the meat. Trim the excess fat from the meat. An untrimmed 2-lb. skirt steak yields approximately 1¼ lb. of trimmed meat. →

MEAT

Cleaning and stemming spinach, 7
How to use caul fat, 8–9

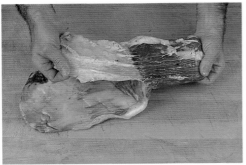

2 **For the untrimmed flank steak:** <u>Pull off the skin on both sides.</u> Notice that the skin will separate from the thicker, meatier side lengthwise and should be pulled down and off. Most of these pieces of meat, unless purchased directly from a slaughterhouse, will come trimmed from your local butcher. They may, however, not be as trimmed as they are in this photo. If so, trim further until completely clean for grilling.

3 At the thin end of the flank steak, there is mostly fat. <u>Trim the steak into an oval shape, removing most of the fat, especially at the tail end.</u> A 2½-lb. untrimmed flank steak will yield a trimmed steak of about 1¾ lb. (approximately ¾ lb. of fat and sinew).

4 **For the hanging tenderloin:** When untrimmed, this piece of meat is covered by a thick skin, especially at the tail, where there is a big lump of fat. Clean away the excess fat, <u>pulling the layer of skin and fat from the meat.</u> A 3-lb. hanging tenderloin yields approximately 1½ lb. of completely trimmed meat.

5 Here are 3 pieces of meat, trimmed: the <u>skirt steak on top, the flank steak in the center, and the hanging tenderloin on the bottom.</u>

MAKING THE CREPINETTES

6 **Beef crépinettes:** <u>On the right are 2 tsp. of browned coriander seeds and, on the left, 2 tsp. of unbrowned coriander seeds.</u> To brown, spread the seeds in a roasting pan and place in a preheated 375-degree oven for 12 to 15 minutes. Reduce to a powder in a spice grinder. The browned seeds will taste quite different from the unbrowned seeds. Combine the ground beef with the salt, pepper, sherry, scallions, coriander powder, and fresh bread crumbs.

7 **Pork crépinettes:** Remove the large stems from the spinach. Moreover, <u>if the stems are particularly large and fibrous, pull them off the back of the leaves by folding the leaves in half lengthwise with one hand and pulling up on the stems with the other.</u> Wash the spinach thoroughly.

Melt the butter in a large skillet, add the onions, and sauté for a few minutes. Add the garlic and sauté for 10 seconds, and then add the spinach fresh from the washing water. (The water will produce enough moisture for the spinach to cook.) Cook the spinach over high heat about 1 to 2 minutes, uncovered, until it begins to wilt. Cover and continue cooking 3 to 4 minutes over high heat. Set aside to cool. Process the chicken livers in a food processor until puréed and combine with the ground pork, salt, pepper, and the cooled spinach mixture.

8 If the caul fat is cold, place it in a bowl of lukewarm water to make it easy to separate and extend. If not soaked, it will have a tendency to tear. <u>Spread the caul fat on the table and cut into 5-in. squares.</u> Divide the pork mixture and the beef mixture into 4-oz. patties, 7 or 8 of each.

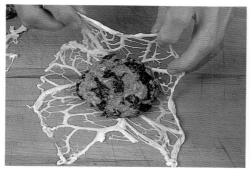

9 Place each patty on a square of caul fat and fold the fat on top of it to encase completely.

GRILLING THE STEAKS

10 Sprinkle each of the 3 steaks with 1 tsp. oil and ¼ tsp. salt. Season the hanging tenderloin with ¼ tsp. pepper. Sprinkle the skirt steak with seasoning no. 1 (1 tsp. mustard seed, ½ tsp. cardamom powder, 1 tsp. paprika, ⅛ tsp. cayenne pepper, and ½ tsp. fennel seed ground into a powder), and the flank steak with seasoning no. 2 (½ tsp. cumin, ½ tsp. thyme, 1 tsp. peppercorns, ¼ tsp. powdered cloves, and ½ tsp. coriander seeds ground into a powder). The steaks are now ready to be placed on the hot grill.

11 The barbecue should be started ahead so at the time of cooking there are only very hot ashes left underneath without much visible flame. The wood should burn at least 30 minutes beforehand to become glowing charcoal. (See Grilled Sole with Herb Butter, page 133, and Grilled Leg of Lamb Robert, page 253.)

12 Place the patties and the hanging tenderloin on the hot grill. Notice that the patties are cooking on a flat, solid piece of metal, as opposed to the open grill where the steak is cooking. The patties are cooked more easily this way but can also be cooked on the open grill.

Place the seasoned flank steak and the skirt on the hot grill next to the tenderloin. Cook the skirt steak 2 to 3 in. from the hot ashes approximately 1½ minutes on each side. This should be long enough to mark it well and brown the exterior. Place on a tray. Cook the flank steak, which is a bit larger, approximately 2 minutes on each side (4 minutes total). Place on the tray with the skirt steak. The hanging fillet should cook approximately 4 minutes on each side (total of 8 minutes) as it is thicker. Place it next to the skirt and flank steaks on a tray. The 3 steaks can now be kept hot and the cooking completed in a 130- to 150-degree oven. The meat will continue cooking in its own juice and relax so it is pink throughout and some of the cooking juices flow outside onto the tray. It should be kept in the warm oven for at least 30 minutes but can be kept there as long as 1 hour.

Grill the patties, or crépinettes, on the griddle over coals that are not as hot as those used for grilling the steaks (or the patties will burn) for about 5 to 6 minutes total for the beef crépinettes and 10 to 12 minutes total for the pork crépinettes. Keep warm by placing next to the steaks in the oven.

13 At serving time, melt the 1 Tb. butter for the shallot garnish to be served with the hanging tenderloin. When hot, add 1 c. sliced shallots, dash of salt and pepper, and sauté for about 3 minutes over medium heat, until the shallots soften. Add 3 Tb. chopped parsley and 2 Tb. wine and stir into the shallots.

14 Pour the shallot garnish directly onto the hanging tenderloin. Serve with the crépinettes and the stuffed onions (recipe, step 17). →

15 Cut the flank steak on the bias into thin slices (about ¼ in.). Serve also with the stuffed onions and crépinettes.

16 The skirt steak can be cut a little thicker than the flank steak as the slices are usually narrower. Serve, again, with the stuffed onions and the crépinettes.

17 **To make the stuffed onions:** Peel the 2¼ lb. of onions but leave the root ends. Cover the peeled onions with water, bring to a boil, and simmer at a gentle boil for about 30 minutes, until the onions are tender but still a bit firm. Drain and set aside to cool.

18 When cool, cut off a ½- to ¾-in. slice from the top of each onion so the opening will be larger. Using a small spoon, scoop out the inside of each onion, leaving about 2 or 3 outside layers for strength. Remove the root ends. You now have a receptacle for the stuffing.

For the stuffing: Chop the onion trimmings coarse. You should have about 2 c. Melt the 2 Tb. butter and add 1 Tb. oil to it in the skillet. When hot, add the chopped onions. Sauté over medium to high heat 4 to 5 minutes. Peel the cooked potato and chop coarse (you should have a good c.). Add to the onions in the skillet and continue cooking, tossing occasionally, for 5 minutes longer.

19 Add the ½ tsp. salt, ¼ tsp. pepper, 4 oz. cream cheese, and 2 Tb. chives, and crush the mixture with a fork so it is well mixed. Remove from the heat.

20 Place in a gratin dish. Using a spoon, stuff the hollowed-out onions with the stuffing mixture. Sprinkle with the 1 Tb. Parmesan cheese and place in a 400-degree oven for about 15 minutes if the stuffing is still hot when placed in the onion receptacle. If cold, leave the onions in the oven for at least 25 minutes. Finish for 1 to 2 minutes under the broiler to create a nice brown crust. Serve with the steaks and crépinettes, as explained above.

A LEANER VERSION

In step 10, omit the oil on the skirt, flank, and hanging tenderloin and cook according to the recipe. In the shallot garnish, reduce the amount of butter from 1 Tb. to 1 tsp. and proceed according to the recipe. Omit the beef and pork crépinettes and the potato-cheese–stuffed onions.

ARTICHOKE BOTTOMS OR HEARTS

Nowadays, the globe artichokes we eat are almost all grown in Castroville, California, their acknowledged capital, owing to the happy mix of sea mist and heat along the coastal field between San Francisco and Monterey. Artichokes can be served whole, stuffed or unstuffed, in lemon butter, or cold in vinaigrette.

Usually, artichokes that are starting to get yellow and are not too firm are used to make artichoke bottoms. Not nice enough to be served whole, they are less expensive and ideal for making bottoms. Artichoke bottoms or hearts are widely used in elegant meals, served as garnishes or vegetables with meat or fish, in purées or soups, but most often as receptacles. Filled with eggs (poached or scrambled) or spinach as well as mushrooms, as in the recipes here, they can be served as a first course or as an accompaniment to most roast meat and poultry.

Globe artichokes and Jerusalem artichokes (also called Sunchokes) have no botanical similarity. The Sunchoke is a tuber and the globe artichoke is a bud.

8 medium artichokes, about ½ lb. each
¼ c. lemon juice

COOKING STOCK FOR 8 ARTICHOKE BOTTOMS

3 c. water
1 Tb. flour
2 Tb. peanut oil
¼ c. lemon juice
½ tsp. salt

1 The goal is to retrieve as much of the "meat" from the leaves and bottoms as possible. Break off each leaf high enough so that the meat remains attached to the body of the artichoke.

2 If you pull the leaf off instead of breaking it off, the lower white part of the leaf with the meat attached will come off as shown in the photograph. Be sure to fold the leaf down and pull down to break it off, leaving the meat attached to the heart.

3 When all of the heart is exposed, cut the center leaves of the artichoke at the level of the choke.

4 Using a vegetable peeler or a small, sharp knife, trim the remaining green from the heart. Rub with lemon juice to prevent discoloration.

5 Here is another peeling method that is often used by professionals but requires training and practice. It is shown in photographs 5 to 8. The outside leaves are trimmed off the heart with a knife at greater speed than by using the method explained in steps 2 to 4. Place the blade on the side of the artichoke, the point at a slight angle facing the center of the leaves. Roll the artichoke, cutting the leaves all around without getting into the heart.

6 Trim the center leaves off at the level of the choke, as explained in step 3.

7 Using a sharp paring knife or vegetable peeler (as shown in photograph 4), trim the remaining leaves from the bottom of the heart . . .

8 and on the top to expose the choke. Rub with lemon to prevent discoloration.

9 Combine the cooking stock ingredients (3 c. water, 1 Tb. flour, 2 Tb. peanut oil, ¼ c. lemon juice, and ½ tsp. salt) thoroughly, making sure the flour is dissolved, and add the bottoms. Bring to a boil and boil gently for 20 to 25 minutes, until the bottoms are tender but still firm to the touch. Let cool in the liquid. When cold enough to handle, remove the chokes from the bottoms and place the bottoms back in the cooking liquid until ready to be used.

→

MEAT

10 As a vegetable accompaniment to meat or fish, the artichoke heart can be cooked in pieces. About 2 in. of the stem can also be left on the heart, providing the artichoke is young enough for the stem to be tender. <u>Trim all around the heart, as explained above, and around the stem.</u>

11 Cut the trimmed heart into 4 pieces and <u>remove the choke with the point of a knife</u>. Rub with lemon juice to prevent discoloration. Cook the hearts according to instructions above.

A LEANER VERSION

Omit the flour and peanut oil in the cooking stock and proceed according to the recipe. The hearts can be served hot from the stock.

FLORENTINE ARTICHOKE BOTTOMS MORNAY

Yield: 6 servings

6 artichoke bottoms, cleaned and kept warm in the stock
Mornay sauce

SPINACH WITH BROWN BUTTER

1½ lb. spinach, cleaned (about 1¼ lb.)
¼ tsp. freshly ground black pepper
½ tsp. salt
2 Tb. butter

MORNAY SAUCE

2 tsp. butter
2 tsp. flour
1 c. milk
¼ tsp. salt
⅛ tsp. pepper
Dash grated nutmeg
¼ c. grated Swiss cheese
¼ c. heavy cream
1 egg yolk
1 Tb. grated Parmesan cheese

12 Place about ½ in. of water in a stainless-steel skillet, add a dash of salt, and bring to a boil. Add the spinach and cook 4 to 5 minutes, stirring until wilted and soft. Drain, cool under cold water, and press into a ball. Chop the spinach coarse and sprinkle with pepper and salt. Melt the butter in a skillet and, when it turns dark brown, add the spinach. Break up with a fork and sauté the spinach just to heat through. Spoon equal portions of the spinach into the artichoke bottoms.

For the Mornay sauce: Melt the butter in a heavy saucepan and add the flour. Mix well with a whisk and continue cooking over medium heat for 30 seconds. Add the milk all at once and <u>mix well with the whisk</u>. Add salt, pepper, and nutmeg, and keep mixing and stirring until the mixture comes to a boil. Boil gently for 30 seconds and add the Swiss cheese. Mix well until it melts. Remove from the heat. Mix the cream and yolk together thoroughly with a fork. Add to the hot sauce all at once, stirring with a whisk.

13 <u>Coat the filled artichoke bottoms with the sauce.</u> Sprinkle with the Parmesan cheese, and place under the broiler for 3 to 4 minutes, until browned.

14 The artichoke bottoms are ready to serve.

1 The larger, flatter piece of meat on the left is called the "flat" and the elongated piece of meat on the right is called the "eye round." Both pieces are attached together in the back leg.

2 Cut the flat into 2 pieces approximately 5 lb. each. The 3 pieces are of approximately equal size, and any one of them could be used in our pot roast.

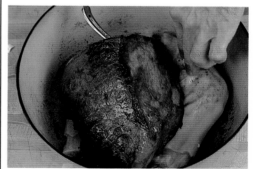

3 Melt the butter in a large cast-iron pot and brown 1 piece of the flat over medium to high heat for approximately 15 minutes, turning it every few minutes or so to brown it all around. Add the split calf's foot, 1 tsp. salt, and 1½ c. water. Bring to a boil, cover tightly, and place in the middle of a preheated 275-degree oven for 3 hours. →

CONNECTICUT POT ROAST

A braised piece of bottom round, cooked slowly in its own juices with vegetables around it, is an ideal family or bourgeois dish. It can be served at the table directly from the braising pot or sliced beforehand and served, coated with the lightly thickened juices, with the vegetables, as in the recipe here.

The bottom round, a fairly dry, lean piece from the back leg, is perfect for this dish. The whole bottom round is made up of 2 pieces of meat. The one used here weighs 14½ lb.: 4½ lb. for the eye round and 10 lb. for the flat. The eye round is elongated, narrow, and quite fibrous. The "flat," larger and moister, is used in the recipe here. It is better to use an adult animal for pot roasts as well as for any braised meats. Young animals do not produce the right juice, texture, and taste.

To be good, a pot roast has to cook slowly (at a low temperature) for a long time. It is important to first brown the meat all around so that the juices are caramelized, giving the meat and the juices taste, texture, and color. Although brown stock could be used for a stronger sauce, water is perfectly adequate for creating steam and softening the meat. Through the long cooking process, the protein eventually softens in the meat and, with the moisture around, produces a moist, flavorful, and tender piece of

meat. Use a Dutch oven or a pot with a tightly fitting lid to prevent the meat from drying out.

Calves' feet or beef feet add taste and gelatinous texture to the juice. The feet are usually boned and served with the roast or on the side. Vegetables are added 2 hours before the roast has finished cooking so they are tender, moist, and flavorful but still retain their shape. The pot roast is excellent reheated or served cold with mustard and a salad.

Yield: 10–12 servings

FOR MY ROAST

1 piece, about 5 lb., from the flat
3 Tb. butter
1½ lb. calves' or beef feet (1 calf or beef foot), split in half lengthwise
1½ tsp. salt
3 c. water
12 red-skinned potatoes (about 1¾ lb.)
1 lb. carrots (about 5), peeled
1 lb. pearl onions (about 2 doz. the size of small Ping-Pong balls), peeled
7 oz. shiitake or other mushrooms
2 tsp. potato starch dissolved in 2 Tb. red wine

GARNISH

1 Tb. coarsely chopped parsley

MEAT

227

4 Wash the potatoes and peel completely or peel off only a strip of the skin around the middle, leaving the remaining skin on the top and bottom to give more color. Cut the carrots into 1½- to 2-in. chunks and split the chunks into pieces about 1 in. thick. Peel the onions and remove the stems from the shiitake mushrooms. (The stems are fibrous and will be too tough for this recipe, but they can be used in stocks.) Add the carrots, onions, mushrooms, and potatoes to the pot with 1½ c. more water and ½ tsp. salt. Cover tightly and place in the oven for 2 hours.

5 After 5 hours of cooking, the pot roast should be fork tender and the vegetables well done but still holding their shape. Remove the calf's foot, and when cold enough to handle, bone it and dice the meat into ½-in. pieces. Return the meat to the pot with the roast and vegetables.

6 Setting the lid slightly ajar on the pot and using it to hold the meat and vegetables down, pour the juices into a saucepan. You should have between 4 and 5 c. of liquid. Keep the meat covered in a warm place while you boil the liquid in the saucepan down to reduce it to 3 c. Add the dissolved potato starch to the reduced juices and bring the mixture to a boil to thicken it. Pour the sauce back around the pot roast. Keep warm until serving time.

7 At serving time, cut the meat into slices and arrange on a platter with the vegetables around it. Coat with the sauce. Decorate with parsley and serve immediately.

A LEANER VERSION

In step 2, trim the meat all around, removing all fat. Omit the 3 Tb. of butter and place the meat in the cast-iron pot and under the broiler. Broil for 30 minutes, turning the meat occasionally until browned all around. In step 6, skim the 4 to 5 c. of liquid of any fat that comes to the surface. Proceed according to the recipe.

PORK AND HAM

PORK STEAKS WITH PORT AND PRUNES

Pork is one of the most versatile of all meats and nothing on it is wasted. Since the trimmings are ideal for making pâtés, dumplings, or crépinettes (page 221), the well-trimmed meat used in the recipe here doesn't represent a waste of money.

The whole loin, as shown in photograph 2, extends from the shoulder blade to the pelvic area at the beginning of the back leg (the ham). The color of the meat should be a fresh pink. It is more difficult to buy pork than beef or veal, where one can choose a prime and higher quality by paying a higher price. Pork is not available in prime, choice, or Grade A at the local supermarket, and one has to rely on the reputation and honesty of the butcher.

Pork is cooked until well done, although when all the sinew and fat have been removed, as in the recipe here, the meat doesn't have to be cooked to an internal temperature of 180 degrees as is usually indicated in cookbooks. Trichinosis is killed at around 138 degrees, and since the inside of the steaks in my recipe reaches approximately 155 degrees internal temperature, the meat is cooked enough and tends to be more moist and tender than when it is overcooked. If, however, the meat is less trimmed and is roasted or cooked as pork chops (photographs 3 to 7), it should be cooked longer because of the fat on it.

Pork bones roast well and make a nice addition to braised or boiled beans (see Epigrams of Lamb with Stewed Beans, page 250, and Black Bean Soup Augier, page 17). A standard stock made with pork bones tends to be cloudy but is perfectly fine for soup.

The sweetness of the port wine and prunes cuts down on the richness of the meat and complements it, as does the stew of apples, onions, raisins and vinegar, which is ideal also for most game and rich poultry like duck and goose. The apple stew can be made ahead and reheated or served cold as a condiment (more highly seasoned, with perhaps a dash of cayenne pepper) with a roast of pork or other poultry. →

Yield: 8 servings

1 lb. very large prunes (about 30) with
   pits in
1½ c. water
1 c. port wine
1 pork loin (about 7½ lb.)
½ tsp. salt
½ tsp. freshly ground black pepper
3 Tb. butter

(1 extra pork rack, 4 lb., cut into 8 chops,
each 1 in. thick and weighing 5 to 6 oz.;
not used in this recipe. Freeze and use in
another recipe.)

DARK PRUNE SAUCE

Drippings from cooking the steaks
2 Tb. chopped shallots
Juice from prunes
1 c. demi-glace (page 7)
½ tsp. potato starch dissolved in 1 Tb.
   water, if needed
Salt and freshly ground black pepper, if
   needed

APPLE AND ONION STEW

1 lb. onions
2½ lb. apples (about 5 large white-fleshed
   and acidic apples such as Cortland,
   McIntosh, Stayman, or Opalescent)
⅓ stick butter
1 Tb. vegetable oil
½ c. raisins
½ c. cider vinegar
1 tsp. freshly ground black pepper
1½ tsp. salt
2 Tb. sugar

1 Prepare the prunes. Bring 1½ c. water
to a boil and pour over the prunes. Let
stand for 1 hour, then add the port wine.
Cover and let macerate overnight.

2 The whole strip loin, which is the part
from the shoulder blade to the leg or the
fresh ham, is divided into parts. In this
photograph, I am cutting it in the center
to separate the rack from the loin. The
rack goes from the center of the strip up to
the neck part, and this is what is shown in
the upper right. The end of the strip as it
reaches the shoulder has the flat shoulder
blade bone in it, and that piece is often
boned out and used as a shoulder blade
roast, sometimes called the loin blade
roast.

3 Cut chops approximately 1 in. thick
from the rack. They will weigh about 6
oz. each trimmed.

4 To clean the center pork chops elegantly,
cut off the little strips of sinew along the
inside of the bone, as they are stringy and
tough. The trimmings can be reserved to
be ground for pâtés or dumplings.

5 Cut around the chine bone (the backbone) and, using a cleaver, sever the lump
of vertebrae at the base of the chop. The
only bone remaining is the rib itself.

6 The end of each chop will have a lump of
fat; cut around it and scrape it off the bone
to remove it. Again, reserve for another
use.

7 The pork chops are now completely
clean and weigh about 6 oz. each, depending on their thickness. As you can see, this
is the center eye of the rack with just a
little piece of bone projecting from it. The
chops can now be used in different recipes
but should be cooked slightly longer (10
to 12 minutes in a skillet) than the steaks
below because of the fat, sinews, and
bones still on them. (Freeze the chops
individually wrapped.)

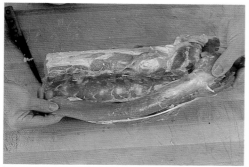

8 Bone out the loin roast, which is the piece that extends from the first rib to the back leg. That piece contains the fillet and has the T-bone in the center. Run your knife around the bone to remove the fillet in one piece.

9 Continue boning the loin, following along the bone with your knife. Remove the meat in one piece.

10 Remove all the fat and sinew on top of the boned-out loin roast, as shown in the photograph. The whole strip is divided into a shoulder blade roast, in front on the right, and some trimmings to be used in pâtés or dumplings, next to the roast. In back of the trimmings, on the left, is the fillet, and, behind, the loin being cleaned of fat. On the right are the bones, to be used in stocks or soups. (The chops are not shown.)

If there is still some meat left on the bone, use a spoon to scrape it off, as shown

in the recipe for the Saddle of Lamb (page 237, step 11) and the Rognonnade of Veal (page 286, step 7). This scraped meat can be used in ground meat or in stuffings.

11 For the recipe, the loin is now completely cleaned of any fat and so is the fillet above it.

12 Cut the loin into 5-oz. steaks (6 pieces) and the fillet into 2 pieces to make a total of 8 steaks. Pound the steaks to a uniform thickness with a meat pounder, dampening it first with a little water so it slides on the meat and doesn't tear it. The steaks will be about the thickness of the fillet. Sprinkle the steaks with ½ tsp. each salt and pepper.

13 Melt the 3 Tb. butter in 1 very large or 2 smaller, heavy (aluminum or copper) saucepans. When very hot, add the steaks and cook over medium to high heat for approximately 2½ minutes on each side, a total of 5 minutes at the most.

14 At this point, the steaks will not be completely cooked in the center but will be nicely browned on both sides. Transfer the steaks to another saucepan, cover, and set aside on the corner of the stove or in a warm oven (150 degrees) and let them continue cooking in their own juices while making the sauce. A lot of juice will seep out of the steaks while they rest, and this should be added to the sauce. Remember that there is no fat or sinew on this meat so they can be cooked less than a regular pork chop.

15 For the sauce: To the drippings in the saucepan, add the 2 Tb. chopped shallots, sauté for about 1 to 2 minutes, and add the juice from the prunes. Bring to a boil

→

MEAT

231

and boil for 2 to 3 minutes, scraping the pan to melt all the solidified juices. Reduce to about 1 c. Add to the pan any of the juices that have accumulated around the steaks. Add the 1 c. demi-glace. Bring to a boil and reduce the mixture to 1½ c. If too thin (depending on the demi-glace), add ½ tsp. potato starch dissolved in 1 Tb. water to the sauce to achieve the right consistency. If needed, add salt and pepper.

18 Melt the ⅓ stick butter in a large skillet with 1 Tb. oil. When hot, add the onions and sauté over high heat for 5 to 6 minutes, until the onions are lightly browned, wilted, and almost cooked. Add the apples, ½ c. raisins, ½ c. vinegar, 1 tsp. pepper, 1½ tsp. salt, and 2 Tb. sugar, cover, and cook 10 minutes, tossing occasionally. If there is a lot of liquid coming out of the mixture, remove the cover and cook 2 to 3 minutes over high heat to reduce some of the liquid.

16 Place the prunes in a saucepan and strain the sauce on top of them. Bring the mixture to a boil and set it aside until serving time.

19 Arrange a ring of the apple stew around each plate. Place a steak in the center, garnish with a few prunes, and coat with the sauce. Serve immediately.

17 To make the apple and onion stew: Peel and slice the 1 lb. of onions thin (⅛ in.). Cut 2½ lb. of apples in half and core. The skin should be left on to give some chewiness and texture to the mixture. Cut the apples into ⅜-in.-thick slices.

HAM GEORGIA

A whole ham is impressive and ideal for a buffet or large party. The ham used here is bought fully cooked but does improve considerably when cooked again in water. After recooking, the ham should be allowed to cool in the water and can be served plain, warm, or cold, or baked again with a peach-mustard glaze, as done here. The peach sauce is optional but is delicious made with large, ripe, yellow Georgia peaches.

In French country inns, ham is sometimes poached with fresh hay to give it an earthy, country flavor. This step is optional.

Yield: 20 servings

1 store-bought fully cooked ham
   (16½ lb.)
1 large handful fresh hay (optional)

PEACH-MUSTARD GLAZE

⅓ c. peach preserves
½ tsp. freshly ground black pepper
2 tsp. dried mustard
Dash ground cloves

PEACH SAUCE

1 c. drippings (from cooking ham)
3 c. demi-glace (page 7)
3 Tb. butter
2 lb. peaches (about 10), cut into
   1-in. wedges
1 Tb. sugar
4 oz. dried peaches, julienned
1 Tb. cider vinegar
1 tsp. salt

1 Tb. cognac
1 tsp. potato starch dissolved in
   1 Tb. water, if needed

1 <u>Place the ham in a large stockpot with the hay.</u> Fill the pot with enough cold water to cover the ham. Bring the water to approximately 180 degrees. (Do not boil the water or the ham will crack open at the joint.) Cook at that temperature for 2½ hours.

2 Lift the ham partially from the water to test for doneness. Next to the shank bone there is a second smaller bone. <u>With pliers, twist it and pull it out.</u> If it comes out in one piece, the ham is done inside. If not, cook another hour. Let cool overnight in the cooking water.

3 Remove the skin. If the ham has been cooked with hay, the skin will be more discolored than it would be otherwise, but it can still be reserved for stews or soups, or for cooking with pea beans, black beans, or split peas. <u>Trim the fat and dark surface skin from the underside,</u> leaving only a very thin layer of fat.

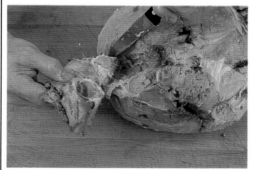

4 Keep trimming the surface of the meat where it is brown and skinlike around the shank bone. To make carving easier later on, <u>remove the pelvis or hip bone by running a knife around it</u> (see Leg of Lamb, page 254, step 3). →

MEAT

5 <u>Remove most of the fat from the top,</u> leaving only a thin layer of white fat. The extra white fat can be used in soups, stews, or to enrich casseroles and bean dishes.

8 Pour off accumulated fat in the roasting pan and add 1 c. of water to the drippings in the pan, stirring to loosen the solidified juices. Add the demi-glace and bring to a boil.

For the peach sauce: Heat 3 Tb. butter in a large skillet. When hot, add the 2 lb. of peach wedges and sauté 2 to 3 minutes. Sprinkle with 1 Tb. sugar and continue cooking for 3 to 4 minutes longer. <u>Add the 4 oz. dried julienne of peach and</u> <u>stir to mix.</u> Strain 1 c. of the drippings and the 3 c. demi-glace mixture on top of the peaches, add 1 Tb. cider vinegar, 1 tsp. salt, and 1 Tb. cognac. Stir to mix and set aside. (If the sauce is too thin, add 1 tsp. potato starch dissolved in 1 Tb. water to the mixture and bring to a boil.)

10 <u>Slice the ham on the bias, stopping at</u> <u>the cut edge,</u> and arrange the meat on a platter.

6 Run your knife in a criss-cross pattern through the remaining fat on top of the ham, cutting slightly into the surface of the meat. This scoring will help the glaze adhere to the meat while cooking.

Mix together the preserves, pepper, mustard, and cloves. <u>Spread the coating</u> <u>mixture on top of the ham,</u> position it in a roasting pan, and place in a preheated 350-degree oven for 30 minutes. Reduce the heat to 325 degrees and continue cooking for 1 hour and 30 minutes, a total roasting time of 2 hours.

11 Serve about 3 or 4 slices of ham per person. Spoon 2 to 3 Tb. of the peach sauce around and over the meat. Serve immediately.

9 To make the carving easier, <u>cut down</u> <u>into the ham approximately 1 in. above</u> <u>the shank bone.</u> The object is to make a guard that will give a clean bottom edge to the slices and also protect your hand from the knife in case it happens to slide while you are slicing the meat.

7 <u>The ham is now ready to be carved.</u>

LAMB

SADDLE OF LAMB
WITH SAGE-MOUSSE STUFFING

The best-tasting lamb is so-called spring lamb, an animal slaughtered when from 5 to 10 months old. The meat has reached maturity and peak taste and is usually served medium rare for the leg, rack, saddle, etc. The breasts or other pieces, where there is a layer of fat in the middle of the meat, are cooked well done.

Older lamb, which is called mutton, is usually stronger in taste and is often stewed, braised, or roasted until medium or well done. Baby lamb, "hot-house" lamb, or "milk" lamb comes from an animal approximately 3 to 6 weeks old, and should never be more than 20 lb. for a whole lamb. The uncooked meat will be pinkish white and you should not, therefore, cook it "rare" as the meat itself doesn't have that red color associated with mature beef. It should be cooked like veal, just medium and slightly pink at the bone.

The whole lamb saddle, also called the double loin or the short back, is the piece that extends the length of the fillet from the first rib of the rack to the pelvic bone of the

back leg. The rack and lamb chop recipes (pages 244 and 247) are variations of the recipe here, using the same stuffing, but the methods of preparation and cooking are different.

There is a basic difference between the technique used in roasting the saddle and the one used in roasting the rack. For the saddle, the mousse is placed on the loin and the flanks are brought back on top of the mousse to enclose it. It makes three layers: the flank, the mousse, and the loin. If the saddle were cooked in the usual way in the oven, the loin would be cooked much sooner than the mousse. To avoid this, the saddle is pan-fried, stuffed side down, on top of the stove first for about 30 minutes to partially cook the stuffing. Then it is finished in the oven so that both the stuffing and the loin are properly cooked — the loin rare and the stuffing well done.

The boned and stuffed rack (page 244), however, is roasted the standard way in the oven. The flank of the rack is cleaned of fat and sinews and used as a "wrapper" for the mousse and loin. Since the loin is in the center of the roast, the rack can be cooked in the conventional way. Roasting in the oven is by concentration (the heat comes from the outside of the meat and cooks it gradually from *the outside to the center), so the loin in the center will be cooked last, thus remaining pink while the wrapper and mousse will be well done.*

The stuffed rib is pan-fried and the heat, going through the stuffing, eventually cooks the loin, although it remains rare in the center. It is imperative that before serving any one of these cuts it be allowed to rest first. As it cooks, the meat contracts, squeezing the juice and pushing it toward the center. Letting it rest allows the meat to relax and open so the juices can run throughout, making the meat pink throughout. The larger the piece of meat, the longer the resting time; allow at least 20 to 30 minutes for the saddle, 15 to 20 minutes for the rack, and 10 minutes for the chops.

Yield: 8–10 servings

1 saddle of lamb (about 10 lb. with kidneys, fat, and flanks)

LAMB-SAGE MOUSSE

½ c. ½-in.-sliced leeks
½ c. peeled and very thinly sliced carrots
½ c. water
2 oz. spinach, washed
1 lb. meat (12 oz. lamb trimmings, 4 oz. chicken meat)
2 eggs
1 tsp. salt
½ tsp. freshly ground black pepper
½ c. heavy cream
6–9 sage leaves (about 2 Tb. loose)

FOR THE ROASTING OF THE SADDLE

⅛ tsp. salt
⅛ tsp. pepper

ONION-TOMATO SAUCE

1 c. chopped onions
1 c. dry white wine
2 c. chopped tomatoes
2 tsp. chopped garlic (about 3 or 4 cloves)
2 c. water
2 tsp. potato starch dissolved in 2 Tb. water

PREPARING THE MEAT

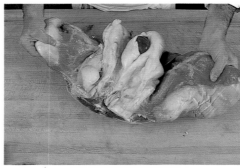

1 This is a saddle of lamb, untrimmed, as seen from underneath. The 2 large lumps of fat encase the kidneys, and the flanks are on the sides.

2 This is the saddle of lamb as seen from the top, the place where one sits down when horseback riding.

3 Pull out the 2 kidneys, trim them, and set aside. (They can be removed from their envelope of fat and used in another recipe, page 301.) Held in the back is the spleen on the right side and a lump of meat called the hanging tenderloin, both of which can be used for stew.

4 With the saddle flat and upside down, trim about 5 in. off each end of the flank. For use in this recipe, these pieces should be trimmed of sinews and fat. Holding your knife so the blade is flat and parallel to the table, cut the flank. The meat can be separated into layers. Lift up one layer and cut it off. Set aside for later use.

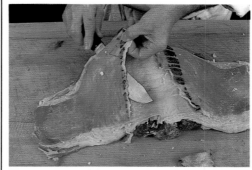

5 Turn the saddle over and trim off the reddish skin (called the "fell" or the "pell") from the top and remove most of the fat.

6 The saddle is now completely clean on both sides, with just enough flank to protect the fillets during cooking.

7 With the flanks folded back onto the fillets, the saddle could now be roasted in the usual way and carved at the table. The 10-lb. saddle weighs 5 lb. when completely cleaned.

8 For this recipe, however, the saddle is completely boned. To bone, place the saddle on its back, and cut off the two fillets by following the contour of the central bone. They should come off easily.

9 Slide your knife flat underneath the bone where the fillets sat and cut, following the contour of the bone to loosen one loin.

10 Repeat on the other side and, finally, lift up the central bone and separate it from the meat. The rim in the center of the bone is against the top skin part of the saddle. Be careful not to make holes in the top of the saddle while boning.

11 If you have left some meat on the bone while boning, use a spoon to scrape it off and set it aside for the stuffing.

12 Clean up the two fillets. Notice that each fillet separates into two pieces, the fillet and the "chain" of the fillet, which should be scraped with a knife or spoon to separate the meat from the sinews. (This scraped-off meat can be used in the mousse.) The fillets themselves can be cut in half. Keep the thicker part of the 2 fillets to place in the center of the saddle. The tails can be kept for the stuffing.

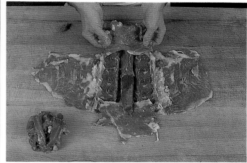

13 After the fillets have been arranged in the center of the saddle (there is a space from the removal of the bone), place the 2 extra pieces of flank on either side of the loins for use as a wrapper for the mousse. →

PREPARING AND COOKING THE STUFFED SADDLE OF LAMB

14 **For the mousse:** Cover ½ c. each sliced leeks and carrots with ½ c. water, bring to a boil, cover, and cook 3 minutes. Then add 2 oz. spinach and cook about 1 minute longer. Most of the moisture will have evaporated, and the mixture should be almost dry. Spread on a large platter or cookie sheet to cool quickly and thus retain the color of the vegetables.

15 Place the 12 oz. of lamb trimmings and 4 oz. of chicken meat into a food processor, and process for about 5 seconds. Clean the meat from the sides of the bowl with a rubber spatula and add 2 eggs. Process for 10 seconds longer, until very smooth. Add 1 tsp. salt and ½ tsp. pepper, and while the machine is operating, add ½ c. cream through the feed tube. Process briefly, just long enough to blend.

16 Pile 6 to 9 sage leaves together and shred them into a fine julienne. Combine the mousse with the shredded sage. Press the cold vegetables with your hands to extract more liquid (too much liquid will make the mousse break down) and mix with the mousse.

17 Sprinkle the saddle and fillets with ⅛ tsp. salt and ⅛ tsp. pepper and spread the mousse on top. The filling should be about 1 in. thick.

18 Bring back the extra pieces of flank from above and below to cover the mousse and fold in the 2 flanks from either side to enclose the mousse entirely on 4 sides.

19 Using kitchen twine and the half-hitch technique (see page 168, steps 16 to 18), tie the saddle without squeezing it too much so there is room for the stuffing to expand.

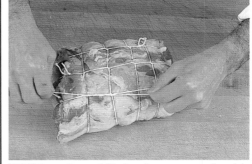

20 When the saddle has been secured, add 2 extra pieces of string the length of the saddle to hold the stuffing in place during cooking.

21 Lift the saddle up by the string and place in a roasting pan on top of the stove, stuffed side down. Cook in this position for 25 minutes, first over high heat for about 1 minute and then over low heat for the remainder of the cooking time. Spoon some of the drippings on top of the saddle and place in a preheated 400-degree oven for 30 to 35 minutes.

22 <u>The saddle is now cooked.</u> Lift it out of the roasting pan and place on a platter to rest in a 130-degree oven or on the side of the stove where it's warm. Let it rest for at least 20 to 30 minutes before carving.

Meanwhile, **make the sauce:** Remove most of the fat from the roasting pan and add the 1 c. chopped onions. Sauté for about 5 to 6 minutes, until the onions are quite brown. Add the 1 c. white wine, 2 c. tomatoes, 2 tsp. garlic, and 2 c. water, and bring to a boil. Boil gently 8 to 10 minutes on top of the stove. Add 2 tsp. potato starch dissolved in 2 Tb. water and strain. You should have approximately 1¾ to 2 c. of sauce remaining.

24 Arrange the saddle on a large platter with the Eggplant and Stewed Tomatoes (see page 244) surrounding it. Coat the meat with the sauce and serve immediately.

23 When ready to serve, <u>slice the saddle in pieces about ½ in. to ¾ in. thick. Hold the slices with one hand while you cut from behind with the other hand. This will help the slices to hold their shape.</u> The saddle can be cut into 8 to 10 nice slices.

RACK OF LAMB PROVENCALE

The double rack in our picture is a "primal" cut (a piece directly from the slaughter-house), going from the shoulder blade to the saddle or the last rib. That double rack is complete here with the breasts, and some-times this piece takes on the name of "brace-let." It usually has 8 ribs and weighs approximately 10 to 11 lb. whole for a spring lamb. Without the two breasts, it weighs approximately 7 to 7½ lb. untrimmed. Each single rack, completely trimmed (we'll have 2 single racks with a double rack), will weigh approximately 1¼ lb. and serve 3 to 4 people. Although racks of lamb are usually bought split and trimmed, the professional cook may want to prepare it from the beginning. A rack of lamb is beautifully complemented by the Artichoke Bottoms Helen on page 242.

Yield: 3–4 servings per rack

1 single rack of lamb, trimmed (about 1¼ lb.)
¼ tsp. salt
¼ tsp. freshly ground black pepper
2 shallots, peeled and minced (2 Tb.)
3 Tb. chopped parsley
1 small clove garlic, minced (¼ tsp.)
⅛ tsp. dried thyme or herbs of Provence (a mixture of dried thyme, sage, ore-gano, and savory)

1 slice fresh bread, crumbed in the food processor (½ c.)
2 Tb. butter, melted
½ c. demi-glace (page 7)

GARNISH

Sprigs of watercress

CUTTING UP THE LAMB

1 This is the double rack seen from the shoulder side. As you may notice, there are layers of fat which should be removed in the meat and the shoulder blade.

2 This is the double rack seen from the saddle side. It is a solid piece of meat without fat. When buying lamb chops that are cut from the rack, the preferred choice is the chops cut from the side of the saddle.

3 Using a hacksaw, remove the breast on each side of the rack. The breasts will weigh approximately 1¾ lb. each. See page 243 for my recipe for stuffed breast of lamb.

4 Using a sharp, pointed knife, cut straight down on each side of the back-bone, or chine bone, going as deep as you can. The tip of the knife should touch the bone underneath. Keep cutting so the backbone is well separated from the meat on each side.

COOKING AND CARVING THE LAMB

5 Place the rack so the ribs are facing you, and using the point of a sturdy cleaver, start cutting on each side of the backbone where the ribs join. Keep cutting to separate the rack completely from the backbone. If the double rack is split right in the center, each of the single racks will have the chine, or backbone, underneath, and every time one cuts between the ribs, the backbone must be cut also. The object is to remove the backbone completely so that the only bones remaining are the ribs, which one can cut between easily.

6 Lift the layer of meat and fat from the top of the loin with your hand. It should separate easily. Then slide a knife between the layer and the loin to separate the whole top in one piece and expose the loin and the ribs.

7 Trim the surface of the ribs where there is still some fat remaining.

8 The layer removed from the top of the rack can be used. Insert your finger between the meat itself and the top layer of fat and pull the meat. It should separate into one layer of meat plus the shoulder blade. Set it aside. It can be used in stuffing or in stew. Discard the fat.

9 To dress up the rack, the meat can be trimmed away from between the top of the ribs. Remove approximately 1 in. of meat and fat from between each of those ribs and scrape the point of the ribs to make them clean. Reserve scraps.

10 Complete division of the whole rack: On the left, the 2 single racks, one with the ribs dressed up and the other without; in the center background, the backbone, which can be used in soup or stock; in the center, the layer of meat from the top of the racks, which can be used in stuffing and stew; and, on the right, 2 breasts of lamb, 1 stuffed and 1 unstuffed, which can be used in stew or broiled.

11 Sprinkle one rack with the salt and pepper and place in a skillet on high heat. Brown, meat side down, and then, holding the rack with tongs or a pincer, sear it also on the bottom. This does not cook the rack but simply sears it all around. There is no need for fat in the skillet since there is enough remaining on the rack for it to brown in its own fat.

12 Mix the 2 Tb. chopped shallots, 3 Tb. chopped parsley, ¼ tsp. garlic, ⅛ tsp. dried thyme, ½ c. fresh bread crumbs, and 2 Tb. melted butter lightly with a fork. Place the rack flesh side up and press the bread crumb mixture lightly over the top. Roast in a preheated 450-degree oven for 12 to 15 minutes. If the bread crumbs are not browned enough, place under the broiler for approximately 1 minute to make them a bit darker. Transfer the rack to a plate and keep uncovered on top of the stove or in a warm oven (about 140 to 150 degrees). The rack should rest 10 to 15 minutes before carving so the meat is pink and moist throughout. Remove excess fat from the cooking skillet and add the demiglace. Melt all the solidified juices and strain into a little saucepan. →

MEAT

241

13 For an alternative recipe, the rack can be cooked dressed up by cleaning the ribs but without using the bread crumb mixture. <u>Sear it on top of the stove in the same manner (as explained in step 11).</u> Then roast and let it rest (as explained in step 12).

14 At carving time, serve the lamb on very hot plates, making certain that the juice is very hot also. <u>Carve in between the ribs.</u>

15 A second method is to remove the whole loin in one piece and cut it into thinner slices. Then separate the ribs. Four or 5 thin slices of the lamb can be served per person with 2 of the ribs next to the slices, the juice, and a watercress garnish.

16 The finished plate, garnished with a little bit of watercress and the lamb (see opening photo for alternate presentation as described in step 15).

A LEANER VERSION

Clean the lamb according to steps 1 through 10. Cook as explained in step 3 without the top breading. Make the sauce according to step 2, making sure that all the fat is removed from the skillet first. Proceed according to recipe instructions.

ARTICHOKE BOTTOMS HELEN

Yield: 6 bottoms

2 Tb. butter
2 c. mushrooms, cut into ½-in. slices
  (about 6 oz.)
1 Tb. cognac
½ c. heavy cream, plus ¼ c., whipped for
  use at the end
⅛ tsp. pepper
¼ tsp. salt
1 Tb. chopped fresh tarragon and parsley
  mixture
½ tsp. potato starch dissolved in 1 Tb.
  cold water
6 artichoke bottoms, prepared according
  to directions on page 225, cleaned of
  chokes and kept warm in the stock

1 Melt the butter in a saucepan and add the mushrooms. Cook until the liquid from the mushrooms has evaporated. Add cognac and cook 1 minute. Add ½ c. of the cream, pepper, salt, and herbs, and bring to a boil. Boil gently 2 to 3 minutes. Add the dissolved starch and mix well. Boil to thicken. Whip the remaining ¼ c. cream until stiff. Fold rapidly into the mushroom mixture and fill the artichoke bottoms immediately. Place under the broiler for 2 to 3 minutes, until nicely browned.

2 The artichoke bottoms ready to serve.

2 Stuff the breast, pushing the stuffing into the pocket, and tie it with 2 or 3 pieces of string. Don't worry if some of the stuffing is still visible; it will not leak out. In a large saucepan (aluminum or copper), brown the meat, fat side down, over medium heat for about 5 minutes. Add ½ c. water, cover, reduce the heat to low, and keep browning slowly for 45 minutes. Discard all the fat that has accumulated in the pan.

BREAST OF LAMB LYONNAISE

The breast can be left completely untrimmed, whether it is stuffed or cut into pieces to braise, providing it is first cooked over low heat for 45 minutes to 1 hour to melt as much fat as possible from the untrimmed meat. Discard the fat.

Yield: 3–4 servings

1 breast of lamb, untrimmed (about 1¾ lb.)

FOR THE STUFFING

1½ c. meat trimmings from the top of the rack (see preceding recipe), cut into pieces (about 6 oz.)
1 egg
½ c. chopped onion
2 cloves garlic, peeled, crushed, and chopped fine (about 1 tsp.)
¼ c. chopped chives
¼ c. chopped parsley
1 tsp. dried thyme
½ tsp. salt
½ tsp. freshly ground black pepper
1 c. fresh bread crumbs (about 2–2½ slices crumbed in the food processor)
½ c. water

TO FINISH THE DISH

¾ lb. onions (about 4 onions), peeled and thinly sliced
20 cloves garlic (approximately), peeled
1½ c. water
½ c. dry white wine
½ tsp. salt

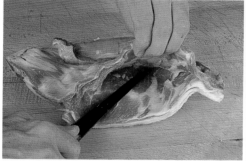

1 Place the breast flat on the table and cut with a knife directly on top of the ribs to create a pocket.

Make the stuffing: Process the meat trimmings with the egg in the food processor for a few seconds. The mixture should still be a bit coarse. Mix with the onion, garlic, chives, parsley, thyme, salt, pepper, and bread crumbs.

3 Add the sliced onions and the garlic to the meat and cook, uncovered, about 5 minutes over medium heat. Add the remaining water, wine, and salt, cover, and cook for 30 to 40 minutes longer on low heat until very tender.

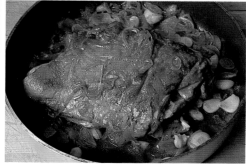

4 The meat, when completely done, should be moist and tender. Slice between the ribs and serve with the natural gravy, onion, and garlic mixture.

MEAT

243

LOIN OF LAMB IN SAGE-MOUSSE STUFFING WITH EGGPLANT AND STEWED TOMATOES

Although this recipe is made with a boned rack, it could also be made with a half saddle, using the same technique.

The eggplant and tomato garnish is served hot but is also excellent cold, sprinkled with olive oil, studded with black olives, and topped with fresh basil leaves. Be sure to start preparing it while the lamb is cooking, or even before.

Yield: 6 servings

1 single rack of lamb (5½ lb.), whole, untrimmed, including the breast

FOR THE MOUSSE

About 6 oz. meat trimmings
3 oz. chicken meat (from 1 leg or 1 breast, skinned)
1 egg
¼ c. heavy cream
½ tsp. salt
Dash freshly ground black pepper
3 or 4 leaves of sage
1 c. cooked vegetables (a mixture of carrots, leeks, and spinach, cooked according to the recipe Saddle of Lamb with Sage-Mousse Stuffing, page 238)

TO ROAST THE RACK

⅛ tsp. salt
Dash freshly ground black pepper

SAUCE

Rib bones
½ c. chopped onions
1 large tomato, coarsely chopped (or the juices and skins of tomatoes used in the stewed tomatoes, below)
½ c. white wine
1 tsp. chopped garlic
1 c. water
½ tsp. potato starch dissolved in ½ Tb. water
Salt and freshly ground black pepper to taste

FOR THE EGGPLANT

1½ lb. eggplant (1 or 2 eggplants, depending on size)
2 tsp. salt
½ c. peanut oil

FOR THE STEWED TOMATOES

2½ lb. tomatoes (about 6 or 7 fairly large tomatoes)
4 Tb. olive oil
1 c. chopped onions
2 tsp. chopped garlic
2 Tb. tomato paste
1 tsp. salt
¼ tsp. freshly ground black pepper

GARNISH

Sage leaves

PREPARING THE MEAT

1 The rack here is complete with the breast. Most of the time, the breast will have been removed from the rack when purchased. If it is not included, a breast can be purchased separately. The pieces of breast meat are needed for the wrapper in this recipe.

Saw off about 5 in. from the breast and set aside (see Breast of Lamb Lyonnaise, preceding recipe).

2 Sliding your knife behind the rib, separate the loin from the rib.

3 Now lift up the loin, a cylindrical piece of meat about 2 in. in diameter. It will slide out.

4 There is a section on top of the loin that will lift up and should be separated from the loin. Clean the loin and that extra piece of meat of all sinews.

5 When the section of meat from the top has been cleaned, butterfly it by slicing it almost in half and opening it.

6 Separate the layer of meat from the layer of fat on the flank and breast.

7 Separate the meat from between the thin layers of fat around it. Discard the fat.

8 Cut out the little layers of meat between the ribs and set aside with all the scrapings of meat for use in the mousse.

9 The meat is now completely divided. In the center, top right, are the flat layers of meat and the piece held (about 1 lb. total). On the top left side is about 6 oz. of meat to be used for the mousse. In the front row are the rib bones (weighing about 8 oz.) on the left, the loin (about 9 to 10 oz.) in the center, and, on the right, the breast (weighing about 1 lb.), which can be used for soup or stew.

PREPARING AND COOKING THE STUFFED LOIN OF LAMB

10 Make the mousse according to the instructions included in the Saddle of Lamb with Sage-Mousse Stuffing recipe (page 238). Arrange all the flat pieces of lamb wrapper on the table, one slightly overlapping another, and spread the mousse on top of them. The mousse will, in a sense, be the cement that will hold everything together. Sprinkle the loin with ⅛ tsp. salt and a dash of pepper, and place in the center of the mousse.

11 Using a dough scraper or a spatula, gently lift up the wrapper, now covered with mousse, and encase the loin with both sides.

12 Using the half-hitch trussing technique described on page 168, steps 16–18, secure the loin with kitchen twine. Do not tie it too tight since the stuffing will

MEAT

245

expand during cooking. Cover any areas where the mousse is visible with aluminum foil to hold it inside.

Place the bones in a skillet and fry on top of the stove for about 10 minutes. Gently lift up the roast by the string and place it in the center of the skillet with the bones around it.

13 Brown it over medium heat for approximately 5 minutes, rolling it over gently so it browns on all sides. Place the roast in a preheated 400-degree oven for about 20 minutes, basting it after 10 minutes. Then lift it out of the roasting pan and place it on a platter to rest in a warm oven (about 150 degrees) for at least 15 to 20 minutes.

14 For the sauce: Remove most of the fat from the roasting pan. Add the ½ c. chopped onions and brown for 4 to 5 minutes. Then add 1 chopped tomato, ½ c. white wine, 1 tsp. chopped garlic, and 1 c. water, and cook for 6 to 7 minutes. Remove the bones. Add ½ tsp. potato starch dissolved in ½ Tb. water to thicken, bring to a boil, and add salt and pepper to taste. Strain through a fine strainer. You should have about 1 c. of sauce.

15 To prepare the eggplant: Cut a 1½ lb. eggplant into 1¼-in. slices.

Line a cookie sheet with paper towels and sprinkle 1 tsp. of the salt on top of the towels. Score the eggplant slices on one side to a depth of approximately ⅛ in. in a criss-cross pattern with the point of a sharp knife. Place the slices, scored side down, on the salted paper towels. Score the other side of the eggplant, sprinkle with another tsp. of salt, cover with paper towels and another cookie sheet, and place a 5- to 6-lb. weight on top. Set the eggplant aside for approximately 30 minutes.

Remove the covering. Note: The salt will have drawn the moisture out of the eggplant slices and removed bitterness.

16 Heat the ½ c. peanut oil in a large skillet or saucepan. When hot, add the eggplant in one layer and cook over high heat for about 3 to 4 minutes. Reduce the heat and cook 5 minutes longer. Turn the slices over, cover, and continue cooking on the other side for 10 minutes, or a total of 18 to 20 minutes' cooking time. The eggplant should be soft and darkly browned.

To prepare the stewed tomatoes: Lower the 2½ lb. of tomatoes into a pan of boiling water, removing them after 15 to 20 seconds. Peel the tomatoes, cut them in half, and squeeze the seeds out, reserving the seeds and skin for stock (Shrimp Madison, page 83). Chop the tomato flesh into ½- to 1-in. dice.

Place the 4 Tb. olive oil in a saucepan. When hot, add the 1 c. chopped onions and sauté for 2 minutes. Add the 2 tsp.

chopped garlic, stir for a few seconds, and add the tomatoes and 2 Tb. tomato paste. Sauté for about 1½ minutes, just enough to heat the tomatoes. Season with 1 tsp. salt and ¼ tsp. pepper.

17 Slice the roast into ½-in. slices and arrange on a large platter. Spoon the sauce around the meat and serve immediately with eggplant slices topped with the stewed tomatoes and garnished with sage leaves.

A LEANER VERSION

For the stewed tomatoes: reduce the amount of olive oil from 4 Tb. to 1 Tb. and proceed according to recipe instructions.

FAVA BEANS NEYRON

2 lb. fava beans (about 8 or 9 oz. out of the pods and shelled)
4 cloves garlic, peeled and sliced (¼ c.)
1 small escarole (or half a large one), cleaned and cut into 1-in. pieces (about 4 c.)
1 Tb. butter
½ c. chicken stock
¼ tsp. salt
¼ tsp. freshly ground black pepper

LEEK AND MUSHROOM PIE
DOUGH

3 c. flour (16 oz.)
5 oz. duck fat
½ tsp. salt
⅓–½ c. cold water

1 egg (for egg wash)
FILLING
1 Tb. butter
1 large leek (6 oz.), washed and sliced thin
½ c. water
6 oz. mushrooms, sliced (3 c.)
½ tsp. salt
¼ tsp. freshly ground black pepper
¼ tsp. dried thyme leaves
½ c. heavy cream

LAMB CHOPS IN AMBUSH, FAVA BEANS NEYRON, LEEK AND MUSHROOM PIE

These lamb chops are ideal for a party. They can be prepared ahead with the stuffing around them, covered with plastic wrap, and cooked at the last moment. This recipe extends one rack of lamb a great deal. One rack usually serves only 2 or 3 people, allowing at least 2 or 3 tiny chops per person, but with the mousse around the ribs, you get what will look like 6 very large chops from one rack, one per person, which is ample within the context of a full dinner. If the fava beans and leek and mushroom pie are served with the lamb chops, the beans should be shelled and the pie prepared ahead so only the lamb chops have to be sautéed at the last moment.

Fava beans are available fresh in the spring. Although they can be cooked with the skin left on after removal from the pod, this skin is quite tough and the beans will require 30 to 40 minutes of cooking to be tender. Peeled, as in the recipe here, they will cook in about 2 minutes, making it worth the extra work beforehand.

The leek and mushroom pie can be served by itself and is also an ideal accompaniment for roasted or stewed meat. The dough in my recipe is made with duck fat, but it could be made with lard as well as butter.

Yield: 6 servings

1 rack lamb (5½ lb.), whole, untrimmed, including the breast
FOR THE MOUSSE STUFFING
8 oz. lamb trimmings
4 oz. chicken meat
1 egg
⅓ c. heavy cream
1 c. cooked vegetables (a mixture of carrots, leeks, and spinach, cooked according to the Saddle of Lamb recipe, page 238)
4 or 5 leaves of sage, shredded into a julienne
½ tsp. salt
¼ tsp. freshly ground black pepper
FOR COOKING THE CHOPS
2 Tb. butter
SAUCE
½ c. chopped onion
1 large tomato, coarsely chopped
½ c. white wine
1 tsp. chopped garlic
1 c. water
1 tsp. potato starch dissolved in 1 Tb. water
Salt and fresh ground black pepper to taste

1 Cut the breast of the rack as shown in photograph 1 in the Loin of Lamb in Sage-Mousse Stuffing recipe (page 244) and lift up the layer of fat on top of the meat and ribs, as shown in photograph 2. Clean the sinews from the top of the rack so it is completely clean. Clean the extra breast, saving the meat for the mousse and discarding the fat. You will notice here (as in the Loin of Lamb with Sage-Mousse Stuffing recipe) that one end of the loin has a double layer of meat on top. Lift it up and clean it of all sinews. →

MEAT

247

2 Cut the rack into 6 chops. <u>Scrape the bones where the meat ends so they are completely clean</u>, and save the scrapings for the stuffing. You should have 8 oz. of lamb trimmings for the stuffing, including the above double of meat layer.

3 As explained in step 1, there is a layer of meat that is separate from the loin. When cutting the 6 chops, the piece removed and cleaned from the top of the loin should be cut and <u>added to the chops where it belongs</u>. Even though some chops are now made of 2 pieces of meat, this won't be visible with the stuffing around them.

4 Make the mousse according to the directions in the Saddle of Lamb with Sage-Mousse Stuffing recipe (page 238). <u>Pile a good 2 Tb. of mousse on top of each chop</u> and reverse onto a plastic-wrap-lined cookie sheet.

5 Pile the remainder of the stuffing on the other side of the chops, dividing it among them. <u>Wet your finger with water and press the stuffing all around the edges</u> and along the rib, so the stuffing completely surrounds the meat and joins on both sides. Cover lightly with plastic wrap and refrigerate until ready to cook. (You should use approximately 4½ to 5 oz. [about ⅔ c.] of stuffing per chop.)

6 At serving time, heat the butter in 1 large or 2 smaller skillets and, when hot, add the chops. Cook over low heat for about 5 minutes and <u>turn gently, using a flat spatula</u>. Cook for another 5 minutes. Remove the chops, place on a warm plate, and set aside in a warm place for at least 10 minutes so they can continue cooking in their own heat.

Make the sauce in the drippings in the skillet, following the instructions given in the Loin of Lamb in Sage-Mousse Stuffing recipe (page 246).

7 **To prepare the fava beans:** <u>Remove the beans from the pods.</u>

8 You will notice that even after the beans are out of the pods, there is still a shell on them. With your fingernail or <u>the point of a sharp knife, slit this skin and pull it off.</u> See how the beans inside are more tender and delicate, and a brighter green. If you want to cook the beans with the shells on, there is a yellow germ on one side that should be removed, as it tends to be bitter. When shelled, fava beans can be served raw as crudités or hors d'oeuvre with a bit of salt or a little vinegar and oil.

9 Peel the garlic and slice it thin (you should have ¼ c.). Use escarole that is as white as possible and wash it thoroughly, lifting it up out of the water. <u>Melt the butter in a skillet</u> and, when hot, add the garlic, and sauté for about 1 minute. Add the escarole and stir and cook for about 1 minute longer, until the escarole is wilted. Add the ½ c. chicken stock, fava beans, and ¼ tsp. each salt and pepper. Bring to a boil, cover, and boil gently over medium heat for about 2 minutes. Uncover and cook another minute or so to reduce the sauce lightly. Set aside until serving time.

10 **The leek and mushroom pie**

For the dough: Combine the 3 c. flour (scooping it out of the flour bin and leveling it off with your hand) with the 5 oz. duck fat. Mix with your fingertips until the fat is completely incorporated into the flour. Add the ½ tsp. salt and, finally, the water (⅓ to ½ c., depending on the moisture in the flour). Mix the water as little as possible with the mixture, just enough for the dough to hold together. Set aside to rest while making the filling.

Filling: Place the Tb. of butter in a large skillet and, when hot, add 6 oz. sliced leeks and ½ c. water. Bring to a boil and cook for a few minutes, until the water has evaporated. Add the 3 c. sliced mushrooms, ½ tsp. salt, ¼ tsp. each pepper and thyme, and ½ c. cream, stirring to mix. Bring to a boil and boil over medium to high heat for 3 to 4 minutes, until half of the cream has evaporated and the mixture has thickened. Spread the mixture out on a plate and cool in the refrigerator.

Divide the dough in half. On a floured board, roll out one half until very, very thin (no more than ¹⁄₁₆ in.) into a circle measuring about 13 in. in diameter. Transfer the dough to a cookie sheet and arrange the stuffing in the center of the circle, spreading it to within 1 in. of the edge. Wet the edge of the pastry all around with water.

11 On a floured board, roll out the remainder of the dough into a circle of equal size and thickness, roll it back on the pin, and then unroll it over the filling. Press around the edge to seal the pastry and enclose the filling.

12 Using a lid as a guide, trim away the rough edges of dough to create a uniform circle. The trimmings can be frozen for later use. Break an egg into a bowl and remove half of the white so the proportion of yolk is greater than white (which will give a nice brown color to the dough) and beat it with a fork. Brush the entire top with the egg.

13 With a sharp knife, mark the dough concentrically from the edge toward the center and, finally, press around the edges with the tines of a fork to score the dough and create a design.

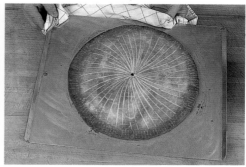

14 Place in a preheated 400-degree oven and cook for 45 minutes. The crust should be very crisp and crunchy. Cut into wedges at serving time.

15 Arrange the fava beans on individual plates and place a chop in the center of each. Top with the sauce and serve with the leek and mushroom pie.

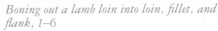

Yield: 6 servings

LAMB FLANK

1 flank, about 1 lb. trimmed, 12 oz. after
  blanching
1½ c. bread crumbs (4 or 5 slices)
2 scallions
2 large cloves garlic
½ tsp. freshly ground black pepper
1 egg
¼ tsp. salt

STEWED BEANS

1 lb. dried navy or pea beans
1 tsp. salt
6 oz. bacon, cut into lardons (¼-in.
  strips)
1¾ c. coarsely chopped onions (2 onions)
1½ c. quartered tomatoes, seeds removed
  (2 medium or 4 small tomatoes)
½ tsp. dried thyme leaves

TO SAUTE THE FLANK

1 Tb. butter
1 Tb. oil

FOR LAMB LOIN AND FILLET

2 Tb. butter
1 loin of lamb, 1 lb. cleaned (about 6 lb.
  with flank, fillet, fat, and kidney)
1 fillet (about 5 oz. cleaned)
¼ tsp. salt
⅛ tsp. freshly ground black pepper
½ c. demi-glace (see page 7)

EPIGRAMS OF LAMB WITH STEWED BEANS

This recipe goes back to the beginning of the nineteenth century. In this instance, the epigram is not a witty or sharp saying, as it usually is in literature, but a lamb dish. It is recorded by culinary chroniclers that during a dinner party at a wealthy lady's house in Paris, the guests mentioned during the meal that they "had been 'served' delicious epigrams" the day before at another party. The lady, not too keen on language, assumed this was something they had eaten and insisted that her chef prepare épi-grammes to serve at her next party. The poor chef, not knowing what these were, decided – intelligently – to serve a loin of lamb and with it the flank of the lamb cooked in another fashion, and he baptized this dish "Epigrams of Lamb à la Monselet," since Monselet was his name.

This is a sensible combination, which cuts down on the price of the dish. The loin of lamb fillet is quite expensive while the flank is usually used in restaurants for stew or stock – or sometimes it is discarded altogether. The flank has different layers of fat and here it is boiled gently a long time in water to eliminate most of the fat. It is then flattened, breaded, and sautéed and served as an accompaniment to the medium-rare loin and fillet.

The white beans do not need presoaking. These small dried so-called pea beans, navy beans, or white beans that are found in supermarkets are usually from the previous year's crop and are not dry enough to require soaking. In fact, long soaking makes the beans ferment and contributes to flatulence or other gastric disturbances sometimes attributed to dried beans. The stewed beans, flavored with bacon, onion, tomato, and garlic, are ideal with the lamb dish. They could also be transformed into a cassoulet with the addition of sausages and poultry.

1 Above, the saddle, sometimes called the short back or double loin, is split in half. Each half has the kidney, fat, and flank attached to it. In the recipe I use 1 loin, which weighs approximately 6 lb. with the kidney, fat, fillet, and flank attached.

2 Remove the kidney (page 301) and cut away the large pieces of fat around the loin in the kidney area and discard them. Slide your knife along the bone to separate the fillet from the bone; it should come out in one piece.

3 Continue boning out the piece of meat, running your knife along the bone lengthwise, and the loin will come out in one piece. You will have approximately 1 lb. of fat and kidney.

4 Remove the loin meat and clean of any sinews and fat.

5 On the flank, remove the red skin, the "fell" or "pelt" of the flank, and the layer of fat underneath and on top. Clean off as much fat as you can. Clean the fillet, also, of any sinew and fat.

6 The loin completely cleaned should weigh approximately 1 lb.; the fillet, cleaned and "chain" removed, about 4 to 5 oz.; the flank, completely cleaned, about 1 to 1¼ lb.; and the bones approximately 1 lb. Discard the extra fat and skin and freeze the bones to use for stock or soup.

7 Place the flank in a saucepan, cover with cold water, and bring to a boil. Cover with a lid, reduce the heat, and cook very slowly at a gentle boil for about 45 minutes. Drain, reserving the liquid to cook the beans, and rinse the flank under cold water. Place on paper towels in a pan, cover with another length of paper towel, and put another tray on top. Place a weight of 5 to 6 lb. on top and let the flank cool under refrigeration this way so it is very flat.

When cooled, remove any extra skin or visible fat from the top or sides.

8 For the sautéed lamb flank: Process the bread crumbs, scallions, garlic, and pepper in a food processor until mixed. Place the mixture on a large tray or cookie sheet. Beat the egg with the salt and dip the flank into it, coating it all over with the egg. Place the flank in the bread crumb mixture and pat the crumbs onto the flank until well coated on both sides. Refrigerate until serving time. →

9 **To prepare the beans:** Remove any pebbles from the 1 lb. of beans and discard damaged beans. Wash under cold water and place in a kettle with the reserved liquid from boiling the flank and enough cold water to amount to 8 c. total. Add 1 tsp. salt, bring to a boil, and simmer gently, uncovered, for 45 minutes.

In a heavy saucepan, place the 6 oz. bacon lardons (made by cutting the piece of bacon into slices about ¼ in. thick and then packing the slices together and cutting them into ¼-in. strips). Cook 8 to 10 minutes over medium to high heat, until nicely browned. Add the 1¾ c. chopped onions and cook for 1 to 2 minutes longer.

10 Add the 1½ c. tomatoes, the ½ tsp. thyme leaves, and the partially cooked beans. Bring to a boil and simmer gently for 45 minutes, until the beans are tender.

11 Place approximately 1 c. of the bean mixture in a food processor and process until puréed. Return the purée to the saucepan with the remaining beans. This

will serve as a thickening agent to make the beans the right consistency. If the beans are still too liquid, cook them in the pan, uncovered, over high heat for a few more minutes to reduce the liquid further. If, on the other hand, the beans are too thick, add a little water to thin.

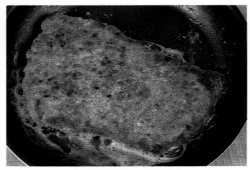

12 At serving time, heat the Tb. of butter and the Tb. of oil. When hot, add the flank and sauté over low to medium heat for 10 minutes, 5 minutes on each side. Keep warm.

13 **To prepare the lamb loin and fillet:** Meanwhile, melt the 2 Tb. of butter in a heavy saucepan. Season the cleaned loin and fillet with ¼ tsp. salt and ⅛ tsp. pepper and brown on top of the stove for 1 to 1½ minutes, just enough to sear it lightly all over. Place in a preheated 450-degree oven for 3 minutes, then remove the fillet and set it aside. Turn the loin on the other side and continue cooking for another 3 minutes. Remove it and place it next to the fillet on a pan and let rest in a warm place on top of the stove or in a 140-degree oven to continue cooking in its own heat. It should rest at least 10 to 15 minutes before carving. The juice coming out of the meat can be added to the saucepan along with the ½ c. demi-glace. Heat to the boil, strain through a fine sieve, and set aside.

14 At serving time, arrange a ring of beans around each individual plate. In the center, place a little piece of the fillet, a piece of the loin, and a piece of the breaded flank with some of the sauce around them. Serve immediately.

A LEANER VERSION

Omit the stewed beans and the lamb flank recipe. To sauté the loin and fillet, reduce the amount of butter from 2 Tb. to 2 tsp. in step 13 and proceed according to directions. Serve the meat with a steamed vegetable or a salad.

PUREE OF SPINACH WITH CROUTONS AND EGGS

Yield: 8–10 servings

2½ lb. spinach, cleaned, with stems on
1 c. water
1 tsp. salt
2 tsp. potato starch dissolved in 2 Tb. water
¼ c. milk
¾ c. heavy cream
⅛ tsp. powdered nutmeg
¾ tsp. salt
¼ tsp. freshly ground black pepper
4 slices white bread
1 Tb. butter
1 Tb. oil
4 hard-cooked eggs (see Gratin of Eggs Loute, page 31)
2–3 Tb. juice rendered by cooked lamb

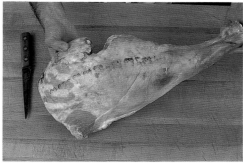

1 The leg of lamb seen from above. Notice there is still a part of the tail with the pelvis area on the left and the whole pelvis bone.

GRILLED LEG OF LAMB ROBERT

A leg of spring lamb comes from an animal between 5 and 10 months of age when slaughtered. It should have white, waxy fat, and the color of the meat should be pinkish red. See information on lamb on page 235. The whole leg, including the pelvis and shank bones, will weigh approximately 8 to 9 lb. The standard gigot, a roasted leg of lamb studded with garlic cloves and sprinkled with rosemary, is a classic French country dish, and the meat is trimmed as explained in steps 1 to 5. But in the recipe here, the leg is completely boned out and butterflied, so it cooks faster and has a large flat surface ideal for grilling.

The marinade mixture is strongly flavored. No salt is needed because of the soy sauce. The amount of jalapeño peppers can be reduced or increased, or they can be omitted altogether, to suit your taste buds. This marinade is also excellent for flank steak and chicken that is to be broiled or grilled.

As with flank, skirt, and hanging tenderloin of beef as well as shoulder of veal, it is imperative that the meat rest after cooking on the barbecue. The meat is cooked briefly on the grill, just long enough for it to acquire a charred color and absorb the taste of the grilling, and then it must continue cooking in its own juice in a pan placed in a warm oven. If you are outdoors and an oven is not available, the meat can be placed on the side of the barbecue, covered with a piece of aluminum foil, and allowed to rest in this manner until serving time. It should rest for at least 30 to 45 minutes but can stay in a warm place for longer than 1 hour before being served.

For the spinach purée, the stems as well as the leaves are used and some of the lamb drippings are sprinkled on top at the end. The croutons and eggs, a nice addition, are often served in home or country-style French cooking.

Yield: 8–10 servings

1 leg of lamb, 8 to 9 lb. with pelvis and shank bone (about 3½ to 3¾ lb. boned)

MARINADE

1 medium onion, peeled
3 cloves garlic, peeled
1 piece ginger, peeled (about same amount as garlic)
½ seeded medium jalapeño pepper
¼ c. soy sauce
¼ c. honey·
2 Tb. peanut or cottonseed oil

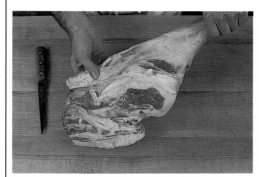

2 The untrimmed leg of lamb, seen from underneath. There is a lot of fat on the outside of the leg and most of it should be removed, as the strong taste of lamb that people often object to is mostly found in the fat. →

MEAT

253

3 With the underneath of the leg showing, run a knife along the bone of the pelvis to loosen it. Notice that the bone is attached not only to the meat around it but also to the socket in which it lies, where the femur bone connects with the pelvis. The bone can be cleaned of most of the fat, cut into pieces, and used to make Scotch barley soup or any lamb-flavored soup.

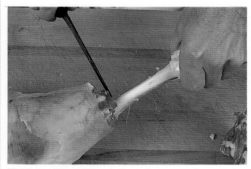

4 If the leg of lamb is to be served unboned whole, cut into the shank 2½ to 3 in. from the end of the bone, and scrape the pieces of shank meat off the bone. The clean bone can now be used as a handle for holding the roast while you carve. This step is done more for aesthetic reasons than anything else. The pieces of cut-off shank can be placed in the roasting pan and cooked beside the lamb.

5 A lot of fat has been removed from the underside and the top part of the leg, most of it from the top of the hip. Leave only a minimum layer of fat here and there. Notice that there is practically no fat on the meat next to the shank bone. There is just a thin layer of skin, which should be left on. The leg trimmed in this fashion can now be roasted whole in the oven.

6 For the grilled leg of lamb, however, the leg should be boned completely. With the underside up, start cutting along the femur bone, following the bone to the joint of the knee.

7 Cut around the joint so the second bone stays attached and both bones are removed together.

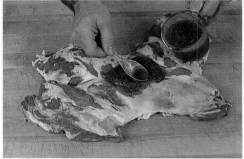

8 Remove the knee joint. The meat is now completely boneless. Trim away lumps of fat and sinew that are visible underneath and on top. Two areas of the leg will be thicker: one is the top round and the other the knuckle. Cut down into these large muscles to a depth of about 1 in., and spread the meat open so the whole leg of lamb is approximately the same thickness throughout (about 2 to 2½ in. thick).

9 Place the onion, garlic, ginger, and hot pepper in the food processor, and process until the mixture is puréed. Add the soy sauce, honey, and peanut oil, and mix just enough to combine. You should have 1 c. of the marinade. Spread it on both sides of the leg of lamb.

10 If time allows, place the meat and marinade in a plastic bag, close the bag, and refrigerate overnight, turning the bag two or three times so the marinade gets all around the meat.

11 **To grill the leg of lamb:** Have the grill very clean and very hot with the ashes red and white. Place the meat directly on the grill, skin side down, and grill 4 to 5 minutes on one side no more than 2 to 3 in. from the ashes. Turn and grill 4 to 5 minutes on the other side, a total of 8 to 10 minutes. At this point, the meat should be nicely browned and seared on both sides.

12 Place on a jelly roll or roasting pan in a preheated 170- to 190-degree oven and let cook in its own juice for a minimum of 30 minutes and as long as an hour before serving. The internal temperature should be around 130 degrees. Notice in the photograph the juices that have accumulated around the roast after the meat has been set aside to rest. The leg of lamb is now relaxed and pink throughout.

13 **Meanwhile, make the spinach purée:** Clean the 2½ lb. of spinach several times in water, lifting the leaves from the water to ensure that the sand is released from the spinach. Bring 1 c. of water with 1 tsp. salt to a boil in a saucepan (preferably stainless steel). When boiling, add the spinach fresh from the washing water, cover, and cook for about 10 minutes over high heat. Drain in a colander and press with a spoon to remove some of the water from the spinach. Place in a food processor and process to purée fine. Put back in the saucepan and add 2 tsp. potato starch dissolved in 2 Tb. water to the spinach along with ¼ c. milk and ¾ c. cream. Add the ⅛ tsp. nutmeg, ¾ tsp. salt, and ¼ tsp. pepper, and bring the mixture to a boil, stirring almost constantly to prevent the spinach from burning and splattering. It should come to a good boil for the potato starch to cook properly.

14 **For the croutons:** Trim the 4 slices of bread and cut into halves. Melt 1 Tb. butter and 1 Tb. oil in a large skillet and add the pieces of bread. Sauté approximately 1½ minutes on each side over low to medium heat to brown nicely.

For the eggs: Cook 4 eggs as described on page 31 (Gratin of Eggs Loute) and shell.

15 At serving time, place the eggs back in boiling water for 1 minute to reheat. Arrange the spinach in a gratin dish with the egg halves and croutons around the edge, and sprinkle some of the juice rendered from the lamb on top.

16 Carve the lamb into slices ¼ in. thick. Notice that there is no sinew and no waste.

17 The carved lamb in its own juice is ready to serve with the purée of spinach. Serve on very hot plates.

A LEANER VERSION

For the marinade, reduce the amount of honey from ¼ c. to 2 Tb. and omit the 2 Tb. of peanut or cottonseed oil. Proceed according to the recipe. For the Purée of Spinach with Croutons and Eggs: Replace the ¾ c. of cream with ¾ c. of low-fat milk. Omit the butter and oil and toast the bread in a toaster or oven. Proceed according to the recipe.

MEAT

255

ROAST BABY LAMB
WITH SHALLOT SAUCE

A tiny baby lamb, also called milk lamb or hothouse lamb, should be approximately 4 to 6 weeks of age when slaughtered and weigh, gutted, from 18 to 22 lb. with skin and head removed. Baby lamb is usually available in the spring, around Easter, and is often roasted whole, stuffed with a mixture of couscous and fruits or with a bread stuffing. Often the "baron," which is the whole saddle with the back legs, or the "double," made up of both back legs held together by the pelvis bone, is roasted whole. (See information on lamb, page 235.)

Most commonly, however, the baby lamb is divided into the pieces I have in the recipe below. The 2 back legs are separated, the pelvis bone removed, and the whole saddle (sometimes called the double loin) is left whole or split in half, as I do here, to make 2 single loins which are used in the recipe here, where they are boned and stuffed. The 2 racks are usually separated and the 2 front shoulders roasted whole or boned and stuffed, as done below. Remaining is the chuck (i.e., the meat directly above the shoulder and around the neck area), which is excellent for stew; the breasts, which are usually stewed with vegetables; and, finally, the head (a delicacy in Greek cooking), which can be roasted in the oven. The

brains can be poached or sautéed, the tongue boiled, and the bones and sinews can be transformed into a stock or a soup, such as Scotch barley soup.

Just as a calf, which is baby beef, has pale meat, a baby lamb has pale meat also and so is cooked to medium. Undercooked baby lamb tends to be sour, spongy, and chewy. Because the meat is white, it will not ever be red like a spring lamb or a piece of beef, even if undercooked. It should be slightly pink at the bone and the center of the roast, like veal.

The meat goes well with herbs and dressings, accented with seasonings like garlic and leeks, because it is a bit bland and needs some accents to heighten its flavor. The extra pieces of meat should be wrapped individually in layers of plastic wrap and aluminum foil and frozen but should be defrosted slowly under refrigeration before being cooked.

The photographs that deal with the making of the garlic bread, artichokes, and vegetable tempura are placed at the end of the lamb recipe to keep the lamb sequence

together. If used with the lamb, the artichokes should be prepared ahead and braised at the same time as the lamb. Either a whole or a half artichoke can be served per person, depending on the menu.

The vegetable tempura is best cooked at the last minute, although the vegetables and the batter can both be prepared a few hours ahead. The artichokes as well as the tempura can be used as a garnish for most meat or fish dishes. The tempura can also be served as an hors d'oeuvre by cutting the vegetables into smaller pieces and making a tiny tempura that can be passed around as soon as it is fried.

Yield: 10–12 servings (½ lamb)

FOR MY RECIPE

1 rack baby lamb, from 1 baby, milk, or
    hothouse lamb, about 23 lb. gutted,
    but including the head and fleece
1 single loin, boned out
1 leg (back)
1 shoulder (front leg)

BREAD STUFFING FOR THE LAMB

¼ stick butter
1 c. finely sliced leeks
1 c. coarsely chopped onions
1 c. bread crumbs (made in food processor
    from 2 slices bread)
1 c. diced lamb offal (mixture of sweet-
    breads, kidneys, and heart)
2 Tb. chopped parsley
¼ tsp. crushed dried sage or 1 tsp. shred-
    ded fresh sage
½ c. chopped dried morels or other dried
    wild mushrooms (½ c.), soaked ½ hour
    in 2 c. tepid water
½ tsp. salt
½ tsp. freshly ground black pepper

FOR ROASTING

2 Tb. butter
1 tsp. salt
¼ tsp. freshly ground black pepper

BROWN SHALLOT SAUCE

Pan drippings (from cooking the lamb)
About ½ c. water from soaking the mush-
    rooms
2 Tb. butter
8–10 shallots (½ c. chopped)
½ c. chopped parsley
½ tsp. potato starch dissolved in 1 Tb. of
    water, if needed

GARLIC-BREAD ARTICHOKES

8 firm medium-sized artichokes
Lemon half
2 qt. water
STUFFING
2 Tb. butter
¼ c. peanut or corn oil
4 or 5 shallots, finely chopped (⅓ c.)
3 or 4 cloves garlic, finely chopped
2 c. fresh bread crumbs (about 4 or 5 slices
   bread)
¼ tsp. freshly ground black pepper
¼ tsp. salt

2 Tb. olive oil
1 c. water

VEGETABLE TEMPURA

BATTER
2 c. flour
1 tsp. baking powder
2 egg yolks
¼ tsp. salt
2½ c. ice-cold water
VEGETABLES
1 medium carrot, peeled
½ medium onion, peeled
1 small zucchini
½ c. loose mushrooms
½ c. fresh corn kernels
1 c. loose parsley
1½ c. loosely packed spinach, washed and
   stems removed, loose
TO COOK
Approximately 1 Tb. corn oil for each
   large tempura
Salt

1 Here is the whole baby lamb, just gutted. The meat does not need to age more than a day or so. The omentum is a lacy membrane that connects the stomach to other organs. It can be used to wrap pâtés or crépinettes (see Beef-Coriander Crépinettes and Pork-Spinach Crépinettes, page 222). The organs are, starting at the left front: the round sweetbread (pancreas gland) and, above, the 2 small kidneys, used in the stuffing. In the second row are the lungs, which are excellent stewed with red wine. In the third row front is the spleen, also good in stew, and, above, the heart, used in the stuffing. Finally, there is the liver, excellent sliced and sautéed (see Calves' Liver Slivers with Grape and Currant Sauce, page 295).

Total weight of the offal is about 2 lb.

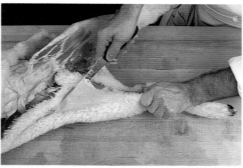

2 To remove the skin, place the lamb on its back and cut through the skin the length of the leg with a pointed knife. Pull off the skin. It should come away from the flesh easily (see skinning of rabbit in Rabbit Blanquette, page 197). To help release the skin, cut the membrane between the skin and the flesh with the point of a knife as you are pulling. After the legs are free, pull off the skin along the back.

3 Continue to pull until the front shoulders of the lamb are uncovered. Pull the skin down the front legs and cut at the joint of the knee. Cut at the neck. The head can be kept, as shown in step 16, or discarded. If the head is kept, remove the skin and eyes.

4 Remove both front legs at the shoulder joints by pulling and cutting between the shoulders and the body of the lamb. The front legs should separate easily.

5 With the baby lamb on its back, cut with a knife and a cleaver through the bones just above the 2 back legs to separate the legs from the rest of the body. →

MEAT

257

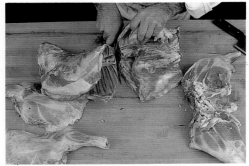

6 Cut across the first rib to remove the saddle. It is the piece that extends from the back legs to the ribs. The fillets, which are inside the saddle, extend from the back legs (head of the fillet) to the first rib (tail of the fillet). The length of the fillets is the same as that of the saddle.

7 Cut the breast off the rack, leaving approximately 2 in. of bones on the ribs. The breast can be cut, bones and all, into 2-in. pieces and used for stew.

8 Separate the double rack from the neck.

9 Remove the pelvis bone, which holds the back legs together.

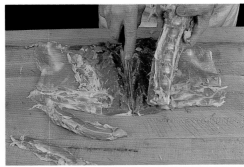

10 Bone out the saddle (see Saddle of Lamb with Sage-Mousse Stuffing, page 235). Remove the 2 fillets first and, following the bone, cut so that the whole central bone comes out in one piece. Lift the bone off the saddle and cut in the center to have 2 single loins.

11 Bone out the front legs or shoulders: Follow the bone of each shoulder blade, cutting around it to separate it from the flesh.

12 When loose on top and around, pull the bone out. Continue to remove the bones of the front legs so the shoulders are completely boneless.

13 To separate the double rack into 2 single racks (see Rack of Lamb Provençale, page 240), place the rack on the table and slide your knife along each side of the chine bone.

14 Cut with a cleaver down the chine bone on each side to separate both racks. The racks are completely boned out except for the ribs and can be cut through easily at serving time.

15 Here is the whole baby lamb, boned out. From left to right, first row front, the chuck meat from around the neck, to be used in stew (about 1 lb.). Behind, the breast, also used for stew, cut (bones and all) into 2-in. pieces (about 1 lb.). Next the 2 boned-out shoulders, one above the other (2¾ lb. for both). Next are the 2 racks, ready to cook, one above the other (1¼ lb. for both) and, next to them, the saddle, cut in half, one loin above the other (about 1¾ lb. for both). On the far right are the 2 back legs, one above the other (about 4½ lb. for both). Finally, in the last row, are the bones and sinews, to be used in stocks and soups (about 4 lb.).

16 The lamb's head, split in half, and the brain and tongue (about 2 lb. total). Not pictured is the skin or fleece, which weighs approximately 4¾ lb., for a total weight of about 23 lb. for the whole baby lamb.

17 To stuff the shoulder, place it flat on the board, skin side down. If there is any part of it that is thicker, butterfly the thicker part so that the shoulder is of approximately equal thickness throughout.

18 **To make the bread stuffing:** Heat the ¼ stick butter in a saucepan. When hot, add 1 c. each sliced leeks and onions and sauté over medium heat for about 5 minutes.

Place 1 c. bread crumbs on a cookie sheet in a preheated 400-degree oven or under a broiler and cook for 4 to 5 minutes, until nicely browned. Add 1 c. diced offal to the leek-onion mixture and sauté for 1 to 2 minutes. Add 2 Tb. parsley, ¼ tsp. sage, the bread crumbs, ½ c. drained mushrooms (reserving the liquid), and ½ tsp. each salt and pepper. Toss gently and cool. This is enough stuffing for 1 shoulder and 1 loin.

19 Place the loin and the shoulder on the board and sprinkle both pieces with 1 tsp. salt. Divide the stuffing between the 2 pieces of meat.

20 Roll up the loin and the shoulder so the stuffing is held inside. If some of the loose stuffing falls out at the ends, a small piece of aluminum foil placed at either end will help hold it in.

21 Tie the shoulder and the loin with string, using the half-hitch technique (see page 168, steps 16 to 18). Don't tie too tight; the stuffing should have room to expand a little.

22 Here are all the pieces, ready to be cooked. (This will be enough for 10 to 12 servings.) From left to right: the leg, the rack, the boned-out stuffed loin, and the boned-out stuffed shoulder. →

MEAT

259

23 **To cook the meat:** The pieces of meat are first browned in butter on top of the stove in a large skillet. Next, they are roasted in the oven, for different lengths of time, depending on size and length of cooking required. They all come out of the oven at the same time. Place 2 Tb. butter in a very large sauté pan. Sprinkle the meat with 1 tsp. salt and a dash of pepper. When the butter is hot, brown the pieces all around over high heat. The rack should be just lightly browned for 2 to 3 minutes and removed to a plate. The 2 stuffed roasts should take 6 to 7 minutes and the leg about 8 to 9 minutes to brown. Keep the leg (the largest piece) in the sauté pan and place in a preheated 400-degree oven for about 20 minutes. Then add the stuffed roasts in a separate pan and cook at the same temperature for another 20 minutes. Baste the pieces, then add the rack and cook for 10 minutes longer. Total roasting time is 10 minutes for the rack, 30 minutes for the stuffed roasts, and 50 minutes for the leg. Remove from the oven. The internal temperature of the lamb should be approximately 140 to 150 degrees. Remove to a pan and allow the meat to rest in a warm place (150-degree oven) and continue cooking in its own juices.

24 **For the brown shallot sauce:** To the drippings in the pan add the ½ c. of liquid from the mushrooms and bring to a boil while stirring to loosen all the solidified juices. Boil 1 minute and strain. You should have about 1½ c.

Heat 2 Tb. butter in a skillet. When hot, add ½ c. chopped shallots and sauté 3 to 4 minutes, then add ½ c. chopped parsley and the reduced sauce (above). If the sauce is too thin, thicken with ½ tsp. potato starch dissolved in 1 Tb. water.

Remove the string from the roasts and cut into ½-in. slices. Arrange on a serving plate and spoon some sauce on top. Serve with the artichokes and vegetable tempura (below).

On the plate, from left to right: the stuffed shoulder, the leg, the stuffed loin, and the sliced rack.

25 **For the artichokes:** Cut about 1 in. off the top of the artichokes and cut off the stems. Peel the fibrous skin from the stems and reserve the centers. Rub cut parts with lemon to prevent discoloration.

26 Using scissors, cut off the top third of each artichoke leaf. These leaf tips are tough, and each has a "needle" in the center. Wash the artichokes under cool water. Bring 2 qt. of water to a boil in a stockpot. Add the artichokes, cover, bring to a boil again, and boil gently 8 to 10 minutes. Drain in a colander and rinse under cold water.

27 When cool enough to handle, grab the center of each artichoke and pull out the center leaves in one clump.

28 Using a spoon, remove the choke, the hairy material inside at the base. The artichokes are not yet completely cooked and may require some scraping to remove the choke.

29 The centers of the artichokes are clean.

30 Stuffing: Melt the 2 Tb. butter and ¼ c. peanut or corn oil in a large skillet. When hot, add ⅓ c. chopped shallots, 3 or 4 chopped garlic cloves, and 2 c. bread crumbs, and sauté, stirring almost continuously, for 4 to 5 minutes over medium to high heat, until the bread turns a nice brown color. Add ¼ tsp. each pepper and salt. The base of the center leaves is tender. Cut away the tender parts and add to the stuffing.

31 Spoon about 2 Tb. of the stuffing into each artichoke, placing some in the cavity and some in between the leaves. When they are stuffed, place the artichokes side by side in one layer in a saucepan. Sprinkle with 2 Tb. olive oil, add 1 c. of water, and place the stems around the artichokes. Cover, bring to a boil, reduce heat, and cook approximately 30 minutes. By then, most of the moisture should have evaporated and only the olive oil will remain

with the gently stewing artichokes. If there is still liquid in the pan, remove the lid and continue boiling until the remaining moisture has evaporated.

32 Arrange the artichokes on a platter with the stems around. The artichokes can be served alone as a first course or with the baby lamb.

33 For the vegetable tempura: Mix together the 2 c. flour, 1 tsp. baking powder, 2 egg yolks, ¼ tsp. salt, and 1 c. of the ice water with a whisk. The batter should be very thick at this point; work with the whisk until smooth. If the batter is thick enough, the threads of the whisk going through it will break up any lumps of flour and produce a thick but smooth batter. Add the remaining 1½ c. ice water and mix to combine. The mixture should be about the thickness of a crêpe batter.

The vegetables used here are excellent for the tempura, but other vegetables, from cabbage and eggplant to turnips, can be used also. Slice all the vegetables except the parsley and spinach very thin by hand or in a food processor fitted with the 1-mm. blade.

34 At serving time, combine the vegetables and the batter. Heat 1 Tb. of corn oil in each of two 7-inch-bottom non-stick skillets and, when hot, add approximately ½ c. of the vegetable-batter mixture to each skillet. Spread the mixture with a spoon so the pancakes are very thin. Cook on one side from 1½ to 2 minutes over high heat, until nicely browned.

35 Turn the pancakes and cook on the other side for 1 minute. Sprinkle lightly with salt and serve immediately, or place on a cookie sheet and keep warm in a hot oven or under the broiler for a few minutes while you finish cooking the remainder of the pancakes.

36 For an individual serving, arrange a few pieces of lamb on a very hot plate: a piece of stuffed loin on the top left, a piece of leg in the front, and a rib on the right. Place half an artichoke at each end and halved pancakes on the sides. Spoon sauce over the top and serve immediately.

VEAL

VEAL CHOPS

The double rack of veal comprises half of the back of the animals. Our double rack weighs 20 lb. without the breast.

Veal is ideal as a mainstay for fine restaurants because it is adaptable to many different preparations and accompaniments. The best-quality veal is delicate, lean, and usually expensive, and goes under a variety of names, including fancy veal, nature veal, milk-fed veal, Plume de Veau, and Provimi veal (for protein-vitamin-mineral). The young animal, fed only milk and a formula rich in protein, vitamins, and minerals, is slaughtered when about 12 weeks old and weighing between 300 and 350 lb.

Veal chops, like other veal cuts, should never be overcooked or drastically undercooked; coming from young calves, veal is not a red meat and, consequently, cannot be cooked rare, as fully grown beef often is. Veal chops should be served slightly pink at the bone and juicy.

When veal chops are grilled over an open flame or broiled, they should be exposed to direct heat only briefly to avoid toughening the meat. After the crust (caramelized juices) is formed for taste, the meat is transferred to a gentler heat and continues cooking in its own heat.

Cooking en papillote, or in an oiled paper pouch, is one such gentle cooking method, for the paper — when properly oiled or buttered and sealed, with plenty of air inside — provides something akin to a small pressure-cooker environment. The heat is far less intense than a pressure cooker's, but the principle at work — moist, hot air circulating around the food — is the same. Parchment paper, nonporous and strong enough to withstand considerable heat, is preferable to foil, which can alter both taste and color if the food it encases contains acid. En papillote cookery, illustrated here with Veal Chops Ménagère in Papillote, is not limited to veal but is equally useful for fish or vegetables.

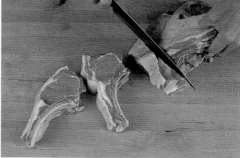

4 Cut the racks into ribs, a relatively easy task now that the backbone has been removed. Notice that of the 7 or 8 ribs, the 4 cut on the side of the loin are the nicest and are usually referred to as the "first." The ribs cut on the side of the shoulder are referred to as the "second."

TWO RECIPES FOR VEAL CHOPS

GRILLED VEAL CHOPS WITH SHALLOTS AND BEANS

Yield: 2 servings
2 veal chops (11 to 12 oz. each)
1 Tb. peanut oil
½ tsp. herbs of Provence (a mixture of dried thyme, sage, oregano, and savory)
Salt and pepper to taste
½ lb. small, thin, firm green beans, cleaned
3 Tb. butter
2 Tb. peeled and chopped shallots
¼ tsp. salt
⅛ tsp. freshly ground black pepper
½ tsp. lemon juice

2 To separate the 2 single racks, run your knife along each side of the backbone (see Rack of Lamb Provençale, page 240) so each rack is attached to the backbone only at the end of the ribs.

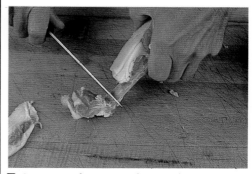

5 Trim along the ribs inside each chop.

6 Cut around the tip of each rib and scrape the meat off to expose about 2 in. of the tip of the ribs. This is done for aesthetic reasons and also because the meat around the tip of the ribs is fatty and tough. →

1 A double rack of veal weighs about 20 lb. It extends from the loin (side down) to the shoulder blade.

3 Stand the rack up and, using a cleaver, cut down on each side of the central bone to sever the ribs from the backbone. Each rack will weigh approximately 9 lb.

MEAT

263

7 Here the rack is cut into 7 chops with the 4 "first" on the left and the 3 "second" on the right. The trimmings of the ribs and the meat from the top of the rack (both seen in the back) can be used to make a stew or ground for pâté or dumplings. The central bone (not shown) can be made into white stock or brown veal stock (see pages 19 and 7).

8 For the grilled veal chops: Prepare a barbecue with wood or wood charcoal. Clean the grill thoroughly with a metal brush.

Rub the chops with oil and herbs, and allow to macerate for a few minutes. At cooking time, sprinkle lightly with salt and pepper and place on the hot grill. Cook approximately 2 to 3 minutes, repositioning the chops after a minute or so to create a criss-cross pattern. Turn and repeat on the other side. At this point, the chops are not completely cooked but it is best to finish them in the oven to prevent them from drying out.

Arrange on an ovenproof platter and place in a preheated 300-degree oven for about 6 to 8 minutes to continue cooking and to "relax" the meat.

9 For the shallots and beans: Bring a pot of salted water to a boil and add the ½ lb. beans. Cover the pot so the water comes back to the boil quickly. When the water boils, uncover the pot and cook over high heat for 4 to 5 minutes, depending on the freshness and size of the beans. (They should be cooked until al dente—still firm to the bite.) Remove with a slotted spoon and place in ice water to cool. Drain and set aside until serving time.

At serving time, melt the 3 Tb. butter in a skillet, add 2 Tb. chopped shallots, and cook for about 1 minute. Add the beans, ¼ tsp. salt, and ⅛ tsp. pepper, and toss just until heated through. Add the ½ tsp. lemon juice. Arrange on each plate with a veal chop in the center.

A LEANER VERSION

Reduce the amount of oil from 1 Tb. to 1 tsp. in grilling the chops (step 8) and reduce the amount of butter from 3 Tb. to 2 tsp. in sautéing the green beans (step 9). Proceed according to the recipe.

VEAL CHOPS MENAGERE EN PAPILLOTE

Yield: 2 servings

1 Tb. butter
2 veal chops, trimmed (about 11 to 12 oz. each)
Salt and pepper to taste
¼ c. dry white wine
⅓ c. heavy cream
About 12 peeled small baby carrots (6 per person)
About 12 peeled medium-sized white onions (6 per person)
2 rectangles of parchment paper, each about 24 in. by 15 in.
1 tsp. freshly chopped parsley

1 Prepare the veal as in steps 1 to 7 of the preceding recipe. Melt 1 Tb. butter in a heavy skillet. Sprinkle the chops lightly with salt and pepper and sauté over medium to high heat for 1½ minutes on each side. They should be nicely browned. Set aside. The sautéing crystallizes the natural sugar of the meat and forms a light crust, which improves the flavor.

Deglaze the skillet with the ¼ c. white wine and cook until most of the mixture reduces. Add ⅓ c. cream, bring to a boil, and season with salt and pepper.

Meanwhile, cover 12 peeled carrots and 12 onions with cold water and bring to a boil. Boil for 30 seconds and drain. (The liquid can be retained for stock or soup.)

2 Oil the paper rectangles lightly on one side; this helps browning in the oven. Fold each rectangle in half with the oil on the outside. Place a chop on the unoiled side of the paper with about 6 carrots and 6 onions and half the sauce. Fold the other half of the paper over the chop to enclose it. Repeat with the other chop.

3 Twist the edges of the paper all around to secure the chop inside. Be sure the edges are double-folded so the package will not leak during cooking and will "lock in" the moisture to ensure juicy meat.

4 Open the paper slightly at one end and, using a straw, blow some air inside the casing to inflate it. (The paper should not touch the top of the meat, as it would dry out while cooking.) The paper should be inflated to create a "hothouse," allowing moisture to rise and fall back on the meat and vegetables during cooking and, in effect, basting the meat continuously.

5 To prevent air from escaping, secure the opened pointed end by twisting it into a "pig's tail."

6 Place on a cookie sheet in a preheated 400-degree oven for 10 minutes. Serve immediately, all puffed, as they come from the oven, directly on the plate . . .

7 or cut the paper casing and slide the chop and vegetables onto a warm plate. Sprinkle with chopped parsley and serve immediately. The vegetables should be tender but slightly firm and the chop slightly pink and moist.

A LEANER VERSION

Reduce the amount of butter from 1 Tb. to 1 tsp. and omit the cream (step 1). Add 2 Tb. of water instead of the wine to loosen the juices in the pan. Proceed according to the recipe.

MEAT

BONING OUT A LEG OF VEAL

The purpose of boning out the leg is to divide the different muscles. Some muscles are tenderer than others, and the fiber of the meat goes in one direction for one muscle and in the other direction for another. When all the pieces are separated, each can be cut properly, usually against the grain, and used in different ways: The tenderest part is best for steak or a sauté of <u>escalope</u>, and the drier, tougher parts are better braised. The gelatinous, moist pieces are good for stew as well as for boiling or roasting.

A veal leg can weigh between 35 and 50 lb. The veal leg I am cutting up here weighed about 38 lb. The same boning technique can be used for a leg of beef, a leg of pork (a whole ham), and even a leg of lamb, some parts of which can be used for a shish kebab and some for roasting or for stew.

1 Here is the whole leg of veal as seen from the top.

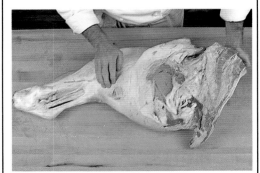

2 Here is the whole leg of veal as viewed from the inside. Notice on the inside by the tail and the pelvic bone the thick, white, waxy, hard fat and the pink, pale color of the flesh, both of which are signs that the meat is of high quality.

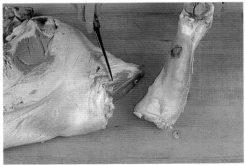

3 Remove the shank by cutting with a sturdy knife through the first joint at the knee. To make the famous Italian dish called *osso bucco,* cut the unboned shank into pieces about 1½ to 2 in. thick (about 3 or 4 per shank). The shank can also be braised whole with the bone in and then brought to the table and carved. In this instance, the carving will be done the long way, standing the bone straight up and cutting down to remove the shank. This will make a very tender, moist piece of braised meat. In this case, we are making a stew with the shank.

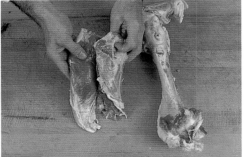

4 To make the stew, bone out the shank, sliding your knife around the bone. It will come out in one piece. This piece of meat (weighing approximately 2 lb.) can be rolled on itself and roasted or braised or cut into serving-size pieces for our Veal Curry, page 283. As you bone out the leg, be sure to set the bones aside. They can be cut into pieces and used for stock (see Veal Stock, page 7) or frozen for later use.

5 Along the inside of the pelvic bone by the tail, the tip of the fillet is lodged within the pelvic area. <u>Run your knife all around to dislodge it</u>. This piece of tenderloin, weighing approximately 1 lb., is only the head or top of the fillet and is the tenderest part of the whole back leg. Clean the piece of fillet of any sinews and fat, and set aside for the veal *escalope*. The rest of the fillet is part of the loin or saddle and is not shown in our picture.

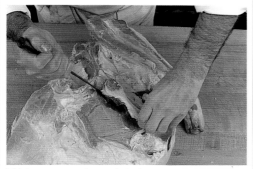

6 To remove the pelvic bone, <u>run a sturdy, sharp-pointed knife along the bone to loosen it from the flesh</u>. Cut gently and work slowly to make certain that you don't cut into the meat too much and that you follow the contours of the bone.

7 <u>When the bone is loose all around, pry it out</u>. Notice that in the socket, where the end of the femur bone is lodged, there is a large sinew. Gut the sinew to remove

the bone more easily. Keep pulling and cutting until the entire pelvic bone is separated from the leg. Cut the bone into pieces and set aside for stock or soup.

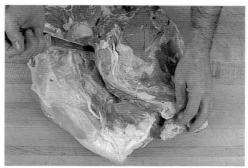

8 To remove the largest muscle of the leg – the top round – place the leg of veal inside up flat on the table. <u>Cut next to the head of the femur bone (where the bone is closest to the surface of the meat), and continue cutting with your knife along the bone</u>. As you cut and pull on the meat, you will see that the meat separates by itself into different muscles. Follow the separation of the meat to scoop out the large rounded muscle called the top round.

9 <u>Lift the top round from the meat and separate</u>. This is one of the choicest parts of the back leg and weighs between 4¼ and 4½ lb.

10 The top round has an upper layer of skin and meat, which should be separated from it. <u>As you start cutting, you will see the separation</u>. This layer of meat and skin closest to the surface of the leg is tougher. However, braised or cleaned and ground, it can be used for fricadelles (Fricadelles of Veal Renée, page 272) or paupiettes (Paupiettes of Veal Sara, page 279) or for making pâté as well as quenelles or stuffings. Clean the entire surface of the top round and set aside. I will use some of the top round cut into thin slices to make the Veal Vienna, page 277.

11 Now that the top round has been removed, you will notice that on the lower part of the leg, where the shank was removed, there is still a rounded, sinewy piece of meat. <u>This is also a part of the shank and should be separated from the leg</u> and used with the other piece of shank in the Veal Curry, page 283. Weighing about 2 lb., it is moist, gelatinous, and ideal for braising or stewing. →

12 The large bone, being now almost completely visible, is easy to remove. Cut on each side, sliding your knife underneath and cutting gently all around the bone until it is completely separated from the meat. Cut the bone into pieces by sawing or breaking with a hammer, and set the pieces aside for stock or soup.

13 Remove the top knuckle (a round, moist piece of meat close to the shank). This tender piece will be used for roasting and served with braised lettuce (Veal Roast with Braised Lettuce, page 281). Start pulling and cutting around the muscle to remove the entire large, roundish piece of meat, weighing about 4½ lb. Although I am roasting the top knuckle, it can also be used for *escalopes* or steaks.

14 On the side of the hip, remove the top sirloin or hip steak, the tenderest part of the leg except for the fillet. This piece of meat will be smaller, weighing approximately 2 lb., and will be cut into steaks.

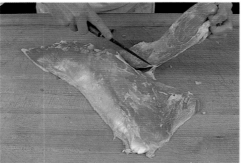

15 Finally, remaining on the table is the bottom round to be divided into two parts: the roundish, long, cylindrical muscle called the "eye round" and, attached to it, a flatter, wider piece called the "flat." The eye round is the toughest part of the leg and is often braised with stock or wine to give it some tenderness. It can also be ground for use in pâté. The flat, a tenderer piece, is often braised or roasted. The bottom round of the veal is used for pot roast or, in this case, for the *escalopes* in the Paupiettes of Veal Sara, page 279. (The whole flat weighs about 2 lb.)

16 Here are all the muscles of the leg, divided into pieces. From left to right in the front are the pieces of shank together, the fillet, the cleaned top round, and the roundish, solid top knuckle. In the back, on the right above the top knuckle, is the hip or top sirloin, to be used for steak, and, next to it, the bottom round divided into the eye round (the small cylindrical piece) and, below it, the flat.

17 As you divide and bone the leg into pieces, set aside separately the cleaned meat trimmings, the fat, the sinews, and the bones. In the meat trimmings, such as the layer from the top round, notice the surface of the meat. One can see the fibers, long and very visible, that indicate toughness. Flavorful but tough, these pieces have to be braised a long time or can be used ground in pâté or fricadelles as well as in mousses or paupiettes. The closer it is to the surface of the skin, the tougher the meat will usually be. Weighing almost 40 lb. then, this leg of veal divides into almost 10 lb. of bones (frozen for stock or soup); 3½ lb. of white, waxy fat (for use in dumplings or pâté); 3 lb. meat trimmings, completely cleaned (to be ground); 1½ lb. pieces of sinews and nerves (for use in a sauce for the Veal Roast, page 281); 4 lb. total (2 pieces) of shank; 1 lb. of fillet; 5 lb. top round, completely cleaned; 4 lb. of top knuckle; 2 lb. sirloin; and 5½ lb. bottom round, divided into the eye (1½ lb.) and the flat (4 lb.).

2 Peel the carrots and onions. Notice that a little of the green stem is left on the carrots; it is sweet-tasting and looks good in the dish.

Separate the meat lengthwise, following the lines of the sinew and nerves. You will notice that the meat lends itself to being separated into lengthwise strips. Cut each of the shanks into 6 pieces and remove any extra fat. There will still be some sinew remaining in the meat, but most of it will melt during cooking, as this cut is very gelatinous and moist.

COCOTTE VEAL SHANKS ANNIE

Cocotte is the French word for a Dutch oven, usually made of enameled cast iron. It is excellent for browning and cooking meats like the shank. As the meat cooks covered in a cocotte, it browns while its juices are released, making for a very moist and tender stew.

Shank meat is ideal for this type of cooking. In addition to the shank shown in photograph 1, which comes from the shoulder of veal, I added another shank to make a total of 4 lb. of meat (8 lb. with the bones).

The simple garnish of onions and carrots flavors the meat, and in turn these vegetables are flavored by the juice coming out of the meat. There is no need to add wine, stock, or water to the meat, because when it is cooked this way it renders enough juice to create its own natural gravy.

Yield: 6–8 servings

2 veal shanks (4 lb. each, unboned,
  2 lb. each, boned)
2 doz. baby carrots, peeled (about 10 oz.),
  with a little green left on top
12–15 small (Ping-Pong-ball size) onions
  (about 14 oz.)
½ tsp. salt
¼ tsp. freshly ground black pepper
3 Tb. butter
2 tsp. chopped garlic
1 Tb. coarsely chopped flat parsley

A LEANER VERSION

Reduce the 3 Tb. of butter to 1 Tb. and proceed according to the recipe.

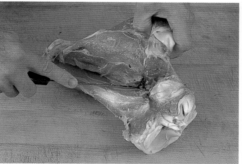

1 Slide your knife along the bone to detach it from the meat of the shank. The meat should come out in one piece. The bone can be broken with a big cleaver or hammer and frozen to use later in stocks, soups, or Brown Stock (page 7).

3 Sprinkle the meat with salt and pepper and melt the butter in a heavy Dutch oven. When hot, add the shank pieces and brown on all sides over high heat for 10 minutes. Cover, reduce the heat to low, and cook for about 30 minutes. Add the onions and garlic, cover again, and cook 10 minutes longer. Add the carrots and cook an additional 10 minutes.

4 Arrange the shank pieces and vegetables on a platter and pour the natural gravy (you will have 1¼ to 1½ c.) over them. Sprinkle with parsley and serve.

MEAT

269

1 Here are the fillets. Clean the tops of them of any sinews and nerves and cut into 8 pieces, each about ¾ in. thick and weighing 2 oz.

ESCALOPES OF VEAL COLETTE

The escalopes in this recipe are made with a piece of fillet (about 1 lb.). Escalopes can also be cut from the top round, the flat part of the bottom round, the top sirloin, as well as the top knuckle. The garnish can be changed according to what is available or the needs of a specific menu. My recipe uses colorful and flavorful red Swiss chard, although green Swiss chard or spinach can be substituted. The potatoes Parisienne are done in the classic way, finished with a reduction of stock, which glazes them and makes them particularly flavorful.

As an alternative, serve the escalopes with the Braised Endive, page 273.

The escalopes, especially when made with the fillet, should not be overcooked; they should be sautéed gently in moderately hot butter so they stay moist and tender.

Yield: 4 servings

1 piece of veal fillet (1 lb.)

POTATOES PARISIENNE

4 or 5 large Idaho potatoes, peeled
2 Tb. butter
1 Tb. oil
3 Tb. demi-glace (page 7)
Dash salt

RED SWISS CHARD

8 oz. young, tender red Swiss chard,
   washed in cold water
2 Tb. butter
Dash salt

TO SAUTE THE VEAL

2 Tb. butter
¼ tsp. salt
⅛ tsp. freshly ground black pepper
½ c. demi-glace
½ tsp. lemon juice

2 To avoid tearing the meat when pounding it, wet the cutting board and the metal meat pounder. Pound the meat slices lightly to spread the *escalopes* to approximately ¼-in. thickness. You will notice that it is easy to pound fillet as it is a very tender piece of meat. You will have to apply more pressure and strength when pounding pieces from the bottom round or top round.

3 **To prepare the potatoes Parisienne:** Use large potatoes, preferably, and a melon baller. Twist and press the melon baller (notice the little hole on top to prevent air from getting trapped inside) until it is practically embedded in the potato. Use your thumb to push it firmly into the potato.

4 Turn the melon baller around to make an almost completely round potato ball. If the balls are not round it's usually because the melon baller has not been pressed firmly enough into the potato before being twisted around. The trimmings of the potatoes can be kept for soups, mashed potatoes, croquettes, etc. Place the potato balls and the trimmings in cold water to prevent discoloration. These can be prepared to this point a day ahead of serving. When ready to use, drain the potatoes, cover with fresh cold water, bring to a boil, and boil 2 minutes. Drain. This blanching of the potatoes will prevent them from discoloring when out of the water and will put some moisture into them. With the additional moisture, the potatoes will cook faster when sautéed in butter and have a softer, nicer consistency.

6 **For the red Swiss chard:** Although I have used small-leaved red Swiss chard, green Swiss chard as well as spinach could be used in the same manner. Cut the Swiss chard so all the pieces cook in the same amount of time. Since the leaves will cook faster than the stems, which are tougher, cut the leaves into large pieces and the stems into thin slices about 1½ to 2 in. long.

Place about ½ in. of water in a large saucepan and bring to a boil. Add the Swiss chard, return to the boil, cover, and cook about 3 minutes. Drain and place the Swiss chard directly in ice water or under cold water to stop the cooking and retain the vegetable's beautiful color.

8 **For the veal:** Meanwhile, heat the 2 Tb. of butter. Sprinkle the *escalopes* lightly with salt and pepper and place in the foaming (but not too hot) butter and sauté for 1 minute on each side. Remove to a platter and let sit for a few minutes. During that time, add the ½ c. demi-glace to the drippings in the skillet, bring to a boil, and add ½ tsp. lemon juice.

Arrange Swiss chard on each serving plate, surround with the potato balls, and place 2 *escalopes* in the center, on top of the Swiss chard. Spoon the sauce over the meat and serve immediately.

5 When ready to serve, melt the butter and oil in a skillet and, when hot, add the potato balls. They should be in one layer. Sauté for about 10 minutes over medium to high heat, shaking the skillet so the potatoes brown evenly on all sides. When they are tender, drain the fat out of the skillet and add the demi-glace. Continue to cook the potatoes over high heat, shaking the pan occasionally so the demi-glace reduces and forms a glaze that coats the potatoes. Salt lightly.

7 At serving time, heat the 2 Tb. butter in a skillet. Notice that when the foam subsides the butter turns a light brown. Continue cooking the butter until it turns dark brown, and then add the Swiss chard, squeezed lightly first between your palms to extract the excess water from washing. Toss the Swiss chard in the butter with a dash of salt and cook just long enough to heat through.

A LEANER VERSION

Reduce the amount of butter from 2 Tb. to 1 tsp. in sautéing the Swiss chard (step 7). After the Swiss chard is tossed in the hot butter, add 1 Tb. of water to give it some moisture and help heat it up. Proceed according to the recipe. Omit the Parisienne potatoes.

Reduce the amount of butter from 2 Tb. to 2 tsp. in sautéing the veal (step 8), using, if possible, a non-stick skillet.

2 Process the trimmed bread pieces in a food processor for a few seconds, until you have fluffy bread crumbs. Remove and set aside.

In the food processor, process half the veal (unless you have a very large processor and can do the entire mixture at one time). Add half the cream slowly with the machine running. Then add half the pepper and salt, and mix just enough to incorporate. Remove the veal mixture to a bowl and repeat with the remaining veal, cream, salt, and pepper. Combine with the first batch and stir in the vegetables.

FRICADELLES OF VEAL RENEE

Yield: 6 servings

5 or 6 slices white bread, trimmed of crust
    (which can be reserved for stuffing or
    other breading needs)
½ c. leeks
1 c. ½-in.-diced carrots
1 c. ⅜-in.-diced zucchini
2 c. loose spinach
MOUSSE
1¼ lb. very lean veal
1½ c. heavy cream
⅛ tsp. pepper
¼ tsp. salt
Cooked vegetables (see above)
2 Tb. butter
2 Tb. corn oil
SOUR CREAM SAUCE
½ c. onions
¼ c. red wine vinegar
½–¾ c. cream
⅛ tsp. salt
⅛ tsp. pepper
GARNISH
3 large carrots
1½ medium zucchini
1 Tb. butter
Dash salt

1 Prepare all your ingredients and cut the trimmed bread into pieces for crumbling. Note: The crusts are removed so the bread crumbs in this recipe will be uniformly white.

Put about ¼ in. of water in a saucepan, preferably stainless steel. Add the leeks and carrots, and cook 2 to 3 minutes. Then add the zucchini and spinach, and cook for another minute or so, until the spinach is wilted. Run the vegetables under cold water for a minute to stop the cooking, drain in a colander, and set aside. If too wet when ready to use, squeeze the vegetables in a towel or between your hands to extract surplus water, because too much moisture in the vegetables may cause the mousse of veal to break down.

3 After wetting your hands first so the veal doesn't stick to them, form veal patties, each about ¾ in. thick and weighing 5½ to 6 oz. for a main course. Press them lightly into the fresh bread crumbs, to coat them all around.

Melt the butter and oil in a large saucepan and, when foaming, add the patties. Lower the heat and cook over medium to low heat for about 10 minutes on one side; they should be nicely browned. Turn and cook for another 3 to 4 minutes on the other side, just enough to cook the patties through. They should remain very moist inside. Remove the patties to a platter.

4 For the sauce: Increase the heat under the skillet used to cook the veal patties and add the chopped onions to the drippings in the pan. Cook over high heat for 1 to 2 minutes, until the onions are nicely browned, stirring to dissolve the solidified juices. It is perfectly all right if a few pieces of onion are slightly scorched and dark, since this gives taste and intensity to the sauce. Add the red wine vinegar and cook for a minute or so, until most of the vinegar has evaporated. Add the ½ c. cream, bring to a boil, and strain through a fine strainer into a small saucepan, being sure to press the solids with the back of a spoon to extract as much liquid as possible. Add salt and pepper and a little water if the mixture is too thick (1 or 2 Tb.). You should have approximately 2 Tb. of sauce per person.

5 For the garnish: While the veal is cooking, peel the large carrots and cut them into 2- to 2½-in. pieces. Cut the zucchini into 2- to 2½-in. chunks and then into ⅛-in. slices. Cover the carrots with cold water, bring to a boil, and boil gently for 10 minutes. Drain. The carrots should be cooked but still firm. Slice into ⅛-in.-thick slices. In a large skillet, heat the butter and, when foaming, add the zucchini. Sauté for about a minute, until the pieces begin to wilt. Add the carrots and a dash of salt and continue cooking over medium heat for about another minute. Set aside.

6 Create a design with the hot vegetables around a platter and pour approximately 3 Tb. of sauce in the center. Position the veal patties on top. Serve immediately.

BRAISED ENDIVE

Braised endive is a delicious accompaniment to stews, like the Rabbit Blanquette (page 197), or to roasted meats. It can be served hot from the cooking stock as is or transformed into other dishes, such as endive Flemish-style, where the cooked endive is wrapped in slices of ham, covered with a light cream sauce and cheese, and glazed under the broiler. In my opinion, most meat is best served by the taste of the endive when just poached in its natural broth.
Yield: 8–10 servings
2 lb. endive, trimmed of damaged leaves and washed
Rind of 1 lemon, removed by peeling with a vegetable peeler
1 Tb. lemon juice
2 Tb. butter
2 tsp. sugar
1 tsp. salt
¾ c. water
2 Tb. butter, to finish the dish
GARNISH
Bunch of basil or parsley

1 Place the endive in a large kettle, either stainless steel or enameled cast iron. Arrange them so they fit very tightly. Sprinkle with the pieces of lemon skin, lemon juice, 2 Tb. butter, sugar, salt, and water.

2 Cover with a piece of paper cut to fit, so that the steam that rises during the cooking will just touch the paper and fall back on the endive without any space between. It makes for a moister dish and prevents the endive from discoloring.

To prepare the paper so it fits, fold a square piece of parchment or waxed paper in half, then in half again.

3 Starting in the center, where there is no opening, fold on the diagonal to create a triangle. Fold again and again, 2 or 3 more times, to make a smaller and smaller triangle. →

4 Then, from the point in the center of the pot, measure the radius of the saucepan or kettle and trim the paper at the end to fit. Open the piece of paper. It should fit inside the pot. Butter at least half of the paper on one side and fold it on itself to butter the other half. Prepared as indicated, the paper can be kept until ready to use. A buttered piece of paper is particularly useful when baking a whole fish. The buttered paper, covering and tucked all around the fish, will prevent it from drying during baking. As the moisture from the fish and seasonings rises, it touches the paper and falls down onto the fish, keeping it moist by creating a hothouse effect.

6 At serving time, remove the endive from the liquid, drain, and arrange on a platter.

7 Melt the remaining 2 Tb. butter and pour over the endive. Arrange a little bunch of basil or parsley in the center as a garnish and serve immediately.

A LEANER VERSION

In step 1, omit the 2 Tb. of butter and the sugar and proceed according to recipe instructions. At serving time (step 7), use only 2 tsp. of butter and proceed according to the recipe.

5 Open the folded and buttered paper and place, buttered side down, on top of the endive. Place a plate that fits inside the kettle upside-down on top to press on the endive and keep them submerged in their juices while they are cooking. Cover with a lid and place on the stove. Bring to a boil, turn the heat to low, and boil gently for 15 to 20 minutes. Remove to the side of the stove.

2 **For the artichoke bottoms:** The artichokes take longer to prepare than the veal steaks and should be prepared first. Trim the artichokes according to the technique on page 225. Remove the choke, however, before cooking, using a small spoon to scoop it out. Slice the bottoms into ¼-in. slices. Melt the butter in a large skillet, add the artichokes, water, and salt. Cover and boil over high heat for 1 to 2 minutes. Remove the lid and continue cooking the artichokes until all the water has evaporated and the artichoke slices are lightly browned in the butter.

GRENADINS OF VEAL HELEN

Yield: 6 servings

6 veal steaks, preferably from the top sirloin, each about 5 to 6 oz. and ¾ in. thick
2 oz. dried morels, about 6 mushrooms per person
¼ tsp. salt
¼ tsp. pepper
3 Tb. butter
2 Tb. chopped shallots
1 Tb. cognac
1 c. soaking water from morels (retain other c. for stock or soup)
1 c. demi-glace (page 7)
Tarragon leaves for garnish

SLICED ARTICHOKE BOTTOMS

6 artichokes
3 Tb. butter
⅓ c. water
¼ tsp. salt

1 The wild morel mushroom is readily available dried and is one of the most flavorful of the dried mushrooms. Although they are expensive, 2 oz. of morels will be more than enough for 6 people. You should have approximately 6 morels per person. The small, pointed black specimens with rounded ends are the best quality.

Cover the dry morels with 2 c. of cold water and set aside for 30 minutes. Lift the morels from the water, pressing them lightly to extract excess water. Strain the soaking liquid through a paper towel and reserve 1 c. of it for use in the sauce. Any extra can be used in stock or frozen for future use.

3 Sprinkle the steaks with salt and pepper. Melt the butter in a large, sturdy skillet and, when the butter foams (but is not too hot), add the steaks. Cook over medium heat for 2½ to 3 minutes on one side, depending on the thickness (my steaks were ¾ in. thick). Turn the steaks and cook for an additional 2½ to 3 minutes. The steaks will still be pink on the inside. Remove to a hot platter, cover, and set aside in a warm oven (130 to 150 degrees) so the steaks relax and continue cooking in their own heat.

Meanwhile, add the shallots to the skillet, toss, and cook for about 30 seconds. Add the cognac and flame it. Then add 1 c. of the soaking liquid from the morels and cook over high heat until the liquid is reduced again to a glaze. →

MEAT

4 Add the demi-glace, the morels, and the juice that has come out of the veal. Bring to a boil, taste, and add salt and pepper, if needed.

5 The veal steaks can be served on a platter with the slices of artichokes, the morels, and the sauce on top. Sprinkle with tarragon leaves and serve.

6 Or 1 veal steak can be placed in the center of each individual plate, topped with the sauce and morels, sprinkled with tarragon leaves, and surrounded with artichoke slices for immediate serving.

A LEANER VERSION

Reduce the amount of butter from 3 Tb. to 1 Tb. in sautéing the steaks (step 3) and proceed according to the recipe.

For the artichoke bottoms, reduce the amount of butter from 3 Tb. to 2 tsp. and increase the water from ⅓ c. to ¼ c. Proceed according to the recipe.

VEAL VIENNA

Although small <u>escalopes</u> of veal can be breaded and sautéed, Veal Vienna is made with 1 large slice (about 4 to 5 oz.) per person. The slices are pounded very thin, breaded, and cooked quickly.

Yield: 6 servings

1 piece veal (2½ to 3 lb.) from the top
    round, completely trimmed
¼ tsp. salt
⅛ tsp. pepper
½ c. flour

DIPPING MIXTURE

2 eggs
1½ Tb. water
1 Tb. oil
3–4 c. fresh bread crumbs from about
    10 to 12 slices of bread, crusts removed

GARNISH

1 lemon
6 anchovy fillets
6 olives, preferably Greek or Spanish-style
2 hard-cooked eggs, yellow and white
    chopped separately
⅓ c. fresh chives
2 Tb. capers, drained (optional)

THE BRUSSELS SPROUTS

1 lb. Brussels sprouts
2 Tb. butter
Dash salt

TO FINISH THE VEAL

6 Tb. butter
6 Tb. oil
½ c. demi-glace (page 7)

1 Cut the large, thin pieces of veal needed for the breaded veal from the top round. Using a long, thin, sharp knife slice right across the top round, cutting the veal into pieces about ½ in. thick. The slices should weigh approximately 4 to 5 oz. each. If the surface is too large, slice from one side to the center of the meat, then slice the other.

2 If you do not have very large, thin pieces of veal, Veal Vienna can be made with smaller pieces, provided they are completely cleaned of all sinew and fat. Take the smaller pieces, as shown here, and butterfly them by slicing them almost completely through the center. Each piece is sliced into "halves" that still hold together along one edge, and the piece of meat is then opened like a book to form one large slice.

3 When a piece is butterflied, it is cut so it opens on the table. The pieces should weigh about 2 oz.

4 Dampen the table, the meat pounder, and the meat with a little water. Pound the meat, driving the pounder straight down and then out. If the pounder does not come down flat on the meat, its edge will tear the piece. The amount of pressure needed to pound down and out depends entirely on the tenderness of the meat. It

MEAT

277

will require less strength to pound the pieces of fillet and more pressure for the top round, which is tougher.

5 If, after the meat has been pounded, you have small pieces (as shown in photographs 2 and 3), place them together, overlapping slightly, to create a large piece.

6 Using your dampened meat pounder, pound the pieces gently where they overlap to make them adhere to one another. When cooked, they will look like one large piece, provided there is no sinew or fat attached to make them curl up or move during cooking. The finished pieces should measure about 8 to 9 in. long by 6 to 7 in. wide.

7 **Prepare the dipping mixture:** Mix the 2 eggs, 1½ Tb. water, and 1 Tb. oil together with a fork until combined. Sprinkle salt and pepper on the veal. Dust the pieces lightly with flour (shaking off the excess) and dip gently into the egg mixture, letting the excess drip off.

8 Place the veal in the 3 to 4 c. of bread crumbs. Press lightly on one side, turn, and press lightly again to coat both sides with the bread crumbs. If desired, using the dull edge of the blade, mark the top to create a lattice design. This refinement is optional, as the design often disappears in the cooking process. Place the pieces of veal on a large cookie sheet, separating layers with waxed paper so the breaded slices don't stick together. The veal can be refrigerated at this point.

9 **For the garnish:** Peel the lemon completely, removing all the white skin underneath, and cut into ¼-in. slices. Roll an anchovy around each of the 6 olives and place in the center of a lemon slice. Chop fine (or push through a sieve) first the yolks and then the whites of 2 hard-cooked eggs. Chop the ⅓ c. chives.

10 **For the Brussels sprouts:** Clean the 1 lb. Brussels sprouts of any damaged leaves; trim the ends and wash under cold water. Bring about 1 in. of water to a boil in a large, shallow stainless-steel saucepan. Add the Brussels sprouts, cover, and cook for about 7 minutes at a high boil. Drain and set aside on a plate until cool enough to handle, then cut each sprout into 3 slices.

At serving time, melt 2 Tb. butter in a skillet. Add the sliced sprouts and a dash of salt, and cook just until the sprouts are heated through. Do not brown.

11 Prepare your plates ahead of serving (since it takes a little time), arranging the garnish of egg yolks, chives, and egg whites in triangular patterns.

At serving time, heat 6 Tb. butter and 6 Tb. oil in 1 or 2 very large skillets and, when hot, place the breaded veal (scored side down) in the skillets. Cook over medium heat for approximately 2 minutes, turn, and cook 2 minutes on the other side.

Arrange the veal in the middle of each plate with a slice of lemon and an anchovy-wrapped olive on top. Surround with Brussels sprouts and, if desired, drained capers. Place ½ c. demi-glace in the cooking skillet, warm to a boil, and spoon the mixture around the veal. Serve immediately.

PAUPIETTES OF VEAL SARA

These paupiettes are an ideal family dish because they can be made ahead and are excellent reheated or served cold for a picnic. The eggplant is good hot and can also be added to salad or served cold sprinkled with a dash of vinegar.

Yield: 4 servings

STUFFING MIXTURE

¾ lb. chopped veal
6 oz. veal fat
2 Tb. fresh tarragon
¼ c. crushed ice (or small cubes)
1 egg
¼ tsp. salt
⅛ tsp. freshly ground black pepper

THE ESCALOPES

8 small veal *escalopes* from the bottom round
3 Tb. butter
1 c. ¼-in.-diced carrots
1¼ c. ½-in.-diced diced onions
1 tsp. fresh thyme, chopped
1 c. demi-glace (see page 7)
½ tsp. salt
⅛ tsp. freshly ground black pepper

SAUTEED EGGPLANT

1¼ lb. small eggplants (about 5), stem ends removed
⅓ c. corn oil
¼ tsp. salt

GARNISH

Chopped parsley

1 I use the flat, which is part of the bottom round of veal, for this recipe. It makes very nice *escalopes*. Cut the veal into slices weighing approximately 2½ oz. each and, using a meat pounder and a little water, pound the pieces to make 8 *escalopes* that are approximately ⅛ in. thick. Spread a little water on the board and wet the pounder, so the meat slides and expands rather than tears during the pounding. Each *escalope* should be about 7 in. long by about 5 to 6 in. wide.

2 The filling for the *escalopes* is called *godiveau*. It is a stuffing made with veal, veal fat, ice, and eggs. The ice lightens the mixture and makes it spongy and tender without imparting any richness to it. Make the stuffing in 2 batches in your food processor.

Place half of the veal, fat, tarragon, and ice in the food processor and process for 10 to 15 seconds, until the ice is incorporated and the mixture is smooth. Beat the egg with a fork and pour half into the processor along with half the salt and pepper. Process for 5 to 10 seconds longer, just enough to make the mixture smooth and bind it together. Repeat with the remaining half of the ingredients and mix the batches together in a bowl.

3 Place about ⅓ c. of the stuffing mixture in the center of each *escalope*. Fold the edges of the *escalopes* around the stuffing, wrapping as securely as possible. If the meat has been cleaned of all fat and sinews and is well pounded, it won't shrink or move during the cooking process.→

4 Tie the stuffed <u>escalopes</u> like a package with string, knotting it on the top or the <u>bottom.</u>

5 Heat the butter in a large skillet and, when hot, add the paupiettes and <u>brown gently all around for 5 to 6 minutes. The butter should not be too hot.</u>

Transfer the paupiettes to a plate and add the carrots, onions, and thyme to the skillet. Increase the heat and cook over high heat for 3 to 4 minutes and add the demi-glace. Return the paupiettes to the pan, add salt and pepper, and bring to a boil. Lower the heat and simmer very gently for 15 to 20 minutes. The paupiettes should be just cooked on the inside. Set aside.

6 **For the eggplant:** Cut all the small eggplants in half lengthwise. Place the corn oil in a large skillet and, when hot, add the eggplants, cut sides down, with the salt. Sauté for 5 minutes over medium to high heat. <u>Turn and cook for 5 minutes on the other side.</u>

7 At serving time, remove the paupiettes from the skillet and discard the string. Pour the juice and fat into a smaller saucepan and remove as much of the fat from the surface as you can. Boil down the mixture to thicken it. You should have approximately 2 c. of sauce remaining. It should contain a lot of vegetables and not be too liquid.

Arrange the paupiettes on a large platter. Place the eggplants around them, and spoon the sauce over the paupiettes. Sprinkle them with chopped parsley and serve immediately.

VEAL ROAST WITH BRAISED LETTUCE

A moist veal roast with a rich gravy embodies for me the essence of bourgeois cooking. Braised lettuce, elegant and subtle, is the perfect accompaniment, although it could be served with most roast meat or poultry.

Yield: 10–12 servings

About 1½ lb. veal trimmings (mostly
  sinews and tendons); if not available,
  use chicken backs and bones
½ stick unsalted butter
1 top knuckle veal roast (about 4 to
  4½ lb.)
½ tsp. salt
¼ tsp. freshly ground black pepper
2 c. coarsely cut onions
1 c. coarsely cut carrots
3 c. water
2 c. chicken stock
1½ tsp. arrowroot or potato starch dissolved in 3 Tb. water

BRAISED LETTUCE

5 heads Boston lettuce (about ½ lb. each)
½ stick butter
¼ tsp. salt

1 Place the trimmings in a heavy aluminum roasting pan, about 11 in. wide by 16 in. long. Add the butter and cook on top of the stove over medium to high heat for about 20 minutes. The trimmings should be well roasted and brown.

Set the oven at 400 degrees. Sprinkle the roast with salt and pepper. Make space in the center of the roasting pan and brown the roast lightly on top of the stove on all sides for about 5 minutes. Place in the center of the oven for 15 minutes, then turn the roast over.

2 Cook another 15 minutes, then baste with the pan juices and sprinkle the onions and carrots around the roast. Cook 45 minutes longer, basting every 15 minutes (total cooking time 1 hour and 15 minutes, about 15 to 18 minutes per pound). Remove the roast when it reaches an internal temperature of 130 degrees. Place on a platter and set in a warm place on top of the stove to rest for at least 20 minutes.

3 Meanwhile, place the vegetables, trimmings, and juices in a saucepan and deglaze the roasting pan with the water, scraping to remove all the coagulated juices. Add this mixture to the saucepan along with the chicken stock, bring to a boil, and boil gently for 30 minutes, skimming occasionally to remove most of the fat. Strain through a fine strainer. (You should have approximately 3 c. left.) Boil this liquid down to reduce it to 1½ c. Season to taste with salt and pepper. Add arrowroot or potato starch dissolved in water and stir to thicken. Set aside. →

MEAT

4 **For the braised lettuce:** Be sure to wash the Boston lettuce carefully. Soak the heads in a lot of water and trim off the outside leaves, which may be dark or soiled. Clean the inside of the heads by opening them carefully and holding them under running water or by plunging them up and down in a sink full of water so the water gets inside the lettuce and washes away any sand or dirt between the leaves.

5 Place the lettuce in a large kettle of boiling water, return to the boil, and cook for approximately 12 to 15 minutes, depending on the size and tenderness of the lettuce. It should be just tender but still firm when pierced with the point of a knife. Lift the lettuce out of the water and place in a bowl of ice-cold water, being careful to keep the heads intact.

6 Lift the lettuce by the cores out of the cold water, then press gently between the palms of your hands to extract the water and firm up the shape.

7 Place the lettuce on the table and cut lengthwise into 2, 3, or 4 pieces, depending on the size of the heads. The object is to have all the sections of lettuce approximately the same size.

8 Flatten each piece of lettuce lightly with the edge of a knife at the green end. With the point of a knife, lift about 1 in. of green end and fold it over on top of the lettuce. Lift up the root end and fold onto the green so that the lettuce is folded onto itself in thirds.

9 The end of the lettuce segments can be trimmed so the packages are triangular and uniform in size, although if the lettuce is tender and young it is not necessary to trim the cores.

10 Heat the ½ stick butter in a very large skillet and, when sizzling, place the lettuce rounded side down in the pan. Sprinkle with ¼ tsp. salt and sauté for 2 to 3 minutes, until lightly browned on top. Turn and sauté gently 2 to 3 minutes on the other side.

11 Pour some of the sauce from step 3 into the bottom of a large platter and place the roast in the center. Arrange the lettuce around it. Glaze the roast and the lettuce with some of the sauce. Slice and serve immediately with extra sauce on the side.

A LEANER VERSION

Omit the ½ stick of butter in browning the trimmings (step 1). There should be enough fat released when browning the trimmings so the roast can be browned on top of the stove as explained in step 1. Proceed according to the recipe.

For the braised lettuce, omit the butter. In step 10, arrange the lettuce packages in a gratin dish and place in a preheated 400-degree oven for 6 to 8 minutes to evaporate most of the moisture and heat the lettuce. Arrange the lettuce and roast on a serving platter, as indicated in step 11 and moisten with the sauce.

1 lb. apples (about 4 small), unpeeled, stems and cores removed, cut into ½-in. dice (2½ c.)
6 cloves garlic, chopped fine (1 Tb.)
2 bananas, peeled and sliced (1½ c.)

GARNISH

Mint

BROWN RICE

2 Tb. butter
1½ c. coarsely chopped onions
2 cloves garlic, chopped (1 tsp.)
½ c. raisins
1½ c. short-grain brown rice
3½ c. light chicken stock
½ tsp. salt

OKRA

½ lb. okra
1 c. vinegar
2 qt. water
1 Tb. butter

VEAL CURRY WITH PEAR CHUTNEY AND BROWN RICE

The shank is ideal for stewing or braising because it is moist and tender when well cooked. The amount of curry powder used and the hotness of the curry mixture can be varied to suit one's own taste. Some of the spices in the curry powder come whole and some are already powdered; when possible, buy the whole seeds and grind them yourself for a fresher and better seasoning.

Yield: 8 servings

CURRY POWDER (⅓ CUP)

1 Tb. whole coriander seeds
½ tsp. hot pepper flakes
2 tsp. black peppercorns
½ tsp. whole cloves
1 tsp. mustard seeds
1 Tb. cumin powder
2 tsp. ground turmeric
1 tsp. cinnamon

PEAR CHUTNEY

½ tsp. allspice berries
12 cloves
1 tsp. mustard seeds
½ tsp. coriander seeds
⅛ tsp. cayenne pepper
¼ tsp. black pepper
¾ c. white distilled vinegar
2 Tb. grated onion
¾ c. golden raisins
½ c. sliced almonds
¼ c. honey
¼ c. molasses
1 lemon, quartered and cut into thin slices
1½ lb. pears, well ripened (3–5, depending on size), peeled and cut into 1-in. pieces

FOR THE STEW

4 lb. shank of veal
3 Tb. butter
1½ tsp. salt
⅓ c. curry powder (recipe above)
2 Tb. flour
½ c. ¼-in.-diced onions
1 c. chicken stock
2 c. water
1½ c. tomatoes, seeds removed, coarsely chopped (2 large tomatoes)

1 Place the coriander, peppers, cloves, and mustard in a spice grinder and grind to a powder. Add the remaining curry powder ingredients. Mix to blend. Keep in a tightly covered jar.

2 Grind the allspice, cloves, mustard and coriander seeds, and peppers to a powder in a spice grinder or coffee grinder. Add the remaining pear chutney ingredients.

Place all the pear chutney ingredients in a saucepan and bring to a boil. Cover, boil gently for 30 minutes, then uncover and cook to reduce the juices, so the mixture is just moist with no excess liquid (about 20 minutes). Place in a jar and cool. The chutney tastes better after a few days and will keep for weeks in the refrigerator.

3 For the stew: Cut the veal into 12 portions approximately 4 to 6 oz. each. (They could be cut into smaller portions but are easier to serve and more attractive on the plate when cut into large pieces like this.) If shank is not available, the shoulder of veal would be very moist and good for this stew.

4 Heat the butter in a large saucepan. When hot, add the meat in one layer. Sprinkle with salt and brown on all sides over medium to high heat for about 10 minutes.

Combine the curry powder with the flour and add with the onions to the meat in the pan. Stir to mix and allow to cook for 1 to 2 minutes.

5 Add the stock and water and the rest of the stew ingredients. Bring to a boil, cover, and boil gently for 45 minutes. (The meat should be tender when pierced with the point of a knife; if still tough, cook a little longer.) If too much liquid remains, boil gently, uncovered, to reduce the sauce further.

6 For the rice: Heat the 2 Tb. butter in a sturdy saucepan and, when hot, add 1½ c. chopped onions and 1 tsp. chopped garlic and sauté for 2 minutes. Add ½ c. raisins and 1½ c. rice, stirring well to coat the rice with butter. Add 3½ c. chicken stock and ½ tsp. salt and bring to a boil, stirring occasionally, so the mixture doesn't scorch. As soon as it boils, lower the heat to very low, cover, and cook for 45 minutes. The rice should be cooked but the grains should have some firmness.

7 For the okra: Okra is sometimes used in stew (like the gumbo in New Orleans cooking or the lamb stew in Africa) since the viscous juice it exudes tends to thicken sauces. Remove the tips of ½ lb. of okra and slice it in half and then quarters lengthwise. To eliminate some of the sliminess, place in a plastic bag and cover with 1 c. vinegar. Leave for 30 minutes. Remove the okra and rinse well under cold water.

Bring 2 qt. of water to a boil, add the okra, and return to the boil. Boil for 5 minutes uncovered. Strain in a colander and refresh under cold water. At serving time, heat 1 Tb. butter in a skillet, add the okra, and sauté gently, just enough to heat through.

8 Place the veal mixture on a large serving platter. Scatter the warm okra and a few mint leaves on top and serve with the rice and pear chutney on the side.

A LEANER VERSION

For the pear chutney: Reduce the amount of honey from ¼ c. to 1 Tb. and the amount of molasses from ¼ c. to 1 Tb. Omit the raisins and almonds and proceed according to the recipe.

Omit the brown rice.

For the stew: Omit the butter. Instead of browning the veal as explained in step 3, place the meat in one layer in a saucepan and brown lightly under the broiler for 12 to 15 minutes, turning the pieces so they brown evenly all around. Omit the flour, add the rest of the ingredients, and proceed according to the recipe.

For the okra: Omit the butter (step 7). At serving time reheat the okra in a warm oven or in boiling water for 1 to 2 minutes and proceed according to the recipe.

THE WHEAT SQUARES

3½ c. milk
1 tsp. salt
½ tsp. freshly ground black pepper
⅛ tsp. ground nutmeg
3 eggs
½ c. heavy cream
1 c. regular Cream of Wheat
1 c. finely grated Swiss cheese
1 tsp. corn oil (for oiling jelly roll pan)

TO SAUTE THE WHEAT SQUARES

2 Tb. butter
2 Tb. corn oil

THE PATTYPAN SQUASH

1½ lb. miniature pattypan squash, trimmed
1 Tb. butter
¼ tsp. salt

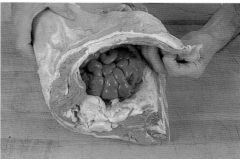

1 One single loin (sometimes called half a saddle) weighs approximately 14 to 15 lb. (depending on the size of the animal) untrimmed, with fat, kidney, flank, and bone in.

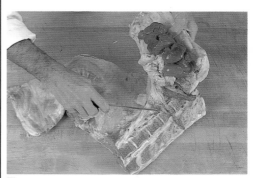

2 Pull off the whole block of fat that encases the kidneys and remove the kidneys from the fat. This white, waxy fat is sometimes rendered. It is good for deep-frying potatoes and can be used in mousse as well as fish mixtures (see Pike Quenelles, page 103). Set aside about 3 oz. for the mousse.

ROGNONNADE OF VEAL WITH WHEAT SQUARES

<u>Rognonnade</u> takes its name from the word <u>rognon</u> ("kidney" in French) because the loin of veal in this recipe is cooked with the kidney tucked inside the roast. Since it is placed in the center of the veal, the kidney is the last to cook. When carved, the veal should be moist and juicy and the kidney pink in the center. (See information in Grilled Veal Chops, page 263.) The loin is an expensive cut of meat, especially when from milk-fed veal, but prepared in this manner, using the loin, fillet, kidney, flank, and trimmings (in a mousse), it makes a large roast, enough for 10 to 12 people for a special dinner party.

The miniature pattypan squashes are just steamed briefly and buttered. They could be served with other roast meat as well as fish. Slices of zucchini or pieces of pattypan squash can be used in the same manner if the miniature squashes are not available.

The Cream of Wheat could be served like a polenta with melted butter, as shown in photograph 14. The polenta for the sautéed squares must be made ahead so it has a chance to cool and harden. It is served, below, with the veal roast and natural gravy, but can also be served with a light tomato sauce by itself or as an accompaniment to sautéed meat and fish.

Yield: 10–12 servings

½ veal saddle (also called single loin roast), complete with kidney, fillet, fat, and flank (about 14 to 15 lb.)
¾ tsp. salt
¼ tsp. freshly ground black pepper
1 Tb. butter

FOR THE MOUSSE

2 slices white bread
⅓ c. milk
10 oz. veal trimmings
3 oz. veal fat
1 egg
1 clove garlic, crushed and finely chopped
3 Tb. chopped chives
1 Tb. chopped fresh oregano or 1 tsp. dried oregano
¼ tsp. freshly ground black pepper
½ tsp. salt

NATURAL SAUCE

Cooking juices from the veal
1 tsp. potato starch dissolved in 1 Tb. water
Salt and freshly ground black pepper to taste

3 Cut approximately 6 in. from the flank. This extra piece can be used in stew but is butterflied in my recipe and placed at the ends of the roast to hold in the stuffing. Reserve all the trimmings of lean meat to use for the mousse.

4 Run your knife around the bone to remove the fillet in one piece. Separate the chain from the fillet. The chain is that long, narrow strip of meat attached to the fillet, and it is full of sinews; scrape it with a knife to remove as much meat as possible for use in the mousse (see page 206).

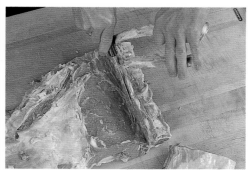

5 Run your knife behind the ribs and central bone to loosen the loin.

6 Remove most of the fat from the inside of the veal.

7 When the bone is loose, use a spoon to scrape any remaining meat from it and reserve the meat for the mousse.

8 In this roast, the flank is narrower than the loin, and it should be as wide in order to encase the stuffing and overlap the loin. Butterfly the flank and open it until it is approximately as wide as the loin. Split the fillet and kidneys in half lengthwise.

9 The whole loin is now boned out: In the back row, from left to right are: 3 lb. of fat, 2 lb. of bone and sinews together, and about 1 lb. of extra flank, cut into pieces, on the right. In the front, on the left, are the trimmed roast and flank together (about 4 lb.), the kidneys (12 oz.), and the fillet of veal (about 6 oz.), with about 10 oz. of trimmings, behind.

10 **To make the mousse:** Soak the 2 slices of white bread in ⅓ c. milk for a few minutes. Place 10 oz. of veal trimmings and 3 oz. fat in the food processor and process about 15 seconds. Add 1 egg and process another 5 to 10 seconds. Add the soaked bread, 1 chopped garlic clove, 3 Tb. chives, 1 Tb. fresh or 1 tsp. dried oregano, ¼ tsp. pepper, and ½ tsp. salt, and process just enough to mix well.

Sprinkle ¼ tsp. salt and ¼ tsp. pepper on the meat and kidneys. Spread a layer of the mousse (using about half) where the flank joins the loin. Place the kidneys on top of it and the fillet alongside with some mousse in between.

11 Place the 2 pieces of butterflied extra flank one on each side (top and bottom in the above photograph), tucking them under the kidneys. Spread the remainder of the mousse on top and bring these two pieces of meat back over the mousse to encase it with the kidneys. Bring the flank back over the stuffed loin to encase it completely.

12 To tie: Attach one loop of the twine at one end of the roast to secure. Then, using the half-hitch technique (see page 168, steps 16 to 18), secure across and lengthwise to hold the stuffing inside. The weight of the roast should be approximately 8½ lb. now.

At cooking time, arrange the bones and the sinews from the saddle in a roasting pan and place in a preheated 400-degree oven for 30 to 45 minutes.

13 For the wheat squares: The wheat squares can be prepared ahead, ideally the day before, and spread on a jelly roll pan to cool before being cut into squares.

Bring the 3½ c. milk, 1 tsp. salt, ½ tsp. pepper, and ⅛ tsp. nutmeg to a boil in a saucepan. While the mixture heats, mix 3 eggs and ½ c. cream together in a bowl until incorporated. When the milk boils, off heat add 1 c. Cream of Wheat, stirring with a whisk. Return to the heat and cook 3 to 4 minutes, stirring with the whisk until the mixture gets thick.

14 Remove from the heat and whisk in the egg-cream mixture. Return to the stove and bring to a boil, stirring with the whisk.

15 Oil a jelly roll pan. Stir 1 c. grated Swiss cheese into the boiling mixture and pour into the oiled pan. Spread with a spatula so the thickness of the mixture is about ½ in. To help spread and smooth the mixture, place a piece of plastic wrap on top of it and press and spread with your hand. Refrigerate until thoroughly cold.

16 When the bones are browned, push them to the sides and position the roast in the center of the pan. Sprinkle it with ½ tsp. salt and rub 1 Tb. of butter on top. Place in a 400-degree oven for 30 minutes.

17 Turn the roast over, reduce the oven temperature to 350 degrees, and continue cooking 1 hour. →

18 Turn the roast over again and continue cooking 45 minutes longer (about 2 hours and 15 minutes total). The roast should have an internal temperature of 130 to 140 degrees as it comes out of the oven. The temperature will continue to rise 5 to 10 degrees as it rests. Lift up the roast, place it in another roasting pan, and set it on the side of the stove or in a 140-degree oven to keep warm and relax.

19 Pour off as much of the clear fat as possible from the drippings in the roasting pan and discard it. Place the remaining drippings and bones in a saucepan, add 1 qt. water to the roasting pan, and scrape with a wooden spatula to melt the solids. Add these to the saucepan with the bones, bring to a boil over high heat, and boil gently 25 to 30 minutes.

20 Notice that after the meat has rested for 15 to 20 minutes a lot of juice has come out of it. The juice is red because of the kidney inside, which has been resting and releasing juices. Add the juices to the

bones, which are being boiled for the sauce.

After the bones have been boiled for about 30 minutes, strain the stock, let it rest for a few minutes, and remove most of the fat from the top. Return the stock to high heat and reduce it to 2 c. Add 1 tsp. potato starch dissolved in 1 Tb. water to the reduction and bring to a boil. Taste the sauce for seasonings and add salt and pepper, if needed.

21 When it is cold and hard, cut the wheat mixture into pieces about 3 in. square.

22 In 1 very large or 2 smaller skillets, heat the 2 Tb. of butter and 2 Tb. corn oil. When hot, add the squares and cook over medium to high heat until a nice crust is formed, about 5 minutes. Turn and cook another 5 minutes on the other side.

For the miniature pattypan squash: Wash the 1½ lb. of squash and place in a stainless-steel pan with about ½ in. of water. Bring to a boil. When boiling, cook, covered, for about 4 to 5 minutes, and drain. Toss with 1 Tb. butter and ¼ tsp. salt.

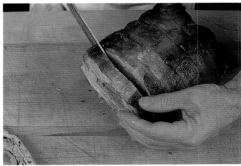

23 Cut the string around the roast and remove it. Transfer the roast to a cutting board and cut into slices approximately ¾ in. thick. Notice that one hand is cutting while the other is holding the roast in front to catch the slice of meat as it is released.

24 Place the roast on a large platter with the sliced pieces in front and the wheat squares around. Spoon some of the sauce over the roast and pass the rest at table. Serve immediately with the steamed pattypan squash.

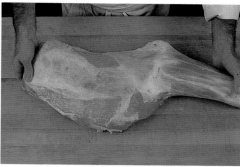

1 The whole leg of veal as seen from the top, including the shank. It will weigh approximately 15 lb.

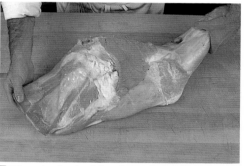

2 Here is the inside of the shoulder. You can recognize the shoulder blade and a lump of the fat in the center. Except for that lump of fat in the center, near the shoulder blade joint, there is basically nothing to remove or trim except the shank, should you decide to remove it.

GRILLED SHOULDER OF VEAL WITH HERB BUTTER

A large piece of grilled meat is ideal for a big summer party. The shoulder of veal featured here will serve about 16 people. Although the shank can be cooked with it, it tends to be sinewy and tough when grilled and, therefore, I removed it to use in Cocotte Veal Shanks Annie, page 269. The recipe here is easy to make since the shoulder is not boned out. Except for the removal of the shank, it is placed on the barbecue just as it came from the market.

The front leg or shoulder is relatively inexpensive and, although it will probably have to be specially ordered from a butcher or obtained from a meat wholesaler, it is readily available. The shoulder may not look exactly as it does in photographs 1 and 2. Sometimes the shank has already been removed, while other times more of the neck and less of the lower part of the leg are present. In any case, the round piece with the flat shoulder blade is always there.

The shoulder will weigh from about 12 to 20 lb. whole. Buy veal that is white and of good quality – the so-called fancy veal, nature veal, <u>Plume de Veau</u>, or Provimi veal (see information on veal, page 262, Veal Chops).

The potato and corn packages (see the following page) can be cooked in a gratin dish but are ideal done in individual aluminum-foil packages on the barbecue and are easy to serve this way. The packets can be prepared while the veal is cooking and placed on the barbecue to cook alongside the meat when it is half cooked. The herb butter can be made ahead and even frozen. It can also be used to flavor steaks, stews, sauces, and fish.

Yield: About 16 servings

1 whole shoulder of veal, about 15 lb. with shank
Salt (optional)
HERB BUTTER
2 c. mixed herbs (1 c. parsley and 1 c. mixture of fresh tarragon, basil, chives, and chervil)
2 sticks butter
1½ Tb. lemon juice
1 Tb. freshly ground black pepper
1 tsp. salt

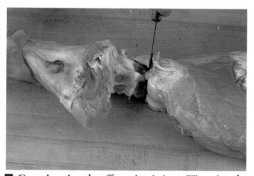

3 Cut the shank off at the joint. The shank will weigh approximately 4 lb. with the bone in. Of those 4 lb., 2 lb. will be meat and 2 lb. will be bones. The bones can be cut and frozen or reserved for stocks or soups (see Brown Stock, page 7). →

MEAT

4 Have a strong fire going on the grill that can last and withstand long cooking. Push the hot coals to the side so the place where you put the shoulder is not too terribly hot. (Otherwise, the exterior will get too dark during cooking.)

Place the shoulder top side down and cook approximately 30 minutes, then turn to brown on the other side. Continue cooking, turning the roast every 30 to 45 minutes, for 2 to 2½ hours longer. When finished, the internal temperature should be approximately 125 to 130 degrees. Remove the veal from the grill, place on a tray, and keep in a 140-degree oven to continue cooking slowly in its own juices and resting for 45 minutes longer. If you can't transfer it to an oven, you can place it covered with a piece of aluminum foil in a warm place off to the side of the barbecue to continue cooking.

POTATO AND CORN PACKAGES

Yield: 16–18 packages
4 lb. medium potatoes, peeled, washed, and sliced thin
1 Tb. chopped garlic
6 c. milk
2 c. heavy cream
2 tsp. salt
1 tsp. freshly ground black pepper
4 ears corn, cut off the cob (see page 13)

5 In a large kettle or Dutch oven, place the thinly sliced potatoes (wash after peeling but not after slicing to preserve the starch needed for proper texture). Add the garlic, milk, cream, salt, and pepper. Bring the mixture to a boil, stirring occasionally so it doesn't stick to the kettle, and let boil for 1 to 2 minutes, just long enough for the mixture to thicken.

Cut the corn off the cob with a knife and reserve until ready to use.

6 Line small bowls with 12-in. squares of aluminum foil. Press the squares into the bowls and, using a scoop, fill each with about ¾ c. of the potato mixture and ¼ c. of corn kernels. Pinch the ends together (enough to seal but not too tightly so the steam can expand a little). Place the packages on the side of the grill over medium heat and cook for 35 to 40 minutes.

7 For the herb butter: In a food processor, place the 2 c. of mixed herbs and process for about 10 seconds. Add the butter, lemon juice, pepper, and salt. Process until well homogenized.

At serving time, slice the veal, brush with the soft herb butter, and serve with the potato and corn packages.

A LEANER VERSION

Grill the shoulder of veal as explained in step 4. Omit the herb butter. After the veal is grilled, sprinkle it with the 2 c. of chopped herbs and place it in a 140-degree oven, as indicated in step 4. Omit the potato and corn packages. Potatoes could be cooked (unpeeled) on top of the grill and served plain with the veal.

INNARDS

BRAISED BEEF TONGUE WITH LENTILS

Beef tongue cooked with beans, lentils, or potatoes makes an excellent winter dish, easy to prepare ahead and flavorful when reheated. The beef tongue itself can also be sliced cold for sandwiches or served at a buffet, glazed in an aspic.

The beef tongue I use in my recipe is already cured but uncooked, as tongue is found in most markets.

Yield: 8–10 servings

1 3¾-lb. cured beef tongue
8 oz. salt pork, cut into ½-in. dice
¾ lb. onions, cut into 1-in. chunks (2 or
    3 medium onions)
10 oz. carrots, cut into 1-in. chunks
    (about 3 medium carrots)
2 Tb. rosemary
1 lb. lentils
6 c. chicken stock
Salt, if needed, depending on saltiness of
    stock, tongue, and salt pork

1 Place tongue in a kettle and cover with cold water. Bring to a boil and simmer gently, just under the boil, for a good 2 hours. Remove the tongue and let cool for at least 30 minutes, until cool enough to handle.

2 Peel the tongue and remove the bones toward the throat. (They are the only bones left in the meat.)

3 Cover the little pieces of salt pork, called lardons, with water. Bring to a boil and boil about 1 minute, drain in a sieve, wash under cold water, and place in a large Dutch oven. <u>Cook over medium to high heat for about 10 minutes, until they are nicely browned and most of the fat has been rendered</u>. Add the onions and carrots and continue cooking for about 3 minutes. Then add the tongue and the rosemary, lentils, and chicken stock to the pot. Simmer gently for 1 hour with the pot covered almost completely except for a slight opening. It is better to cook this dish ahead and let it sit for at least 30 minutes before carving.

5 Arrange the tongue on a large serving platter with the vegetables and lentils. (If any lentils are left over, they can be puréed with some water in the food processor. Some of the tongue or sausage or ham can be diced and combined with the puréed lentils to make a very flavorful soup.)

4 Remove the tongue from the lentils and <u>cut into ½-in. slices</u>.

TWO RECIPES FOR POACHED CALVES' BRAINS

The brains of calves and lamb are the tastiest. Pork brains tend to be mushy and beef brains are spongy and elastic. Calves' brains are readily available in butcher shops and even supermarkets nowadays and are inexpensive and very good.

Although brains can be just poached as purchased, it is nicer to remove the membrane from the surface. If left on, the membrane will darken as it cooks and make the top of the brains tougher. After the brains are poached, they can be kept in their cooking liquid in the refrigerator for a week. When needed, they can be reheated in the liquid and served with melted or black butter, or with a sauce, such as the one in Calves' Brains Financière (next recipe). You will note that in the following 2 recipes, only one large brain is used, but you could, of course, double either of the recipes.

Yield: 4 servings

TO POACH THE BRAINS

2 large calves' brains (about 1½ lb.)
¼ c. white wine vinegar
3 c. water
2 large sprigs fresh thyme
1 c. finely sliced onions
3 bay leaves
½ tsp. pepper
1 tsp. salt

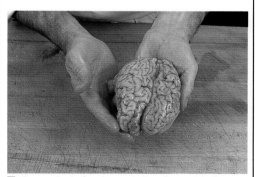

1 One whole brain weighs about ¾ lb.

2 Cut each of the brains in half. The half on the right shows the surface of the brain and the half on the left the inside.

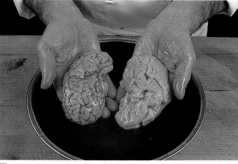

3 Holding the brain halves under running water, slide your index finger and thumb through the folds and crevices to remove the thin membrane from the surface until the brain is completely clean. Then wash again under water. The brain should be white and clean. <u>Notice the half brain on the right is cleaned and the one on the left still has the membrane.</u>

4 Place the vinegar, water, thyme, onions, bay leaves, pepper, and salt in a saucepan, preferably stainless steel, and bring to a boil. Boil for approximately 5 minutes. Then drop the brains into the boiling liquid and bring the mixture back to the boil. Lower the heat and poach gently at a bare simmer for about 8 to 10 minutes. <u>Lift out of the stock when ready to use.</u>

Although the recipe can be doubled or

MEAT

tripled easily, I am giving here recipes for 2 servings, which is 1 brain, approximately 12 oz., already poached as shown in the procedure above.

CALVES' BRAINS FINANCIERE

This recipe calls for 1 brain for 2 servings. Instead of serving it on individual plates, however, both halves are placed on a platter and coated with the sauce. The financière *sauce can also be served with dumplings or fish quenelles as well as sweetbreads or even sautéed breast of chicken.*

Yield: 2 servings
¼ c. pitted and coarsely chopped green olives
2 Tb. butter
1 Tb. chopped shallots
½ tsp. chopped garlic
2 c. button mushrooms, cleaned
¼ c. white wine
½ c. demi-glace (page 7)
⅓ c. ⅛-in.-diced boiled ham
⅓ c. peeled, seeded, and diced tomatoes
¼ tsp. pepper
¼ tsp. salt
1 whole calf brain, about 12 oz., cut into halves and poached as explained above

GARNISH

Parsley

A LEANER VERSION

Reduce the amount of butter from 2 Tb. to 2 tsp. (step 2) and omit the ham. Proceed according to the recipe.

1 Blanch the olive pieces so they won't impart a bitter taste to the sauce: Place them in a saucepan, cover with water, bring to a boil, and boil for 15 to 20 seconds. Drain in a sieve and rinse under water. Set aside.

2 Melt the butter in a saucepan. Add the shallots and sauté for about 30 seconds. Add the chopped garlic and the mushrooms. Sauté until the juice starts coming out of the mushrooms, for about 3 to 4 minutes, then add the wine and demiglace. Bring to a boil, boil gently for 1 minute, then add the ham, tomatoes, and olives, bring to the boil again, and season with pepper and salt.

3 Remove the brains from the hot broth and drain. Arrange on a platter, coat with the sauce, decorate with parsley, and serve immediately.

CALVES' BRAINS WITH BROWN BUTTER

Yield: 2 servings
1 whole calf's brain, about 12 oz., cut into halves and poached
2 Tb. flour
3 Tb. butter
1 Tb. oil
1½ Tb. capers, drained
1 tsp. red wine vinegar
2 Tb. shredded fresh basil

1 Remove the brains, which should be lukewarm or cold, from the poaching liquid. Each piece of brain is half a brain. Hold each piece flat and cut it with a knife to butterfly it – that is, open it in half, which makes it approximately ½ in. thick.

Sprinkle the flour on a plate and dip each piece of brain into the flour. Melt 1 Tb. of the butter and the oil in a large skillet and put the 2 portions of brain into it. Sauté over medium to high heat for about 2 minutes on one side and turn and sauté on the other side for 2 minutes. It should be nicely crusty and brown on each side.

2 Arrange the brains on 2 serving plates and discard the juices in the pan, which would turn black, especially with the flour. Clean up the pan with a piece of paper towel and cook the remaining 2 Tb. of butter. Arrange the capers around the brains, sprinkle with the red wine vinegar and, when the butter in the skillet turns quite brown, pour it on top of the brains. Top with the shredded basil and serve immediately.

CALVES' LIVER

C alves' liver is a delicacy, excellent ground in pâté or sautéed in large steaks or thin slivers. It should not be over-cooked.

A good-quality calves' liver will have a pale pink color, as opposed to steer or beef liver, which is much darker, stronger, and drier. Although it is not readily available whole, a whole liver from one calf will weigh from 2½ to 6 or 7 lb., depending on the size of the calf. The best calves' liver comes from milk-fed veal (see page 262 on milk-fed veal).

The recipe here can be made with duck or chicken liver as well as lamb liver. It is excellent served with fresh pasta, such as fettuccine; the dough should be made first and allowed to dry. To make fettuccine, use half the recipe for the ravioli dough on page 297. Or if you happen to be making ravioli, use the trimmings to make fettuccine, as I have done here. Fettuccine cooks very quickly, and so does the liver. You'll find it easiest to cook the pasta first and keep it warm while you quickly sauté the slivers of liver.

The ravioli itself could be served with the liver instead of fettuccine, if you wish. When ravioli is filled with a smooth mixture such as squash stuffing or fish mousse, it can be made using the technique I show in the recipe – with or without the special rolling pin. However, if the stuffing is coarse – with ground bits of mushrooms, fish, or meat – you should make small mounds of the filling at regular intervals on the dough, using a pastry bag or spoon; that way you leave space in between the two layers of dough so you can stick them together and then cut out neat squares.

CALVES' LIVER SLIVERS WITH GRAPE AND CURRANT SAUCE AND FETTUCCINE OR RAVIOLI

Yield: 6 servings

1½ lb. calves' liver

FETTUCCINE (ENOUGH FOR 4 SERVINGS)

About 6 oz. dough trimmings from the ravioli (see next recipe) or make fresh dough
Approximately ⅓ c. flour
½ tsp. salt

BUTTER SAUCE (4 servings)

2 Tb. butter
⅛ tsp. freshly ground black pepper
⅛ tsp. salt
1 Tb. Parmesan cheese

TO SAUTE LIVER SLIVERS

½ tsp. salt
¼ tsp. freshly ground black pepper
2 or 3 Tb. butter
2 or 3 tsp. peanut oil

GRAPE AND CURRANT SAUCE

Drippings from sautéing liver
⅔ c. chopped onions
½ c. red wine vinegar
½ c. white wine
1¼ c. demi-glace (see page 7)
2 c. seedless green grapes

¼ c. dried currants (dried "currants," are tiny seedless Corinth grapes)
2 Tb. butter
¼ tsp. salt, if needed
⅛ tsp. freshly ground black pepper, if needed

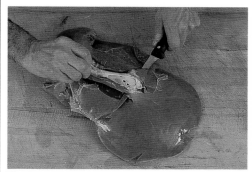

1 Place the calves' liver upside down on the table (the sinewy side on top). Insert your knife and remove most of the large sinews. Then start peeling off the skin. →

Peeling, slicing calves' liver, 1–3   *Cutting fettuccine by hand, 5*

side. Remove the liver to a plate and keep warm while you prepare the sauce.

    Place the onions in the drippings in the skillets and brown over high heat for about 4 to 5 minutes, until the onions are dark brown. Add the vinegar and the wine, and cook over high heat to reduce by half, about 3 to 4 minutes. Add the demi-glace. Bring to a boil.

2 When the skin on the underside has been removed, turn the liver over and <u>peel the skin from the top.</u> Although some cooks do not remove this thin veil of skin, removing it makes the liver much more tender.

5 Return the dough to the board, fold it in half or fourths, and <u>cut it into strips approximately ⅜ in. wide to make fettuccine.</u> The less it is dried, the faster the fettuccine will cook. Bring 3 to 4 qt. of water to a strong boil with ½ tsp. salt. Add the fettuccine, return to the boil, stir with a fork to separate the strands, and cook approximately 2 to 3 minutes, depending on the dryness of the pasta, until the fettuccine is cooked al dente (still firm to the bite).

    While the pasta is cooking, prepare the **butter sauce:** Melt the butter in a large bowl over hot water and add the pepper and salt. When the pasta is cooked, drain it in a colander and toss it with the butter. Sprinkle the top with the grated Parmesan cheese and toss again. Keep warm in a 150-degree oven while you sauté the calves' liver.

7 <u>Strain the sauce into a saucepan, directly on top of the grapes and currants.</u> Bring to a gentle boil, swirl in the 2 Tb. of butter until it is combined with the sauce, and add salt and pepper, if needed.

3 <u>The liver can be cut into 24 small (1-oz.) slivers, as in the foreground here, for use in my recipe,</u> or it can be cut in larger, thicker steaks, each weighing about 4 to 4½ oz. Properly packaged with a layer of plastic wrap and then aluminum foil, liver can be frozen for a few weeks, and if it is defrosted slowly under refrigeration, the quality should remain quite good.

8 Arrange the liver slivers on individual plates, spoon the sauce around them, and surround with the warm fettuccine.

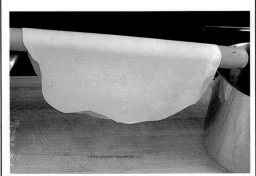

4 **For the fettuccine:** Place the soft ravioli trimmings (I had 6 oz. left from my recipe) in the food processor with ⅓ c. flour and process until the mixture forms into a ball (about 10 to 15 seconds). Place the dough on a floured board and roll very thin – mine came out to a 13- by 16-in. rectangle. <u>Place directly on the rolling pin to dry for at least 15 to 30 minutes.</u>

6 Sprinkle the slivers of calves' liver with the salt and pepper. Heat up at least 2 skillets, each containing 1 Tb. butter and 1 tsp. peanut oil. When very hot, sauté approximately 8 pieces of liver in each skillet, being careful not to overcrowd the skillet. <u>Cook the liver over very high heat for approximately 45 seconds on one side,</u> turn, and cook 45 seconds on the other

SQUASH-STUFFED RAVIOLI

Yield: 6 servings

SQUASH FILLING

1½ lb. butternut squash (approximately 1¼ lb.), peeled, seeded, and cut into 2-in. pieces
½ c. heavy cream
½ tsp. salt
¼ tsp. freshly ground black pepper
1 Tb. cornstarch dissolved in 1 Tb. cold water

RAVIOLI DOUGH

2 c. flour
2 egg yolks
1 Tb. oil
½ c. water
Cornstarch (for rolling the dough)

CREAM AND CHIVES SAUCE

1 c. heavy cream
3 Tb. chopped chives
¼ tsp. salt
⅛ tsp. freshly ground black pepper

1 **For the squash filling:** Place the pieces of squash in a saucepan and cover them with cold water. Bring to a boil and simmer 10 minutes. Drain in a colander, and push through a food mill fitted with the fine screen. Place the purée back into a saucepan with the cream, and bring to a boil on top of the stove. Boil for about 5 minutes, stirring to prevent scorching, and reduce the mixture to make it thicker. (Be careful, as it will splatter.) Add the salt, pepper, and dissolved cornstarch. Stir well, bring to a boil, and remove from the heat. Line a large cookie sheet with plastic wrap, place the squash mixture on top, and spread it out to a square of 12 by 12 in. and ⅛ in. thick. Cover with plastic wrap and refrigerate for a few hours.

Meanwhile, make the dough for the ravioli.

2 **To make the ravioli dough:** Combine all the ingredients except the cornstarch in the bowl of a food processor, and process for 15 to 30 seconds, at the most, just until the mixture forms into a block around the blade. Wrap in plastic wrap and let rest for 1 hour, refrigerated, before rolling.

3 When ready to roll the dough, place on a floured board. Roll very thin into a rectangle approximately 13 in. wide by 24 in. long. Roll the dough back on your rolling pin and sprinkle the board with cornstarch, shaking it through a strainer. This prevents the dough from sticking but is not absorbed by the dough as much as more flour would be. Place the dough back on the board. Using the plastic wrap, lift up the cold squash filling . . .

4 and reverse it onto one side of the dough. Peel off the plastic wrap. Spread out the filling a little with a spatula so it is approximately ½ to 1 in. from the border of the dough on the one side.

5 Wet the outer edges of the dough with a pastry brush dipped in water and fold the dough over the filling. Press the edges to seal them and secure the filling.

6 Sprinkle the top of the dough with a little cornstarch and move the dough on the table. There should be enough cornstarch on the top and bottom of the dough so that it does not stick.

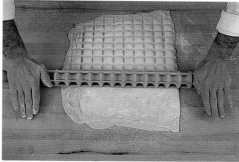

7 Using a special ravioli pin, roll on top of the dough, rocking the pin back and forth while applying pressure to firmly mark the indentations forming the ravioli segments.

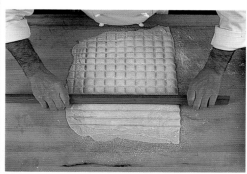

8 If you do not have a ravioli pin, you can use a piece of board about ¼ in. thick at the edge. Press into the dough to divide it into strips, then divide into rectangles or squares by pressing the board in the opposite direction. →

MEAT

9 Trim the dough from around the outside where the squares are only half filled or not filled at all with the stuffing, and reserve the trimmings for fettuccine. Do not worry if some of the filling is mixed into the fettuccine dough.

12 To cook the ravioli, bring a large pot of water (4 or 5 qt.) to a boil, add a dash of salt to it and slide your ravioli in, counting on approximately 8 ravioli per person for a first course. Return the water to the boil, stir, and cook the ravioli for about 4 minutes. If the ravioli is frozen, cook it about 1 minute longer, at the most. Using a slotted spoon, drain the ravioli carefully and arrange it on the plate.

Make a **cream and chives sauce:** Bring the 1 c. cream, 3 Tb. chopped chives, ¼ tsp. salt, and ⅛ tsp. pepper to a boil and spoon over the hot pasta on the plate. Serve immediately.

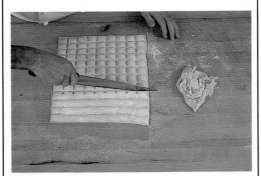

10 If the ravioli is to be cooked right away, divide the dough with a knife, cutting in between the lines to separate the squares or rectangles into individual pieces. (If the ravioli is to be frozen, there is no need to separate it into pieces beforehand; it can be frozen with the squares still attached together and then broken into squares when frozen.)

11 Using a large flexible hamburger spatula, lift up the ravioli and place it on a tray. Cover with plastic wrap to prevent it from drying and place in the refrigerator.

1 **For the tomatoes:** Cut the tomatoes in half lengthwise and squeeze or scoop out the seeds. Place the tomatoes skin side up on the table and flatten them gently with the palm of your hand. Place them on a baking pan, skin side up, sprinkle with salt, and place in a preheated 250-degree oven for 1½ to 2 hours.

2 **For the yellow pepper:** Remove the core and cut the pepper into 8 lengthwise pieces. Remove the seeds, place on a baking tray skin side up, sprinkle with the salt, and place them also in the 250-degree oven for 1½ to 2 hours.

3 When the tomatoes are dried enough (they can be dried more or less, depending on your taste), the skin will have shriveled. The tomatoes are still soft inside and moist, but the flavor is now concentrated into a smaller volume. →

GRILLED DUCK LIVERS WITH HALF-DRIED TOMATOES

This recipe is done with duck livers but other poultry livers or even calves' liver could be prepared in the same manner. The important thing is not to overcook the liver. Notice that it is grilled on the solid surface of the grill, although it could be grilled on the wire rack. The same result could be achieved by sautéing the livers briefly over high heat in a black iron skillet. The liver must be cooked at the last moment and served within minutes to be good. Therefore, it's an ideal dish for a restaurant where every portion is cooked individually.

Half-dried tomatoes and yellow peppers make a nice addition to the duck liver and can also be used in many other dishes. The moisture of the vegetables evaporates in the oven, the taste is concentrated, and the flavor is increased. Tomatoes are usually dried in the sun, in a dehydrator, or in the oven. Drying them overnight in a preheated 200-degree oven gives results similar to the dried tomatoes available at specialty markets. The tomatoes and the peppers for the recipe here should be prepared ahead and reheated a few seconds in the oven at serving time so they are lukewarm rather than cold.

The thinly sliced zucchini, placed in the oven for a few minutes, will soften slightly and render some juice. The vegetable can be used as a garnish, as in the recipe here, but can also be made into a salad by tossing the baked slices with a vinaigrette or another dressing.

Yield: 6 first-course servings

HALF-DRIED TOMATOES

6 plum tomatoes (about 3 oz. each)
½ tsp. salt

HALF-DRIED PEPPERS

1 yellow pepper (¾ lb.)
¼ tsp. salt

GRILLED DUCK LIVERS

6 large livers (8 oz.)
1 Tb. olive oil
¼ tsp. salt

ZUCCHINI

1 small zucchini (4 oz.), cleaned and cut into thin slices
Dash salt

SAUCE FOR LIVERS

½ Tb. ketchup
About 10 drops hot oil or dash cayenne pepper
1 small clove garlic, finely chopped (¼ tsp.)
1 Tb. vegetable oil
1 tsp. Worchestershire sauce
2 Tb. warm water

4 Divide each liver in half and remove the filament and sinew in the center.

5 Sprinkle the livers with 1 Tb. olive oil and salt and rub the mixture all over the meat. Set aside for 5 to 10 minutes to macerate in the oil.

6 Place the oiled livers top side down over very hot charcoal on the center of the grill and cook for about 20 seconds on one side. Turn and cook approximately 15 to 20 seconds on the other side. As mentioned in the introduction, these can also be done in a very hot skillet for the same length of time.

Remove the livers to a plate and set aside in a warm place for 1 to 2 minutes so they can continue cooking in their own heat and juice.

For the zucchini: Meanwhile, spread the zucchini slices out on a large cookie sheet and sprinkle lightly with salt. Place in a 400-degree oven for 5 minutes.

7 On each serving plate, arrange the 2 liver halves, plus another liver half that has been split crosswise and place it in the center to show its pinkness. Place overlapping slices of zucchini on the surrounding pieces and arrange the tomatoes and peppers attractively around the plate. Mix together the sauce ingredients and sprinkle each liver with about 1 tsp. of the sauce. Serve immediately.

A LEANER VERSION

Reduce the amount of olive oil in the grilling of the livers (step 5) from 1 Tb. to ½ Tb. Reduce the vegetable oil in the sauce from 1 Tb. to ½ Tb. Proceed according to the recipe.

1 Mix together all the maître d'butter ingredients.

2 Remove the kidneys from their casings of fat. Pull and cut off the sinew holding them to the fat. Often the kidneys are damaged by butchers or meat inspectors who slice through the meat to check the condition of the animal. Try to get undamaged kidneys.

3 Place the kidneys flat on the table and, with a sharp knife, cut horizontally from the rounded end down to within a half in. of the other side. Open to butterfly.

4 Thread the kidneys on a skewer, going down on one side of the fat and coming up on the other side. Rub with oil and sprinkle with salt and pepper. Set aside until serving time. →

GRILLED LAMB KIDNEYS WITH STUFFED MUSHROOMS

Veal and lamb kidneys are considered the best and most flavorful. Lamb kidneys, especially from older animals, are slightly stronger than veal kidneys and some people never develop a taste for them. Yet kidneys from baby lambs as well as spring lamb are flavorful and not too strong.

Lamb kidneys work quite well grilled. They should not be overcooked but remain pink throughout after being allowed to rest for a few minutes so the meat can relax. If the kidneys are not seared on a very hot grill, they will stick. Furthermore, the meat requires the intense heat to brown outside and have the proper texture.

The mushrooms are stuffed with a light, delicate mixture of shallots, raisins, and coriander. They can also be used as a garnish for other types of grilled meat as well as fish. The maître d' butter is classic with grilled meat or fish; it can be made ahead, even placed in plastic wrap, formed into a cylinder, and frozen for a few weeks.

Yield: 3 servings

9 lamb kidneys
2 tsp. peanut oil
Pinch salt and freshly ground black pepper

MAITRE D' BUTTER

2 Tb. butter, softened
Pinch salt and freshly ground black pepper
1 Tb. chopped parsley
1 tsp. lemon juice

STUFFED MUSHROOMS

6 large mushrooms (1½ oz. each, 9 oz. total)
1 Tb. butter
4 shallots, coarsely chopped (⅓ c.)
2 Tb. raisins
¼ tsp. salt
¼ tsp. freshly ground black pepper
2 Tb. chopped parsley
1 Tb. chopped fresh coriander (also called Chinese parsley or cilantro)
1 small, thin slice bread, crumbed in processor (¼ c.)
1 tsp. oil

GARNISH

1 small bunch watercress

5 **For the stuffed mushrooms:** Use large mushrooms, at least 1½ oz. each. Do not clean the mushrooms ahead, but when ready to use, wash them under water at the last moment if they are dirty. If washed ahead, they will discolor and become spongy. Cut off the stems of the mushrooms with some of the underside of the caps.

7 Gently combine the bread crumbs with the oil, stirring with a fork. The bread should remain fluffy but still be slightly moist from the oil, which will make it brown better in the oven. Stuff the mushroom receptacles with the raisin-coriander mixture and pat the bread crumbs on top. Place under the broiler for 3 to 4 minutes, until nicely browned.

6 Using a teaspoon, scoop out the inside of each mushroom, removing the stem and gills and leaving the cap as a receptacle. Place the caps, open side down, in a roasting pan and place in a preheated 400-degree oven for 6 to 7 minutes so they render their juices. Meanwhile, chop the trimmings of the mushrooms coarse.

Melt the butter in a skillet. When hot, add the chopped shallots, sauté about 30 seconds, and add the chopped mushrooms and raisins. Sauté for about 1 to 2 minutes, until the juices of the mushrooms have been released and evaporated. When the mushrooms start sizzling again, add the salt, pepper, parsley, and coriander. Set aside.

8 Meanwhile, place the kidneys on the very hot grill cut side down, and cook for 1½ minutes, then turn and cook another 1½ minutes (total of 3 minutes). Set aside, covered, in a warm place and let rest 5 minutes before serving.

9 At serving time, arrange 3 kidneys on each plate. Place about a tsp. of the maître d' butter in each of the kidneys, and arrange 2 mushrooms around them. Garnish with a little watercress placed in the center. Serve immediately. The inside of the kidneys should be just pink.

LAMB KIDNEYS IN MUSTARD SAUCE WITH BRAISED CELERY

If the braised celery is to be served with the kidneys, prepare it first. It is important to use celery stalks with the whitest possible hearts, as they will be tenderer and sweeter. The recipe here uses only the lower part of the stalks (about 6 in. up from the base); the top of the ribs and leaves can be reserved for stocks. The braised celery can also be used as an accompaniment to most roasts, sautéed meats, and poultry.

Yield: 4 servings

BRAISED CELERY

2 or 3 whole celery stalks, depending on
   size, as white as possible (about 2 lb.
   trimmed)
Salt
2 Tb. butter
½ c. demi-glace (see page 7)

LAMB KIDNEYS

8 lamb kidneys (about 1 lb.)
3 Tb. butter
½ tsp. salt
¼ tsp. freshly ground black pepper
HOT MUSTARD SAUCE
Drippings from cooking the kidneys
¼ c. chopped shallots
1 tsp. chopped garlic

½ c. robust red wine
1 c. demi-glace
1 Tb. Dijon mustard
GARNISH
A few sprigs parsley

1 Trim the celery, keeping about 6 in. of the root and heart. Reserve the trimmings for stock or soup.

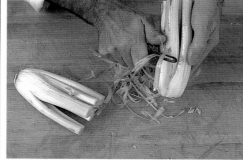

2 Using a vegetable peeler or small knife, remove most of the fiber from around the outside of the celery stalks and trim around the base. Cover the celery with cold water, add ½ tsp. salt, and bring to a boil. Cover and simmer gently for 30 minutes. Drain and cool. (The cooking liquid can be used in stocks or soups.)

3 Cut each celery stalk lengthwise into fourths (for standard celery) or sixths (for larger celery).

4 Melt the butter in a large skillet. When hot, sauté the pieces of celery for about 2 minutes on each side. Add the demi-glace, cover, and simmer 7 to 8 minutes, until some of the demi-glace is reduced and coats the celery. Uncover and cook 3 to 4 minutes to further reduce the demi-glace and coat the celery by rolling and turning it in the liquid. Add salt to taste and set aside.

MEAT

303

5 **For the lamb kidneys:** Split the kidneys in half as shown in the technique for butterflying the kidneys for the Grilled Kidneys (page 301) but cut through completely to separate the halves. Each half will be cut into three pieces. Cut a wedge from one end.

8 Transfer the kidneys to a sieve resting on a plate. The sauce will be prepared in the kidney drippings, and meanwhile, the kidneys will rest and most of the blood will leak out of them. It is strong and, if eliminated, will make the kidneys milder and less assertive in taste.

10 Add the drained kidneys to the mustard sauce and discard the bloody liquid on the plate. Heat the kidneys gently in the sauce but do not bring the mixture to a boil.

6 Cut a wedge from the other side. Remove the lump of fat from the center piece. The kidneys should be sautéed in one layer in a very hot skillet (2 skillets if necessary). The hotter the skillet the better, as the kidneys should sear on the outside without getting soggy and starting to steam. In order to sauté properly, they should be seared in very, very hot butter.

9 **For the sauce:** To the drippings in the saucepan add the ¼ c. chopped shallots. Sauté about 1 minute, then add 1 tsp. chopped garlic and ½ c. red wine, and stir to combine. Cook to reduce until almost dry and add 1 c. demi-glace. Bring to a boil, boil gently 1 to 2 minutes, and strain through a sieve. Add 1 Tb. mustard, stirring gently to incorporate. After the addition of mustard, the sauce should not boil again, as it will tend to break down.

11 Arrange the kidneys on individual plates with the sauce on top and around them. Sprinkle with parsley and place 1 piece of celery on each side of the kidneys. Pass the extra celery at the table. Serve immediately.

A LEANER VERSION

In the braised celery (step 4), replace the 2 Tb. butter with 1 tsp. of vegetable oil, and proceed according to the recipe. In sautéing the kidneys (step 7), replace the 3 Tb. butter with 1 tsp. butter and 1 tsp. vegetable oil, and proceed according to the recipe.

7 Melt the butter until brown and beginning to foam. Add the kidneys and sprinkle with salt and pepper. Sauté over the highest possible heat to sear for about 1½ to 2 minutes, using a slotted spoon to stir them occasionally.

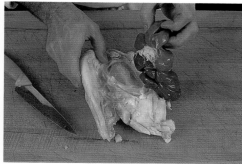

2 Cut the sinew that holds the kidney to the fat. Notice that the kidney will weigh approximately one-quarter of the total weight. There is much more fat than kidney. Set the fat aside.

3 Remove most of the sinews and pieces of fat from the inside of the kidney so it is practically clean.

STUFFED VEAL KIDNEYS BICHON WITH POTATO AND TRUFFLE CAKE

Veal kidneys are particularly tender and flavorful and are very good roasted whole with some of their fat wrapped around them to protect the meat from toughening and keep it tender and moist.

In my recipe, the kidneys are first cleaned of fat and sinews, then stuffed and placed back inside the fat and roasted. They are served with a mushroom and tomato sauce and the accompaniment of a potato and truffle cake.

Yield: 4 servings

4 veal kidneys, whole, each weighing about 1¾ lb. with its fat

STUFFING

2 Tb. butter
2 Tb. chopped onions
1 large clove garlic, peeled and finely chopped (1½ tsp.)
4 oz. mushrooms, cut into ¼-in. dice (about 1½ c.)
⅓ c. finely chopped country cured ham (prosciutto type)
⅓ c. chopped parsley
⅛ tsp. freshly ground black pepper

SAUCE

2 Tb. butter
½ c. finely sliced leeks
2 cloves garlic, chopped fine (1 tsp.)
½ tsp. fresh chopped thyme

⅓ c. red wine
½ c. demi-glace (see page 7)
1 c. peeled and seeded tomatoes, cut into ½-in. dice
Salt and pepper to taste

1 The envelope of fat protecting the veal kidney is very white and waxy. This high-quality fat is good with ground veal for making dumplings and is also used in pâtés or hors d'oeuvre. Notice that since the fat is waxy, it can be separated into small pieces. The fat is held together by small membranes, and if it is to be used in dumplings or quenelles, it should be separated from the membranes (see Pike Quenelles, page 103). For this recipe, remove the kidneys from their envelope of fat.

4 Place the kidney flat on the table and cut down lengthwise through the center to butterfly it and expose all the sinews. →

MEAT

305

5 For the stuffing: Melt the butter in a skillet and, when hot, sauté the onions for about 1 minute. Add the chopped garlic and the diced mushrooms, and sauté for 1 to 2 minutes. Add the ham, parsley, and pepper, and toss well to mix. Set aside to cool. When cool, place the 4 kidneys open on the table and divide the stuffing among them. Then bring the kidneys back on themselves, enclosing the stuffing.

6 Place the fat of the kidney on the table and cut and pound to extend it and make it into a layer approximately ¼ in. thick. Then wrap the stuffed kidney with that layer of fat. If one layer is not large enough, add several and tie them with string into a package to hold the fat together and protect the kidney inside during cooking.

7 Place the wrapped kidneys in a large ovenproof skillet or shallow saucepan and brown on top of the stove over medium to high heat for about 5 minutes, until nicely browned all around. Place in a preheated 400-degree oven for 7 to 8 minutes, turn the kidney packages over, and continue cooking for a total cooking time of 15 minutes. At that point, the kidneys should be medium rare inside. If the kidneys are larger, of course, increase the cooking time. Set the kidneys aside, still in their fat envelopes, for at least 5 to 10 minutes so they can relax and continue cooking slowly in their own heat. Then unwrap.

8 To make the sauce: Heat the 2 Tb. butter in a skillet and, when hot, add the ½ c. sliced leeks and sauté gently for about 30 seconds to 1 minute. Then add 1 tsp. chopped garlic and ½ tsp. thyme and mix well. Add ⅓ c. red wine and bring to a boil. Boil down until most of the liquid has evaporated. To the mixture add ½ c. demi-glace, 1 c. diced tomatoes, and salt and pepper to taste. Bring just to the boil.

Place the kidneys on individual serving plates and spoon the sauce over the top. Notice that the inside of the halved kidney is pink throughout. This is the way the kidneys should look. Serve immediately.

POTATO AND TRUFFLE CAKE

This dish, called Potatoes Sarladaise in France, is named after Sarlat, a town in the southwest of France where a great many truffles are marketed during the winter months. The truffle and potato combination works extremely well, and the entire dish picks up and retains the strong, heady smell and taste of the truffles. For the cook who cannot find or afford expensive truffles, the potato cake can be done in the same way, omitting the truffle, and it then becomes Potatoes Anna.

Yield: 6 servings

1½ lb. potatoes (6 c. peeled and sliced)
1 large truffle or several small ones
5 Tb. butter
3 Tb. corn oil
½ tsp. salt

1 Peel the potatoes and round off the sides of 3 of them to create cylinders of about the same size. Thinly slice (about ⅛ in. thick) the trimmed potatoes by hand or with an automatic slicer. Wash the slices in cold water, drain, and set aside. You should have 2 c. The slices of potato from the cylinders will be round, uniform, and of equal size. They are lined up in the skillet to create a design. The unequal-sized pieces of potato are used for the inside of the cake.

Thinly slice (about ⅛ in. thick) all the other potatoes, including the trimmings from the 3 rounded potatoes. Wash in cold water and set aside.

2 Trim the truffle(s) of all the rough fibrous skin on the outside and chop the skin into small pieces. Thinly slice the centers of the truffles and set aside.

Butter a large (9-in.) skillet, preferably non-stick, with 2 Tb. of the butter. In another skillet, place 1 Tb. of the corn oil and, when hot, add the 2 c. of sliced potatoes of equal size and a dash of salt. Sauté for about 30 seconds, just long enough to coat the potato slices with oil and soften them a bit. Place on a cookie sheet to cool.

3 In the bottom of your buttered skillet, arrange the slices of sautéed potatoes, placing a slice of truffle between every 2 or 3 slices of potatoes. Remember that this will be unmolded and served upside down, so this layer will be the top of the dish. The truffles should be completely covered underneath by potato slices so they don't dry out during cooking. (The truffles will be visible through the thinly sliced potatoes.) Arrange the first layer so the whole bottom of the skillet is covered with the slices of potatoes and truffles.

In the other skillet, add the remaining 2 Tb. of oil and sauté the additional 4 c. of sliced potatoes (including the trimmings) with a dash of salt. Sauté for about 1 minute and add the chopped peelings of the truffles.

4 Place this potato-truffle mixture on top of the arranged slices of potatoes and truffles. Cook on top of the stove over medium to high heat for 2 to 3 minutes to brown the potatoes.

5 Using a large, flat spatula, press the potatoes so they are well packed against the bottom of the pan. Dot the potatoes with the remaining 3 Tb. of butter and cover with a piece of parchment paper or aluminum foil, cut to fit the skillet. With the spatula, press the paper onto the potatoes.

Place in a preheated 400-degree oven for 20 minutes with the paper in position, pressing the paper with the spatula again after 10 minutes to pack the potatoes more tightly.

6 When the potatoes are cooked, set them aside for 4 to 5 minutes to cool and set. Then remove the paper and invert onto a serving platter.

7 Serve the Potato and Truffle Cake, cut into wedges, with the hot Stuffed Veal Kidneys Bichon.

MEAT

307

VEAL KIDNEYS SAUTE MARRAINE

Another way to prepare veal kidneys served here with an accompaniment of fennel.

Yield: 4 servings

FOR THE FENNEL

2 bulbs of fennel (1½ lb. each), cleaned of
   any bruised or damaged ribs and the
   stems trimmed
2 Tb. butter
Salt, if desired

2 veal kidneys, cleaned of fat and sinews
   and sliced to ⅜-in. thickness (cleaned
   weight: about 1 lb. total)
¾ tsp. salt
⅜ tsp. pepper
4 Tb. butter
1 Tb. olive oil
½ c. finely sliced shallots
⅓ c. good-quality port wine
1 c. diced oyster mushrooms (about 4 oz.)
   and 1 c. ½-in.-diced cultivated mushrooms, (or all of one or the other)
¾ c. heavy cream
2 Tb. chopped chives

1 For the fennel: Cut the trimmed and
cleaned fennel bulbs in half and cover the
4 pieces with cold water. Bring to a boil
and boil gently for 10 minutes. Drain.

   Place the butter in a skillet, and while it
is heating, cut the fennel into ¼-in.-thick
lengthwise slices. Place in the skillet, flat
side down, in one layer and sauté over
medium-high heat for about 1 minute on
each side to brown lightly and warm.
Sprinkle with a dash of salt, if desired, and
set aside.

2 Clean the kidneys as explained for the
Stuffed Veal Kidneys Bichon (page 305).
When completely cleaned of any sinews,
slice across into pieces approximately ⅜
in. thick. Sprinkle the kidneys with ½
tsp. salt and ¼ tsp. pepper. Heat the butter and oil in one very large or two smaller
skillets. (The kidneys should fit in one
layer.) When the butter and oil are very,
very hot (almost brown), add the kidneys
and sauté quickly (about 1½ minutes
total) over high heat, stirring, until they
change color, losing any visible red and
becoming whitish and firm. Sprinkle with
the remaining ¼ tsp. salt and ⅛ tsp. pepper, and remove from the skillet with a
slotted spoon. Place in a strainer over a
bowl.

3 To the drippings in the skillet add the
shallots, and cook about 30 seconds. Add
the port wine and cook down until most of
the liquid has evaporated. Add the mushrooms and cook briefly for 1 to 2 minutes.
Add the cream, bring to a boil, boil about
1 minute, and return the kidneys to the
skillet. You will notice that a lot of juice
has come out of the kidneys and accumulated in the bowl. Taste the juice, and if it
is not strong tasting (it shouldn't be from
a tender, young veal kidney), place it back
in the skillet along with the kidneys to flavor the sauce. Warm the sauce and kidneys
until hot but do not boil the mixture or
the kidneys will toughen.

4 Arrange the kidneys on 4 individual plates, sprinkle with the chives, and place 2 pieces of sautéed fennel alongside. Serve immediately with extra fennel on the side.

SWEETBREADS

There are two types of sweetbreads, and both are glands. The elongated, more knobby sweetbread, the throat sweetbread or thymus gland, is found in calves or very young beef. It shrinks to nothing as the animal gets older. The second sweetbread, the "round" or la noix, as the French call it, is the pancreas gland. Unlike the thymus gland, it doesn't disappear as the animal gets older, but gets yellow, spongy, and tough. The best sweetbreads are from milk-fed calves and spring lambs. Although calf sweetbreads are readily available, lamb sweetbreads are, unfortunately, difficult to find in markets.

The texture of the thymus is slightly different from that of the pancreas. The thymus is finer than the more compact, softer pancreas. Some people prefer one, some the other; it is purely a matter of taste. Sweetbreads alone are rather bland in flavor and accommodate themselves well to sauces.

Sweetbreads from freshly killed animals are red and bloody. They should be placed in cold water overnight and the water should be changed periodically to draw out the blood and make them white. If not soaked, they will get very dark and strong in taste during cooking.

Sweetbreads bought at the market do not have the large appendage and sinews that are attached to them (especially the thymus) when they are obtained directly from a wholesaler or the slaughterhouse.

If any sinews are left on, they should be removed. They are easy to recognize because they are tough and outside the gland itself. Store-bought sweetbreads can be used as purchased.

The blanching in water and subsequent pressing improve the texture of the sweetbreads. When not pressed, the meat is rubbery and spongy. After pressing, the meat is compact, tight, and has a better flavor. The blanching and pressing of the sweetbreads can be done several days ahead if desired, but must be done before proceeding with the two recipes below.

In the first recipe, the pancreas gland is used, as it cuts better into large, thin slices, which are brushed with butter, breaded, and sautéed. It is a rich dish, and the tart lemon sauce is a good contrast. The gratin of butternut squash is also rich, and if the two are served in combination, the rest of the menu should be fairly lean — perhaps only a salad and a tart fruit dessert.

In the second recipe, the thymus glands are separated into pieces about one in. each, cooked on a bed of vegetables, and finished with white wine and a demi-glace. The vegetables are cut into tiny dice and are quite flavorful. This is a leaner and tarter dish than the first sweetbread recipe and is served in a little barquette. The dough for the barquette is made with butter, cream cheese, and flour, which make a flaky dough that tends to develop a little like puff paste. Pressed between the little molds, it comes out thin and firm and holds the sweetbread mixture well. For further enhancement, the dish is decorated with fluted mushrooms as a garnish, which should be prepared ahead. The barquettes as well as the fluted mushrooms can, of course, be used for many other dishes.

2 Cover the sweetbreads with cold water. Bring to a boil, lower the heat, and simmer just at a gentle boil for 20 minutes. Then place the sweetbreads under cold water, letting the water run over them until they are completely cold. Arrange the sweetbreads flat on a cookie sheet lined with paper towels. Place another piece of paper towel and another cookie sheet over them. Finally, place a 5-lb. weight on top to press overnight or at least 2 to 3 hours, refrigerated.

BREADED SWEETBREADS WITH TARRAGON SAUCE

Yield: 6 servings

2½ lb. pancreas sweetbreads, yielding
   1½ lb. after blanching and pressing
5 slices bread
1 stick butter
½ tsp. salt
¼ tsp. freshly ground black pepper

TARRAGON SAUCE

1 c. chicken stock (see page 170)
½ tsp. potato starch dissolved in 1 Tb.
   water
2 tsp. lemon juice
½ stick butter
1 Tb. chopped fresh tarragon
¼ tsp. salt
⅛ tsp. freshly ground black pepper

GRATIN OF BUTTERNUT SQUASH

1 large butternut squash (3¾ lb.), peeled
   and seeded (2½ lb.)
1 tsp. salt
¼ tsp. freshly ground black pepper
1 c. heavy cream
3 Tb. Parmesan cheese

1 The sweetbread held is the long, narrow throat or thymus sweetbread, and the one in front on the table is the pancreas sweetbread. Notice that the glands are quite clean and white so there is no need to pull off any sinews or rubbery appendages or to soak to remove blood. These sweetbreads are the pancreas from milk-fed veal and the quality and size are excellent.

3 Pull off any sinews, nerves, or rubbery appendages that may still be attached to the top of the sweetbreads, as shown in photograph 7 of Braised Sweetbreads in Mirepoix (next recipe). Four oz. of sweetbreads is enough per person.

   Cut the round pancreas sweetbreads into ⅜- to ½-in.-thick slices. →

MEAT

4 Trim the crusts from the slices of bread, reserving the trimmings for other types of bread crumbs. Use only the center of the bread to have crumbs that are completely white. Process the bread in the food processor.

Melt ½ of the stick of butter. Sprinkle the sweetbreads lightly with salt and pepper on both sides. Dip them in the melted butter, running each piece of meat along the edge of the pan to remove the excess (they should just be lightly coated with the butter), and dip in bread crumbs so they are lightly covered on both sides. Place the pieces on a plate and refrigerate until serving time.

5 **For the gratin of butternut squash:** Cut off the stem of the butternut squash and split in two at the bottom of the neck. This will make it easier to peel.

6 Peel the cylindrical neck lengthwise with a sharp knife, removing enough skin so the orange flesh appears. (Under the first layer of skin there is a layer of green, which should be removed.) For the round part of the squash, remove the skin with a knife by going around it in a spiral fashion; it is easier to peel a round object in this manner.

7 Cut the rounded part in half and, using a spoon, remove the seeds. With a food processor or knife, cut the squash into ⅛- to ¼-in. slices. Place in a saucepan, cover with water, and bring to a boil. Boil on high heat for 1½ to 2 minutes and drain in a colander. The pieces will break a little. Place the squash in a gratin dish and add the 1 tsp. salt, ¼ tsp. pepper, and 1 c. cream, mixing with a fork to distribute the additions properly. Cover with 3 Tb. Parmesan cheese and place in a preheated 400-degree oven for approximately 30 minutes.

8 While the gratin is baking in the oven, prepare the sauce and sweetbreads.

For the sauce: Place the chicken stock in a saucepan and reduce to ½ c. Add the dissolved potato starch and lemon juice, and bring to a boil. Whisk in the butter, piece by piece, until thoroughly incorporated. Bring back to the boil. Add the fresh tarragon, salt, and pepper, and set aside.

For the sweetbreads: Melt the remaining ½ stick of butter in 2 large skillets. When hot, place the breaded sweetbread slices in the skillets and sauté over low to medium heat for approximately 5 minutes on one side, turn, and continue cooking 5 minutes on the other side.

9 While the sweetbreads are cooking, place the gratin under the broiler for 4 to 5 minutes to brown the top.

10 Spoon the sauce onto warm individual plates. Place 2 pieces of breaded sweetbreads on top and serve immediately with the butternut squash.

2 Keep rolling, extending the dough from the center outward to all sides, rather than just rolling back and forth, which tends to develop the gluten and toughen the dough. This type of dough cannot be extremely thin and should not be thicker than ⅛ in.

BRAISED SWEETBREADS IN MIREPOIX

Yield: 6 servings

CREAM CHEESE BARQUETTES

4 oz. cream cheese
3 oz. sweet butter, softened
1 c. flour (about 5½ oz.)

BRAISED SWEETBREADS

2½ lb. sweetbreads (1½ lb. blanched and pressed, as explained in previous recipe)
2 ribs celery
1 leek
1 large carrot
1 medium onion
3 Tb. butter
1 large or 2 medium tomatoes
1 tsp. chopped garlic
1 c. demi-glace (see page 7)
½ c. white wine
½ tsp. salt
½ tsp. freshly ground black pepper
4 or 5 sprigs fresh thyme
1 tsp. potato starch dissolved in 1 Tb. water

GARNISH

6 large, firm, round mushrooms for fluting
1 Tb. lemon juice
Thyme flowers, if available

1 To make the barquette dough: In a food processor, combine the cream cheese and soft butter. Process about 15 seconds to mix well. Add the flour and process just long enough for the whole mixture to hold together. The dough is better if made ahead and allowed to rest in the refrigerator for a few hours to firm up.

Sprinkle the work surface with flour and roll out the dough, pressing it lightly with your rolling pin.

3 Brush any flour off the dough and roll it onto the rolling pin. Arrange the little barquette molds (about 4 in. long by 2 in. wide) on the table. Unroll the dough on top of the barquettes and press into the molds.

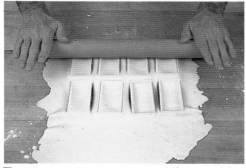

4 Roll the rolling pin on top of the molds to trim off the extra dough. →

MEAT

313

5 If the barquettes are not completely separated, press the dough on the edge of the barquettes to cut it off. To prevent the dough from shrinking, falling on itself, or getting too many bubbles while cooking, press extra molds on top of the dough to thin it further and make it adhere well to the molds. In this way, the dough will conform to the inside of the bottom molds and keep its shape during cooking. Let the barquettes rest for 1 hour before cooking, if possible, to help prevent shrinking.

8 Break the sweetbreads, separating them from the connecting tissue into 1-in. lumps.

11 Flute the 6 mushrooms. Use large, firm, perfectly round mushrooms. It does require practice to flute or carve mushrooms in the elegant spiral pattern and can cost hours of frustration even for professionals to get good results. There are several methods used. Holding the blade of the knife loosely in your fingers, the cutting edge out, place the side of your thumb behind the blade on top of the mushroom.

6 Arrange the molds on a cookie sheet and place in a preheated 400-degree oven for approximately 15 to 20 minutes; by then the dough will have set. Remove the top barquettes and continue cooking in the oven for another 10 to 15 minutes to brown nicely. Remove the barquettes from their molds.

9 Cut the 2 ribs celery, leek, carrot, and onion into tiny dice (about ⅛ in.), a brunoise. You should have 1 c. of each of the vegetables.

12 Using your thumb as a pivot, push the blade forward and down, twisting at the same time in a smooth motion. The slanted cutting edge will carve a strip out of the mushroom cap. The rotation of the mushroom should be smooth and regular. Remove hanging pieces of cap and cut off the stem and base of the cap below the design. Brush the fluted mushroom with lemon juice so it doesn't discolor. Flute the remaining mushrooms and brush with 1 Tb. lemon juice. Cut the trimmings into ¼-in. dice and add to the stewing sweetbreads.

7 Blanch and press the sweetbreads as explained in steps 1 and 2 of the previous recipe. Remove any large sinews and filaments still attached to the sweetbreads.

10 Melt the 3 Tb. butter in a large saucepan. When hot, add the celery, leeks, carrots, and onions. Cook over medium to high heat for about 5 minutes, stirring occasionally, until the vegetables are wilted and soft. Blanch 1 large or 2 medium tomatoes to remove the skin, cut, and seed (see page 83), and add to the saucepan with 1 tsp. chopped garlic, 1 c. demi-glace, ½ c. white wine, ½ tsp. each salt and pepper, 4 or 5 thyme sprigs, and pieces of sweetbreads. Bring to a boil, cover, lower the heat, and simmer at just a gentle boil for 10 to 12 minutes.

13 Add 1 tsp. potato starch dissolved in 1 Tb. water to the sweetbread mixture to thicken it slightly and then add the fluted mushrooms and warm for about 30 seconds in the sauce. Arrange a barquette in the middle of each plate. Fill with sweetbreads and spoon more of the mixture around the plate. Split a fluted mushroom in half and arrange half at each end of the plate. Garnish with a little thyme flower, if available, and serve immediately.

A LEANER VERSION

Omit the cream cheese barquettes and replace, if you desire, with 8 round croutons made from 8 slices of toasted whole-wheat bread. Reduce the 3 Tb. of butter to 1 Tb. (step 10) and proceed according to the recipe.

BLACK SAUSAGE BICHON

Black sausage or black pudding, called <u>boudin</u> in France, is a common country dish and a classic of French charcuterie. My recipe is made with leeks and served with apples and potatoes. In some parts of France, spinach, chestnuts, and even Swiss chard replace the leeks and the dish is often made with heavy cream. Whatever the additions, it is always made with pork blood and fat.

Pork blood is sometimes difficult to get and may come frozen. It should be defrosted slowly under refrigeration. The poached <u>boudins</u> (steps 10 to 12) can be frozen if properly wrapped. They should be defrosted slowly under refrigeration to keep their moist, smooth texture.

Hog casing approximately 1½ in. in diameter is used here. It is thin, delicate, and the right size for <u>boudins</u>. It comes frozen, usually packed in salt, and is easy to use. Although black sausage is often cooked in the casing, which is edible, it is preferable to remove the casing to make the sausage easier to cut and eat at the table.

The purée of white turnips, potatoes, and garlic makes a nice accompaniment. A purée made only with potatoes and a few cloves of garlic is a classic in my family, and the addition of white turnips makes it a delightful variation. At certain times of the year, the turnips are stronger and the proportion of turnips to potatoes can increase or decrease accordingly, but should never be more than two-thirds turnips to one-third potatoes because this amount of potatoes is needed to give body to the purée. When the turnips are particularly strong, the proportions should be reversed.

The recipe below for individual apple-bread charlottes is easier to prepare and more flavorful than the classic version, which directs that you arrange the bread in a pattern around the mold. These delicious little timbales, which are served as a main course accompaniment, are also excellent with rich meat, such as pork or duck, as well as game.

Yield: 16–18 sausages

BLACK SAUSAGES

Hog casing packed in salt
1¼ lb. pork back fat
1¼ lb. onions
3 leeks (about 10 to 12 oz.)
2 Tb. potato starch
3 c. pork blood
1 tsp. salt
½ tsp. freshly ground black pepper

TO SAUTE 8 PIECES OF SAUSAGE

1 Tb. butter
⅓ c. brown stock, if available (page 7)

PUREE OF TURNIPS AND POTATOES

Yield: 8 servings

2 lb. boiling potatoes, peeled
1½ lb. white turnips, peeled
4 large cloves garlic, peeled
1¾ tsp. salt
4 Tb. butter
¼ tsp. white pepper
2 Tb. heavy cream (optional)

APPLE-BREAD CHARLOTTES

Yield: 8 servings

1½ lb. Cortland apples (about 6)
Lemon juice (to rub on apple cores)
2 Tb. butter
2 Tb. vegetable oil
5 c. loose diced bread trimmings (cut into
   1-in. pieces), about 5 oz.
⅓ c. dark raisins
2 Tb. cider vinegar
1 Tb. sugar
½ tsp. salt
½ tsp. freshly ground black pepper
⅛ tsp. grated nutmeg
2 Tb. peanut oil
About 1 Tb. butter (to butter the molds)

GARNISH

Stems of apples

1 The casing usually comes packed in salt. Soak the casing in tepid water for 4 to 5 minutes to remove the salt.

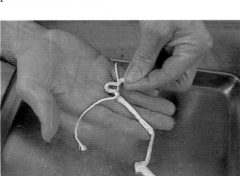

2 Open one end of the casing and secure it around the end of the faucet. Run lukewarm water through it to open and wash the inside of the casing completely. Then place in cold water.

3 To tie off the end of the casing so it will remain securely tied (it tends to be very slippery and will untie with a conventional knot), tie a piece of string (with one knot only) around the casing about 3 to 4 in. from one end. Lap the end of the casing over the knot.

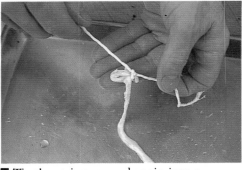

4 Tie the string around again into a double knot, creating a little loop of casing at the end and securing the casing so it won't slip.

5 **To make the sausage mixture:** Cut the pork fat into ½-in. dice. Place half of the fat in a large saucepan and cook over medium to high heat for 4 to 5 minutes, until it starts melting. During that time, slice the onions and leeks thin and add to the melting fat. Continue cooking over medium heat for approximately 15 minutes. Most of the fat will have melted, but don't worry if some of it is still lumpy.

6 Place the onion-leek-fat mixture into the food processor with the remaining unmelted fat and potato starch, and process, pushing the mixture down into the bowl when necessary, until well blended. Place in a bowl and stir in the blood. Add salt and pepper.

7 Attach the open end of the casing to a funnel and fill the casing with the blood-sausage mixture. Do not overfill or the casing will burst. The mixture should flow into the casing; don't force it or the casing will expand too much during cooking.

8 Tie the casing off about every 5 in. with twine to create sections or individual sausages. Some of the casing can be left untied to create a long sausage spiral that can be cut into pieces after cooking.

9 Place all the sausage in a large saucepan to cover the bottom in one layer only. Cover with tepid tap water, place on the stove, and bring to a temperature of about 170 to 180 degrees. Do not let the temperature go higher; if the sausage boils, the casing is apt to burst.

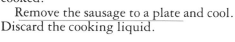

10 The sausage should be done after 15 to 20 minutes. If it tends to rise to the surface during cooking, place a small lid or plate upside down on the surface to keep the sausage submerged. After about 15 minutes, puncture the sausage with a needle. If the juice comes out clear, it is cooked.

Remove the sausage to a plate and cool. Discard the cooking liquid.

11 The sausage may have to be cooked in two batches. Some of the sausage may be in one long spiral rather than individual pieces. Remove to a plate or baking tray and cool.

12 Cut through the casing to separate the individual sausages and cut the long piece into sections of about 4 to 5 in. Although the casing is edible, remove it for a more delicate dish. Cut the casing with a knife the length of the sausage and peel off to remove. The sausage should hold its shape without breaking.

For the purée of turnips and potatoes: Cover the 2 lb. potatoes, 1½ lb. turnips, and 4 garlic cloves with tepid water. Add 1 tsp. salt, bring to a boil, and cook 45 minutes. Push the mixture through a food mill, using the fine screen. Place in a saucepan, mix with the butter, ¾ tsp. salt, ¼ tsp. pepper, and serve immediately. Or cover the top with 2 Tb. cream (so it doesn't form a skin) and set aside until serving time. →

13 **For the apple-bread charlottes:** Core but don't peel the 1½ lb. of apples. (Reserve the cores for use as a decoration, rubbing each with a little lemon juice to prevent discoloration.) Chop the apples coarse. Heat 2 Tb. butter and 2 Tb. oil in a skillet. When hot, add the apples and cook for about 10 minutes. Mix with 5 c. diced bread, ⅓ c. raisins, 2 Tb. vinegar, 1 Tb. sugar, ½ tsp. each salt and pepper, ⅛ tsp. nutmeg, and 2 Tb. peanut oil, then mash the mixture together until well combined. Butter the insides of 8 small ramekins and divide the apple mixture among them (about ½ c. in each), packing it compactly and smoothing the tops. Arrange on a cookie sheet and place in a preheated 400-degree oven for 40 minutes. They should be nicely browned. If the mixture has expanded, press it down into the molds.

15 Arrange a mound of the purée on individual plates with a sausage on top and an apple-bread charlotte on the side, with the stem section of the apple core on top for decoration. Place the brown stock in the sausage pan drippings. Heat and spoon over the purée and sausage.

14 **To sauté the sausage:** At serving time, heat the 1 Tb. butter in a skillet. When foaming, add the sausage pieces and cook 5 minutes over medium to low heat to brown. Turn and cook on the other side for 3 to 4 minutes.

CHITTERLING SAUSAGES
WITH SPICY RICE AND APPLE RINGS

Chitterlings are the small intestine of a pig or calf. The sausages made from chitterlings are a classic delicacy of French charcuterie. Known as <u>andouillettes</u> in French, they are usually grilled or sautéed with a bit of white wine and are often served with mashed potatoes in small bistros. The large chitterling sausages are often served cold under the name of <u>andouille</u> and are recognizable by their thick black skin. In the recipe here, the sausages are made from the small intestine of a pig. Calves' intestines are also used in France but are not usually available in the U.S.

In the traditional recipe, the fatty small intestine is simply bundled up and pulled through a casing to create a sausage. In the version here, the chitterlings are cooked first for two hours in lots of water until tender (you will notice considerable shrinkage at this point), and then the cooked chitterlings are cut into pieces and flavored with shallots, scallions, garlic, mustard, mushrooms, and wine. They are then placed in the casing, poached again briefly in stock and wine, and either served immediately or set aside for later serving. At this point, the chitterlings can be frozen or, as in French charcuterie, placed on a tray, covered with melted lard (pig's fat), and preserved,

immersed in the fat, for several weeks. At serving time, the fat is removed and the sausages are grilled or sautéed.

The spicy rice with little pieces of cured pork and ham is excellent with different types of meat and poultry. The apple rings also are a good complement to fish and sautéed meat or game. Serve one sausage and one apple ring per person as a first course and double the amounts for a main course.

Yield: 15–18 sausages

SPICY PORK SAUSAGE

½ lb. pork shoulder, coarsely ground
1½ tsp. salt
¼ tsp. freshly ground black pepper
1 small clove garlic, chopped
½ tsp. paprika
Dash cayenne pepper

CHITTERLING SAUSAGE

10 lb. chitterlings
8 dried shiitake mushrooms soaked in water for 1 hour, stems removed (and reserved for sauces)
½ c. chopped scallions (about 3)
1 doz. shallots (1 c. sliced)
2 Tb. butter
4 cloves garlic, chopped (1½ tsp.)
3 Tb. chopped parsley (½ c. loose)
1 Tb. finely chopped fresh tarragon (1 large sprig)
4 Tb. good French mustard
2 tsp. potato starch
1½ c. dry white wine
1 Tb. salt plus dash of salt (for unseasoned stock)
2 tsp. freshly ground black pepper
Salted, packed hog casings (see Black Sausage Bichon, preceding recipe)
3 c. white stock (see page 19)

FOR SAUTEING 6 SAUSAGES

½ tsp. butter
2 Tb. white wine
Reserved apple cooking juices
GARNISH

Scallion greens

SPICY RICE

Yield: 6 servings
½ lb. spicy pork sausage (cured); see recipe
½ tsp. fennel seed
1 tsp. dried oregano
½ c. ¼-in.-diced prosciutto ham
1½ c. chopped onions
½ c. sliced scallions (about 3)
2 tsp. chopped hot jalapeño pepper
1 tsp. chopped garlic (2 or 3 cloves)
1 c. long-grain rice
½ c. tomato sauce
2 c. white stock (page 19)
½ tsp. salt

APPLE RINGS

Yield: 6 servings
3 Golden Delicious apples
1 Tb. butter
¼ tsp. salt
¼ tsp. white pepper
1 tsp. sugar

1 Mix together the ingredients for the spicy pork sausage and refrigerate, covered, for 48 hours to cure.

2 Notice that the chitterlings are quite fatty. They should be thoroughly cleaned, then placed in a large kettle and covered with tepid water. Bring to a boil and simmer gently, covered, for 2 hours. The chitterlings will shrink considerably.

3 Cut the chitterlings into ½-in. pieces.

4 Drain and chop the mushroom caps and chop the scallions. Slice the shallots. Melt the butter and, when hot, sauté the scallions and shallots for 2 to 3 minutes. Add the mushroom caps and cook 1½ minutes longer. Then add the chopped garlic and combine the mixture with the chitterlings. Add the parsley, tarragon, mustard, potato starch, ½ c. of the wine, the 1 Tb. salt, and pepper.

5 Soak the entire casing in lukewarm water for 4 to 5 minutes. Fit one end of the casing on the end of a faucet and run tepid water gently through the casing to open it, as if filling balloons with water (see Black Sausage Bichon, preceding recipe, photograph 2).

Tie the casing at one end, as explained in Black Sausage Bichon recipe, page 316, steps 3 and 4. Place the chitterling mixture in a pastry bag with a plain 1-in.-wide opening. Push the mixture into a plastic funnel onto which the casing is fitted or squeeze it directly from the pastry tube into the casing.

6 As the mixture goes into the casing, push it down by squeezing it gently with your fingers toward the far end of the casing. When most of the casing is filled, press with your hand (not too much or it will burst) to compact the stuffing and, using a trussing needle or another needle, prick where you see little bubbles of air so the mixture is compact. Tie off with twine about every 4 to 5 in. to divide the stuffed casing into individual sausages.

7 To cook the chitterling sausage: Arrange the sausage in a spiral in a large saucepan. It should cover the bottom in one layer. Pour the 3 c. white stock and the remaining 1 c. wine on top; there should be just enough to cover. Add a dash of salt, as the stock is not seasoned. Place over medium heat and bring to 170 degrees. Poach at that temperature approximately 12 minutes. Do not let the mixture boil or the casing will burst. Let cool in the stock for a few hours. Remove to a platter and cut where the sausages are tied, into individual pieces. After cooling, the filling is set and the casing cooked. The stuffing will not pop out of each end. The stock can be used to reheat the sausages or for sauces or soups.

8 To cook the spicy rice: Break the spicy pork sausage into 1-in. pieces. Place in a sturdy saucepan and sauté over low heat for about 12 to 15 minutes, until well browned. Add the ½ tsp. fennel seed, 1 tsp. oregano, ½ c. diced prosciutto, 1½ c. onions, and ½ c. sliced scallions, and cook for 3 to 4 minutes. Add 2 tsp. chopped jalapeño pepper and cook for another minute. Finally, add 1 tsp. garlic and 1 c. rice. Mix well, add ½ c. tomato sauce, 2 c. white stock, and ½ tsp. salt and bring to a boil, stirring occasionally. As soon as it boils, cover and cook over very low heat for 30 minutes.

9 When the rice is cooked, it should be fluffy but holding together and highly spiced.

10 **To cook the apples:** Leaving the skin on, cut 3 apples crosswise into approximately 1-in. slices. Golden Delicious are ideal for this. Using a round cookie cutter or the large side of a pastry tip, remove the apple core to create a ring.

11 Heat the 1 Tb. butter in a large skillet. When hot, add the apple slices. Sprinkle with ¼ tsp. each salt and pepper, and 1 tsp. sugar, and sauté the apples about 5 minutes on one side. Turn and cook 5 minutes on the other side, until nicely browned and tender. Remove the slices to a plate and set aside. Add ½ c. water to the pan to deglaze the juices and set aside.

12 Prick the sausages all around with a fork before sautéing to prevent them from bursting. Heat the ½ tsp. butter in the same skillet used for sautéing the apples. When hot, add the sausages and cook over very low heat for 5 minutes. Add 2 Tb. wine, cover, and continue cooking for about 1 minute over low heat. (If the heat is too high, the sausages will burst.)

13 Add the apple juices to the sausages. Arrange the rice in the centers of individual plates with 2 sausages beside it and apple slices at either end. Spoon a little of the sauce over the apples, garnish with a sprig of scallion stuck into the center of the rice mound, and serve immediately.

MUSTARD PIGS' FEET
WITH GATEAU OF POTATOES

Traditionally, pigs' feet are poached, brushed with mustard, covered with bread crumbs, and grilled. They are very gelatinous and the meat tends to shrink and break during cooking. When boning the feet, it is difficult to keep the original shape. Furthermore, they are messy and awkward to eat with the bone in.

In the recipe here, the pigs' feet are boiled in water in a large saucepan for approximately 2½ to 3 hours until tender. Cooking time can be reduced to about 1½ hours if they are cooked in a pressure cooker. The feet are then boned, the meat is coarsely chopped and combined with ground pork, mushrooms, and seasonings, and then reformed into elongated patties. They are finally coated with mustard, breaded, and sautéed. This is a country dish that goes well with everything from beans to mashed potatoes.

The nippy shallot-vinegar sauce is acidic and cuts the richness of the pigs' feet. The gâteau of potatoes, a kind of hash-browned potatoes formed into a cake, is called pommes macaire in French. In this recipe, it is further enriched with cream and cheese before being glazed under the broiler.

The sauce is excellent with pork chops as well as lamb and the potatoes will complement different types of roasts as well as poultry.

Yield: 8 servings

4 pigs' feet, split in half (4 lb.)
3 oz. mushrooms (oyster or cultivated)
1 lb. lean ground pork
½ tsp. chopped garlic
1 tsp. salt
1½ tsp. freshly ground black pepper
3–4 Tb. spicy mustard (for coating patties)
8 slices white bread, crumbed in food processor (3 c. crumbs)

FOR SAUTEING THE PIGS'-FEET PATTIES

2 Tb. corn oil

GATEAU OF POTATOES

2½ lb. potatoes, cooked with the skin on
1 Tb. butter
3 Tb. vegetable oil
¼ tsp. grated nutmeg
¼ tsp. freshly ground black pepper
½ tsp. salt

TO FINISH THE POTATOES

⅓ c. heavy cream
3 Tb. grated Parmesan cheese

NIPPY SAUCE

1 Tb. butter
4 shallots, chopped (⅓ c.)
½ c. red wine vinegar
¾ tsp. freshly ground black pepper
½ tsp. salt
1 c. demi-glace (see page 7)
½ tsp. potato starch dissolved in 1 Tb. water, if needed to thicken

1 The front feet of pigs are considered fleshier than the back feet. Cover the pigs' feet generously with cold water, bring to a boil, and simmer gently 2½ to 3 hours, until tender. Cool in the cooking liquid for a couple of hours.

2 Drain from the liquid. (The liquid can be used for soups or for a rich, gelatinous stock.) The meat should be picked off the bones when still lukewarm, as it hardens when it cools and is more difficult to remove. Be sure to remove all the tiny pieces of bone, feeling the meat with your fingers as you go. The yield should be approximately 1½ lb. of pigs'-feet meat. Chop coarse with a knife into about ¼-in. pieces.

3 <u>Chop the mushrooms coarse.</u> (I prefer oyster mushrooms, but any other type of wild mushrooms or cultivated mushrooms can be used.) Combine the pigs'-feet meat with the ground pork and mushrooms. Season with the chopped garlic, salt, and ½ tsp. of the pepper.

6 Mix the bread crumbs with 1 tsp. of the remaining pepper. <u>Place the patties in the bread crumbs, pressing to make the crumbs adhere all over.</u> Set aside to finish at serving time.

8 Add the ¼ tsp. each nutmeg and pepper, and ½ tsp. salt, and mix well so the potatoes are well coated with the butter, oil, and seasonings. Sauté for about 1 to 2 minutes on top of the stove, stirring the potatoes occasionally so they develop the flavor of the seasonings. Then, <u>using a spatula, press the potatoes to make them lie flat and be more compact in the pan.</u> Place in a preheated 450-degree oven for 35 to 40 minutes, until nicely browned underneath and slightly brown on top.

4 <u>Form the mixture into 8 patties approximately 6 oz. each, wetting your hands first to prevent the mixture from sticking to them and to help you mold the patties properly.</u> Place on a tray and refrigerate for a couple of hours.

7 **For the gâteau of potatoes:** Place the 2½ lb. of washed potatoes in a pot and cover with cold water. Bring to a boil and simmer 30 to 35 minutes, until tender. Drain, and when cool enough to handle, scrape the skin off and chop the potatoes coarse. Melt 1 Tb. butter in a 10-in. preferably non-stick skillet, and add 3 Tb. oil. <u>When hot, add the potatoes.</u>

5 After the patties have been refrigerated, they will be quite firm and easier to handle. <u>Brush generously with mustard on both sides.</u>

9 <u>Place a round flameproof dish upside down on top of the skillet and invert to unmold the potatoes.</u> The potatoes can be served as *pommes macaire,* which means just out of the skillet (as shown in the photograph), or they can be finished with ⅓ c. cream and 3 Tb. Parmesan cheese, as in this recipe. Pour the cream on top of the potatoes, sprinkle with the cheese, and place under the broiler approximately 4 in. from the heat for about 5 minutes, until nicely browned on top.

To sauté the pigs'-feet patties: Melt the 2 Tb. corn oil in 1 very large or 2 smaller skillets, preferably non-stick. When hot, add the pigs'-feet patties and cook over medium to high heat for approximately 6 minutes on one side and 6 minutes on the other side. →

10 For the nippy sauce: Melt the 1 Tb. butter in a saucepan. When hot, add ⅓ c. chopped shallots and sauté for approximately 2 minutes. Add ½ c. vinegar, ¾ tsp. pepper, and ½ tsp. salt, and cook over high heat until the vinegar is reduced almost completely and the shallots just look wet. Then add 1 c. demi-glace and bring to a boil. If thickening is needed, add ½ tsp. potato starch dissolved in 1 Tb. water and bring to a boil.

11 Arrange the sauce on a large serving platter with the patties on top, and serve the potatoes alongside. Serve immediately.

BRAISED TRIPE TITINE

Most cuisines use the insides of animals in savory, earthy dishes, from poultry tripe to <u>pieds paquets</u>, a specialty of the south of France made from lamb tripe. Yet, most of the time, "tripe" refers to the stomachs of oxen or beef. The first and second stomachs are both used. One looks like, and is called, "honeycomb," while the other is smoother and flatter. In France, the <u>feuillet</u>, a "leafy" part of the intestines that is more difficult to clean, is also used but it is not usually available in the U.S.

The tripe available in most markets has already been cleaned and blanched. Tripe is rich and flavorful but difficult to digest, especially if not cooked long enough. The flavor improves with long cooking. Because it takes a long time to cook, it is preferable to cook a large amount at a time and freeze the excess for future use. It freezes quite well and should be defrosted slowly under refrigeration.

Steamed potatoes are ideal with tripe. Boiling potatoes are cut into chunks of approximately equal size and then rounded with a knife to make uniform pieces, or small red potatoes of equal size are used. When steamed, the potatoes absorb less water and are creamier and tastier than if boiled.

Yield: 8 servings

10 lb. tripe (mixture of honeycomb and plain stomach)
1 large beef foot (3 lb.)
1½ lb. carrots, peeled
1½ lb. onions
4 leeks (12 oz.)
1 head garlic (10 to 12 cloves), peeled

BOUQUET GARNI

8–10 bay leaves
1 Tb. peppercorns
2 tsp. dried thyme leaves
½ tsp. whole cloves

2 Tb. salt
1 Tb. jalapeño pepper, chopped
1 tsp. freshly ground black pepper
4 c. dry white wine
4 c. unsalted white stock (page 19)
1 Tb. Calvados or good applejack
⅓ c. flour mixed with 2 Tb. water (to seal terrine)

STEAMED POTATOES

Yield: 8 servings
3 lb. boiling potatoes, peeled
Garlic chives, chopped

1 On the left is the honeycomb tripe and on the right the plain stomach.

2 Leaving it in whole pieces, arrange the tripe in a large kettle. Place the split beef foot, carrots, onions, leaks, and garlic on top. With kitchen twine, tie the bay leaves, peppercorns, thyme leaves, and cloves into a small square of cheesecloth (for easy removal after cooking) and place in the kettle. Add the salt, hot pepper, and ground black pepper, and pour in the wine and stock. Bring to a boil, cover, and cook slowly on top of the stove for 3 hours.

3 Remove all the solids to a tray or cookie sheet when cold enough to handle. Cut the tripe into 1½- to 2-in. pieces. Remove the bones from the beef foot, cut the meat in half, and chop all the vegetables coarse. Place the tripe, meat, and vegetables back into a pot with the stock. Bring to a boil and cook for 1 hour.

4 At this point, the tripe, sprinkled with a little Calvados, can be served with steamed potatoes (steps 8 to 11). It can also be divided and frozen in freezer containers for future use.

5 To get a richer, more concentrated taste, recook the tripe in the oven. Place some tripe mixture in an ovenware terrine (about one good-sized ladle per person) and cover with a lid. Seal the lid tightly to the terrine by smearing with the flour-water paste mixture.

6 Place in a preheated 300-degree oven for approximately 2 hours. Break the seal and spoon off any additional fat that may have come to the top. The tripe should be very tender. Sprinkle lightly with Calvados and serve with the steamed potatoes.

7 If the tripe is allowed to cool, it will become hard like head cheese. It is sometimes sliced and served cold, like head cheese, with a vinegar dressing. At this point, it can also be frozen, reheated, and served with potatoes, prepared as follows.

8 **To make the steamed potatoes:** Cut the 3 lb. of potatoes in half, quarters, or thirds so all the pieces are approximately the same size. (Three lb. of potatoes will yield about 25 to 30 pieces, enough for about 8 people.) On the flat sides of the potato pieces, remove wedges to create rounded tops and sides. Keep trimmings in water for future use in soups, mashed potatoes, etc.

9 Continue rounding up the square edges so the potatoes are uniformly round. →

MEAT

10 Place the potatoes in a steamer above boiling water. Cover and cook about 15 minutes.

11 Ladle the tripe into individual soup plates or bowls. Dip one end of each cooked potato into chopped garlic chives and arrange (about 3 or 4 potatoes per serving) around the tripe. Serve immediately.

PISTACHIO SAUSAGE IN BRIOCHE WITH MUSHROOM SAUCE

Although my sausages are cooked in brioche in this recipe and in water in the following recipes, the same mixture stuffed into a casing and hung to dry makes a conventional salami.

The amount of salt added to the ground meat here is needed to cure the meat. Saltpeter or potassium nitrate is included only to make the sausage an attractive pink color and is optional. It can be omitted without changing the taste.

The sausage can also be served with potato salad or roasted potatoes, a specialty of Lyon. It can be formed into whatever length meets the occasion, and the cooking time won't be affected much, providing the sausage remains 1 1/2 inches in diameter.

Yield: 6 servings

PISTACHIO SAUSAGE

1 1/2 lb. coarsely ground pork, about 1/3 fat and 2/3 lean (The shoulder or Boston butt is ideal.)
2 1/2 tsp. salt
3/4 tsp. coarsely ground black pepper
3/4 tsp. sugar
1/4 tsp. saltpeter (potassium nitrate) for color (optional)
3 Tb. shelled pistachio nuts, with most of the dry skin removed
2 Tb. red wine
1 small clove garlic, crushed and chopped (1/4 tsp.)

BRIOCHE

1 package dry yeast (preferably the quick-rising Red Star brand) (1/4 oz., 2 tsp.)
1/2 c. water, warm from the tap (about 100 degrees)
1 tsp. sugar
1/2 tsp. salt
3 c. flour (1 lb. all-purpose)
4 large eggs
2 sticks butter, softened

FOR FINISHING THE SAUSAGE

Egg wash made with 1 egg with half the
white removed (so proportion of yolk is
greater), beaten with a fork

Flour

1 Tb. butter for buttering the cookie
sheets and aluminum foil

1 slice bread, crust removed, crumbed in a
food processor

FOR THE RED WINE–MUSHROOM SAUCE

2 Tb. butter

¼ c. peeled, chopped shallots

3 c. ¼-in.-diced mushrooms

½ c. fruity red wine

1 c. demi-glace of meat (see page 7)

Salt and pepper to taste

1 Combine the coarsely ground pork
(being sure you have at least one-third fat
and two-thirds lean) with the salt, pepper,
sugar, saltpeter, pistachios, red wine, and
garlic, and mix well. Cover the mixture
with plastic wrap and store in the refrigerator for at least 4 days to cure. (It can be
kept for as long as 1 week.)

2 Shape the mixture into a sausage roll
about 12 inches long and 1½ inches in
diameter. Press the meat together thoroughly to make sure there are no air pock-
ets in the center. For the Pistachio Sausage
in Brioche, shape 1½ lb. of sausage meat
so it is approximately 12 in. long by 1½
in. thick.

To make the brioche: Mix the yeast,
warm water, and sugar together in a large
mixer bowl and let proof at room tempera-

ture for 10 minutes. Add the salt, flour,
and eggs, and mix on medium speed (#4)
with the flat beater of the mixer for about
3 minutes. The mixture will be very elastic, smooth, and shiny. Add the softened
butter, squeezing the butter into the
dough with your hands just long enough
to incorporate it. Don't worry if some of
the pieces of butter are still visible; it will
not hurt the mixture.

The dough is easier to handle and rises
quite well when it is cool and has been
allowed to rise slowly overnight. If doing
this way, wrap the dough in a plastic bag
and place in the refrigerator. If the dough
is to be used sooner, however, leave it in
the mixer bowl, cover it with a damp
towel, and leave at room temperature
(about 72 degrees) to rise for approximately 3 to 4 hours. (It should at least
double in size.)

Punch the dough down slowly to eliminate the air inside and use immediately.

3 Finishing the sausages: Spread the
dough on a lightly floured board. (If the
dough is freshly made, it will be softer and
more flour will be required in the rolling
than when it is made ahead. The freshly
made dough also may have to be spread by
hand rather than rolled.) Roll it with a
rolling pin or spread it with floured hands
into a rectangle large enough to enclose
the sausage (approximately 10 in. wide by
13 to 14 in. long). Brush the center with
the egg wash and sprinkle with a little
flour. Place the sausage on top and brush
again with the egg mixture and sprinkle
with a little flour. The flour and egg mixture will form a type of glue, which will
tend to hold the brioche tightly against
the sausage without separating.

4 Fold one side of the brioche on top of the
sausage and brush it again with the egg
wash.

5 Then fold up the other side of the
brioche, overlapping it on top. Press out
the 2 ends of dough to make them thinner,
brush with the egg wash, and fold them
on top of the package.

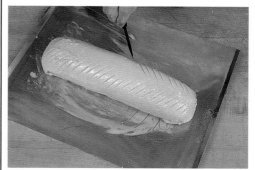

6 Butter a large aluminum cookie sheet
and, turning the sausage package over,
place it seam side down on the cookie
sheet. There is a double layer of dough
underneath now, and only one layer on
top. By the time the dough has risen, the
sausage will have sunk a little and be
approximately in the center of the dough
when it finishes cooking.

Brush the top of the package with egg
wash and score the dough with the dull
edge of a small knife if you want to make a
design on top. →

MEAT

7 Make 3 holes on top of the dough; this will permit the steam to be released and prevent the dough from cracking too much during cooking.

Tear off a long sheet of aluminum foil (long enough to go completely around the sausage) and fold it into thirds lengthwise. Butter the strip on one side, and wrap it loosely around the sausage, butter side in. Secure it loosely with a string, being careful you don't make it too tight since the brioche needs room to expand. Sprinkle the top with 2 to 3 Tb. of bread crumbs to give a nice finish to the top and set aside.

9 Let the sausage cool in a warm place by the stove for at least 20 to 30 minutes before slicing. Using a serrated knife, cut into 1-in.-thick slices.

10 Although the sausage can be served without any sauce, it is a bit more special when served with a sauce.

To make the red wine–mushroom sauce: Place the 2 Tb. butter in a large skillet and, when hot, add ¼ c. chopped shallots. Sauté for about 1 minute, add 3 c. diced mushrooms, and sauté for 2 minutes, until the mushrooms have rendered most of their juice. Add ½ c. red wine and boil down until most of the liquid has evaporated. Add 1 c. demi-glace and bring to a boil. Season with salt and pepper to taste.

Place 1 slice of sausage in brioche on each warm plate and surround with 2 to 3 Tb. of sauce. Serve immediately.

8 Let the sausage-stuffed brioche rise for a good hour at room temperature (about 72 degrees). Set the pan in the center of a preheated 375-degree oven and cook for about 15 minutes. By then, the brioche will have expanded and set. Remove the string and foil and continue to bake for an additional 20 minutes (approximately 35 to 40 minutes total baking time).

A NOTE ABOUT THE AUTHOR

Jacques Pepin was born in Bourg-en-Bresse, near Lyon, and began cooking at the age of thirteen when he apprenticed in his parents' Lyon restaurant, Le Pelican. He went on to study in Paris at the Meurice restaurant and then the famed Plaza-Athénée, where he trained under Lucien Diat. From 1956 to 1958, Mr. Pepin was the personal chef to three French heads of state: Gaillard, Pflimlin, and de Gaulle.

In 1959, Mr. Pepin came to the United States. He studied at Columbia University and earned a B.A. and an M.A. in eighteenth-century French literature.

Mr. Pepin appears frequently as a guest speaker on radio and television food programs and has written about food and cooking for *The New York Times, Bon Appétit, Food & Wine, House Beautiful,* and *Travel & Leisure.* For the past two and a half years *Gourmet* magazine has featured excerpts from this book.

He lives in Madison, Connecticut, with his wife and their daughter, Claudine, although he spends almost thirty weeks out of the year traveling around the country to give cooking demonstrations.

A NOTE ON THE TYPE

The text and display types were chosen for their appropriateness, clarity, beauty, contrast to each other, and association with France. They also represent the best in type design of two vastly different eras and are part of a long tradition and history.

The text was set in a digitized version of Garamond, which is based on letter forms originally created by the Frenchman Claude Garamond (c. 1480–1561). He was a pupil of Geoffroy Tory and may have patterned his letter forms on Venetian models.

The display type was set in a digitized version of Frutiger, which was designed by the Swiss Adrian Frutiger in Paris in 1976. It is based on the signage type he created in 1970 for the Roissy-Charles de Gaulle Airport and was originally produced in the United States by Mergenthaler-Linotype and in Frankfurt by Stempel. Frutiger also designed Univers and Serifa type faces.

Composition by Graphic Composition, Inc., Athens, Georgia
Printing and binding by Toppan Printing Company, Tokyo, Japan

Photography by Tom Hopkins

Design by Stephanie Guiomar Tevonian, Works design group